D0416201

Trade, Environment, and the Millennium

A Note to the Reader from UNU/IAS

Trade, Environment, and the Millennium reflects the core mission of the United Nations University Institute of Advanced Studies (UNU/IAS). In April 1996, the UN Secretary-General inaugurated the UNU/IAS as an in-house community of scholars, established to vigorously pursue knowledge at the intersection between societal and natural systems. The programmatic theme of the IAS was created to be dynamic and flexible, focusing on finding creative solutions to the pressing global issues arising at this nexus. As an overarching theme, the IAS adopted the concept of *Eco-restructuring*, an approach to sustainable development that envisions shifting technological and societal systems towards a greater equity between developing and developed countries, between human-kind and the environment, and between current and future generations. An integral component of the IAS Eco-restructuring dynamic involves the examination of global institutions, regimes, values, and policies relating to sustainable development. These issues are dealt with under the programmatic sub-theme of *Environmental Governance and Multilateralism*. Within this programme, in-depth theoretical research is combined with relevant policy studies and the formulation of practical policy options. A strong capacity-building component that to seeks enhance the participation of policy actors in global environmental negotiations has also been built into the programme.

This book has been put together within the framework of the Environmental Governance and Multilateralism Programme. The IAS has strategically focused upon trade and environment in the belief that this will constitute a crucial aspect of environmental policy as we enter the new millennium. The debate is synonymous with the complex tensions that exist between current societal structures that emphasize increased economic growth and prosperity, with the need to ensure that we do not degrade the environment beyond its restorative capacity, or deny its natural resources to future generations. The next round of trade negotiations could provide an opportunity to reconcile these seemingly mutually exclusive imperatives. A sustainable consensus, however, must be based on globally accepted principles such as common, but differentiated responsibility, the polluter pays principle, and the precautionary principle. It must also be recognized that the industrialization models of this century are not viable in the long term and that a more sustainable model of development must be sought.

Trade, Environment, and the Millennium

Edited by
GARY P. SAMPSON and
W. BRADNEE CHAMBERS

**United Nations
University Press**

TOKYO • NEW YORK • PARIS

United Nations University Press
The United Nations University
53-70, Jingumae 5-chome,
Shibuya-ku, Tokyo 150-8925, Japan
Tel: +81-3-3499-2811   Fax: +81-3-3406-7345
E-mail: sales@hq.unu.edu
http://www.unu.edu

United Nations University Office in North America
2 United Nations Plaza, Room DC2-1462-70, New York,
  NY 10017, USA
Tel: +1-212-963-6387   Fax: +1-212-371-9454
E-mail: unuona@igc.apc.org

United Nations University Press is the publishing division of the
United Nations University.

Cover design by Joyce C. Weston

Photograph by Pacific Press Service

Printed in Hong Kong

UNUP-1043

ISBN 92-808-1043-X

Library of Congress Cataloging-in-Publication Data

Trade, Environment, and the Millennium / edited by Gary P. Sampson and W. Bradnee Chambers.

p. cm.

"Trade, Environment, and the Millennium reflects the core mission of the United Nations University Institute of Advanced Studies (UNU/IAS). This book has been put together within the framework of the Environmental Governance and Multilateralism Programme." Includes bibliographical references (p.) and index.
ISBN 928081043X
1. International trade-Environmental aspects. 2. Commercial policy-Environmental aspects. 3. Environmental policy-Economic aspects. 4. World Trade Organization. I. Sampson, Gary P. II. Chambers, W. Bradnee. III. Institute of Advanced Studies. IV. Environmental Governance and Multilateralism Programme.
HF1379 .T723 2000
382'.92–dc21
99-050491

CONTENTS

Acknowledgements

Trade, Environment, and the Millennium was prepared with the assistance of many people. First and foremost we would like to thank the authors for their contributions, and Janet P. Boileau and Manfred Boemeke of UNU Press for their flexibility, hard work, and initiative in getting this volume published. We would like to express our appreciation to Risa Schwartz and Shona E. Dodds for their dedication in assisting us with the editing of the chapters. We would also like to thank Miho Komiyama, who continues to lend her valuable support and help to the Environmental Governance and Multilateralism Programme of the Institute of Advanced Studies (IAS) of the United Nations University.

Lastly, we would like to thank Professor Tarcisio Della Senta, Director of the IAS, who gave his full commitment and support to this book from the very beginning.

ACRONYMS

APEC	Asia-Pacific Economic Cooperation Conference
ASEAN	Association of South East Asian Nations
BAT	best available technology
BTA	border tax adjustment
CAA	Clean Air Act (USA)
CAP	Common Agricultural Policy (EU)
CBD	Convention on Biological Diversity
CFCs	chlorofluorocarbons
CITES	Convention on International Trade in Endangered Species of Wild Fauna and Flora
CPC	Central Product Classification (UN)
CSD	Commission on Sustainable Development
CTBT	Committee on Technical Barriers to Trade
CTE	Committee on Trade and Environment
CWA	Clean Water Act (USA)
DPG	domestically prohibited good
DSB	Dispute Settlement Body
DSU	Dispute Settlement Understanding
EC	European Communities
ECJ	European Court of Justice
EFTA	European Free Trade Association
EIA	environmental impact assessment
EIS	Environmental Impact Statement
EMIT Group	Group on Environmental Measures and International Trade
EPA	Environmental Protection Agency (USA)
EST	environmentally sound technology
EU	European Union
FAO	Food and Agriculture Organization of the United Nations
FCCC	Framework Convention on Climate Change
GATS	General Agreement on Trade in Services
GATT	General Agreement on Tariffs and Trade
GMO	genetically modified organism
ICJ	International Court of Justice

IGO	intergovernmental organization
IPOA	International Plan of Action (FAO)
IPRs	intellectual property rights
ISO	International Standards Organization
ITO	International Trade Organization
LCA	life-cycle analysis
MAI	Multilateral Agreement on Investment
MEA	multilateral environmental agreement
MFN	most-favoured nation
MRA	mutual recognition agreement
MTS	multilateral trading system
NAFTA	North American Free Trade Agreement
NEPA	National Environmental Policy Act
NGO	non-governmental organization
NPR-PPMs	non-product-related processes and production methods
ODS	ozone-depleting substances
OECD	Organization for Economic Cooperation and Development
PIC	prior informed consent
PPMs	processes and production methods
PVP	Plant Variety Protection
S&D	special and differential (treatment)
SCTE	Sub-Committee on Trade and Environment
SMEs	small and medium enterprises
SPS	Sanitary and Phytosanitary measures
TBT	Technical Barriers to Trade
TRIPS	Trade-related Intellectual Property Rights
UNCED	United Nations Conference on Environment and Development
UNCTAD	United Nations Conference on Trade and Development
UNEP	United Nations Environment Programme
UPOV	Union for the Protection of New Varieties of Plants
WEO	World Environmental Organization
WTO	World Trade Organization
WWF	Worldwide Fund for Nature

Introduction and Overview

Gary P. Sampson and W. Bradnee Chambers

Just a few weeks prior to the start of the next millennium, ministers and heads of government from the 134 member governments of the World Trade Organization (WTO) will meet in Seattle to decide the agenda for future multilateral trade negotiations. Given the increasing attention paid to the WTO by many environmentalists, and the ongoing debate over the apparent conflict in trade and environment policy, it is clear that trade and environment issues will loom large at the Seattle meeting. How governments choose to deal with these issues will have important implications for both trade policy and environment policy well into the twenty-first century.

The issues raised in this debate are complex and touch on some of the most fundamental aspects of WTO concepts, principles, and rules. The complexity is further increased owing to the diversity of views and the number of stakeholders involved. Although all parties assign a fundamental priority to the protection of the environment, the perceived role of the WTO in achieving these objectives differs greatly across groups. Reaching agreement on significant changes in rules and practices will not be an easy task in an organization where decisions are adopted on the basis of consensus.

Many environmentalists, for example, are of the view that the WTO rules—and trade liberalization generally—accelerate unsustainable consumption and production patterns that cause resource depletion, loss of species, and other environmental degradation. They argue that WTO rules constrain domestic legislators from protecting the environment by using trade measures to enforce environmental standards internationally. The inability in the WTO to discriminate between products on the basis of how they were produced runs contrary to the objectives of many environmentalists. Some environmental non-governmental organizations (NGOs) perceive the WTO as an instrument of globalization that is non-transparent and unaccountable to the public at large.

For their part, many developing countries are deeply suspicious of what could follow from changing the WTO rules and processes to meet the concerns of environmentalists. Restricting trade on the basis of how goods are produced for export, for example, may mean poorer countries being obliged to adopt standards applied by their developed counterparts in their own production processes. These standards may not be appropriate in the sense of reflecting the development priorities of the countries producing the goods, their resource endowments, or their available technology. In addition, it is feared that, although such policies may well be construed with good intentions in mind, they might also fall captive to protectionist interests. Further, if standards relating to the environment are accepted as a basis for trade discrimination in the WTO, why not other standards that relate to production methods such as labour standards?

On the other hand, many in the trade community (developed and developing countries alike) argue that the General Agreement on Tariffs and Trade (GATT)—and now the World Trade Organization—has been successful over the past half-century at doing what it has been clearly mandated to do. The WTO has two primary objectives: first, progressively to remove trade restrictions and distortions that protect uncompetitive producers and deny consumers the possibility to purchase goods and services at the most competitive international prices; secondly, to maintain the open and liberal multilateral trading system based on non-discriminatory rules as a means to ensure predictability and stability in world trade. They point to the fact that more than 6 trillion dollars worth of goods are traded according to WTO rules and almost 2 trillion dollars of world services. This figure represents 26 per cent of the world total output and is projected to increase to 45 per cent by 2010. Through eight rounds of trade-liberalizing negotiations, tariffs on industrial goods have been reduced from 45 per cent in 1947 to an average of approximately 4 per cent today. International trade increased at a rate faster than economic growth by an average 2 per cent per annum between 1948 and 1997,[1] leading to higher standards of living and levels of employment and greater prosperity in many countries. The argument continues that trade liberalization is not a cause of environmental degradation, but rather a source of increased real resources that can be directed at the national level towards effective environmental management policies.

Although WTO rules (and those of GATT prior to it) may have brought stability and predictability to the world trading system, the sorts of objections raised by the environmental community, as well as the concerns of developing countries in addressing them, cannot be ignored. The challenge is how to deal with these concerns without severely damaging the credibility and usefulness of the WTO and the carefully negotiated Uruguay Round Agreements based on non-discrimination. Conducting international trade according to rules—rather than commercial or political power—is accepted by all WTO members to be one of its most important characteristics.

Not only is accommodating the perceptions of the role of the WTO held by the stakeholders complex, so too are the issues that are the subject of the trade and environment debate. In recent years much of the discussion has centred on the possibility of there being a natural, or in-built, potential for conflict between trade policy and policies relating to the environment. The numerous examples include: higher environmental standards in an importing country than an exporting country leading to a loss of international competitiveness; a lowering of environmental standards to gain international competitiveness; compensatory border adjustment measures to offset environmentally driven taxes or subsidies conflicting with trade rules; trade liberalization and economic growth leading to resource depletion and environmental degradation; cross-border pollution or damage to the global commons, with trade sanctions as retaliatory measures; disguised protection, with domestic standards tailored to discriminate against imports; and conflicting obligations in multilateral environment agreements and trade agreements. To these can be added: health concerns and the future WTO legitimacy of measures to restrict trade where standards differ across countries (e.g. with respect to trade in products derived from genetically modified organisms); the role of precaution in the justification of these differing standards; the extent to which labelling products according to the process used to produce them provides a solution; and whether or not such labelling is in fact WTO legal.

WTO members recognized some time ago the complexity of the relationship between trade policy and environment policy. As a result of discussions that coincided with the later stages of the Uruguay Round, a Committee on Trade and Environment (CTE) was established by the WTO General Council in January 1995. The CTE terms of reference are far-reaching and indicate an early concern on the part of WTO members with ensuring that WTO rules are consistent with, and supportive of, environmental policies. The CTE reported to the first biennial meeting of the Ministerial Conference, and its work and terms of reference were reviewed in the light of its recommendations. This report was heavily negotiated, forwarded to ministers, and adopted in Singapore in December 1996. Although the work as described in the report has been comprehensive and addressed many of the complex issues described above, it has fallen short of fulfilling the expectations of those who saw it as a means to resolve the issues of concern of environmentalists. The work of this committee provides a reference point for the current thinking in the WTO. It is described in some detail in Appendix I.

The motivation behind this book is the belief that, for a variety of reasons, there is now a window of opportunity to move the debate on trade and environment forward. First, the WTO Seattle Ministerial Meeting in December 1999 will provide the opportunity for serious consideration of the issues to be addressed in whatever form the multilateral negotiations take in the year 2000. Secondly, a great deal of groundwork has been done in the WTO, by environmental NGOs, by various international organizations (e.g. the UN Conference on Trade and Development, the UN Environment Programme, the Organization for Economic Cooperation and Development), and elsewhere to introduce change if thought necessary. Comprehensive proposals on most of the major issues have been discussed at length in the WTO and many are described in the report of the CTE to ministers in Singapore. Thirdly, a great deal of work is already under way in the regular bodies of the WTO, such as the General Council and the Dispute Settlement Body, addressing many of the concerns of the environmental community.

These include increasing the transparency of WTO operations, accelerating the derestriction of documentation, and intensifying the contact between the WTO and public interest groups.

Also of considerable importance is the apparent political awareness in the industrialized countries that something needs to be done to build public support for future negotiations in the WTO, and possibly for a new round of multilateral trade negotiations. The United States President, in his message to the 1999 WTO High Level Symposium on Trade and Environment, emphasized the need to strengthen environmental protection; to ensure that trade rules support national policies providing for high levels of environmental protection and effective enforcement; and to achieve greater inclusiveness and transparency in WTO proceedings. In its communiqué from the 1999 meeting in Cologne, the G-8 urged WTO members to "fully take account of environmental considerations in the next round" and to clarify the relationship between key multilateral environmental agreements and principles and WTO rules.

Expressions of political will from the leaders of the industrial countries, however, are not enough to set a process of change in motion. As will be argued by some of the authors of the following chapters, many of the proposals related to trade and environment put forward by developed countries have lacked sensitivity to the needs of developing countries. They frequently do not pay due regard to core principles, such as: common, but differentiated, responsibility; the right to development; or even the right to basic human needs such as food, health, and education that developed countries take for granted. In other words, they do not respond to the concerns of developing countries. In a consensus-based organization where two-thirds of the membership comprises developing countries, their concerns cannot be ignored.

The intention of this book is to provide a constructive input into future WTO negotiations by elaborating the concerns of both developing countries and environmentalists. The intention is also to raise the awareness of a number of the key issues that will have to be addressed in any future negotiations. Meeting this objective has provided the chapters with a strong policy orientation. The contributors have been drawn from academia, government, and civil society, and each is a leading authority in his or her particular field. In providing the substantive chapters of this book, the contributors have been asked to utilize their wealth of knowledge and experience in an effort to provide clear policy recommendations that will be useful within the framework of future WTO negotiations.

The book contains 11 chapters. The first chapter is a visionary overview by Rubens Ricupero of some of the principal considerations in the trade and environment debate. The next three chapters describe the various viewpoints on trade, environment, and the WTO of two groups of stakeholders—developing countries and environmental NGOs. Chapter 5 describes and comments on the WTO dispute settlement process, considered by many to be the heart of the WTO, and a key element in most of the policy chapters that follow. Each of the following chapters addresses a specific issue that will be central for any future multilateral trade negotiations that bear on trade and the environment.

Chapter 2, by Magda Shahin, examines trade and environment issues from the perspective of a developing country negotiator with considerable experience in how the debate has evolved in the WTO. The author raises many of the questions and expresses many of the concerns voiced by developing countries. She poses the question of whether developed countries are genuinely concerned over social and environmental issues at the international level or, rather, is it hegemonic and commercial interests that are the real motivators. Is linking trade to environment a justified concern with honest environmental goals or are additional protection measures at play? Irrespective of the answer to this question, the author draws attention to the difficulties of developing countries in dealing with the complex issues, given their resource constraints, poor information flows, and lack of scientific knowledge.

The author elaborates the position of many developing countries on specific topics addressed in the WTO; for example, the relationship between the provisions of the multilateral trading system and trade measures pursuant to multilateral environmental agreements (MEAs) , and the relationship between environmental measures and the WTO Agreement on Trade-related Intellectual Property Rights (TRIPS). She also addresses market access issues and the concerns that have been expressed by many developing countries over the effect that eco-labelling schemes could have on their access to developed countries' markets. She cautions that multilateral environmental regimes and measures that go beyond a country's own borders, for the sake of protecting the environment, are "a flagrant violation of WTO rules and regulations, which do not allow for extra-territorial measures." Today "we see growing concern by environmental groups at the national level forcing the issue of *national sovereignty* against the country's obligations to abide by WTO judgements."

In much of this chapter, a common theme is a concern over changing WTO rules to permit the regulation of trade on the basis of processes and production methods (e.g. with respect to the use of eco-labelling schemes) rather than on the characteristics of the products themselves. Justifying discrimination between "like products" and making market access for exports conditional on complying with production standards "would upset the entire trading system and would have devastating effects, in particular on developing country exports." This is a statement of the importance ascribed by developing countries in general to avoiding any discrimination in trade according to the manner in which exports are produced. In this sense, developing countries are not "natural allies" for those environmental NGOs that are critical of the WTO for not permitting discrimination according to production methods (e.g. on the basis of life-cycle analysis).

In fact, this concern emerges as a key issue not only in this chapter but in many other parts of the book—with respect to, for example, the accommodation of MEAs by the WTO, the use of unilateral measures to impose certain standards in other countries, revising the WTO exceptions provisions to accommodate environmental concerns, justifying standards on the grounds of protection of the environment, eco-labelling schemes based on acceptable methods of production, and many others. In offering advice to developing countries, the author states that they have to remain firm on their positions on trade and environment in regard to changing of the rules; "such a move would only serve as a prelude to the integration of the 'social clause' in the WTO, which has wider implications for developing countries and should be of more serious concern." Maintaining the consensus-based nature of the WTO and maintaining control over policy in the hands of its members (as against, for example, the Appellate Body deciding policy through litigation) are also important themes that express the concerns of many developing countries.

In chapter 3, Veena Jha and René Vossenaar point out that most developing countries are strongly resisting the inclusion of trade and environment in future trade negotiations and acknowledge that there may be sound reasons for them to oppose broad WTO negotiations based on environmental considerations. They add that developing countries may have good strategic reasons for opposing the inclusion of environment in the build-up to the Seattle Ministerial Conference. However, the authors also argue that it may be difficult for developing countries to sustain their opposition to addressing the environment in future WTO negotiations. Therefore, the authors provide the elements of an initiative by the Secretary-General of UNCTAD to promote a "Positive Agenda" as an alternative approach to future trade and environment negotiations. Although the authors warn that the potential for consensus between developing countries may be limited, they suggest that such a positive agenda should promote, at least, the principle of common, but differentiated, responsibility and the closer integration of developing countries into the global economy.

Before outlining the elements of the agenda, the authors present what they consider to be the legitimate apprehensions of developing countries with respect to the WTO debate on trade and the environment. The authors assess the costs and benefits of engaging in discussions on trade and environment, and find that there is scope within the current framework to accommodate the concerns of developing countries. The approach adopted by the authors is to identify the points of entry for developing countries into a debate that they characterize as having been polarized so far.

It is not surprising that there is a considerable concordance of view with the previous chapter, particularly in identifying issues of concern to developing countries. Although a number of concerns are addressed, the authors assign priority to: accommodation, through a change in WTO rules, of trade measures taken pursuant to multilateral environmental agreements; accommodation of trade measures based on non-product-related production methods on environmental grounds, particularly in the context of eco-labelling; and greater scope for the use of the precautionary principle. All these issues are taken up in some detail in later chapters.

The authors also address an issue raised on a number of occasions in later chapters of the book, particularly the chapter by Daniel Esty: the pressure exerted by the non-governmental community for greater access to the WTO processes; for example, to its dispute settlement mechanism through the submission of *amicus briefs*. The authors note that civil society—both non-governmental organizations and the business community—can play an important role in promoting a balanced trade and environment agenda. They flag, however, one of the reasons for resistance on the part of developing countries to proposals to open the WTO to greater participation from public interest groups. A number of proposals "that may be labelled under the heading 'transparency,' such as the those facilitating the submission of *amicus curae* briefs to dispute settlement panels, could, in practice, accentuate certain imbalances . . . because NGOs in the South have fewer financial resources to avail themselves of such opportunities." In the preceding chapter Magda Shahin expressed the same reserve but rather in the context of maintaining the intergovernmental character of the WTO and its tradition of being an organization where policy is decided by the member governments alone.

In chapter 4, Daniel Esty presents the view of many non-governmental organizations: broadly speaking, it is in the interests of the WTO itself to be more receptive to NGO views and involvement. In so doing, however, he first acknowledges the important role the WTO has to play as a facilitator of economic interdependence, but notes that, if the WTO is to play its role effectively, it must be seen as having legitimacy, authoritativeness, and a commitment to fairness. "Absent these virtues, decisions that emanate from the WTO will not be accepted as part of the process of global decision-making." To achieve this, the author considers it necessary for the WTO to become better connected to the non-governmental organizations that represent the diverse strands of global civil society.

The author proceeds to elaborate how the WTO could increase its legitimacy by demonstrating that it has genuine connections to the citizens of the world and that its decisions reflect the will of the public at large. In this respect, non-governmental organizations represent an important mechanism by which the WTO can reach out to citizens and build the requisite bridge to global civil society. The WTO could increase its authoritativeness through increased inputs from NGOs that have in-house analytical and technical skills and whose "*raison d'être* is to sharpen thinking about policy issues." They also provide an "important oversight and audit mechanism"—they can "act as watchdogs on national governments and report on whether they are fulfilling their WTO obligations." In the view of the author, fairness can be enhanced through providing opportunities for the public to submit views to the dispute settlement process in the form of *amicus briefs* and to observe how outcomes are reached in the dispute process.

The author is aware that his case for the WTO to have broader links with non-governmental organizations will be challenged. He therefore sets about stating the points of resistance (some of which were raised in chapters 2 and 3), and offers his rebuttals. In short, his conclusion is that some of these arguments "represent little more than traditional trade community cant. Other concerns have a more serious foundation. But none of the claims bears up under scrutiny."

In chapter 5, William Davey makes the important observation that it would "make little sense to spend years negotiating the detailed rules in international trade agreements if those rules could be ignored." In the commercial world, security and predictability are viewed as fundamental prerequisites to conducting business internationally. For this reason a system of rule enforcement is necessary. Because the same WTO dispute settlement process is common to the enforcement of all its agreements, it is not surprising that it is referred to on numerous occasions in the following chapters.

The author describes the WTO dispute settlement process by outlining its four basic phases: consultations, the panel process, the appellate process, and the surveillance of implementation. He points to the fact that the WTO dispute settlement process differs in important ways from that of GATT. In particular, automaticity comes from the new rules under the Dispute Settlement Understanding (DSU) on the adoption of decisions taken in the WTO. The DSU also offers a more structured approach, with stricter timetables and greater surveillance to ensure that the panel or Appellate Body rulings are implemented. In the view of the author, the WTO dispute settlement system has operated well; WTO members have made extensive use of the system, suggesting that they have confidence in it.

Faced with the challenge of greater transparency for WTO operations, the author draws attention to the fact that "panel and Appellate Body reports (and all other WTO documents relating to specific disputes) are issued as unrestricted documents and placed on the WTO website immediately after their distribution to members." There have, however, been proposals, particularly by non-governmental organizations, that the WTO dispute settlement proceedings be open to the public, that submissions be made public, and that non-parties be permitted to file "friend-of-the-court" submissions to panels. As argued by Esty in chapter 4, the credibility of the system would be much enhanced if it were more open and that openness would have no significant disadvantages. A similar concern is expressed in chapter 5. In addressing these concerns, the author reminds readers that "some members view the WTO system as exclusively intergovernmental in nature and hesitate to open it to non-governments. In their view, if a non-governmental organization wants to make an argument to a panel, it should convince one of the parties to make it and, if no party makes the argument, those members would view that as evidence that the argument is not meritorious."

The author discusses the ongoing review of the DSU, the principal concern of developing countries being the resource difficulty that many of them face when they participate in the dispute settlement system. The DSU addresses this problem by requiring the WTO Secretariat to provide legal assistance to such countries and by conducting training courses that either include or are exclusively focused on dispute settlement. The author considers the best hope for a significant improvement in dealing with inadequate developing country resources to be the proposed Advisory Centre on WTO law, which would be an international intergovernmental organization providing legal assistance to developing countries in respect of WTO matters.

Chapters 6 to 11 address a number of areas that are highly relevant for future WTO negotiations. What they all have in common is that they bear directly on important issues in the area of trade and environment. In chapter 6, David Schorr addresses one of the most discussed topics in the Committee on Trade and Environment; namely, the manner in which the removal of trade restrictions and distortions can lead to a "win–win" outcome. The first win comes from the fact that the removal of certain trade restrictions in developed countries will be beneficial to the environment of those countries themselves. The second win follows if the products facing the trade restrictions and distortions are of current or potential export interest to developing countries. In a win–win scenario, improvement of the environment in developing countries coincides with export expansion in developing countries. In this chapter, the author presents the results of his research on a particular case-study that represents a potential win–win scenario: the removal of government subsidies to fisheries. A particularly interesting feature of this chapter is that it demonstrates that it is possible to find areas where there is potential for WTO rules to be used positively to deal directly with environmental problems.

According to estimates cited by the author, 60 per cent of the world's fisheries are overexploited or already exploited at maximum rates, largely because there are "too many fishing boats chasing too few fish." His answer to the question of what keeps so many fishing boats afloat as fish stocks shrink is "huge government payments that promote excess harvesting capacity and reward unsustainable fishing practices." The link with the WTO is that many of these subsidies are "administered in open violation of existing international trade rules [and] constitute a profound failure of both economic and environmental policy." Removing these distortions would be beneficial for the preservation and building up of fish stocks worldwide. As far as developing countries are concerned, fish and fish products are an important export item for them as they account for over one half of world trade in these products and represent a large net export-earner for developing countries collectively.

The author describes the nature and extent of the subsidies paid to the fisheries sector as well as the relevant WTO obligations with respect to what is prohibited by WTO rules, what is actionable under the WTO, and what is non actionable. In his view, the Subsidies Agreement appears to create significant opportunities for challenges to fishery subsidies, although substantial questions about the legal limits on such challenges remain.

The broader question is whether there is a role for the WTO in addressing the problem in the case of fisheries. He concludes that "there are good reasons to contemplate a more direct role for the WTO on the fishery subsidies issue. First, fishery subsidies do cause trade distortions . . . The WTO has experience with handling subsidies-related disputes and with negotiating subsidies disciplines (e.g. the Agriculture Agreement). The operations of the WTO Subsidies Committee (including oversight of the notification process) could also provide the seed of a structure for a fuller notification and monitoring system on fishery subsidies. Finally, the WTO system offers a ready-made process for binding dispute resolution and a plausible context for negotiations to forge new fishery subsidies rules." The author, however, cautions that the WTO does not hold all the solutions. It is clear that several classes of important fishery subsidies appear "unlikely" to be disciplined under these rules, whereas some environmentally beneficial subsidies remain subject to attack.

One of the principal obstacles to developing countries in accessing the markets of developed countries is meeting the required standards for their exports. Thus, chapters 7, 8, and 9 all deal with mandatory and voluntary standards to protect the environment and health. The two key agreements covering standards under the WTO are the Agreement on Sanitary and Phytosanitary Measures (SPS) and the Agreement on Technical Barriers to Trade (TBT). Within both of these agreements, an attempt has been made to strike a balance between the sovereign right of members to adopt legitimate standards to protect to their citizenry and the adoption of standards that serve as unnecessary obstacles to trade. Striking the right balance is the difficult task that confronts trade officials when interpreting and enforcing the two agreements. The standards provided for under the agreements and their relationship to the legitimacy of WTO labelling are also an issue of considerable importance, particularly for developing countries whose market access could depend upon the status of these requirements.

In chapter 7, Steve Charnovitz analyses what promises to be one of the most important WTO agreements in coming years, namely, the Sanitary and Phytosanitary (SPS) Agreement. This is particularly the case for developing countries, and the author notes that there are surely "numerous questionable SPS barriers that impede exports to industrial countries." He expresses some surprise that so far there has been no SPS litigation involving a developing country. In his view, this is certainly related to the complexity of the subject-matter and the "complicated" nature of dispute settlement when it comes to SPS matters. He observes that rich countries "with large governmental legal staffs that are repeat litigants will have the advantage in SPS adjudication."

The author sets about explaining the SPS Agreement against the backdrop of three cases that have been dealt with by WTO panels: the complaint by the United States and Canada against a European Commission ban (begun in 1989) on the importation of meat produced with growth hormones; the complaint by Canada against an Australian ban (begun in 1975) on the importation of uncooked salmon; and a complaint by the United States about a Japanese phytosanitary measure (begun in 1950) that banned imports of apples, cherries, nectarines, and walnuts potentially infested with coddling moth.

The author explains the SPS rules in terms of seven disciplines. First, any SPS measure is to be based on scientific principles. Second, governments are to ensure that their SPS measures are based on risk assessment. Third, distinctions in the levels of health protection are not to result in disguised restrictions on international trade. Fourth, SPS measures are not to be more trade-restrictive than required to achieve their appropriate level of protection. Fifth, SPS measures are to be based on international standards. Sixth, an importer is to accept an exporter's SPS measure as equivalent to its own if it achieves the level of protection. Finally, the WTO is to be notified of regulations and affected governments must be allowed to make comments.

As in other chapters, the author finds a flaw in an otherwise "reasonable" dispute settlement process—its secretive, closed nature. His view is that it "seems contradictory for governments to make sanitary decisions with open, transparent procedures and then have them reviewed at the WTO behind closed doors." Although this problem is common to all WTO dispute settlement, in his view it is perhaps most acute in the area of health and environment. He notes that "not only are panel sessions closed, but panels so far have been unwilling to entertain *amicus curiae* briefs submitted by non-governmental organizations. For example, when an NGO submitted an *amicus* brief to the *Hormones* panel, it was rejected by the WTO Secretariat."

The author considers that there are at least three controversial issues that should be addressed in any future WTO negotiations. The first is the highly intrusive regulatory consistency requirement, which provided the grounds on which the defendants in both the Australian *Salmon* and the Japanese *Agricultural Products* lost their cases. Second is the precautionary principle. The use of the precautionary principle is increasing under international law and has become the basis for environmental protection in several multilateral agreements such as the Biodiversity and Climate Change Conventions. The principle remains highly theoretical, however, because no practical implementation guidelines have been established. Several key questions in regard to its practical application remain unanswered. These questions include the definition of "irreversible damage," the level of certainty necessary to justify action, and the issue of how to balance costs against potential damage. The third issue raised in chapter 7 relates to product labelling. This transcends both the SPS and the TBT agreements and is dealt with, more comprehensively, in the chapters by Arthur Appleton and Doaa Abdel Motaal.

With respect to improving the accessibility of developing countries and the protection offered to them by the SPS Agreement, the author is sceptical of the progress being made. Despite a recognition in the March 1999 report of the SPS Committee, the author believes that the Committee has made very little progress on enhancing technical assistance to developing countries, particularly with regard to human resource development, national capacity-building, and the transfer of technology and information. Consequently, the author proposes that, in Seattle or any subsequent negotiations, the Committee could be invigorated by giving it a broader mandate and authorizing more coordination with external agencies. The author concludes by noting that, although high SPS standards are needed throughout the world, "it is in developing countries that the regulatory regimes are weakest. By working with those countries to implement international food safety standards, the WTO could reduce potential barriers to food exports by those countries."

In chapter 8, Arthur Appleton examines eco-labelling schemes, the goal of which is to discriminate against products that are perceived to be less environmentally sound. Although the overall goal of eco-labelling schemes—using market forces to improve the environment—is laudable, the author analyses why they are of both systemic and commercial concern to developing countries. From a commercial perspective, producers in developing countries lack the resources and political expertise to influence the development of foreign labelling criteria. Also, developed countries may formulate eco-labelling criteria on the basis of conditions in their own countries that are not appropriate for developing countries. Further, wage considerations, regulatory requirements, and the enforcement of regulations are often viewed as sources of comparative advantage. Labelling schemes that alert consumers to serious discrepancies in the above may disadvantage developing countries and be based on what can be very subjective factors.

From a systemic perspective, the author introduces one of the "most controversial trade issues" which has been a recurring theme in this book; namely, "whether a WTO member should be permitted to apply its trade policy to influence the selection of manufacturing processes in other countries." He notes that WTO members have little problem with the idea that a particular state can regulate production processes within its own jurisdiction, or that a member can establish performance-related environmental standards applicable to products within its own jurisdiction. Controversies arise when a member seeks to apply its laws to influence production processes and methods outside its jurisdiction.

The relevance of this issue relates to the fact that certain environmental labelling schemes provide a means of discriminating between products by informing consumers when production methods do not meet particular environmental, labour, or other criteria. From the trade law perspective, this issue is intertwined with the "like product" distinction made in WTO agreements that restrict the right of importers to discriminate between and among foreign and domestic like products on the basis of how they were produced. The result has been that "processes and production methods" that cannot be detected in the final product are not relevant in making a like product determination. The author provides a comprehensive legal analysis of the consistency or otherwise of eco-labelling schemes with key GATT provisions, such as most-favoured-nation treatment, national treatment, and limitations on the use of quantitative restrictions, as well as the Technical Barriers to Trade Agreement.

In the view of the author, whereas from an environmental or labour perspective the disregard for the manner in which a product was produced may be subject to criticism, from the trade perspective it is justified on the grounds that differentiating between goods based on production methods would increase trade barriers and result in increased trade discrimination. Developing countries have been particularly adamant in opposing trade restrictions based on production methods out of fear that they would lose economically.

However, the author notes that, although the policy considerations presented above are serious, at this point there is little evidence to suggest that eco-labelling schemes have significantly altered consumer buying habits or manufacturing practices. Instead, fears concerning labelling schemes currently appear exaggerated. He concludes from this that, from the developing country perspective, the strong opposition in many quarters to labelling schemes may be a strategic decision. By keeping the attention of the trade community focused on eco-labelling, other more important issues, such as the internalization of environmental externalities and labour-related labelling, have been kept off the agenda.

In chapter 9, Doaa Abdel Motaal outlines the manner in which eco-labelling has been discussed in the Committee on Trade and Environment (CTE) and the Committee on Technical Barriers to Trade (CTBT) and, as such, provides insights into the extent to which there can be different interpretations on the part of various delegations of key WTO terminology. In the CTE, eco-labelling has been examined within the broader context of all product-related environmental requirements, and in the CTBT within the context of the Agreement on Technical Barriers to Trade (TBT).

The author identifies two main questions that have been raised by WTO members. The first concerns the coverage of the TBT Agreement; some members have questioned the extent to which the Agreement covers eco-labelling schemes. The second concerns the consistency of eco-labels with the provisions of the TBT Agreement. What has been discussed with respect to both these viewpoints has been the extent to which such schemes differentiate between products on grounds that are accepted by the WTO; namely, the manner in which the goods were produced.

The author points to a number of arguments to support the avoidance of differentiation on the basis of production methods. The first relates to the preservation of territorial sovereignty, because preventing discrimination on the basis of production methods is to prevent intervention from the outside in rule-setting within national boundaries. The author notes that it is "precisely because the WTO is able to offer such security to its members that its membership has expanded to the size it is today." The second is that avoiding differentiation based on production methods "allows countries to set standards (environmental or otherwise) that are appropriate for their level of development"; it "allows countries to trade their developmental needs against their needs for environmental protection in a manner that is consistent with how they themselves value these needs (and not on the basis of how others value them for them)." Finally, "differences in environmental absorptive capacities, priorities and problems in different parts of the world can be taken into account" through providing for different production processes.

The author notes that, although it is "often stated that a North–South divide characterizes trade and environment discussions in the WTO . . . [n]umerous standpoints have been taken in the CTE on the extent to which eco-labels are covered by and are consistent with WTO rules . . . Although it may be argued that there is a distinctly Southern perspective in the CTE on this issue, it cannot be stated that a distinctly Northern viewpoint has emerged." Among the views that have emerged in the WTO are that: eco-labels are both covered by and consistent with the TBT Agreement; they are not covered by the TBT Agreement but scope needs to be created for them; they are not covered by the TBT Agreement and creating scope for them could endanger the trading system; and they are inconsistent with the TBT Agreement and should not find any accommodation within the WTO system.

In chapter 10, James Cameron examines the Precautionary Principle and its importance and relevance with respect to trade agreements. He identifies the principle as "part of a system of rules designed to guide human behaviour towards the ideal of an environmentally sustainable economy. Fundamentally, it provides the philosophical authority to take public policy or regulatory decisions in the face of scientific uncertainty." The author notes that the "precautionary principle began to appear in international legal instruments only in the 1980s, but it has since experienced what has been called a meteoric rise in international law." He describes it as a statement of commonsense, "with utility in balancing the competing concerns of economic development against limited environmental resources. The economics of globalization continue to place ever-increasing demands on resources while increasing the efficiency of their use. This essential paradox, together with well-organized opposition to trade liberalization from the environment lobby, has informed the search for balance between trade and environment policy."

This chapter details a brief history of the principle, as evidenced in the usage of explicit precautionary language in law. It then analyses in some detail the core concepts inherent in the precautionary principle and examines the status of the principle in international law. It discusses a number of procedural aspects of implementing the principle, and finally reviews the precautionary principle in international trade situations, specifically those within or related to the WTO.

The author recognizes that the principle is an "elusive concept," and therefore has questionable status in international law, or "at present . . . is not a term of art." However, the precautionary principle "does have a conceptual core"; it reflects "a lack of certainty about the cause-and-effect relationships or the possible extent of a particular environmental harm. If there is no uncertainty about the environmental risks of a situation, then the measure is preventative, not precautionary. In the face of uncertainty, however, the precautionary principle allows . . . for the state to act in an effort to mitigate the risks. Put best, 'the precautionary principle stipulates that where the environmental risks being run by regulatory inaction are in some way uncertain but non-negligible, regulatory inaction is unjustified'."

According to the author, the WTO has already adopted sustainable development—and the notion of the precautionary principle—as an orientation for trade liberalization. He draws attention in this respect to the Preamble to the Agreement Establishing the WTO, which refers to "the optimal use of the world's resources in accordance with the objective of sustainable development, seeking both to protect and preserve the environment and to enhance the means for doing so in a manner consistent with their respective needs and concerns at different levels of economic development." The importance of the precautionary principle for international trade agreements is also underscored by the fact that it is directly relevant for two WTO agreements: the Agreement on the Application of Sanitary and Phytosanitary Measures and the Agreement on Technical Barriers to Trade. At issue with respect to these agreements is the extent to which measures can be taken to restrain trade in the absence of scientific evidence, a consideration also taken up by Steve Charnovitz in relation to the SPS Agreement. Additionally, the exceptions provisions of GATT can be informed by the principle, and the author outlines its significance in some of the most controversial WTO dispute settlement cases. The author also draws attention to the extent to which the precautionary principle has become an important principle for some of the most important multilateral environment agreements, some of which are identified by Duncan Brack in the following chapter as being potentially inconsistent with WTO rules.

In chapter 11, Duncan Brack examines the key issues in the debate over how best to reconcile the two objectives of environmental protection and trade liberalization as they emerge in two bodies of international law—that found in multilateral environmental agreements (MEAs) and those of the multilateral trading system overseen by the WTO. Trade liberalization and environmental protection may both be desirable objectives, but the legal regimes that govern them are developing largely in isolation. In the view of the author, "a failure to resolve the *potential* conflict between them can lead only to actual conflict, undermining both. The time to act is now." This chapter summarizes the key issues at stake, examines various options for the resolution of the debate, and concludes that a new WTO Agreement on MEAs would provide the optimal solution.

The view of the author is that "the biggest danger in this debate is that no political impetus will be given to it and nothing will in the end be resolved. It is entirely possible to argue, for example, that most MEAs do not contain trade provisions, that there has never been a WTO dispute involving an MEA, and that recent panel and Appellate Body findings have shown that the WTO is sensitive to the environmental imperative; therefore, no action is required." Also, the authors of both chapters 2 and 3 elaborated the misgivings of a number of WTO members with respect to modifying WTO rules to accommodate inconsistent WTO measures as contained in MEAs.

The author is of the view that inaction in this important area "would be a profound mistake. MEAs are growing in number, in scope and in importance, matching the growing evidence of global environmental degradation. In some cases they will need to impact international trade if they are to be implemented effectively." The author considers that there have already been too many instances of multilateral trading system incompatibility arguments "being used as weapons in MEA negotiations to retard their development."

Nearly 200 MEAs now exist, with memberships varying from a relatively small group to about 170 countries—which means in effect the whole world. The main global MEAs include: the 1973 Convention on International Trade in Endangered Species (CITES); the 1987 Montreal Protocol on Substances that Deplete the Ozone Layer; the 1989 Basel Convention on the Control of Transboundary Movements of Hazardous Wastes; the 1992 Rio agreements (the Framework Convention on Climate Change, the Convention on Biological Diversity, and the Convention to Combat Desertification). Others agreed recently, but not yet in force, include the 1997 Kyoto Protocol on climate change and the 1998 Rotterdam Convention on hazardous chemicals in international trade. There are also draft MEAs still under negotiation, including the convention on the control of persistent organic pollutants, and the Biosafety Protocol to the Biodiversity Convention.

The author poses the question of whether the use of trade measures in these MEAs against WTO members be regarded as an infringement of WTO rights. The author concludes that "there is a *potential* for conflict"; for example, WTO members are not permitted to discriminate between traded "like products" produced by other WTO members, or between domestic and international "like products," yet CITES, the Montreal Protocol, and the Basel Convention discriminate between countries on the basis of their environmental performance, requiring parties to restrict trade to a greater extent with non-parties than they do with parties.

The author examines various possible routes to resolving the issue and concludes that the "distinctly preferable" route is to create a new WTO side agreement. The advantage is that "it avoids attempting to amend existing rules, with probable implications for a wide range of topics; it creates a very clear set of rules which would apply only to MEAs (i.e. which would not encourage further unilateral actions); and it is probably easier to negotiate." The author elaborates on the content of such a WTO side agreement to accommodate MEAs in the WTO context.

Note

1. These data are drawn from http://www.wto.org/wto/anniv/intro.htm.

1

Trade and Environment: Strengthening Complementarities and Reducing Conflicts

Rubens Ricupero
Secretary-General of UNCTAD

It is with great pleasure that I have accepted the invitation by the United Nations University to contribute a chapter to this important book on Trade and Environment.[1] The fact that it is to be launched before the Ministerial Conference of the World Trade Organization (WTO) in Seattle is both a challenge and a reason for caution. On the one hand, I think that the conference and its preparatory process provide a good opportunity to reflect on progress made in trade and environment and on what is needed to move towards further integration of the trade and environment regimes. This is particularly important in the process of greater trade liberalization that is likely to follow. At the same time, however, many of my friends among developing countries' negotiators in Geneva are deeply concerned about the prospect that trade and environment could be included in a possible new round of multilateral trade negotiations.

This does not mean that developing countries are not interested in trade and environment issues. On the contrary, our experience at the United Nations Conference on Trade and Development (UNCTAD) shows that developing countries attach great interest to them. This can be observed in their strong interest in policy analysis and technical assistance for capacity-building and in their efforts to benefit from new trading opportunities that are arising on account of environmental concerns. Developing countries have nevertheless expressed concern about developments in trade and environment issues in the context of the multilateral trading system (MTS).

In this chapter I will first address the question of why there is not much excitement among developing countries in Geneva over the prospects of a new round of multilateral trade negotiations, particularly where environmental issues are concerned. The intention is not to spread pessimism among those who see the round as an opportunity to make progress on specific issues, but rather to warn against excessively high expectations that later may turn into unnecessary disappointment and unjustified frustration. Then I will reflect on the extent to which trade and environment regimes are either complementary or in potential conflict with each other. Finally, I will make some suggestions about what can be done to move ahead on trade and environment, both within and outside the MTS.

1. A new round: Little enthusiasm among developing countries, in particular when it comes to the environment

With regard to the prospects of a new round of trade negotiations, I have already mentioned that developing countries are not exactly thrilled by the idea.[2] In a recent speech at a seminar organized by Columbia University,[3] I highlighted that the reasons for that attitude generally fell into one of four categories: the financial and economic crisis; problems with the functioning of the world trade system; the revival of protectionism; and a growing frustration with the gap between the promise and reality of trade liberalization.

Turning now to the reasons that many developing countries are so deeply concerned about the prospects of trade and environment being included in a new round, they largely overlap with those mentioned above. But there are also additional reasons, such as the failure of developed countries to live up to the commitments made at the United Nations Conference on Environment and Development (UNCED) in Rio de Janeiro in June 1992. Let us discuss some of them.

The resurgence of protectionism

Developing countries are concerned that the recent international economic and financial crisis appears to be inducing renewed recourse to protectionism and unilateral measures, including measures taken under the guise of environmental concerns. There is also concern about continued pressures to accommodate the use of trade-restrictive measures for non-trade purposes. It is feared that such pressures may also spill over into other areas, such as labour issues.

Concerns about the resurgence of protectionism cannot be dismissed as being based on a lack of information or on exaggerated fears that legitimate environmental policies in developed countries will have widespread adverse effects on the competitiveness of products exported by developing countries. On the contrary, such concerns have emerged first and foremost because of the renewed recourse to old-fashioned protectionism. First, making progress on agriculture has proven far more difficult than anticipated. For example, speaking before the US House Agricultural Committee, Ms. Charlene Barshefsky accused the Common Agricultural Policy (CAP) of the European Union (EU) of responsibility for 85 per cent of the world's agriculture export subsidies. Ms. Barshefsky referred to this practice as "the largest distortion of any sort of trade." A few months earlier, the Cologne meeting of the EU had already confirmed how difficult it would be to undertake a serious reform of the CAP as a necessary basis for future liberalization of agricultural trade. There has also been a resurgence of protectionism in some industrial sectors. In steel products, for example, we are now witnessing what I personally consider the worst single setback since the Uruguay Round: the return of so-called "voluntary" export restraint agreements; in other words, the comeback in force of "managed trade." Here we have a clear-cut case of prohibited grey-area measures that are resurrected.

If we add to what could be called "grandfather protectionism" the "New Wave" variety (that is, the serious danger that legitimate concerns about the environment and labour will inevitably be misused as protectionist tools), we will understand why so many developing countries fail to see any promising prospects of redressing past imbalances in a new round.

Systemic issues

There are concerns about systemic issues. The difficulties encountered in some cases (e.g. bananas) are well known. Let me go straight to the environmental issues. Recent decisions by Appellate Bodies of the WTO have fundamental implications that still need further analysis, for example with regard to subparagraph (g) of Article XX of the General Agreement on Tariffs and Trade (GATT) 1947 and the issue of trade measures based on non-product-related process and production methods (PPMs). Although welcomed by many in developed countries, these measures have generated new concerns in developing countries, which believe they are being used to impose the environmental policies and priorities of developed countries on developing country trading partners. They have also created some alarm about the implications of clarifying trade and environment issues on the basis of case-law and Appellate Body decisions.

In this context, it should be noted that many developing countries have now become more committed to the defence of the multilateral trading partners than the major trading partners, for whom unilateralism is always an alternative and a temptation. Attempts to amend existing trade rules, for example to accommodate trade measures under multilateral environmental agreements (MEAs), may have implications for a wide range of topics. Similarly, pressure from some to make the WTO treatment of non-product-related PPMs a central and systemic issue causes deep concern to the developing countries, because it implies very substantive changes in the operation of the multilateral trading system.

The deal struck at Rio

At Rio it was agreed that all countries have a responsibility and must cooperate to achieve environmental and sustainable development objectives, based on the principle of common but differentiated responsibilities. Thus, developed countries took on a commitment to provide improved access to their markets for products from developing countries and to promote access to environmentally sound technologies and finance. It is widely recognized that MEA negotiators should consider a package of measures focusing on supportive measures and, in some cases, trade measures. However, there is some concern that "accommodation" of MEA trade measures in the WTO may deter the search for supportive measures, such as transfer of technologies, financial assistance, and improved market access, including for environment-friendly products.

Avoiding excessively high expectations

It is sometimes argued that a new round of multilateral trade negotiations is an important opportunity to move on trade and environment. The reason given is that in a broad process of negotiations, covering a range of issues, trade-offs can be identified. I would nevertheless argue that we should be careful not to create excessively high expectations.

First, there is still no broad consensus on the need to modify the provisions of the multilateral trading system for environmental purposes. For example, several years of deliberations in the Environmental Measures and International Trade group and the WTO Committee on Trade and Environment have not resulted in any concrete recommendations to modify the existing provisions of the multilateral trading system. I will come back to the issue of compatibility/conflict between trade and environment regimes in the next section.

Second, developed countries are in a difficult bargaining position with regard to the lion's share of issues being proposed for future negotiations. Thus, they may simply not have sufficient concessions to offer to enable trade-offs between issues of interest to them vis-à-vis issues being proposed by developing countries.

Third, the current trade and environment debate seems to lack balance. Proposals made so far seem to focus on accommodating measures that could restrict trade, rather than on measures that promote trade. As long as developing countries fear that engaging in negotiations on trade and environment could result in further accommodation of trade-restrictive measures on environmental grounds, thereby limiting their market access, it is unlikely that they would be inclined to accept a trade-off between environment and market access. After all, what would be the deal?

Fourth, as mentioned above, UNCED already tried to strike a deal between developed and developing countries. However, the recent assessment of progress in the implementation of Agenda 21 by the United Nations General Assembly showed that little progress has been made on what Agenda 21 calls "implementation issues," such as finance, access to environmentally sound technologies, and, perhaps to a lesser extent, capacity-building. This leaves us with the following question: if the Rio commitments have not so far been implemented, what would be different in a new trade-off? What appears to make this question even more relevant are the doubts often expressed by developed countries over the extent to which so-called supportive measures (such as access to and transfer of technology) can be specified in WTO agreements.

Fifth, many of the solutions to problems related to the interface between trade and environment should perhaps be sought outside the multilateral trading system. I will come back to this in the final section.

Having said this, I do not want to be misunderstood. The multilateral trading system has to be responsive to legitimate environmental concerns. If there were consensus among WTO members that certain provisions of the MTS stand in the way of achieving sustainable development objectives, we should together examine possible adaptations, based on equity and other Rio principles.

The WTO Ministerial Conference is an important opportunity to raise further awareness, including on the need to ensure that the resulting trade liberalization process is as friendly to the environment as possible. This means that we have to continue to pay high priority to trade and environment, carry out policy analysis, and build consensus throughout the negotiating process. We should also step up capacity-building efforts.

2. To what extent do trade and environment regimes conflict?

We should not create the impression that the major problems for the environment stem from international trade or the rules of the multilateral trading system. The plain fact is that, although there are more than 200 multilateral environmental agreements, fewer than 20 of them have trade provisions, and there has not been a single case of differences between these agreements and the GATT/WTO agreements that member countries have considered of great importance. Thus, to postulate conflicts between the trade and environment regimes is to indulge in abstractions that have yet to be proven to be grounded in reality.

Analysis carried out by UNCTAD for many years has confirmed that compatibility between trade and the environment is the rule; conflict is the exception. And, where conflict has arisen, current rules have often provided an appropriate setting for their settlement. *Causes célèbres,* such as the so-called "eco-dumping" controversy, or unfair competition induced by lax environmental regulations, have in reality proven to be non-issues or largely exaggerated. Equally exaggerated have been fears that MEA trade measures may be challenged in the WTO.

It is important to consider collectively, and in a coordinated fashion, the international rules needed to ensure that the trade and environment regimes are mutually supportive. Given the number, variety, and forcefulness of the non-governmental organizations involved in environmental policy-making, it seems that only good can come out of such a process.

However, we should keep in mind that all this will require time for analysis and consensus-building, including in the context of the international environmental agenda. In the environmental arena we are still far from the consensus achieved in the multilateral trading system. For instance, one needs only to remember the strenuous last-minute efforts that had to be made before Rio to bring the United States on board for the Framework Convention on Climate Change, and how similar efforts failed in the case of biodiversity. More recently, negotiators in Cartagena, Colombia, failed to negotiate a Biosafety Protocol, which *inter alia* involves the sensitive issue of trade in genetically modified organisms. By contrast, in the multilateral trade talks the United States has consistently used its unrivalled power to steer and drive the negotiations. Thus, as far as environment is concerned, the biggest hurdles to overcome have mostly been created by the most powerful players of the international trade system, not by less influential developing countries.

3. Looking ahead

Opinions on what has been achieved so far on trade and environment vary widely, in accordance with differing perspectives and expectations. Whereas many observers have expressed disappointment about the lack of clear results in the WTO Committee on Trade and Environment, others have found that it was more important to initiate an educational process. The limitations and opportunities of the WTO system to provide remedies in order to accommodate environmental concerns are also becoming apparent. The debate has highlighted the fact that remedies often lie outside the WTO system and are to be found in the very framework of environment policy-making at both the national and multilateral level.

Some progress has nevertheless been made. First, whereas the earlier debate was characterized largely by fears of major contradictions between trade and environment policies, the post-UNCED debate has focused on exploring the scope of the complementarities between trade liberalization, economic development, and environmental protection. Secondly, conceptual and empirical analyses have helped to avoid inappropriate policy choices, for example on the competitiveness issue. Thirdly, the debate has become much more participatory. It is noteworthy that the current debate seems to have attracted the attention of a very large range of stakeholders, including at the levels of different government ministries, NGOs, the business community, and academic institutions in both developed and developing countries. This has allowed the international community to engage in a much more knowledge-based and constructive agenda.

At the national level as well, many developing countries are adopting a proactive approach to trade and environment issues. One reason is that they have become increasingly aware that they cannot embark on successful development processes without paying appropriate attention to environmental protection and the sustainable management of their natural resources. It is also becoming clear that trade-offs between environmental protection and trade liberalization have to be resolved nationally. The benefits of environmental protection in terms of development, trade, and other economic gains are also gaining currency in the developing countries.

Seattle and subsequent trade negotiations could create more awareness and promote trade and environment coordination at the national and multilateral levels. UNCTAD and the United Nations Environment Programme (UNEP) could make an important contribution, for example through a joint programme of capacity-building on trade, environment, and development. The two institutions are envisaging the creation of a task force with the explicit aim of building capacity by pooling the technical expertise of these two organizations. Such a joint programme could bring together various stakeholders who could articulate concrete steps that should be taken to further the process of consensus-building around these issues.

The economics of the environment

National economic policies are inevitably concerned about employment creation, tax revenues, and economic growth, all of which push environmental concerns to the bottom of the list of priorities. It is necessary to focus on creating incentive structures to move environment up the priority list, in other words, to "reinvent the economy." Markets and accounting systems should recognize natural resources as assets in the true sense of the term, or should value resource-based goods and services properly. For example, in the context of biodiversity, economic incentives and better pricing of the products and services derived from biodiversity would better meet conservation and sustainable development objectives. Misleading information about scarcity values, conveyed through low prices of genetic resources and the know-how based on traditional knowledge, can seriously endanger biodiversity. This in turn can create a faulty decision-making process for the management, utilization, and enhancement of natural resources. In the absence of well-defined property rights for public goods, to which access is generally open, such as clean air, clean water, and biodiversity, these goods can be overused in productive activities; preventing such overuse requires judicious government intervention as well as effective market signals.

Creating an effective market for environmental goods and services can also help to meet environmental objectives. Creating a market for the products derived from traditional knowledge, for example, may generate market premiums and hence incentives for conservation. Similarly, in the context of climate change, creating markets for energy-efficient products and alternative sources of energy might be a cost-effective way of reducing carbon emissions at the global level.

Strengthening policy coordination at the national level

The vast majority of environmental problems are not global, or even regional, but local. They do not involve an international dimension, or, *a fortiori,* a trade dimension. To deal with real-life environmental problems, we should literally start at the national level.

Concerns such as the reduction or elimination of perverse subsidies, distortions affecting the management of natural resources, and the distorting effects of macroeconomic mismanagement are best tackled at home. Growing economies, many of which are developing countries, are in a better position to bring about the necessary shifts in resources, employment, and government revenue required to accommodate desirable environmental objectives. In this context it is worth noting that, left to itself, the market system provides incorrect signals and misleading information and therefore needs to be complemented by well-designed government intervention. The role of strengthening policy coordination between different ministries is particularly important in guiding government intervention to correct for market failures. Such intervention should seek to ensure that levels of costs and benefits reflect the fullest information about scarcity, rights and responsibilities, and actions and consequences. Coordination between civil society and government is crucial in generating the information needed to make such intervention meaningful. The pragmatic and timely use of such information by society is a precondition for the promotion of sound long-term management of natural resources. Iterative dialogue procedures between government and civil society, including the private sector, are important for ensuring that such information is fed into decision-making procedures at the right time. The role of the media should also be highlighted in these decision-making processes.

What can be done in the context of future trade negotiations?

I very much support the view that the new round should be a Development Round. Development is needed to eradicate poverty; it also implies the need to pay greater attention to environmental quality, for example by strengthening infrastructure and by ensuring the availability of adequate sanitation and drinking water. The principle of common but differentiated responsibilities, which gives high priority to the concept of equity, should be fully taken into account.

Progress could be made on a number of issues. First, there could be further trade liberalization in areas where possibilities for "win–win" results—i.e. improved trading opportunities and enhanced environmental protection at a global scale—have been identified. Secondly, in accordance with the principle of common but differentiated responsibilities and the concept of equity, any consideration of the environmental implications of negotiations concerning specific WTO agreements should be accompanied by an examination of developing countries' needs in terms of technology, finance, and capacity-building. Thirdly, there should be further trade liberalization in sectors of key export interest to developing countries. Fourthly, progress should be made in the areas of technology and special and differential treatment, as well as in the effective implementation of corresponding WTO provisions.

The positive agenda

In my report to UNCTAD X, I emphasized that "environmental considerations have come to interact with trade policies, and this trend is likely to continue. UNCTAD can play a role in helping developing countries identify areas in which they can take advantage of trading opportunities that may arise on account of environmental concerns, and in helping developing countries work out a positive agenda on trade and environment issues."[4]

The chapter in this book by my colleagues Veena Jha and René Vossenaar (chap. 3) examines possible elements of a positive agenda on trade and environment. Speaking about the positive agenda—not in the context of trade and environment, but in general—in my statement on the next trade negotiating round, I said the following: "I know that some of my friends among developing countries' negotiators will think that our positive agenda is a losing proposition and that we only risk legitimizing an essentially flawed and unbalanced process."[5] They may think this in particular when the environment is involved. But in the same statement I said that, "As you can judge from some of my comments, I am not unaware of the pitfalls and dangers of the exercise. I believe, however, with Albert Schweitzer, that one may be pessimistic in knowledge, but optimistic in hope and action."[6]

Notes

1. These comments are made in my personal capacity.
2. The concerns of developing countries are largely threefold. First, they stress that the Uruguay Round and its implementation process did too little to improve market access for developing country exports of goods and services. Secondly, many developing countries feel that the new WTO rules have been imbalanced in several important development-related areas, such as the protection of intellectual property rights and the issue of industrial subsidies, while special and differential treatment for them in the WTO agreements has been inadequate and needs revision. Thirdly, weaker human and institutional capacities, as well as a lack of financing, have prevented developing countries from using the WTO system to pursue their interests, particularly in making use of the dispute settlement mechanism, and also from complying fully with their multilateral obligations.
3. Rubens Ricupero, "Why Not a Development Round This Time, for a Change?" Keynote luncheon statement delivered at the New York Seminar "To the Next Trade Negotiating Round, Examining the Agenda for Seattle," Columbia University, 23 July 1999.
4. "Report of the Secretary-General of UNCTAD to UNCTAD X," TD/380, 29 July 1999.
5. Ricupero, "Why Not a Development Round This Time, for a Change?", op. cit.
6. Ibid.

2

Trade and Environment:
How Real Is the Debate?

Magda Shahin

Globalization and liberalization are the twin processes marking the beginning of the twenty-first century. Today, we are confronted with maxims such as "Making Globalization Social and Green"[1] or "Globalization with a Human Face." A myriad of new standards is in the making to handle the devastating effects of globalization on developed and developing countries alike. Yet, without a doubt, developed countries are the front-runners. Green consumers, healthy consumers, and safe consumers are now in the driving seat. Today, trade wars are erupting even between the United States and the European countries on genetically altered crops and modified food, threatening trade and investment flows accounting for more than US$2,000 billion annually and providing 14 million jobs on both sides of the Atlantic.[2] What are the underlying motives? Are they truly anxiety and concern for food safety, the environment, morality, and concern for human kind? Or are these kinds of trade wars driven by world hegemony and by commercial interests with billions of dollars at stake? Is linking trade to environment a justified concern with genuine environmental goals? Or are additional protection measures at play? Where do the developing countries fit into all this, with their resource constraints, poor information flows, and lack of scientific knowledge?

1. Background

The relationship between trade and environment is complex and critical.
It is over-burdened with suspicion and strained by misunderstandings
that need to be addressed and clarified. To that end, it is appropriate to
go back as far as the issuing of the Brundtland report in the mid-1980s.
Brundtland, the Prime Minister of Norway at that time, chaired a group
of eminent personalities. In her famous report, she drew the attention of
the international community to the interface between environment and
development in the newly introduced phrase "sustainable development."
When introduced at the 39th General Assembly in 1985, it was met
with a great deal of scepticism on the part of developing countries in
general. The notion of sacrificing today's development to preserve the
environment for the development of future generations was viewed with
resentment and misgivings. It took the international community several
years and a huge effort to work out a smooth relationship between
development and environment and to establish close linkages between
them. This culminated in an Agreement at the UN Conference on
Environment and Development (UNCED) held in Rio de Janeiro in
1992. The Agreement has established fundamental principles to be
observed and specific measures to be undertaken for the attainment of
environmental goals, all framed in a detailed programme of action:
Agenda 21. Some of the key principles of the Rio Declaration are
particularly pertinent to our discussion:

> The right to development must be fulfilled so as to equitably meet
> developmental and environmental needs of present and future gen-
> erations. (Principle 3)
>
> Eradicating poverty is an indispensable requirement for sustainable
> development. (Principle 5)
>
> States have common but differentiated responsibilities in regard to
> promoting sustainable development. (Principle 7)
>
> There should be a diffusion and transfer of technologies. (Principle 9)
>
> States should co-operate to promote a supportive and open interna-
> tional economic system that would lead to economic growth and
> sustainable development in all countries. (Principle 12)[3]

Agenda 21 set out specific measures on trade; in particular, the promotion of "an open, non-discriminatory and equitable multilateral trading system that will enable all countries—in particular, the developing countries—to improve their economic structures and improve the standard of living of their populations through sustained economic development."[4] In addition, a range of measures was agreed for the transfer of technology and the provision of new and additional financial resources to the developing countries for the implementation of the programme. Hence Agenda 21 set the basic principles as well as the overall framework within which the international community shoulders its burden of responsibility and has to work in order to protect, preserve, and enhance the environment together with the development process, particularly in developing countries.

Nevertheless, in parallel to that event and far away in Geneva, while trade representatives were busy negotiating the Uruguay Round Agreements of the soon to be World Trade Organization, environmentalists were determined to integrate environment in the trade debate. Their intentions and motives were questioned at a time when the Rio Conference had just been successfully concluded. Were developed countries thinking of backtracking on the commitments and obligations they had agreed to within the framework of the UN Conference? Were developing countries justified in their apprehensions about the trade debate? Were these apprehensions legitimate? It did not take long for such doubts to be proved well founded. In addition to the persisting divisions in the ongoing debate in the World Trade Organization, the lack of progress in the mid-term review of the Rio Programme of Action in New York in 1997 was yet further proof of the doubts and suspicions aired by developing countries. There has been obvious, and regrettable, backtracking on the obligations undertaken by the developed countries, especially in regard to improving market access for developing country exports, the transfer of technology, and the provision of new and additional resources. (In regard to financial resources, it was estimated that the developing countries would require US$125 billion, in the form of grants and concessions, from the international community to implement the activities specified in Agenda 21. This requirement remains unmet.) Moreover, in the view of many developing countries, developed countries are in effect retreating from the holistic approach to sustainable development agreed at Rio. Their focus is now on unilateral measures and on environmental conditionalities attached to trade and investment. This trend is inimical to the attainment of both developmental and environmental goals.[5]

2. The trade and environment debate in the WTO

Though initially developing countries resisted debating the trade/environment relationship in the World Trade Organization (WTO), they reluctantly came to an agreement towards the end of the Uruguay Round. A decision was issued at the Marrakesh Ministerial Conference (1994) to that effect. A Committee on Trade and Environment was established to cool the heat created by the non-governmental organizations (NGOs) and to allow for a smooth signing and ratification of the Uruguay Round Agreements and the creation of the WTO. Dealing with the relationship between trade and environment in the WTO has gone through various phases, at some points being a leading priority in the framework of the WTO work, at other times being less attractive and thus occupying a lower profile. At no time were developing countries the *demandeurs;* on the contrary, they succumbed to pressure on many occasions.

In all this, the central question remained how to bring the trade and the environmental systems closer together without undermining either system, knowing that they are not necessarily always compatible. In fact, the two regimes are often even in conflict. The environmental regime allows for measures that go beyond a country's borders, for the sake of protecting the environment, whereas such a measure would amount to a flagrant violation of WTO rules and regulations, which do not allow for extra-territorial measures. The problem goes even further. Today we see growing concern by environmental groups at the national level forcing the issue of *national sovereignty* against the country's obligations to abide by WTO judgements. A case in point is the well-known dispute regarding "Import Prohibition of Certain Shrimp and Shrimp Products" between the United States on the one hand and Thailand, India, Pakistan, and Malaysia on the other hand. Unhappy with rulings on the matter by the WTO dispute settlement panel and the Appellate Body, a coalition of

US environmental groups raising the issue of national sovereignty succeeded in winning a ruling from the US Court of International Trade that went against the WTO panel. There is no doubt that this ruling from the Court of International Trade will handicap US efforts to comply with the WTO panel and Appellate rulings.[6] The environmentalists believe that the United States is compromising its national sovereignty for the sake of its international obligations.

Today, after five years of intensive discussion and learning about the relationship between trade and environment, many continue to have mixed feelings about how to go about this relationship. Traders and environmentalists have many a time stood helpless and perplexed in front of this conundrum, which turns on how to accommodate environmental concerns in trade policy without tampering with the trade rules. Striking a balance between the need for governments to protect and preserve the environment, on one hand, and avoiding the usage of environmental measures as a new trade protection measure, on the other hand, remains a sensitive and highly controversial issue.

It was only after long and informed reasoning that many realized beyond a doubt that the two systems could not remain under the same roof, because their objectives vary as well as their methods of implementation. That does not mean, however, that trade and environment are not mutually supportive. In many instances they are. Nevertheless, all the efforts to incorporate environment within the WTO system were to no avail. Based on this, Renato Ruggiero, the outgoing WTO Director-General, was brave enough to come up with a solution, which is—to my mind—straightforward and simple. He explained that all we need is a multilateral rules-based system (similar to that of the WTO) for environment—a World Environment Organization to be the institutional and legal counterpart to the WTO. Such a proposal has been put forward on a number of occasions, the last being the High Level Symposium on Trade and Environment in the WTO on 15 March 1999.[7] There has been agreement with this viewpoint. "Indeed, nothing would advance 'trade and environment' harmony more than the creation of a Global Environmental Organization to work alongside the WTO," wrote Daniel C. Esty of Yale University in his presentation to the High Level Symposium.[8]

Realizing the immense difficulties involved in resolving the trade and environment relationship and easing the tension that had developed in the

WTO in this regard, the European Commission proposed a high-level "political" conference to bring trade and environment ministers together in the WTO. Because the debate in the WTO seemed burdened with suspicion and scepticism, developing country representatives in Geneva felt that the timing was not propitious, especially in light of the fact that many issues remained unsolved in this relationship. In their mind, this needed further technical work before it could be brought to a political forum. Together with developed country delegations, they agreed after long deliberations to turn the high-level "political" conference into a non-official, non-conclusive symposium involving a wider spectrum of the public, notably NGOs and academia, in a brainstorming session with a view to airing all positions, including those of civil societies.

It is astonishing that, in spite of the general view that further work needs to be undertaken on all items of the agenda of the CTE, pre-determined positions are still taken. Such positions continue to press for amending the WTO rules to accommodate environment or call for the legitimization of the processes and production methods approach in the GATT system, irrespective of the wide-ranging and serious implications for developing countries and their methods of production. In addition, little tribute is paid to the concerns of developing countries in general. Market access and the new environmental conditions are key in this respect. The pretext that competition among nations is creating downward pressure on environmental standards is causing new protectionist measures to be arbitrarily imposed. The debate has revolved around these and other issues for the past few years. Developing countries have defended their interests and stood firm for positions that today might warrant more explanation and definition. The next phase of negotiations will be not less but certainly more controversial, and developing countries will again have to aggressively defend their positions.

3. The basis of the WTO trade/ environment debate

It is worth noting that the trade and environment debate in the WTO is set within a consensual framework and based on three essential premises. These I would call the three Cs: Consistency with the level of development, the Competence of the world trading system, and allaying fears of additional Conditionality. Let me elaborate further.

First, no one denies the importance assigned to the protection and preservation of the environment in the Preamble of the Marrakesh Agreement Establishing the World Trade Organization.[9] But, it is equally true that the Preamble emphasized that this be done in a manner consistent with the needs and concerns of countries at different levels of economic development. What is of significance here is that the importance accorded to environment was not absolute, but linked to countries' levels of development. I could even argue that priority was given to development, because the protection and preservation of the environment can be achieved only to the extent that this is consistent with the level of development.

It is not difficult to draw a comparison between the WTO Preamble and Rio Principle 7, cited earlier, concerning the common but differentiated responsibilities of states in regard to promoting sustainable development. This principle was the anchor for the UNCED. It accepted that the Northern countries had a greater responsibility for meeting the costs of adjustment because of their larger role in environmental degradation as well as their economic capacity to absorb more costs. The developing countries still needed to grow and develop (sustainably, of course) to meet their people's needs. The North also made a commitment to provide adequate financial resources and technology transfer to facilitate the South's transition to sustainable development.[10]

Secondly, the Marrakesh Ministerial Decision on Trade and Environment[11] was clear in setting the terms of reference for WTO work on trade and environment. The fourth paragraph of the Preamble stipulates that the coordination of policies in the field of trade and environment should be done without exceeding the competence of the multilateral trading system. Again of utmost significance here is that the negotiators were adamant that the "competence of the multilateral trading system" is limited to trade policies and those aspects of environmental policies that may result in significant trade effects for its members.

Thirdly, in order to allay any possible fears of a new "green conditionality" attached to market access opportunities, thus nullifying the benefits accruing from trade liberalization within the context of the Uruguay Round, the 1996 Singapore Ministerial Report on Trade and Environment[12] stressed the following:

1. the WTO is not an environmental protection agency and it is assumed that the WTO itself does not provide an answer to environmental problems;

2. environmental problems require environmental solutions, not trade solutions;

3. no blank cheque for the use of trade measures for environmental purposes;

4. trade liberalization is not the primary cause of environmental degradation, nor are trade instruments the first-best policy for addressing environmental problems;

5. GATT/WTO agreements already provide significant scope for members to adopt national environmental protection policies, provided that they are non-discriminatory;

6. secure market access opportunities are essential to help developing countries work towards sustainable development;

7. increased national coordination as well as multilateral cooperation are necessary to address trade-related environmental concerns adequately.

It is worth stressing that the first WTO Ministerial Conference was keen to elucidate the reality of the relationship and its rightful stance in the multilateral system. It was clear from the ongoing debate at the time that there was no quarrel with depicting the WTO as an environment-friendly organization. In fact, the GATT allows for any action to be taken at the national level to protect the environment, provided it is in compliance with its basic rules and regulations. Article XX ("General Exceptions"),[13] the Agreement on Technical Barriers to Trade (TBT),[14] and the Agreement on the Application of Sanitary and Phytosanitary Measures (SPS)[15] are all cases in point: they give each country the right to set the level of protection that it deems appropriate on environment, provided it does not act against the basic principles of the WTO as stipulated by Article I ("Most-Favoured-Nation Treatment") and Article III ("National Treatment"). In addition, it should not constitute an unnecessary barrier to trade. I should emphasize that the "Trade and Environment" Report adopted at the first Ministerial Conference remains as valid as ever and constitutes the backbone of the ongoing debate on trade and environment. However, one thing developing countries were keen to elucidate was that the report does not represent a legal instrument, hence does not alter or touch upon the rights and obligations of WTO members.

I shall now turn to a few of the specific issues that were subject to intensive debate at the CTE. I start with the interrelationship between multilateral environment agreements and the WTO, followed by the complex relationship between the Agreement on Trade-related Intellectual Property Rights (TRIPS) and environment. I then deal with eco-labelling as a life-cycle analysis and the problem of process and production methods. Finally, I address market access and competitiveness as prime issues of interest to developing countries in the trade and environment debate.

4. Some specific issues in the debate

The relationship between multilateral environment agreements and the WTO

The relationship between the provisions of the multilateral trading system and trade measures for environmental purposes, including those pursuant to multilateral environmental agreements (MEAs), was a topic that was extensively debated and subject to the most controversy. In spite of the long and tedious discussions throughout the previous five years or so, little rapprochement, if any, was achieved. Views on a number of issues were and remain wide apart; the definition of MEAs, Article XX, the issue of process and production methods, the effectiveness of trade restrictions and whether they were the most appropriate instruments to advance environmental policies are but a few of these issues.

The relationship between the multilateral trading system and the multilateral environmental agreements raised numerous difficulties and controversies. These ranged from issues of hierarchy and compatibility between the two entities to the comprehensive framework of the MEAs, which combine a mixture of incentives and trade measures to deal with environmental externalities. In the framework of MEAs, positive measures—such as improved market access, capacity-building, additional finance, and access to and transfer of technology—were considered to be effective instruments to assist developing countries to meet multilaterally agreed environmental targets. This was in sharp contrast to the much-disputed effectiveness of trade measures applied as sanctions under the purview of the WTO. The scope for trade measures pursuant to MEAs under WTO provisions and their unilateral application to address environmental problems that lie outside a country's national jurisdiction led to wide disagreement and were strongly contested.

In this debate, developing countries had to defend themselves on a number of fronts. First, developing countries continued to argue against developed countries' intentions of arming the WTO with additional power to protect the environment, because this would have the effect only of elevating trade measures, i.e. sanctions to be considered as priority tools for the environment. This would undermine the international consensus reached on a whole range of positive measures negotiated at length within the framework of the multilateral environmental agreements. Isolating the trade measures would not serve the purpose and could prove to be detrimental to the environment because they deprive developing countries of an assured source of resources. Such resources could be directed, among other things, towards the protection of the environment. Furthermore, in order to determine the necessity and effectiveness of the trade measures, these would have to be assessed together with other measures in a holistic framework, such as the one provided for by the multilateral environmental agreements. Countries cannot press for the use of trade measures just because they are less expensive and hence more appealing to politicians, without weighing the pros and cons of such usage in an objective and comprehensive manner. On the contrary, MEAs should provide developing countries with the "carrot" to entice them to comply with their obligations under such agreements, if—as proclaimed—the ultimate goal is to preserve and protect the environment.

Secondly, regarding the issue of hierarchy, at the Singapore Ministerial Conference of the WTO in December 1996,[16] developing countries succeeded in undermining the attempts by developed countries to give the MEAs superiority over the WTO's settlement of disputes. The underlying reasons were clear: developing countries refused the dominance of environmental considerations, as advocated in the MEAs, over the WTO Dispute Settlement Understanding (DSU) as guided by the key principles of the trading system, notably most-favoured-nation and national treatment, as well as the rejection of unilateral measures. Developing countries felt that on no account should they give up or weaken their inalienable rights to have recourse to the WTO DSU by giving primacy to settling disputes through the MEA. That did not mean, however, that MEAs were disregarded. They remain a viable option for disputants to settle their disputes, if they so wish.

The repeated attempts by the European Commission to reinterpret or even add an amendment to the WTO rules that would prioritize environment or make it an exception through what they would like to perceive as an "environmental window" were doomed to failure. Developing countries have stood firm against any amendments to the WTO rules in order to legitimize inconsistent trade measures in the WTO. They insisted that any effort to reopen the WTO rules would mean imposing environmental conditionality on trade and would give sufficient ground for unilateral measures that would amount to protectionism and restriction of market access under the disguise of protecting the environment. It was also recognized that, in principle, trade measures taken pursuant to MEAs were not to be challenged by the WTO membership, because the majority are also members of the MEAs. Furthermore, trade measures within the MEAs—as multilaterally agreed upon—were tolerated, and many of them were even pushed by developing countries themselves. This was the case with the Basel Convention and the Prior Informed Consent Convention on Hazardous Chemicals.

It is surprising that voices are still raised in favour of effecting substantive changes in the GATT. The first of these would involve amending Article XX on the pretext that, as it is currently applied, it gives prominence to trade goals over environmental ones. In my view this is the wrong way to look at things. The WTO's main concern is implementing trade goals. It is entitled to rectify any wrong-doings in the area of trade, but it is not within the competence of the organization or its trade representatives to deal with issues going beyond trade and trade-related issues, be they environment, human rights, child labour, or other social issues. In addition, it has been stated that Article XX is flexible enough to accommodate legitimate environmental concerns. It was precisely with this in mind that negotiators stressed the competence of the multilateral trading system in the fourth paragraph of the Preamble of the Marrakesh Ministerial Decision on Trade and Environment.

Another substantive amendment to the current GATT structure that would facilitate peace between the trade and environment camps would involve the recognition by GATT that, in an ecologically interdependent world, *how* things are produced is often as important as *what* is produced. In particular, environmental standards that relate to processes and production methods (PPMs) cannot always be rejected and judged indiscriminately to be violations of GATT.[17] On the other hand, accepting the introduction of PPMs in GATT/WTO would amount to the imposition of a country's domestic environmental values or policies on other countries. As environmental standards and PPMs are based on values that differ from one society to another, it would be difficult to internationalize PPMs and require all countries to follow the same production methods. On the other hand, we have to distinguish between environmental standards that are product related, such as disposal and handling, with which I have no quarrel, and non-product-related standards, which do not affect the final product.

The risks of setting and accepting ecological standards for PPMs in GATT today are twofold. First, these standards would most likely be the ones used in developed countries, thus allowing environmental standards to be easily manipulated for protection purposes. Second, setting ecological standards for PPMs could be used as an opening for over-stretching the concept in the future and taking it as a precedent to incorporate other non-trade-related goals, such as labour standards, human rights, good governance, and all sorts of other domestic pressures that have hardly any relationship with the WTO.

The Shrimp-Turtle *dispute*

It is worth referring briefly to the *Shrimp-Turtle* dispute. In this case, the two rulings (by the dispute settlement panel as well as by the Appellate Body) are precedent setting. The dispute was the first concerning a trade embargo based solely on domestic environmental legislation forced by the United States as the only country that interprets Article XX so broadly as to allow for extra-territorial measures to protect the environment beyond its territories. It was obvious from the very beginning that the issue at stake was not a trade measure mandated by an MEA (in this case the Convention on International Trade in Endangered Species of Wild Fauna and Flora [CITES]), but a measure to address a global environmental concern applied unilaterally by one country.

For the United States, the case involved the right of WTO members to take measures under Article XX (b) and (g)[18] of GATT 1994 to conserve and protect natural resources, as reaffirmed and reinforced by the Preamble to the WTO Agreement. For the complainant, it was a case about the imposition of unilateral trade measures designed to coerce other members to adopt environmental policies that mirrored those in the United States. The United States based its entire defence on Article XX, which allows countries to take measures contrary to GATT obligations when such measures (a) are necessary to protect human, animal or plant life or health; (b) relate to the conservation of exhaustible natural resources.

In this case, the United States argued that a trade measure was necessary because sea turtles were threatened with extinction and the use of turtle excluder devices on shrimp nets was the only way effectively to protect them from drowning in shrimp nets. The panel, however, stressed the WTO's preference for multilaterally negotiated solutions.[19] Furthermore, the panel focused its analysis on the headnote or "chapeau" of Article XX, which requires legitimate trade restrictions to be applied "in a manner, which would not constitute a means of arbitrary or unjustifiable discrimination between countries where the same conditions prevail or a disguised restriction on international trade." The panel found that interpreting the chapeau in a way that would allow importing countries to restrict market access according to exporters' adoption of "certain policies, including conservation policies" would mean that "GATT 1994 and the WTO Agreement could no longer serve as a multilateral framework for trade among Members." Such an interpretation, the panel felt, could lead to "conflicting policy requirements" because exporting countries would need to conform with different domestic policies in importing countries, thus threatening the "security and predictability of trade relations" under WTO agreements. It therefore drew the conclusion that "certain unilateral measures, insofar as they could jeopardize the multilateral trading system, could not be covered by Article XX."[20]

The panel reaffirmed the logic of developing countries that the WTO cannot be made responsible for safeguarding all kinds of different interests. This would give leeway to members to pursue their own trade policy solutions unilaterally, thus reinstating power politics. This would certainly amount to an abuse of Article XX exceptions, as the panel put it, and thus threaten the preservation of the multilateral trade system based on consensus and multilateral cooperation. It is worth recalling at this juncture that to do away with a power-based system and replace it with a rule-based one was an essential objective of the seven-year Uruguay Round of negotiations, which hardly anyone would want to give up today.

Without much ado, the Appellate Body also concluded that the US measure was "unjustifiably discriminatory."[21] In its ruling, the Appellate Body was more cautious and less blunt than the panel. Trying to find some "political" justification for the US measure, it characterized the ban "as an appropriate means to an end," although its application was at fault. It attributed the unjustifiable nature of the discrimination to the failure of the United States to pursue negotiations for consensual means of protecting and conserving sea turtles, resulting in the "unilateral" application of its trade measure. The Appellate Body further agreed that the United States had applied the measure in an "arbitrary and discriminatory" manner between countries where the same conditions prevail, contrary to the requirements of the chapeau of Article XX. The application was discriminatory in giving a longer grace period to Caribbean countries than to Asian nations, in not transferring technology to them on similar terms, in its lack of transparency, etc.

The Appellate Body then stressed that it had not decided that the sovereign nations that are members of the WTO cannot adopt effective measures to protect endangered species, such as sea turtles; "Clearly, they can and should."[22] It stressed that protection and preservation of the environment are of significance to WTO members, provided that "they [sovereign states] act together bilaterally, plurilaterally or multilaterally, either within the WTO or in other international forums." Finally the Appellate Body decided that, "although the measure of the US in dispute in this appeal serves an environmental objective that is recognized as legitimate under paragraph (g) of Article XX of GATT 1994, this measure has been applied by the US in a manner which constitutes arbitrary and unjustifiable discrimination between Members of the WTO, contrary to the requirements of the chapeau of Article XX."[23]

Although the US ambassador to the WTO hailed the Appellate Body's ruling as a success for the US position, a similar sense of victory was neither felt nor expressed by US environmental NGOs, which, as mentioned earlier, had brought the case to the US Court. The Appellate Body ruling, in my view, does not amount to a reversal of the panel ruling, as some would like to have it, but rather falls under what the Singapore Ministerial meeting attempted to elucidate. GATT/WTO agreements do provide significant scope for national environmental protection policies, provided they are not discriminatory in nature. Moreover, countries should seek joint and not unilateral action. This is how, I believe, the Appellate Body findings and conclusions should be regarded. This decision is an attempt not to overturn the consensus reached in the WTO CTE, but rather to strengthen it. In fact, the Appellate Body pronounced itself clearly against WTO-inconsistent trade measures applied unilaterally to address extra-jurisdictional environmental problems. It thus underlined what WTO members had succeeded in injecting into the factual part of the Singapore report. It was explicitly mentioned that "all delegations except one"[24] stated that they consider that the provisions of GATT Article XX do not permit a member to impose unilateral trade restrictions that are otherwise inconsistent with WTO obligations for the purpose of protecting environmental resources that lie outside its jurisdiction. In any event, arguments in favour of reinterpreting Article XX to address environmental concerns (as put forcefully by those who want to see Article XX amended or reinterpreted) for fear of the trend by the Appellate Body to expand—on its own—the meaning of Article XX, remain void. There is no doubt that neither the Appellate Body nor the panels are entitled to attempt to interpret the WTO rules. *Interpretation of the rules is the sole right of the membership.*

The environment and trade-related intellectual property rights

The relationship between environment and trade-related intellectual property rights (TRIPS) is yet another example of the underlying conflict in the WTO between the urge to protect the environment on the one hand and the tools made available for such an objective in the framework of the TRIPS Agreement, on the other hand. Here the case is quite the reverse. The TRIPS Agreement as negotiated and pushed for by the developed countries has proven to be unfriendly to the environment. In fact, reading carefully through the TRIPS Agreement, one cannot fail to realize that environmental concerns did not really occupy a priority at the negotiating table then. It has become clear only over the past few years that a number of provisions in the TRIPS Agreement go against the objectives of Agenda 21 and the various multilateral environmental agreements in regard to access to and transfer of technology to help maintain and protect the environment. The outcry came first from non-governmental organizations engaged in development and environment in developed and developing countries alike.

India was one of the few countries that, at an early stage in the work of the CTE, recognized the real problem in reconciling intellectual property protection, as laid down in the TRIPS Agreement, with the objectives and provisions on transfer of technology incorporated in some of the MEAs.[25] It failed, however, to summon the necessary backing on the part of the developing countries on this topical issue. The primary reason was the complexity of the issue itself. Hardly any developing countries were grabbed by this difficult and composite relationship, because they were still struggling with other outstanding commitments emanating from the Uruguay Round. Coping with the various provisions of the TRIPS Agreement was not a priority, because they felt they had ample time until the transitional period expired.

As we get closer to the implementation of the TRIPS Agreement and with environment looming as a topic in the Millennium Round, developing countries ought to look more seriously at this issue. Let me hasten to say that at no point in my argument should it be taken that developing countries are trying to back-pedal on their commitments. It none the less remains a fact that the TRIPS Agreement as negotiated was put in a very narrow context and with limited objectives, i.e. to lay down minimum standards for the protection of the owner, the titleholder, and the patentee, conferring on them exclusive rights. This goes against a whole myriad of legitimate and valid concerns; topping the list are socio-economic and developmental issues, the environment, technology transfer, and fair and open competition. It is no secret that, for these as well as other reasons, developing countries remained inimical to such an agreement until the eleventh hour. It was only under pressure of the "Single Undertaking" commitment that they were obliged to accede to it.

Addressing the relationship between the TRIPS Agreement and environment, the CTE focused in its deliberations on two main issues:

1. the generation of, access to, and transfer of environmentally sound technologies, and

2. the contradiction between the TRIPS Agreement and the Convention on Biological Diversity.

In regard to the first issue, the question concerns what happens if TRIPS put such technologies beyond the reach of developing countries. This would undoubtedly have a negative impact on the environment and on the stringent efforts developing countries are making to cope with the environmental requirements. It is true that Article 7 of the TRIPS Agreement stipulates that patenting should encourage the promotion of technological innovation and the transfer and dissemination of technology, to the mutual advantage of producers and users and in a manner conducive to social and economic welfare. This, however, has not yet materialized owing to the fact that developing countries are still benefiting from the transitional period of the implementation of the Agreement. Nor has any empirical evidence sustained this argument so far. Hence, the question remains how TRIPS link up with the objective of facilitating access to and transfer of technology "on fair and most favourable terms"[26] to assist in the conservation of the environment and promote sustainable development.

As for the relationship between the TRIPS Agreement and the Convention on Biological Diversity (CBD), this heads the list of concerns of developmental and environmental NGOs in the North as well as in the South. The contradiction between TRIPS and the CBD is not implicit. There are doubts about the compatibility of the various provisions of the TRIPS Agreement with the clear objectives of the Convention as it relates to the conservation and sustainable use of genetic resources. The underlying disparity between the timely transfer of relevant biotechnology as agreed in the CBD and Article 33 of TRIPS, which provides for a term of protection of at least 20 years, remains a point of contention and a source of serious concern. This is even more so for developing countries when they start implementing the TRIPS Agreement by the year 2000.

It was only after the conclusion of the TRIPS Agreement and after its adoption within the framework of the Uruguay Round that questions regarding the compatibility between TRIPS and the CBD started to surface. Equitable sharing of the benefits arising out of the utilization of the knowledge systems of indigenous communities and fair trade-offs between access to genetic resources and the transfer of technology remain the essence of the CBD, as agreed notably in Articles 15 and 16 of the Convention.[27] However, concerns were expressed about the negative impact of TRIPS in the fields of agriculture, nutrition, and health care, because they would inevitably lead to an extension of the monopoly control of transnationals over production and distribution in these vital areas for developing countries. Moreover, the TRIPS Agreement does not try to curb the commercial exploitation of genetic resources or deal with the sharing on a fair and equitable basis of the benefits arising out of the patenting of genetic resources. Much has been said with respect to the usage and applicability of Article 31(k) of the TRIPS Agreement regarding compulsory licensing for the public domain, as permitting the necessary flexibility. With all the strings attached to this article, however, the question arises whether it truly serves the purpose of facilitating access to and transfer of technology, including biotechnology, on fair and most favourable terms, as stipulated by Article 16.2 of the Biodiversity Convention. This issue undoubtedly requires more in-depth study.

Because of these fundamental controversies and whether or not environment becomes an issue in the next multilateral trading round or is mainstreamed in the various agreements, environment will have to be an integral part of any review process of the TRIPS Agreement. The different available alternatives should be weighed and carefully studied. Three main options, which set the framework for the overall trade and environment debate, come to mind:

1. to agree on the relevance of Article XX as a general exception in the context of the TRIPS Agreement when specifically addressing biodiversity and the sustainable use of genetic resources;

2. to decide whether the TRIPS Agreement or the Convention would prevail in the event of a dispute and how it would work out between parties and non-parties to either; and

3. to keep the issue open, to be addressed and settled on an ad hoc basis by panels in the event of a dispute.

It is worth stressing at this juncture that developmental and environmental NGOs from the North as well as from the South latched on to the issue that developing countries should have been tackling in depth much earlier. Their views should not be neglected, otherwise developing countries might at some point find themselves on the defensive and be confronted with the same kind of arguments raised against the TRIPS Agreement, namely that it was negotiated entirely out of the public view; it might then perhaps be too late. The recent failure of the lengthy negotiations on the Multilateral Agreement on Investment in the Organization for Economic Cooperation and Development (OECD) is a case in point. It clearly denotes the strength and skills of environmental NGOs and, if they feel sidelined, TRIPS could be next in turn.

Eco-labelling

Eco-labelling is another highly controversial issue. Compared with other voluntary standards, such as packaging, labelling, or even recycling requirements, it has attracted much attention in the trade and environment debate in the WTO. In spite of the fact that it was discussed extensively prior to the Singapore Ministerial Conference as well as in the framework of the review process of the Agreement on Technical Barriers to Trade, hardly any decision has materialized to date. The issue has raised a number of practical, conceptual, and systemic problems. It might sound strange and be difficult to comprehend, but the more the debate is focused on the core of the issue at hand, the more the gap between the various views widens.

The complexity of the issue arises from the fact that eco-labelling schemes are based on life-cycle analysis, which involves processes and production methods (PPMs). In other words, eco-labelling is interested in the product during its entire life cycle: the sourcing of raw materials, production, consumption, and disposal.[28] This approach requires, in and of itself, large amounts of information when products or materials are imported, which may cause enormous practical problems, especially for developing countries.[29] In addition, specific PPM-related criteria based on domestic conditions and priorities in the importing country may be less appropriate in other countries. Whereas there is no question that each country has the right to institute domestic regulations on eco-labelling, the concern is that it should not be used for protectionist purposes—applied by some countries selectively to products that are imported or that compete with their own products.

The principal fear of developing countries in dealing with the issue of eco-labelling in the WTO is that an attempt will be made to extend the coverage of such labelling—even though voluntarily—to non-related PPMs. They fear not only the whole range of implications for their exports that such an extension would produce but more the systemic problem it raises in the WTO. It would amount to writing new rules for a system that has so far served the international community and the world trading system well. The problem of subjecting eco-labelling to WTO rules and disciplines lies in the conflict that would arise with the product-based rules of the GATT/WTO trading system. Discriminating between "like products" and making market access conditional on complying with PPMs, thus legitimizing unincorporated PPMs, which are not product related, would upset the entire multilateral trading system and would have devastating effects, in particular on developing country exports.

Developing countries have recognized that what is being put into question—through using eco-labelling as a litmus test—is the basic criteria and characteristics that have so far governed the multilateral trading system. Through eco-labelling, the WTO would become more and more deeply involved in the realm of domestic policy and intervention from the outside would be allowed to set national priorities. On this basis, most developing countries have insisted that eco-labelling is inconsistent and should not be accommodated within the WTO system. This was strongly supported by the fact that the negotiating history of the TBT Agreement upheld their view that unincorporated PPMs were not covered by the Agreement.[30] While admitting the role that equivalence and mutual recognition could play in helping them meet the requirements of foreign schemes, they insisted that accommodating unincorporated PPMs would amount to creating scope for the extraterritorial imposition of national standards. This, they felt, would have significant consequences for the trading system as a whole.[31]

Furthermore, as stated earlier and as emphasized by the Preamble of the WTO Agreement, environmental objectives should be *consistent* with the level of development. The prevention of product differentiation on the basis of unincorporated PPMs allows countries to set standards, whether environmental or otherwise, that are appropriate for their level of development. In other words, it allows countries to trade their developmental needs against their needs for environmental protection in a manner that is consistent with how they themselves value these needs (and not on the basis of how others value them for them).[32]

What I would like to add here is that the debate in the CTE on eco-labelling schemes has triggered a similar heated debate between environmentalists and business groups. The former have criticized what they consider to be the narrow perspective of international trade rules, noting that PPMs are fundamental to minimizing the environmental impact of a product during its life cycle. Business groups see trade rules that distinguish between products solely on the characteristics of end products as relevant and appropriate. Like many developing countries, they view the introduction of PPMs into the trade debate as the beginning of a slippery slope, where loosely related production factors would become the basis for trade barriers.

Lastly, it is essential to recall Principle 11 of the Rio Declaration in this context, which stipulates that environmental standards, management objectives, and priorities should reflect the environmental and developmental context to which they apply. The standards applied by some countries may be inappropriate and of unwarranted economic and social cost to other countries, in particular developing countries.[33] Accordingly, the disciplining of eco-labelling schemes should be on the basis of equivalencies and mutual recognition, where each country sets its standards according to its own values, as stipulated by Agenda 21. The aim of harmonizing or internationalizing PPMs on the basis of any set of multilateral guidelines is in contradiction to what the international community agreed upon unanimously in Agenda 21. What is even more risky is that such an attempt would be detrimental to the trading system, at a time when all countries are embracing and respecting its rules.

Market access and competitiveness aspects of the trade/environment debate

One cannot address the interface between trade and environment without looking at the market access and competitiveness aspects of this relationship. These aspects tended to be underplayed and even overlooked at the beginning of the debate, for the obvious reasons stated earlier. It is needless to reiterate that the whole debate was triggered by developed countries targeting specific issues of concern to themselves. As developing countries gradually became aware of the underlying reasons and objectives of this debate, they rightly pushed issues of their own to the fore. It should be stressed, however, that this move by developing countries was on no account aimed at eventually achieving trade-offs. On the one hand, their refusal to amend or reinterpret Article XX or to introduce non-related PPMs was based on systemic principles, which cannot be subjected to bargaining, because this would alter the very essence of the system. On the other hand, the purpose of bringing in market access and competitive concerns was to add balance to the lopsided debate, and put it in its proper perspective.

From the very beginning the debate on this issue was set in a North–South context. This has harmed rather than helped the debate advance. False allegations continue to be made by firms in countries with high environmental standards and high costs of compliance that they are often undercut by competition from companies based in countries with less strict regulation and lower costs. In theory, this could lead to entire industries departing for countries with lower standards, the so-called "pollution havens." So far, however, there is no evidence of this happening. The reverse—that high environmental standards were a factor in location decisions or have led to the relocation of industry—has also not occurred on a large scale.

The debate on market access from the perspective of developing countries tends to be twofold. They want to ensure first that existing market access conditions are not eroded by emerging environmental requirements and second that additional market access—through what can be perceived as win–win situations—will help promote environmental protection and sustainable development. In this context developing countries have tried to concentrate on identifying sectors of export interest to them. These could be textiles and clothing, leather, footwear, furniture and other consumer goods, and other labour-intensive sectors, where environmental measures could affect existing market access opportunities and thus possibly nullify or impair the Uruguay Round results. In fact, empirical studies, mostly done by the UN Conference on Trade and Development (UNCTAD), show that the sectors of interest to developing countries are those most affected by environmental standards often set unilaterally by the importing governments. Such standards negatively influence developing countries' market access, even though the environmental effects of, say, textile production might mainly be local and do not affect the final characteristics of the product. In addition, there are few—if any—trans-boundary externalities.

Furthermore, UNCTAD's studies have also demonstrated that small and medium enterprises (SMEs) in developing countries have encountered difficulties in complying with environmental policies emerging in the above-mentioned sectors. Such policies have had significant effects on the competitiveness of SMEs in developing countries and have in many instances acted as barriers to trade. A number of reasons have been cited, among them are the following:

- The possibility of compensating for the loss of competitiveness in some sectors by gains in others is higher in economies that are diversified and dynamic, which are not necessarily the main characteristics of developing countries' economies.
- Developing country exporters are normally price-takers, because they compete on price rather than on non-price factors such as technology and ideas. Consequently, any environmental requirement resulting in cost increases reduces export competitiveness. It nevertheless may vary from one industry to another as well as among developing countries at different stages of development and with varying capability to integrate innovative approaches.
- The problems of adjustment are higher for SMEs in developing countries, especially as they are important players in the export promotion strategy for sectors such as textiles, clothing, and footwear. Thus the need to examine the possible conflict between the export promotion strategies of developing countries and the need to comply with environmental requirements and their effects on competitiveness becomes all the more relevant.
- The variable cost component of complying with environmental standards is higher in some sectors than in others. Again, evidence has shown that it is higher in sectors of interest to developing countries, especially leather and footwear, as well as textiles and garment sectors. For example, in leather tanning, the cost of the chemicals required to meet international standards is approximately three times the cost of conventional chemicals.[34]

Two additional topics are germane to the market access and competitiveness debate: the internalization of environmental costs, and charges and taxes for environmental purposes. Though these topics are not new and have in fact been debated at length, they remain contentious and difficult, especially if the idea is to add them to the trading agenda.

The concept of internalization remains difficult to adopt in GATT on the grounds that it interferes with the efficiency of the comparative advantage principle, which is central to the free trading system. The tendency to consider the lack of internalization as a kind of "implicit subsidy" that would be actionable under GATT/WTO is a non-starter. Furthermore, environmental externalities are in principle not distinguishable from other factors, such as education, infrastructure, and social policy, that contribute to the comparative advantages and thus competitiveness edge of an economy. Are we to conclude that the costs of all these factors are to be integrated in production processes under the auspices of the multilateral trading system? The internalization of environmental costs by domestic producers in no way conflicts with GATT principles. However, it becomes problematic under GATT if countries start implementing trade policies on the basis of whether or not foreign producers have internalized their environmental costs. GATT would be more concerned with the trade-distorting or discriminatory effect of such a policy, and with its necessity and effectiveness, rather than with its environmental objectives.

As for charges and taxes for environmental purposes, no one can deny the validity and effectiveness of imposing taxes as such. But what is occurring here is the imposition of taxes on a phenomenon that is not quantitative. Forcing producers to incorporate environmental externalities by imposing taxes on products made with polluting processes is based on the assumption that the costs to the polluting firm and the damage caused by the pollution are known. Moreover, if this is true at the national level, it can only be more complex and difficult if an importing country aims at adjusting such costs at its borders by imposing border tax adjustments on its "like" imports. In addition, the question of what would be an appropriate tax for pollution that would be accepted internationally is still open.

Border tax adjustments (BTAs) should pass the necessity and effectiveness test to find out how pertinent they are to the environment, before even debating how to impose them at the border. The effectiveness of border tax adjustment is doubted and even contradicts the view, widely acknowledged by developing and developed countries alike, that environmental problems should be addressed at source. So how can a tax imposed on final products, as a border tax adjustment, be effective for problems that should be dealt with as far upstream in the production process as possible?[35] As rightly pointed out by UNCTAD, it is generally better if the tax is levied on the production and extraction process causing the environmental problems rather than on the resulting product. In other words, a tax levied internally by the producing country would be more effective at dealing with environmental problems at their source. GATT neither prohibits nor prevents a country from pursuing a policy of taxation or regulation with regard to environmental protection as long as these policies apply only to its domestic consumers and producers. In fact, one can even go one step further. For BTA on imports to pass the compatibility test in GATT, it has to meet the following conditions:

(a) the tax is product related;

(b) the imported product has not been taxed in the country of origin, to avoid double taxation;

(c) the imported product has caused trans-boundary pollution and the polluting input was not consumed domestically.

Similarly to their stance on process and production methods in eco-labelling, developing countries insist that there should be an explicit reference to addressing charges and taxes that relate only to products or product characteristics that are covered by WTO provisions. In any event, the environmental effectiveness and potential trade effects of levying environmental taxes and charges, particularly on market access and competitiveness, remain questions open for debate.

Before concluding, let me state that no one can deny the fact that the relationship between trade and environment has been debated extensively in the WTO. This has undoubtedly helped clarify the status of this relationship in the framework of the organization and shape positions in response to the underlying motives and objectives. Today, even before settling this complex relationship, other more difficult and cumbersome issues are emerging, such as linking trade to labour standards. Though from the very beginning such an inclusion has met with strong objections, it will continue to be pushed in the WTO mainly by the United States—for obvious reasons, which neither time nor space permit to be addressed here. One thing is clear, however. Developing countries have to stand firm on their positions on trade and environment as regards changing the rules. Such a move would only serve as a prelude to the integration of the "social clause" in the WTO, which has wider implications for developing countries and should be of more serious concern.

5. Conclusion

The Seattle Ministerial Conference in December 1999 and the proposed Millennium Round will be a turning point for the trade and environment debate. It will decide on the future course of the debate. One thing remains clear. A great deal of work and education continue to be needed before drawing conclusions or reaching the stage of negotiating rules and disciplines, not to mention changing the rules, as some would like to happen. The trade and environment relationship continues to be an area prone to difficulties, complexities, and most of all sensitivities. Throughout this chapter I have tried to show that so far the CTE has worked within a consensual framework. To try to tamper with this framework in order to incorporate additional objectives will necessitate a new consensual framework. The attempts by the international community to forward some alternatives remain in the very early stages and will need further in-depth study. The following are a few of the options:

1. To carry the debate forwards in the CTE in parallel with the Millennium Round, with a view to bringing the two ends closer. This option is hardly likely to achieve results because, in the view of many people, the CTE has exhausted the debate.

2. The so-called "Ruggiero" option presented earlier: a World Environment Organization to be the counterpart to the WTO. This is a pragmatic and likely workable option in view of the difficulties encountered so far, though it is still resisted by mainly developed countries and their NGOs. Some developed countries, notably the EU countries, Norway, Switzerland, and Canada, continue to believe that the WTO, with its strong and enforceable dispute settlement mechanism, is an

appealing instrument for policy makers, particularly in the field of environment. Many NGOs continue to be convinced that the trading systems should provide the necessary flexibility for the sake of the environment, which is undoubtedly their priority.

3. Mainstreaming environment in the various agreements, such as Agriculture, TRIPS, Textiles and Clothing, and others. The degree of complexity and controversy inherent in this option, which is still to be tested, is difficult to anticipate. However, care should be taken because this option carries with it the inherent risk of doing away with the sensitive balance carefully negotiated in the CTE between issues of interest to developing and developed countries alike, thus thwarting the possibility of trade-offs, if any. With this option, issues of market access would be spread thinly over different agreements, leaving the two topics of concern to developed countries, i.e. the relationship between trade and environment and PPMs, to be negotiated separately.

In spite of tremendous efforts not to label the trade and environment debate as a North–South issue, these have hardly borne fruit. No one can deny that there is evidence of a conflict between developed and developing countries, which will continue and deepen unless the existing doubts about linking environmental interests with protectionism dissipate. *The challenge is to separate protectionism from environment.* The environment cannot be safeguarded and enhanced through trade sanctions. Benefiting the environment must be through access to technology, increased awareness, financial resources, and access to markets, without which developing countries will find it extremely difficult to generate the resources necessary to protect their domestic environments and the global commons.

Let me conclude by stating how Rubens Ricupero, the Secretary-General of UNCTAD, perceives the trade/environment relationship:

Trade and Environment are two poles in a dialectical thesis, where the resulting synthesis should conciliate the two ends. Unlike many would like to believe, linking trade to environment does not come as something natural. To reconcile these two ends necessitates tremendous efforts—and not without sacrifices—where environment should not be treated as a late consideration or an afterthought.[36]

The way to deal with environmental problems is to go to their roots and integrate environment in the decision-making process from the very beginning. This requires the provision of the necessary technology and making available the necessary financing, knowledge, and expertise for the preservation and protection of the environment.

Acknowledgements

Although I am indebted to René Vossenaar, UNCTAD, and Doaa Abdel Motaal, WTO, for their valuable comments and suggestions, which have sharpened the exposition, I wish to exonerate them from any responsibility for the final product. This chapter is my own responsibility and is not meant to reflect Egypt's position.

Notes

1. *Herald Tribune,* 15 March 1999.
2. Stuart E. Eizenstat, US Undersecretary of State for Economic Affairs, "Why We Should Welcome Biotechnology," *Financial Times,* 16 April 1999.
3. Rio Declaration on Environment and Development, United Nations Conference on Environment and Development, Rio de Janeiro, June 1992.
4. "Report of the United Nations Conference on Environment and Development," Rio de Janeiro, 3–14 June 1992, Chapter 1, Objectives 2.9 (a), p. 3.
5. "Trade and Environment: A Developing Countries' Perspective," a paper presented by the Dominican Republic, Egypt, Honduras, and Pakistan to the WTO High Level Symposium on Trade and Environment, 15–16 March 1999.
6. "Legal Wrangle Engulfs US Shrimp Dispute," *Financial Times,* 14 April 1999.
7. Opening remarks by Renato Ruggiero to the WTO High Level Symposium on Trade and Environment, 15 March 1999.
8. Daniel C. Esty, "Economic Integration and Environmental Protection: Synergies, Opportunities, and Challenges," Yale University, 5 March 1999 (draft presented to the WTO High Level Symposium).
9. GATT, *The Results of the Uruguay Round of Multilateral Trade Negotiations, The Legal Texts,* 1994, p. 6.
10. Martin Khor, "Trade, Environment and Sustainable Development: A Developing Country View of the Issues Including in the WTO Context," paper presented to the WTO High Level Symposium on Trade and Environment, 15 March 1999.
11. Final Act Embodying the Results of the Uruguay Round of Multilateral Trade Negotiations, signed Marrakesh, 15 April 1994.
12. WTO CTE, *Report (1996) of the Committee on Trade and Environment,* WT/CTE/1, 12 November 1996.

13. Article XX ("General Exceptions") gives ample opportunity to use measures to protect (a) public morals, (b) human, animal, or plant life or health, etc. The chapeau of the Article stipulates that these measures should not be applied in a manner that would *constitute a means of arbitrary or unjustifiable discrimination between countries where the same conditions prevail, or a disguised restriction on international trade.*

14. The Agreement on Technical Barriers to Trade deals basically with technical regulations and international standards, including packaging, marking, and labelling requirements, and procedures for assessment of conformity. It further makes sure that these regulations and standards should not constitute a means of arbitrary or unjustifiable discrimination between countries where the same conditions prevail or a disguised restriction on international trade.

15. The Agreement on the Application of Sanitary and Phytosanitary Measures forms an integral part of the Agreement on Agriculture. It reaffirms in its Preamble that no member should be prevented from adopting or enforcing measures necessary to protect human, animal, or plant life or health. These measures are subject to the requirement that they are not applied in a manner that would constitute a means of arbitrary or unjustifiable discrimination between members where the same conditions prevail or a disguised restriction on international trade.

16. The 1996 Singapore Ministerial Conference was the first ministerial meeting of the WTO.

17. Esty, "Economic Integration," op. cit.

18. Article XX (b) (g) stipulates that any country subject to the requirement that such measures are not applied in a manner that would constitute a means of arbitrary or unjustifiable discrimination could take measures: (b) necessary to protect human, animal, or plant life or health; (g) relating to the conservation of exhaustible natural resources if such measures are made effective in conjunction with restrictions on domestic production or consumption.

19. *United States–Import Prohibition of Certain Shrimp and Shrimp Products,* Report of the Panel, WT/DS58/R, 15 May 1998, paras. 278–300.

20. Ibid.

21. *United States–Import Prohibition of Certain Shrimp and Shrimp Products,* Appellate Body Report, WT/DS58/AB/R, adopted 6 November 1998.

22. Ibid., para. 185.

23. Ibid.

24. It is no secret that the "one" delegation was the United States.

25. Non-paper by India for the Committee on Trade and Environment, "The Relationship of the TRIPS Agreement to the Development, Access and Transfer of Environmentally-sound Technologies and Products," 20 June 1996.

26. This is a term used in some MEAs and is of particular interest to developing countries because it is interpreted by many of them as meaning "on preferential and non-commercial terms." Indian Non-paper, op. cit.

27. Article 15 emphasizes the sovereign rights of states over their natural resources. It further stresses that access to genetic resources is to take place on terms that are environmentally sound and on a mutually agreed basis, and to be subject to prior informed consent of the party providing the resources, unless otherwise determined by that party. Article 16 implies a central role for access to and transfer of technology in the conservation and sustainable use of biodiversity resources. It further stipulates

that such transfer of technology shall be provided on favourable terms, including concessional and preferential treatment as mutually agreed.

28. See Chapter 9 in this volume, and *Report (1996) of the Committee on Trade and Environment,* op. cit.

29. R.Vossenaar and R. Mollerus, "Eco-labelling and International Trade: Possible Effects on Developing Countries," UNCTAD, ITC/233/lB/96-II-TP, 1996.

30. *Negotiating History of the Coverage of the Agreement on Technical Barriers to Trade with Regard to Labelling Requirements, Voluntary Standards, and Processes and Production Methods Unrelated to Product Characteristics,* WT/CTE/W/10 and G/TBT/W/11, 29 August 1995.

31. Chapter 9 in this volume, p. 233.

32. Ibid., p. 230.

33. This should also apply to ISO schemes, especially ISO-1400, because their unbiased formation is highly doubted by many developing countries. Such schemes cannot be forced into the WTO as internationally agreed ones, as long as developing countries in practice remain outside the effective frame of decision-making in such standard-setting bodies and organizations.

34. UNCTAD, "Environmental Policies, Trade and Competitiveness: Conceptual and Empirical Issues," TD/B/WG.6/6, 29 March 1995.

35. Ibid.

36. Rubens Ricupero, UNCTAD Workshop, Viet Nam, July 1997.

3

Breaking the Deadlock:
A Positive Agenda on Trade,
Environment, and Development?

Veena Jha and René Vossenaar[1]

1. Introduction

The "Positive Trade Agenda" is an initiative of the Secretary-General of the United Nations Conference on Trade and Development (UNCTAD), Rubens Ricupero, taken after the first ministerial meeting of the World Trade Organization (WTO) in 1996 in Singapore. The rationale is that, rather than being passive reactors to agendas set by developed countries, developing countries have to set their own agenda to play a more proactive role in future negotiations.

This chapter tries to define elements of a "Positive Agenda" on trade and environment. This may appear a difficult task, because developing countries have had legitimate apprehensions about engaging in a discussion on trade and environment in the first place. Although the issue has already been on the multilateral trade agenda for some time, work has so far focused on discussions aimed at clarifying trade and environment issues—a process that is still ongoing—not on negotiations. However, there is now some pressure to "mainstream" trade and environment in several WTO agreements and to include the theme, in one way or another, in a possible new round of multilateral trade negotiations (the "Millennium Round").

This creates both risks and opportunities for developing countries. These countries need to be aware of the full implications of engaging in a possible Millennium Round where environment is expected to play an important role. They also need to be aware of the implications of the explicit inclusion of environment in the negotiating agenda.

There is no doubt that developing countries are fully committed to both trade liberalization and enhanced environmental protection. The UN General Assembly's Special Session, in its first five-year review of progress in the implementation of Agenda 21, recognized that "[t]he multilateral trading system should have the capacity to further integrate environmental considerations and enhance its contribution to sustainable development, without undermining its open, equitable and non-discriminatory character."[2] However, developing countries have to strive to ensure that any further accommodation of environment into the multilateral trading system is achieved in a balanced manner and that it takes account of their own environmental and developmental conditions. They may therefore have to resist certain proposals that may run counter to their interests. In particular, developing countries should firmly resist unilateralism and other measures that threaten to undermine the multilateral trading system.

Any Positive Agenda on trade and environment should be based on the concept of sustainable development, which includes both protection of the environment as well as the eradication of poverty. Basic parameters for a Positive Agenda have been set by the UN Conference on Environment and Development, in particular through the Rio Declaration and Agenda 21. A Positive Agenda on trade and environment should promote positive interactions between economic activities, particularly international trade, the multilateral trading system, and the environment. Essentially, it should:

- contribute to the further integration of developing countries, particularly the less developed countries, into the world economy as well as to their growth and development in the short term and the long term;
- help to achieve environmental and sustainable development objectives based on multilateral cooperation and the principle of common but differentiated responsibilities.

These objectives can be achieved only by considering trade and environment interactions within the broader context of development. Recent analysis and debate have indicated that strategies to achieve such objectives may be rendered more effective by:

- strengthening policy coordination at the national and multilateral levels;
- strengthening capacities in developing countries to deal with trade-related environmental issues and environment-related trade issues;
- promoting multi-stakeholder approaches to identify cost-effective and development-friendly options for trade and environment policy integration;
- implementing positive measures, in particular as outlined in Agenda 21.

Although focusing on the trade and environment debate in the WTO, this chapter also emphasizes the WTO's limitations in resolving trade and environment problems. Consequently, the chapter also examines the role that UNCTAD and the Commission on Sustainable Development (CSD) could play in further integrating trade and environment in the pursuit of sustainable development. In this context, it is hoped that this chapter (as well as other papers that will be prepared on specific issues) may also make a contribution to preparations for UNCTAD X.

2. Background

Following the first WTO Ministerial Conference in Singapore in 1996, interest in trade and environment initially seemed to have diminished somewhat. Today, however, the intensity of the trade and environment debate, as measured for example by the number of meetings, seminars, research papers, and technical cooperation projects, seems to be higher than ever before. Much of the renewed interest is focusing on the WTO and how trade and environment will evolve in the context of the multilateral trading system.

Developing countries, however, have expressed grave concerns about recent developments in the debate. Most of them are strongly resisting the inclusion of this issue in future trade negotiations. An important question thus becomes whether their present position obviates the need for the development of a "Positive Agenda" on trade and environment. This chapter argues that developing countries may have sound reasons to oppose broad WTO negotiations based on environmental considerations. In addition, they may have sound strategic reasons to oppose the inclusion of environment in the build-up to the Seattle Ministerial Conference in December 1999. However, the chapter also argues that it may be very difficult for them to sustain their opposition to the entry of environment in a new round for a number of reasons.

First, the recent Appellate Body decision on *Shrimp-Turtle* has generated new uncertainty on how the multilateral trading system will further accommodate environmental concerns. Whereas many observers in developed countries have welcomed the decision as a demonstration of the ability of the multilateral trading system to incorporate environmental considerations, others have expressed renewed concern over the effects of environmental policies, particularly the use of trade measures related to processes and production methods (known as PPMs), on developing countries. Developing countries may be brought to a situation where they have to resort either to a litigious regime (involving clarification of trade and environment issues on the basis of case-law rather than a broad-based consensus) or to a precautionary exploration of trade and environment issues to avert conflicts. In the latter case, a Positive Agenda would be of some help.

Second, proposals have been made to "mainstream" trade and environment issues into existing WTO agreements. This would imply that environment would be addressed in practically all relevant agreements of the WTO, including the built-in agenda and planned reviews of agreements. The risks associated with mainstreaming environmental issues in the WTO for developing countries will be discussed in the next section. However, mainstreaming also implies that developing countries could be forced to engage in negotiations on trade and environment issues, even without an explicit inclusion of environment in the negotiating mandate.[3]

Third, the possibility of a new round of multilateral trade negotiations has triggered renewed concerns about the possible environmental effects of further trade liberalization and hence calls for environmental impact assessments of trade policies and agreements. Similarly, the possibility that there will be a new round has generated new expectations as well as interest among non-governmental organizations (NGOs) to propose issues to be included in the negotiating agenda. Both phenomena may add their own dynamics to the negotiating process. Formulating a positive agenda or alternative positions may help to prevent developing countries being taken by surprise in crucial negotiations.

Current pressures from developed countries that are of particular concern to developing countries would centre on three issues:

1. A review or reinterpretation of GATT Article XX, to provide further accommodation of trade measures (including discriminatory trade measures against non-parties) pursuant to multilateral environmental agreements (MEAs). This may have implications for the use of unilateral measures.

2. Accommodation of trade measures based on non-product-related PPMs on environmental grounds, particularly in the context of eco-labelling.

3. Greater scope for the use of the precautionary principle.

Any or all of these may go against the economic and trade interests of developing countries. There may be two ways of dealing with this pressure. One is to resist the entry of issues by referring back to the Singapore report (and the Rio Declaration and Agenda 21), or to propose solutions outside the multilateral trading system. Another option for developing countries would be to develop their own environmental agenda so that, if this issue comes up for negotiations, they can pursue issues that could yield certain benefits to them. (On many issues, it may be possible to find alliances with certain developed countries).

There is also pressure for greater NGO inputs to the WTO processes, in particular its dispute settlement mechanism. Civil society, both NGOs and the business community, can play an important role in promoting a balanced trade and environment agenda. However, there is a risk that certain proposals that may be labelled under the heading "transparency," such as those facilitating the submission of *amicus curiae* briefs to dispute settlement panels, could, in practice, accentuate certain imbalances in the agenda. This is because NGOs in the South have fewer financial resources to avail themselves of such opportunities.

Environmental considerations have also emerged in the debate on agricultural subsidies, one of the most important issues in the built-in agenda. The Cairns Group and other like-minded countries have used the Committee on Trade and Environment (CTE) as yet another forum to strengthen the case for the elimination of environmentally harmful subsidies. Future trade negotiations, combined with the strong public interest in environmental protection and sustainable development, could provide an opportunity to gain support for the elimination or reduction of some existing trade policy failures, in particular in developed countries, such as trade restrictions and trade-distortive and environmentally harmful subsidies in agriculture and fisheries. These are areas where consensus has already been built between a range of developed and developing countries. Identifying "win–win" scenarios could constitute part of a Positive Agenda, provided that due attention is paid to possible adverse short-term economic effects on certain developing countries.[4]

Except for issues that should be clearly resisted, proposing their own agenda may be a desirable option for developing countries. These countries now have an opportunity to bring greater balance in the treatment of different issues already on the agenda, as well as adding new issues. This should help to strengthen the development dimension in the trade and environment agenda.

Before trying to define elements of a possible Positive Agenda, it is important to understand some of the developing countries' legitimate apprehensions about the WTO debate and to work out those aspects of the current debate that could yield potential benefits. Section 3 therefore analyses some of these concerns in relation to current and future discussions at the WTO and elsewhere for developing countries. It is in this framework that developing countries should assess the costs and benefits of engaging in discussions on trade and environment.

After this assessment has been completed, they should then examine the current discussions and see whether there is scope within the current framework to accommodate their concerns. Section 4 examines some key trade and environment issues with a view to highlighting some questions and issues that developing countries can legitimately ask. It also highlights their points of entry into a discussion that has so far been polarized and develops elements of a positive agenda for developing countries.

Such a positive agenda is however not limited to the arena of the multilateral trading system, but also spans national and regional policies and includes the private sector players. These different approaches are discussed in section 5. Section 6 draws some broad conclusions. An overview of existing problems in the trade and environment agenda, as well as possible solutions—both in and outside the WTO context—from the perspective of developing countries, is provided in Appendix II of this volume.

3. Concerns of developing countries

Given the pressure for the environment to be mainstreamed into the multilateral trading system (MTS) or included in a Millennium Round, it is necessary first and foremost to redress the imbalances in the agenda on trade and environment.

Trade and environment is an important issue for developing countries. Indeed, starting from a position where several developing countries had argued that there was essentially no linkage between trade and environment issues, not only have developing countries acknowledged such linkages, they are proposing a constructive agenda on dealing with these linkages. For example, several of the proposals described in this chapter have already been flagged by developing countries in the CTE. The great interest in technical assistance for capacity-building also demonstrates developing countries' interest in further articulating a proactive agenda. However, mainstreaming environment issues in the WTO also raises some crucial questions for developing countries.

Mainstreaming environment in the WTO?

Some developed countries have proposed including the environment in future negotiations of specific WTO agreements. The European Union (EU), for example, has proposed to examine "the scope for and need to factor environmental concerns into the WTO across the board (mainstreaming)." The EU has argued that "in any future negotiations on trade liberalization there will be no single body within the WTO with the power to ensure that environmental aspects are taken into full consideration throughout the process: the CTE discusses but does not implement policy."[5] Instead, the EU proposes that each relevant WTO committee should deal with environment in the area under its authority. Other countries, such as Canada, Iceland, and Norway, have also made suggestions concerning "mainstreaming."

In the High Level Symposium on Trade and Environment in 1999, the United States (while not mentioning the term "mainstreaming") proposed that the CTE should look systematically and transparently at all the various areas of negotiation on a rolling basis. "The CTE would identify and discuss issues, but not try to reach conclusions or negotiate these issues in the CTE itself. Rather it would provide a report of its discussions to Members and the relevant negotiating groups." The United States also expected that "the CTE's work would play a valuable role in providing input to deliberations at the national level on positions to be taken in the actual negotiating groups."[6]

"Mainstreaming" environmental issues in different WTO agreements could take place either in the context of already planned reviews of specific agreements or in the context of a possible round of new trade negotiations. There are several risks that could arise from such mainstreaming for developing countries.

First, mainstreaming the environment into several committees would make it more complicated for developing countries to participate effectively in corresponding WTO deliberations and negotiations. Developing country delegates would find it difficult to give attention to environmental issues because "environment" would be diffused in several committees and meetings. The capacity of developing country delegates with expertise in environmental issues to service numerous committees in the WTO is relatively limited. Most delegations in Geneva are small and have several meetings to prepare for and attend. Backup support from the capitals would also be lacking in most cases. Moreover, many developing countries are not ready for it, just as they are not ready for the Millennium Round of trade negotiations. This implies that there is an urgent need to build capacity at the national level, a task in which UNCTAD could assist.

Second, maintaining trade and environment within a common framework (as is the case of the CTE) would allow cross-sectoral discussions and the identification of possible trade-offs if negotiations on environment were to be taken up. Diffusing the CTE agenda would mean that several checks and balances would no longer be possible. The CTE process helps to ensure that a balanced agenda is maintained and that every issue is discussed. Although every issue is a stand-alone and systematic issue, the CTE package helps to ensure a holistic treatment.

Third, diffusing the environmental agenda to several committees would imbalance the well-negotiated agenda of the CTE. It is also important in this context to understand what mainstreaming would entail in the context of issues that are of key interest to developing countries on the one hand, and issues that are proposed by certain developed countries on the other.

Developing countries, whether or not in alliance with certain developed countries, are the main proponents of the following three issues:

1. *Additional market access, including through the removal of agricultural subsidies and reduction of tariffs.* These issues are already on the agenda of discussions. Mainstreaming these issues is unlikely to generate benefits that are additional to those that can be obtained through current discussions on implementation issues and the built-in agenda and subsequent negotiations.

2. *Agreement on Trade-related Intellectual Property Rights (TRIPS).* Several issues of concern to developing countries can be pursued in the process of the built-in mechanism for review. These could first be discussed in the CTE, under its current work programme, with a view to exchanging views and building consensus on issues that developing countries could pursue in the review process.

3. *Domestically prohibited goods (DPGs).* Developing countries have to review whether any gains would be politically feasible or whether they should pressurize member countries to honour their previous commitments on notification of DPGs. In any case a moot point is where this would be mainstreamed.

On the other hand, developed countries are the *demandeurs* of further accommodation in the MTS of trade measures pursuant to MEAs (including discriminatory measures), trade measures based on non-product-related PPMs, and trade measures based on the precautionary principle. All of these would facilitate the use of trade restrictions for environmental purposes. In addition, proposals to multilateralize environment impact assessments of trade policies and agreements could all involve a risk that interest groups might seek to use such assessments to introduce obstacles to import liberalization in favour of developing countries.

Developing countries could argue first of all that the existing WTO provisions are sufficient to accommodate environmental concerns. Secondly, to the extent that mainstreaming implies further trade restrictions, it cannot be considered a desirable option because the WTO is about further liberalization not about increasing the scope of trade restrictions. Thus, developing countries may have little to gain and a lot to lose from the proposed option of mainstreaming. Whereas some developed countries argue that mainstreaming provides an opportunity to make progress on certain issues, many developing countries argue that the trade and environment agenda requires greater balance if progress is to be made.

Lack of balance in the trade and environment debate

Lack of balance in the discussions on trade and environment has led developing countries to adopt defensive postures in international debates.

For example, there is considerable dissatisfaction with the fact that, for the most part, the trade and environment debate has explored only some aspects of the linkages. The CTE discussions, for example, have focused largely on issues such as the need to accommodate trade measures pursuant to multilateral environmental agreements (MEAs) as well as eco-labelling based on non-product-related PPMs. Although it is important to ensure a harmonious relationship between MEAs and the MTS, as well as between transparent and non-discriminatory eco-labelling programmes and the MTS, it should nevertheless be noted that "developing country issues," such as safeguarding and further improving market access, controlling the export of domestically prohibited goods, and promoting technology transfer, appear to have received far less attention.

Thus, although in the developed countries there is pressure to accommodate the use of trade measures for environmental purposes within the framework of WTO rules, it appears that there is no concomitant effort actually to control exports of environmentally harmful products and obsolete technologies to developing countries.[7] This is shown by the fact the issue of exports of domestically prohibited goods seems to have been set aside too early as a priority issue for the WTO. Developed countries have argued that this is a technical issue and other forums are better equipped to deal with it. It should be noted, however, that the same arguments could be used to refer a great deal of the discussions on the use of trade measures pursuant to MEAs to the Conferences of Parties of the Conventions.

A challenge for developing countries is to develop a system that facilitates trade restrictions if necessary on such environmental "bads." It is interesting to observe that at the High Level Meeting on Trade and Environment several governments and NGOs called upon the trade community to reorient the trading system to promote safe products and discourage or bar trade in harmful products.

Another feature of the trade and environment debate is that, although there is continuous pressure to legitimize the use of trade restrictions (including unilateral and extra-territorial restrictions), based on non-product-related process and production methods (PPMs), much less attention is given to encouraging the dissemination of environmentally sound technologies (ESTs) that would help developing countries move towards more environmentally friendly PPMs. It is to be noted that at the High Level Symposium a prominent NGO (the Third World Network) pointed out that, rather than being subject to trade sanctions, developing countries should benefit from access to sophisticated environmental technology, technical and political support from the international community, and funding for environmental protection from multilateral lending institutions. The representative of the World Bank noted that allowing unilateral sanctions against pollution or environmental degradation in another country would fundamentally shift the trading system towards one based on power rather than on rules.

Similarly, although some would like an explicit recognition to extend the coverage of the Agreement on Technical Barriers to Trade (TBT) to include eco-labelling schemes (including non-product-related PPMs), there seems to be much less effort to examine how developing countries can benefit from trade in inherently environmentally friendly products that use traditional and indigenous knowledge. This may be a serious shortcoming to the extent that it can be argued that, whereas eco-labelling is a tool to provide information to the consumer as well as some market advantages to products that are relatively less environmentally benign, the promotion of the sustainable trade in products based on indigenous knowledge actually fosters conservation. Not only should products produced using indigenous knowledge be excluded from patentability (which prevents developing countries from exporting these products), an effective branding and labelling scheme should help promote markets for such products.

Furthermore, although some want to accommodate eco-labelling using life-cycle analysis in the TBT Agreement, it has not been possible to make progress on guidelines on the eco-labelling of genetically modified organisms (GMOs), whose environmental and health effects will become known only after several years.[8]

Lack of financial and technological capacity to address environmental concerns

Whereas there has been a lot of attention to the environmental effectiveness of trade and other measures, the capacity-building needs to enable developing countries to meet stricter environmental norms and enhance environmental performance have been underestimated. It is not lack of interest that hinders faster progress on trade and environment integration in developing countries, but the inability of many of these countries to bear the related adjustment costs. Measures and timetables to address global environmental problems may not take sufficient account of the implementation and monitoring capacities of developing countries. Thus, whereas trade measures may be effective in inducing changes in developed countries, the incapacity to monitor would imply that, although the economic effects of trade restrictions are felt by developing countries, the expected environmental improvements do not necessarily occur.

The expectations of some may have been geared too much towards blunt policy solutions, such as trade measures, when the complexity of the issues seems to impose a gradual approach and a priority for enabling measures that create conducive economic conditions for the dissemination and effective use of ESTs. In particular, environmental problems created by the informal sector receive insufficient attention. This is the case despite the fact that the informal sector often accounts for 50 per cent and more of the management of environmentally problematic natural resources, such as heavy metals or hazardous chemicals, and is a key source of pollution.

Developing countries also lack the capacity to build credible certification bodies, with the result that their firms often encounter problems in certifying compliance with international standards. Enforcing environmental standards and norms and monitoring them are also enormous problems for developing countries. The lack of finance, of extension services, of coordinating agencies, and so on, also creates severe bottlenecks in moving towards higher standards. In all these areas UNCTAD has an important part to play.

Although the "precautionary principle" has an important role in environmental policy-making, this should not prevent comprehensive and balanced packages of policy instruments being devised to address all aspects of an environmental problem. There has often been insufficient time to study the underlying economics of environmentally motivated trade measures or other environmental measures that affect trade. In fact, there is a general lack of information on economic and social adjustment costs in developing countries.

Lack of political will

These imbalances in the agenda become especially important because there has been little progress in implementing supportive mechanisms at the multilateral and national levels. The assessment in 1997 of progress on the implementation of Agenda 21 by the United Nations General Assembly showed that little progress has been made on what Agenda 21 calls "implementation issues" such as finance, access to environmentally sound technologies, and, perhaps to a lesser extent, capacity-building. Imbalances in the trade and environment agenda can be addressed only if sufficient emphasis is placed on the development and implementation of such measures.

If the ultimate objective of a trade measure is to fulfil environmental objectives, then such objectives cannot be met by the trade measure alone. In fact, trade measures without supportive measures (such as capacity-building, finance, and access to technology) may further hamper the capacity of developing countries to move towards sustainable development. The argument that supportive measures lie outside the purview of the WTO is no longer sustainable because the purview of the WTO has been broadened considerably by the Uruguay Round agreements on trade-related intellectual property rights, special and differential treatment (S&D), and other provisions concerning technical assistance. The provisions on S&D have so far turned out to be largely empty boxes, and compliance with these provisions by developed countries would allay some fears of developing countries about the use of environmental measures as protectionist devices.

Notwithstanding these concerns, developing countries have to identify the points of entry into the current debate on trade and environment. Whereas some issues must clearly be resisted, there are others where both trade and environmental gains may accrue to developing countries. It is necessary therefore to identify a strategy for trade and environment, either with a view to engaging in negotiations should they arise, or with a view to providing a counter-agenda to avert negotiations.

4. Points of entry into the agenda of the multilateral trading system

Trade provisions in MEAs and the provisions of the MTS

Summary of the discussions so far

The international community has fully recognized the important role that multilateral environmental agreements play in addressing transboundary and global environmental problems, based on international cooperation and the principle of common but differentiated responsibility. There has been considerable debate, however, on the policy instruments used to achieve the objectives of MEAs. Discussions in the Committee on Trade and Environment have focused on the relationship between trade measures pursuant to MEAs and the provisions of the multilateral trading system.[9] Some developed countries may continue to press for an adaptation of GATT Article XX in order further to accommodate the use of trade measures specifically mandated by MEAs. Recent decisions by the Appellate Body may have reduced such pressure, although the Appellate Body decision on *Shrimp-Turtle* may have shifted attention away from subparagraphs (b) and (g) (or the introduction of a new subparagraph) to the headnote of Article XX.

Points of entry for developing countries

- There is a need to improve the implementation of supportive measures under MEAs as well as to examine to what extent the multilateral trading system can help to remove possible obstacles to better implementation. This would be particularly relevant for the transfer of technology provisions in the MEA.

- There should be strengthened cooperation between MEAs and the WTO to avoid future conflicts. This would also obviate the need for Article XX amendments. Such coordination should also examine other WTO rules and aim at strengthening the compatibility of the transfer of technology provisions in MEAs with WTO rules.

- There is a need to examine the consistency of TRIPS provisions and the Convention on Biological Diversity.

- Unilateral and extra-jurisdictional trade measures to address issues of global environmental concern should be avoided. The chapeau test of Article XX should not allow trade measures that constitute arbitrary or unjustifiable discrimination or a disguised restriction on trade. This includes trade measures implemented by one or several countries, purportedly "pursuant to" an MEA, but that may be considered arbitrary or unjustifiable by other countries.

The Agreement on Trade-related Intellectual Property Rights

Summary of the discussions so far

Of special concern to developing countries are provisions in the TRIPS Agreement that deal with the transfer of technology and the protection of biodiversity. Developed countries have emphasized that this agreement is meant to foster innovation. Some have noted, however, that in several cases there may be a trade-off between the positive effects of intellectual property rights (IPRs) on the generation of environmentally sound technologies and the negative effects of IPRs on the dissemination of technologies. The TRIPS Agreement, including through its review mechanism, must find ways and means of balancing these two effects. It is important to bring to the discussion the empirical evidence gathered on the dissemination of ESTs in relation to the use of IPRs. Trademarks and trade secrets may also affect the dissemination of ESTs.

In the manufacturing sector the TRIPS Agreement may:

- adversely affect technology transfer, for example by restricting the use of compulsory licensing mechanisms by governments of developing countries;
- increase the price of goods and technologies because of increased concentration of industries;
- have negative effects on innovation, particularly in developing countries, including in the area of environmentally sound technologies.[10]

Several developing countries argue that the agreement and, more specifically, its implementation do not necessarily promote the dissemination of environmentally sound technologies or the protection of biodiversity. The system of intellectual property protection should also find a way of recognizing indigenous technologies, knowledge, and systems of species preservation because these may be of considerable value in protecting biodiversity.[11] Ironically, the system of IPRs could have adverse effects on research and development on account of several factors. First, innovations in biotechnology for the agricultural sector have traditionally been dependent on land races. Without granting adequate protection to land races, TRIPS may erode the very germplasm that forms the basis of biotechnological innovations. Secondly, granting protection to plant varieties would imply that plant breeders and researchers would be forced to buy patented material at exorbitant prices, if they are allowed access to it at all. This would discourage research, especially in developing countries where there is a cash crunch. Thirdly, granting broad-based protection to life forms instead of to the genes that produce those characteristics would discourage further research into effective ways of producing those characteristics. This would have a particularly chilling effect on public research, for which funding is in most cases difficult to obtain and justify.

Points of entry for developing countries

- Developing countries should exclude all life forms and related knowledge from patentability, as is currently permitted under the WTO.[12]
- There is a need for further analyses of different options for the implementation of effective *sui generis* systems, as called for by Article 27.3(b). In particular, the implications of using the model of the

Union for the Protection of New Varieties of Plants (UPOV)[13] for Plant Variety Protection (PVP) need careful examination. Harmonizing *sui generis* systems to UPOV 91, which *inter alia* imposes genetic uniformity as a legal requirement for IPRs, would be inappropriate for developing countries. These countries should have different options for the implementation of effective *sui generis* systems. For example, they could consider systems such as FAO 1983, which protects land races and traditional medicinal plants as intellectual property. Other *sui generis* systems that meet national conservation objectives should also be encouraged.

- Developing countries may seek additional time for examining the full implications of Article 27.3(b) as well as for a consideration of different options for implementing *sui generis* systems. They may also insist that priority should be given to further examination of the relationship between the provisions of the Convention on Biological Diversity (CBD) and the TRIPS Agreement.

- The WTO TRIPS Agreement should be made consistent with relevant provisions of the CBD, especially in the areas of biological resources and traditional knowledge systems.[14]

- There is a need also to study the application of Article 27.2, which can exclude from patentability technologies that can harm the environment. This would particularly apply to genetically modified organisms (GMOs) that are known to be harmful. It may be necessary to build some scope for a precautionary measure in this Article too.

- In all patent applications for biotechnological innovations, the country of origin of the germplasm should be indicated. It should also be indicated whether prior informed consent was obtained for the biological genetic resource or traditional knowledge, so that mutual benefit-sharing arrangements can be made. Such documentation should also be attached to the patent application.

- Articles 66.2 and 67 of the TRIPS Agreement should be fully implemented. Article 67 obliges developed country members to provide, on request and on mutually agreed terms and conditions, technical and financial cooperation to developing countries. Article 66.2 obliges developed country members to provide incentives to enterprises and institutions in their territories for the purpose of promoting and encouraging technology transfer to least-developed countries. Reviews of the implementation of these two Articles by developed countries should emphasize that these are binding obligations and not just best endeavour clauses. It is also necessary to examine what forms of recourse would be available to developing countries in the event of non-implementation of these Articles.

Market access

Summary of the discussions so far

Market access remains an issue of key concern to developing countries. Safeguarding market access for products exported by developing countries has been discussed extensively at the WTO. It has been pointed out that developing countries may be more vulnerable to environmental measures because of the composition of their exports. They may also find such standards difficult to meet on account of several constraints, many of which have to do with the nature of operation of small and medium enterprises (SMEs), which account for a large share of exports from developing countries.

Preferential market access and other trade preferences are of key importance for many developing countries, in particular the least developed amongst them. The erosion of such preferences, which may be accentuated as the result of the Millennium Round, could have adverse effects on the exports of certain developing countries and reduce their ability to achieve sustainable development through trade.

A lot of emphasis has been placed in this context on identifying win–win opportunities in trade and environment. "Win–win" situations arise when the removal or reduction of trade restrictions (high tariffs, tariff escalation, and remaining non-obstacles to trade) and distortions have the potential to yield both direct economic benefits for developing countries as well as positive environmental results.[15] Much of the discussion so far has concentrated on removing trade distortions in sectors such as fisheries, agriculture, and energy. More research is needed to identify further examples of products where the removal of trade restrictions and distortions might result in "win–win" situations.

With regard to eco-labelling, discussions in the CTE have focused on multi-criteria eco-labelling schemes, especially those that are based on non-product-related PPMs. The effects of "type-1" eco-labelling on the market place and international trade, particularly on imports from developing countries, have so far been limited.[16] It would appear that the interest in eco-labelling in the context of international trade is at least in part attributable to the fact that, from a conceptual and trade policy point of view, it involves many complex issues, such as PPMs, the definition of international standards, and equivalency. So far, little progress has been made in dealing with the PPM issue in the context of eco-labelling (see below). In particular, the debates in the WTO and the International Standards Organization (ISO)[17] have made very little progress on developing the concept of "equivalency."

Points of entry for developing countries

- Under the existing code of good practices, a mechanism could be devised for voluntary measures aimed at avoiding the use of trade discriminatory measures based on PPM-related requirements.
- Greater accountability and WTO discipline is needed for NGO campaigns and policies of local governments—for example in the context of the Plurilateral Agreement on Public Procurement—that might have a potentially significant adverse impact on developing country exports, such as bans on the use of tropical timber imposed by several municipalities.
- There is a need to build consensus on certain concepts to be taken into account in the development and implementation of newly emerging environmental measures with potential trade effects, particularly for developing countries. The role of sound science and the concept of risks that non-fulfilment may create also need to be examined in greater detail, particularly with a view to understanding the appropriate balance between reducing environmental and health risks and adverse effects on trade.[18] Measures that incorporate both these concepts are especially valid for agro-based products and marine products, areas that contribute a significant amount of export earnings to developing countries.
- The concept of proportionality, which is implicit in national environmental policy-making, should be examined in the context of international trade rules.
- It may be necessary to examine whether differential treatment for SMEs is available within the existing framework of WTO rules.

- Guidelines to ensure that eco-labelling processes are transparent and non-discriminatory, and capable of dealing adequately with the trade implications of using criteria based on non-product-related PPMs, need to be further developed. To achieve this, progress has to be made on concepts such as equivalency.
- Two lessons drawn from the eco-labelling discussions are that there may be a need to arrive at a definition of what is "an international standard" and that a true international standard requires effective and representative participation of WTO member states at all levels of development. Similarly, there is a need to support the effective participation of developing countries in international standard setting.

Domestically prohibited goods

Summary of the discussions so far

Many developing countries are concerned about the health and environmental effects of exports to their markets of goods whose domestic sale has been prohibited or severely restricted in the exporting country. Developing country importers need adequate information about the risk that such products could pose to public health and the environment. Apart from information problems, developing countries may also lack the infrastructure (including testing facilities) and other capabilities to monitor and control imports of DPGs. Developed countries on the other hand argue that a number of multilateral agreements and instruments already address this issue. Although duplication is to be avoided, there is a need to examine whether existing instruments, such as the prior informed consent procedure, are sufficient from the perspective of developing countries, in particular with regard to product coverage and procedures. In addition, membership of several multilateral agreements and instruments may be limited, and thus the only option for resolving disputes may be in the WTO.

Points of entry for developing countries

- The definition of DPGs has to be clearly established and agreed upon. It is also necessary to discuss which of the existing DPGs should be considered at the WTO.
- Possible gaps, in terms of product coverage (for example, certain cosmetics and other consumer goods), in existing agreements and

corresponding international notification procedures need to be identified.

- There is still a need to design and implement concrete mechanisms for enhancing transparency. For example, the DPG notification system established by a Ministerial Decision that had been in existence between 1982 and 1990 should be revived (the Decisions taken to establish it remain in force today).

- As recognized in the CTE, technical assistance should be provided to assist developing countries in strengthening their technical capacity to monitor and, where necessary, control the import of DPGs.

Environmental review of trade agreements

Summary of discussions so far

As mentioned above, the possibility of a new round of multilateral trade negotiations (a "Millennium Round") has triggered renewed concerns about the possible environmental effects of further trade liberalization, and hence calls for environmental impact assessments (EIAs) of trade policies and agreements. It is widely recognized that trade liberalization should be accompanied by environmental and resource management policies in order to realize its full potential contribution to improved environmental protection and the promotion of sustainable development through the more efficient allocation and use of resources.

Several suggestions have been made so far. One set of suggestions deals with examining the sustainability implications of the Millennium Round (the European Union and the United States have already announced that they will carry out "sustainability impact studies") and another deals with examining the environmental implications of existing agreements. It has also been suggested that an environmental impact assessment of the Uruguay Round and its agreements should be carried out, in order to draw lessons for future negotiations.

Several developed countries have suggested that an environmental impact assessment of trade policies be included in the Trade Policy Review Mechanism of the WTO. Many developing countries argue that, although EIAs may be useful domestic policy instruments, there may not be a need to multilateralize them.

So far, EIAs have been used mainly in the evaluation of projects. There is little practical experience, particularly in developing countries, with EIAs of trade policies. The challenge is to promote the integration of environment and economics and to anticipate potentially adverse scale effects of trade liberalization. However, there is a need to avoid undue pressures to carry out overly complicated environmental impact assessments that might adversely affect further trade liberalization and distract from emerging efforts in developing countries to integrate environmental considerations into economic policy-making.

Some points need to be stressed. First, it is generally recognized that any assessment of environmental effects should be the responsibility of national governments. Secondly, EIAs are not only a tool for the minimization of negative environmental impacts; their principal objective is to focus on and to be used in promoting sustainable development. In a broad sense, EIAs promote the integration of environment and economics. Thirdly, EIAs should not narrowly focus on scale effects, but also examine income and technology effects. It may also be necessary to examine "with" and "without" scenarios, i.e. what the environmental effects would be of economic growth patterns that might evolve in the absence of the proposed trade agreement.

Points of entry for developing countries

- There is a need to strengthen capacities of developing countries to integrate environmental considerations into economic policies.
- Developing countries could propose an environmental review of the TRIPS Agreement.
- It may be appropriate to carry out an environmental review of the Agreement on Subsidies, especially those relating to agriculture.
- Developing countries could propose an environmental review of trade in "environmental bads" and DPGs.

5. Integrating trade and environment at national and regional levels in developing countries

The integration of trade and environment concerns in developing countries has emerged as one of the priority areas in moving towards sustainable development. Intensive debate and dialogue as well as pilot projects at the national and regional levels have led to the evolution of possible strategies, elements of which are slowly becoming visible. It is now becoming clear that integrating trade and environment in a development-friendly manner needs concrete mechanisms that span several aspects of national and international economic activity. The national and international debate on these issues has also highlighted the fact that the integration of trade and environment is often intrinsically linked to the culture of operation of economic activities at the national level. Hence mechanisms to integrate trade and environment should include initiatives that deal with national and international legislation, national and international policy-making, business partnerships, infrastructure building, civil society participatory activities, and other related activities.

Better policy coordination at the national level can help prevent or defuse conflicts at the multilateral level, as well as maximize the benefits (or minimize the adjustment costs) of measures taken pursuant to multilateral environmental agreements as well as of environment-related measures with potential trade effects adopted in developed countries.

Agenda 21 has already proposed a positive agenda on trade and environment.[19] However, the implementation of that agenda has been disappointing. It seems appropriate to renew commitments as well as to develop new proposals for pragmatic approaches to trade and environment integration. Such an agenda could *inter alia* include the following:

National legislation and policy-making
- promoting policy coordination at the national level;
- identifying packages of measures for SMEs to meet environmental challenges;
- developing legislation and initiatives to mitigate the adverse environmental effects of trade in DPGs;
- identifying packages of measures aimed at supporting developing countries' efforts to join MEAs and complying with national obligations;
- developing effective *sui generis* systems for the protection of traditional and indigenous knowledge as well as effective implementation of Article 27.2, which excludes environmentally harmful technologies from patentability.

Building business partnerships and civil society participation
- identifying how to enhance the contribution that foreign direct investment can make to the dissemination of environmentally sound technologies and better environmental management through the supply chain in the host country;
- building supply capacities for enhanced environmental management at the national and regional levels;
- widening trading opportunities for "environment-friendly" products and services in the context of the greening of consumption patterns in developed countries;
- developing multi-stakeholder approaches in moving towards environmentally friendly production processes and sustainable resource management.

Integrating trade and environment through regional cooperation agreements
- interregional cooperation in developing common positions and approaches in dealing with third countries;
- interregional cooperation in developing mechanisms to cope with national and regional trade and environment problems.

6. Conclusions

From the analysis presented in previous sections, the conclusion could be drawn that several steps should be taken in order to make progress in the trade and environment debate:

- There is a need for greater balance in the trade and environment debate, because it pays insufficient attention to issues of concern to the developing countries.
- The debate should pay more attention to the constraints facing many developing countries in responding to environmental challenges, such as the lack of technical, institutional, and supply capacities, and the fact that many environmental problems in developing countries are of a very different nature.
- There should be sufficient political will to take account of the previous points in building a broad-based agenda on trade and sustainable development in several forums.

• Developing countries need to identify a positive agenda such as that outlined above and to start a process of consensus-building along those lines.

Progress in constructing a more balanced agenda and in strengthening the development dimension can be made only to the extent that countries, in particular developed countries, show greater political will. This includes, for example, the full and timely implementation of the developed countries' Uruguay Round commitments in areas such as textiles. Governments have to adopt larger responsibilities, for example with regard to the notification of exports of DPGs and in reviewing TRIPS for facilitating technology transfer to developing countries. But such political will also has to be shown outside the WTO context, for example through greater progress in providing finance, in facilitating access to and diffusion of ESTs, and in capacity-building, supported by multilateral and bilateral aid programmes.

Developed countries should be aware of the implications of their environmental policies for developing countries and avoid unnecessary adverse effects on developing countries' exports. It is necessary to develop a better understanding of the production conditions in developing countries, their legal systems, and their monitoring capacities. Any calculation of incremental costs under MEAs should take account of these differences.

The role of national governments

The trade effects of environmental standards and requirements raise issues in the area of development and/or *trade promotion policy* as well as in the area of *trade policy*.

In the area of trade promotion policies, for example, governments and the business sector can adopt several policies and measures aimed at promoting standards and quality with a view to enhancing competitiveness. These include *inter alia* establishing and/or improving supporting infrastructure (e.g. appropriate testing, certification, and accreditation facilities), the dissemination of information, promoting cooperation between the government and the business community, promoting cooperation between retailers/importers and producers/exporters, as well as special measures in favour of SMEs. International organizations as well as bilateral and multilateral aid agencies can play important roles in establishing and upgrading national capacities in promoting quality, testing, and certification.

In the area of international trade policy, the emphasis is on reducing the likelihood that standards will restrict trade. Such trade policy measures include the harmonization of product standards whenever appropriate, the maximum possible recognition by importing countries of tests conducted by testing bodies in exporter countries, and the recognition that standards that may have significant effects on trade should be subject to trade rules and disciplines, including provisions for consultation.

The role of UNCTAD

As UNCTAD's special role in the area of trade and environment is to examine issues from a development perspective, it should play an important part in strengthening the development dimension in the trade and environment debate and in helping to identify issues of interest to developing countries. However, developing a positive agenda on trade and environment is first and foremost a responsibility of developing countries themselves.

UNCTAD's work on capacity-building could be of key importance. Strengthening capacities for policy analysis and better coordination between trade and environmental policies could help to reduce some of the obstacles to the achievement of sustainable development in developing countries. Multi-stakeholder approaches are important, in particular where the interests of different groups have to be weighed. UNCTAD's work, including joint activities with the United Nations Environment Programme (UNEP), shows that multi-stakeholder approaches may also help to anticipate the economic and social implications of globalization and trade liberalization and, where necessary, identify suitable packages of measures. The role of UNCTAD is crucial in this context. In particular, UNCTAD, in close cooperation with the WTO secretariat, could play a vital part in research and capacity-building, including on issues listed in the next section.

UNCTAD and UNEP could establish a joint programme of capacity-building on trade, environment, and development. To help implement such a programme, the two institutions could set up a task force with the explicit aim of building capacity by pooling the technical expertise of these two organizations. It could be envisaged that a trust fund might be set up to support technical cooperation activities. The pooling of expertise could assist the two organizations to promote:

- public awareness sessions for policy makers;
- national and regional training workshops for trade and environment officials and civil society;
- demonstration projects to address the environmental and economic effects of trade liberalization at the national level;
- the design of appropriate packages of economic instruments and other policy measures to promote sustainable development;
- developing countries' access to environmentally sound technologies as well as the strengthening of capacities for their indigenous development.

The aim of this task force would be to build capacity for promoting trade expansion in an environmentally friendly manner and to build capacity for trade and MEA negotiations.

A Positive Agenda for the WTO

Finding a certain balance in the terms of reference of the CTE has been a difficult task. This balance could be lost if issues of concern to developing countries were to receive less attention than other issues. In addition, greater attention must be given to measures that take account of the difficulties of developing countries in integrating trade and environment, such as S&D provisions, measures that provide better access to information such as transparency and notification provisions, and measures that might assist small and medium enterprises to respond to environmental challenges. Furthermore, it is important to ensure that all aspects of the issues on the agenda receive adequate attention. For example, attempts to clarify possible inconsistencies between MEAs and the rules of the multilateral trading system should include full consideration of the concerns of many developing countries and of NGOs in these countries with respect to differences in the IPR concepts and regimes in the Biodiversity Convention on the one hand and the WTO TRIPS Agreement on the other.

In the context of a Positive Agenda, there are several specific issues and approaches that merit consideration and could be pursued in the WTO. For example, such an agenda could:

- reconfirm the Rio Declaration and Agenda 21, in particular as they relate to WTO rules;
- strengthen the role of the CTE in clarifying trade and environment linkages, taking into account the need for a balanced and integrated approach as well as the importance of building consensus;
- promote market access for products from developing countries, through safeguarding existing market access (e.g. through an interpretative statement on the concept of proportionality) and creating additional market access, including for environmentally friendly products;
- examine "win–win" areas, taking into account the effects of individual countries, including the net food importing countries;
- enhance the transparency of trade in DPGs, including the revival of notification provisions;
- promote compatibility between the TRIPS Agreement, the diffusion of environmentally sound technologies, and mutual benefit-sharing agreements as prescribed by the Biodiversity Convention.
- seek accommodation in the WTO rules for the special environmental problems and lack of capacity of SMEs;
- promote capacity-building to strengthen capacities for national and regional coordination on trade and environment policies;
- promote a coordinated approach to finding better forms of S&D and implementing the existing provisions of S&D.

A coordinated agenda in several forums

Developing and implementing a Positive Agenda based on the concept of sustainable development requires coordinated efforts in several forums. For example, the WTO debate on the relationship between trade provisions in MEAs and the provisions of the MTS would be more balanced if supportive measures were pursued in forums such as the UN

Commission on Sustainable Development, UNEP, UNCTAD, and the relevant Conventions. These forums could also cooperate in promoting policy coordination as a means of helping to prevent conflicts between trade measures in MEAs and the rules of the multilateral trading system, thereby obviating the need for a modification or reinterpretation of GATT Article XX. The WTO, UNCTAD, UNEP, and other institutions could similarly cooperate in the identification of incentives and supportive measures (rather than trade restrictions) to address issues such as PPMs.

Notes

1. The views expressed in this paper are those of the authors and do not necessarily reflect those of the United Nations Conference on Trade and Development.

2. *United Nations General Assembly Nineteenth Special Session, Overall Review and Appraisal of the Implementation of Agenda 21: Report of the Ad Hoc Committee of the Whole of the Nineteenth Special Session,* A/S-19/29, 27 June1997, para. 29.

3. Note that six Uruguay Round Agreements incorporated explicit references to the environment, even though environment was not included in the Punta del Este mandate: the Agreement on Technical Barriers to Trade (TBT); the Agreement on the Application of Sanitary and Phytosanitary Measures (SPS); the Agreement on Agriculture; the Agreement on Trade-related Intellectual Property Rights (TRIPS); the Agreement on Subsidies and Countervailing Measures; and the General Agreement on Trade in Services (GATS).

4. Due attention should also be paid to food security objectives.

5. See Communication from the European Union, High Level Trade and Environment Meeting, WT/L/273, July 1998.

6. WTO High Level Symposium on Trade and Environment, 15–16 March 1999, "Linkages Between Trade and Environment Policies," Statement by the United States.

7. However, some progress has been made in designing multilateral agreements and instruments to regulate trade in DPGs. These include the Rotterdam Convention on Prior Informed Consent, the proposed Convention on Persistent Organic Pollutants (POPS), and the Basel Convention.

8. Positions vary across countries. The United States (which, however, is not a party to the CBD) is against labelling requirements and other measures that might restrict trade. Countries with strong or growing biotechnology industries, including Argentina (currently the second-largest producer of transgenic crops), Australia, Canada, and Mexico, support the United States. Argentina and Canada, in particular, support the US opposition to the use of labelling to inform consumers about whether food products are genetically modified or not. They argue that this would increase handling, storage, and transport costs by as much as 20 per cent. Others, in particular African countries, Malaysia, and some Latin American countries, favour a restrictive

protocol, based on the precautionary principle. This includes ample testing for risks to human health and the environment before the release of any GMO. The European Union, although wanting to respond to growing public concern about GMOs and to keep the option of controlling imports of certain products, also wants to protect exports of its own GMOs. Source: *The Economist,* 20–26 February 1999.

9. Forums such as the CSD, UNCTAD, and UNEP have emphasized the importance of supportive measures (such as capacity-building, improved access to finance, and access to and transfer of technology) to assist developing countries in meeting multilaterally agreed targets in MEAs, in keeping with the principle of common but differentiated responsibility. It has also been stressed that MEAs may use packages of instruments (which could contain both supportive measures as well as trade measures) to achieve their objectives. Finally, UNCTAD and other institutions have also stressed the need to examine the trade and economic effects on developing countries of different policy instruments used or proposed in MEAs.

10. See UNDP, *Human Development Report 1999,* Chapter 2 on "New Technologies and the Global Race for Knowledge."

11. In accordance with the TRIPS Agreement, in order to be patentable, an invention must be new, involve an inventive step, and be capable of industrial application. It has been argued that the TRIPS Agreement seems to contemplate only the Northern industrialization model of innovation. It fails to address the more informal, communal system of innovation through which farmers in the South produce, select, improve, and breed a diversity of crop and livestock varieties. Thus, Southern germplasm achieves an inferior status to that of contemporary biotechnologists' varieties. The intellectual property of Southern farmers is apparently denied recognition, and hence protection. J. Cameron and Z. Makuch, "The UN Biodiversity Convention and the WTO TRIPS Agreement," WWF International Discussion Paper, Gland, Switzerland: WWF International, 1995.

12. Unless Article 27 of the TRIPS Agreement is interpreted broadly, the patenting of genetic materials could turn more and more life forms into patentable commodities, with long-term environmental, economic, cultural, and ethical impacts. Cameron and Makuch, "The UN Biodiversity Convention," op. cit.

13. UPOV governs an international system of PVP. Some 37, mainly developed, countries are members. The 1978 UPOV treaty allows certain exceptions for farmers and breeders to use protected materials. However, the treaty is being replaced by its 1991 successor, which eradicates the farmers' privilege and gives breeders control over further use of a farmer's harvest of protected seeds. The 1991 treaty came into force on 24 April 1998. As a result, the 1978 version was closed to further signature one year later, on 24 April 1999. See <http://www.upov.int>.

14. The international law of treaties uses various criteria to determine which treaty takes priority. Under the rule that *later treaties take priority over earlier treaties,* the TRIPS Agreement (which was agreed at the end of the Uruguay Round in December 1993 and signed in April 1994) would take priority over the CBD (which was agreed in May 1992). However, under the rule that *more specific treaties take priority over general treaties,* the CBD would take priority because the CBD's language on IPRs in the context of the transfer of technology for biodiversity diversification is more specific than that of the TRIPS Agreement. It is also to be noted that Article 16.5 of the CBD states that: "The contracting parties, recognizing that patents and other intellectual

property rights may have an influence on the implementation of the convention, shall cooperate in this regard subject to national legislation and international law in *order to ensure that such rights are supportive of, and do not run counter to, its objectives*" (emphasis added), Cameron and Makuch, "The UN Biodiversity Convention," op. cit.

15. *Environmental Benefits of Removing Trade Restrictions and Distortions,* Note by the WTO Secretariat, WT/CTE/W/67, 13 March 1998.

16. "Type-1" eco-labels, in the terminology of the ISO, may be awarded by a third party to products that meet (multiple) pre-set environmental criteria, generally following a "life-cycle" approach.

17. In the ISO, progress has been made on developing guidelines on transparency, conformity assessment, and mutual recognition.

18. For example, if reducing the standard of aflatoxins from 5 to 2 ppb increases the risk of cancer by 2 per billion people, then is such a standard appropriate?

19. For example, Agenda 21 called upon all countries to collaborate on global environmental problems on the basis of "common but differentiated responsibilities." It was recognized that developing countries should be provided with improved market access, access to and transfer of technology, and finance.

4

Environmental Governance at the WTO: Outreach to Civil Society

Daniel C. Esty

Trade and investment liberalization promise to bring great benefits to the people of the world.[1] In recent decades, the opening of markets in many regions has lifted hundreds of millions of people out of the abyss of poverty. The gains from trade-driven economic growth offer a promise of improved environmental conditions as well, because wealthier countries are generally both more able and more willing to invest in ecological and public health protection than are poor ones. But there is no guarantee that this link will be made—that development will be environmentally sustainable. Or, to be more precise, carefully considered policies are required to ensure that trade gains do not come at the expense of the environment by causing market failures, welfare losses, distorted economic relations, allocative inefficiency, and unnecessary environmental degradation.[2] Finding ways to achieve these mutual returns and to maximize the synergy between freer trade and better environmental quality stands as an issue of great urgency for the international trading system.[3]

At the centre of this challenge lies the World Trade Organization (WTO). As nations become more economically integrated as a result of ongoing efforts to promote trade and investment liberalization, they need institutional support to promote collective action in response to global-scale risks of market failure. Only the WTO is available to play the role of facilitator of economic interdependence, coordinator of negotiations on the terms of integration, and referee for international economic disputes.[4] In particular, the WTO serves as the forum in which the rules of economic interaction are worked out. By setting the boundaries for appropriate economic behaviour at the global scale, the WTO helps to establish what constitutes a fair or legitimate basis for national comparative advantage. In the environmental realm, for example, some countries have chosen relatively low environmental standards. Are these lax pollution-control and resource-management rules appropriate, given the nation's early stage of development? In some cases, the answer will be yes. But when the harms caused by low standards spill across national boundaries and onto neighbouring countries or the global commons, they should not be considered legitimate. Such spillovers are, in fact, uninternalized externalities that threaten market failure.

The WTO must facilitate regulatory cooperation at the global scale to prevent the economic inefficiency and social welfare losses (not to mention the environmental harms) that might accrue from such trans-boundary pollution. However, the line between legitimate and illegitimate environmental standards will often be unclear, leaving the WTO to sort out which side a particular activity falls on.

Ensuring that the upside of globalization can be achieved without the people of the world suffering from the potentially serious downsides, such as environmental degradation, represents one of the critical public policy challenges of our era. Indeed, the backlash against globalization is already visible.[5] The challenge is particularly acute for the World Trade Organization since it is emerging as one of the central institutions of global governance.

If the WTO is to play its role as a manager of economic and ecological interdependence effectively, it must be seen as having legitimacy, authoritativeness, and a commitment to fairness.[6] Absent these virtues, decisions that emanate from the WTO will not be accepted as part of the process of global decision-making. The WTO's capacity to establish its legitimacy, authoritativeness, and fairness depends heavily on establishing a new relationship not just with the governments of the world, but also with the people around the world in whose name the WTO acts, that is, with civil society. Toward this end, the WTO needs to become better connected to the non-governmental organizations (NGOs) that represent the diverse strands of global civil society.[7]

1. Legitimacy

One key element of the challenge facing the WTO is to establish its *representativeness*. That the WTO takes action only at the direction of its member states is not enough to guarantee public acceptance of its decisions and actions. Public support cannot be founded on government authority. Individual acceptance is what matters. The organization must therefore demonstrate that it has genuine connections to the citizens of the world and that its decisions reflect the will of the people across the planet. Non-governmental organizations represent an important mechanism by which the WTO can reach out to citizens and build the requisite bridge to global civil society.

An essential precondition for acceptance is understanding. NGOs—whether environmental groups, consumer organizations, or labour unions—provide an organized structure for the flow of information. Building a stronger relationship with NGOs therefore offers a significant opportunity for the WTO to increase public understanding of the trading system. In particular, the WTO can use NGOs to disseminate information on the issues that influence the organization's internal deliberations.[8] By informing NGOs about the choices that the organization is facing and the arguments that are being made to push the debate in one direction or another, the WTO can help to ensure that the public are informed about the workings of the international trading system and feel comfortable with the decisions that emanate from it. Explaining what is happening within the trade regime and developing a public appreciation of the work that goes on at the WTO are essential prerequisites for broader public support for trade liberalization in general and for the decisions of the WTO in particular. Currently, there is a great deal of suspicion in many countries about decisions that emerge from the WTO. Critics charge that trade policy is made by a set of faceless international bureaucrats.[9] Environmental opponents of the WTO have staged demonstrations against the WTO in Geneva, Washington, and elsewhere. Better understanding of both the international trading system's procedures and the substantive issues that are under review would help to blunt charges of black box decision-making and to dispel the ignorance that fuels much of the popular criticism of the WTO.

NGOs have the potential not only to transmit information down from the WTO to the public, but also to draw information up into the international trading system. If NGOs were invited to offer opinions on the issues of the day more frequently, there would be fewer policy surprises at the WTO. Knowledge of the concerns that others are bandying about is always valuable and can result in stronger policies refined to address their complaints. Failure to listen to opponents can be fatal, as proponents of the Multilateral Agreement on Investment (MAI) have learned. The OECD negotiations on the MAI came under heavy criticism from the NGO community. Many argue that the international agreement was derailed by a well-coordinated campaign by global grass-roots NGOs.[10] Particularly when issues go beyond technical trade questions and involve connections to other policy domains such as the environment, the small WTO staff in Geneva cannot be expected to have sufficient expertise to recognize and process all of the relevant information. By drawing on submissions from NGOs, the base of information on which WTO decisions are made could be broadened. The organization's sensitivity to public opinion and politics around the world would likewise be heightened.

More importantly, national governments will continue to support international cooperation and the international organizations, such as the WTO, that facilitate collaboration only to the extent that these institutions demonstrate a capacity to deliver collective action gains.[11] And the public are likely to believe that there is a gain from international cooperation only if they perceive that their interests and values are being taken seriously at the global level. Unless this perception exists, national governments will be subjected to criticism by their domestic constituents about the ceding of decision-making to distant officials. Responsiveness, real and perceived, can be provided by public representation at the WTO in the form of NGOs.

A greater role for NGOs at the World Trade Organization would also help to diminish the tension that is created whenever political choices derive from higher (more centralized) levels of government, which are inevitably more distant from ordinary citizens.[12] In providing linkage between individuals and the WTO, NGOs help to reduce the danger that the trading system will be vulnerable to charges of democratic deficit. In particular, NGOs can provide a connective tissue that allows localized citizens to feel better informed and better connected to the distant decision maker.[13]

By broadening the range of voices heard at the WTO, NGO participation will deepen the representativeness of the body and strengthen its legitimacy. Indeed, most of the officials engaged in trade policy-making at the WTO headquarters in Geneva represent national governments.[14] But governments do not perfectly reflect public opinion.[15] Many governments systematically disregard minority viewpoints. Yet a position that is in the minority across many jurisdictions may enjoy a plurality of support at a higher level of aggregation in voting.[16] Permitting NGOs to participate in WTO discussions might also allow the organization to hear important voices that would otherwise be unrepresented or underrepresented in Geneva.[17] By enriching the political dialogue at the WTO, NGO participation would, furthermore, move the international trading system beyond mere pluralism (governance by representative interest groups) toward a model of civic republicanism that emphasizes informed and thoughtful debate and decision-making.[18] This shift toward republicanism and participatory decision-making would add to the legitimacy of WTO governance.

The participation of NGOs in WTO debates could also help to compensate for deficient representativeness at the national level. Weak democratic institutions and other public choice flaws mean that national policies often fail to represent the citizenry's views fairly and accurately. In some cases, authoritarian regimes seek to maintain their hold on power with little regard for public opinion. In other countries, leaders are corrupt. In every country, special interest lobbying, campaign contributions, or asymmetries of resources and political activity among interest groups distort policies and cause some degree of deviation from the true will of the people. It may seem ironic to suggest that the WTO, often criticized for its democratic deficit, could improve the representativeness of decision-making.[19] But, in many cases, the WTO offers a potentially more open, transparent, and pluralistic forum than would be available at the national level. In brief, upgrading the quality of the WTO's political debates through greater transparency and an organized role for NGOs might substitute for the lack of fully functioning democracy in a number of countries around the world.

Perhaps more importantly, many people today do not have their identities determined by the geographic political jurisdiction in which they happen to live.[20] Non-governmental organizations cut across political boundaries and define communities of interest, or what Giddens calls communities of taste, habit and belief,[21] uniting individuals who are committed to human rights, animal welfare, peace, or any number of other causes or viewpoints. In doing so, NGOs provide an alternative form of representation, and they offer a more refined and closely tailored reflection of an individual's views than the one obtained through his or her government. Citizens who care about protecting biodiversity, for instance, will find their views better represented in international forums, such as the WTO, by the Worldwide Fund for Nature than by their own governments.

One of the most important advances in political theory in recent decades is the growing understanding that interactions among people cannot all be mediated through the narrow channel of governments, particularly national governments. Indeed, the liberal critique of traditional realist international relations theory centres on the unwieldy assumption that states are the only actors on the international stage.[22] Quite clearly, a wide variety of other forces now operate internationally, NGOs among them.[23] For the WTO to fail to take cognizance of this transformation or to continue to act as though international affairs were solely a contest of wills among sovereign governments would threaten the international trading system's ongoing viability.[24]

An inclusive approach to NGOs at the WTO also offers important advances from the perspective of the political economy of trade liberalization. Notably, if environmental groups (especially those in North America) and others who have felt excluded from trade policy-making in the past perceive themselves to be included in the process and given a fair opportunity to shape decisions, they are much less likely to obstruct trade liberalization efforts.[25] The benefit of a strategy of inclusiveness was demonstrated during the course of the debate about the North American Free Trade Agreement in the United States. Both the Bush and the Clinton administrations worked hard to ensure that environmental groups were briefed regularly, included in the public advisory groups, and given access to the negotiation process. In the end, a number of environmental groups supported the treaty.[26]

2. Authoritativeness

The credibility and legitimacy of any decision-making body depend on its capacity to make correct decisions. In its core work involving trade liberalization and the settlement of traditional trade disputes, the WTO (and the General Agreement on Tariffs and Trade before it) has an outstanding track record. Over the past 50 years the international trading system has developed a clear underlying economic theory, a well-established set of rules, and a body of dispute settlement precedents to follow. The WTO has both in-house staff and access to outside experts who are capable of providing clear direction and interpretation of the trade rules and of economic law more generally. These assets make the WTO authoritative and thus credible on purely economic issues.[27]

Increasingly, however, the WTO must cope with disputes that involve issues at the intersection of trade policy and other domains, such as the environment. In these cases, the WTO often lacks ready access to the necessary expertise required for well-regarded and widely accepted decisions.[28] Beyond the limited depth of the WTO's own knowledge base, the organization's dispute settlement mechanisms and rule-making procedures lack credibility outside the realm of trade issues. In brief, the WTO faces serious questions about its capacity to deliver substantively correct decisions on trade and environment issues and on other conflicts arising on the periphery of trade law.

To add to the difficulties the WTO faces, policy-making in arenas such as the environment is never easy even in the best of circumstances. High degrees of scientific flux, economic uncertainty, and other complexities surround almost all questions of ecological and public health protection. In the face of this uncertainty, it is extremely helpful to have competing points of view that provide the decision maker with the capacity to triangulate on the truth. The presence of a richer mix of NGO views within the WTO would facilitate this triangulation. In many of these circumstances, the WTO's capacity to produce good policy outcomes that contribute to its reputation for responsiveness and authoritativeness depends on having its deliberations deepened through outside information and multiple policy perspectives. Simply put, the WTO would benefit from considering *competing* policy options.

The benefits of policy competition are well established.[29] In recent years, the gains from bringing competitive forces to bear in the regulatory domain have become a subject of great interest. In the context of international trade policy-making, this theory could translate into a system by which national governments advance competing visions of the direction the World Trade Organization should take. But the limits of horizontally arrayed governments acting as competitors in the regulatory arena have also been recognized.[30] In many policy-making settings, governments do not compete seriously. At the WTO, intellectual competition is particularly limited. Very few governments have sufficient resources to contribute in anything more than a superficial way to WTO policy debates. And this weakness is amplified when the policy questions go beyond the narrow set of trade issues with which the government officials in Geneva are familiar. For example, environmental policy-making often requires careful problem identification, epidemiological and ecological studies, risk assessment, policy design and options development, and cost–benefit analyses. Not many governments in the world can carry out this type of analytically intensive activity. Even fewer have the requisite capacity at hand at the WTO.

NGOs are frequently much better positioned to serve as intellectual competitors than governments are. NGOs often have in-house analytical and technical skills. In many cases, an NGO's *raison d'être* is to sharpen thinking about policy issues. NGOs are, moreover, often more nimble than governments. They work hard to spot new issues and to bring attention to them. In government, the emphasis on following established practices and traditions can translate into inertia. Thus, regulatory competition from outside the governmental domain becomes essential to a sound environmental policy-making process.[31] Fundamentally, the greater the intellectual competition, the more likely it is that policies will be solidly grounded and durable. Better analysis and information also translate into greater authoritativeness and therefore legitimacy.

NGOs also provide an important oversight and audit mechanism. Citizen groups can act as watchdogs on national governments and report on whether they are fulfilling their WTO obligations. With better access to documents and meetings, NGOs would also be in a stronger position to review and critique actions and judgements, by both the WTO and national governments. Although this may not seem intuitively attractive to those in Geneva, the value of peer review and information disclosure is now widely appreciated.[32]

3. Fairness

In addition to substantive correctness, the WTO faces a further challenge of being, and being perceived to be, fair. Fairness has procedural and substantive requirements that must be met if WTO decisions, both in dispute settlement cases and in the negotiation of trade rules, are to have legitimacy.[33] Procedurally, those who believe that they have an interest in the outcomes of decisions must have an opportunity to be part of the decision-making process. This involves opportunities to submit views and to observe how a particular outcome is reached. Substantively, the established rules and precedents must be applied even-handedly over time and across issues, and in a way that does not appear to advantage any particular group or nation systematically.

Again, a broader relationship with NGOs would help the WTO establish a reputation for fairness. In particular, if NGOs believe that they have had an opportunity to participate in the decision-making process, they are much less likely to criticize it. Furthermore, if WTO procedures were more open and accessible to NGOs, it would be harder to argue that special interests dominate the decision-making process. In fact, the belief that the WTO has a pro-business bias would quickly be dispelled if the WTO were to undertake a serious commitment to transparency in all of its decision-making activities. One of the best ways to demonstrate such a commitment would be to allow increased NGO participation.

A more open process would allow both governments and outside observers (including NGOs) to understand the basis on which decisions were being made. An important element of modern governance is that the public have a clear sense of the data and arguments that support a particular decision, including the assumptions that underpin these arguments. Such disclosure at the WTO would go a considerable distance towards ensuring public support of the international trading system.

4. Debunking fears about NGO participation at the WTO

A variety of arguments have been raised against broader WTO links to civil society and a deeper relationship between the international trading system and NGOs. Some of these arguments represent little more than traditional trade community cant. Other concerns have a more serious foundation. But none of the claims bears up under scrutiny.

NGOs as special interests

Perhaps the central fear among trade experts about a broadened role for NGOs at the WTO stems from a belief that many of the groups that might join the trade policy dialogue would represent special interests. More specifically, the trade community sees many NGOs, including most environmental groups, as protectionist and therefore as likely to distort decision-making at the WTO.

It is true that, whenever lobbying of a decision-making body is permitted, there exists some degree of risk that particularized interests will exert influence and steer outcomes in directions that are favourable to them.[34] The tradition of rent-seeking is very long standing indeed. But there is little reason to believe that the current WTO decision process is free of these influences. To the contrary, there is good reason to believe that the level of special interest distortion would be reduced if the WTO's procedures were more open and a broader array of groups was able to exert countervailing influences.

Concerns about opening up the WTO to NGOs are certainly heightened by the perception that many NGOs are unsympathetic to trade liberalization efforts and perhaps are even against free trade.[35] These fears have some basis insofar as a number of environmental groups have aligned themselves with labour unions and other entities that are fundamentally opposed to freer trade. Almost by definition, environmental groups and other non-trade-oriented NGOs have agendas that are not trade centred. These groups bring to trade debates no special commitment to trade or investment liberalization. But forcing trade policy makers to contend with the competing issue demands of the NGO world serves as an important policy discipline and cannot be avoided if the WTO is to be taken seriously as an element of global governance. Political decision makers are always forced to make trade-offs among conflicting goods or values and among competing policy interests. The trade policy choices made at the WTO are no different. Greater NGO participation would therefore complicate WTO decision-making, but a broader base of input would help to ensure a more complete decision process that took cognizance of more of the interests at stake in each decision. This breadth of perspective would ultimately improve the decisions that emanate from the process. With a more diverse set of interests included within the process, interest group manipulation would diminish as the various groups monitored each other and exerted countervailing pressures that would, in general, diminish the prospect of capture of the WTO by any single interest group.[36] A more refined argument along the lines of special interest domination focuses on the need governments sometimes feel to trade off competing domestic interests in order to strike agreements that liberalize trade. Trade officials argue, for example, that they must often go against the needs of domestic interests, particularly those that are hiding behind tariff barriers or other protectionist walls. Indeed, they argue that the capacity to go behind closed doors and cut deals that disadvantage these groups is one of the great strengths of the WTO.

In fact, the argument about the virtues of closed-door deals rests on two faulty assumptions. First, it is by no means clear that the current non-transparent negotiating style promotes freer trade. To the contrary, many protectionist results have emerged from the WTO and from the GATT before it.[37] Secondly, public choice distortions generally become more severe, not less so, when decisions are made out of public view.[38] Transparent decision processes, in which positions are openly disclosed and debated, represent a powerful force in support of outcomes that track the public interest.[39]

The observation that many of the groups that seek access to the WTO are closet, if not overt, protectionists may be true, but it offers no real argument for closed-door meetings or for ducking engagement with civil society. WTO secrecy only serves to heighten anxiety about trade liberalization. Many environmental groups in particular are highly sensitive to process issues, and their opposition to freer trade might well be more muted if they better understood how trade policy decisions are made. A more open WTO process, which involves NGOs, promises considerable advances for the international trading system. Openness and transparency will fuel a broader and more robust WTO politics, which in turn promises to make the decisions that come from the organization more representative, more authoritative, more likely to be perceived as fair, and thus more durable.

The WTO as an intergovernmental body

Some critics of the notion of an expanded role for NGOs at the WTO point to the organization's fundamental structure as an *inter*governmental body as an argument against opening the organization up to civil society. Some commentators[40] suggest that it can be confusing to have statements being issued by constituencies opposing the positions that are being taken by the governments that are supposedly representing them. Others have argued that trade policy works more efficiently when governments can speak clearly to each other without a cacophony of other voices trying to join in the debate. Another strand of the argument turns on the question of whether NGOs might not be getting two bites of the apple if they are allowed to lobby both at the national and at the international levels.

More fundamentally, some analysts argue that the essence of international affairs must be relations among sovereign states.[41] When international bodies attempt to deal with other actors, such as NGOs, their decision processes become murky and the foundation for their legitimacy uncertain. Although this state-centric view of the world might once have been an accurate description of the realm of international law and policy, it is no longer the case. States are, unequivocally, not the only actors that matter in international affairs.[42] And the sovereignty that is important today is not that of governments but rather that of individuals.

In any event, concerns that the presence of NGOs would somehow undermine the WTO's internal logic as an intergovernmental agency miss the point. There is no need to give NGOs a vote at the WTO. Simply by participating in debates and observing WTO goings-on they would strengthen the information flow in and out of the organization.

Representativeness and accountability

A further set of concerns about the role of NGOs in the WTO relates to questions about their accountability and representativeness. Who are NGOs speaking for? How do we know who they really represent? To which groups should WTO officials listen? How do we know the things NGOs say are true?

Concerns about NGO accountability seem legitimate but are, in fact, a red herring. It does not matter how representative NGOs are or to whom they are accountable. NGOs do not purport to *represent* citizens in the same way governments do. Their influence does not derive from being able to cast a vote but arises almost entirely as a function of whether or not the issues and information they present illuminate the issue at hand. There is therefore no need for any external discipline to ensure the accountability of NGOs. A natural market will do the job. In particular, NGOs that present useful information in one set of meetings will find themselves listened to in the next. Groups that present foolish ideas or develop a reputation for presenting inaccurate data or incomplete information will not be taken seriously in future rounds of debate. Perhaps the WTO would need some modest degree of authority over NGOs to ensure that only groups that act within the decorum of the organization (do not conduct demonstrations within the walls of the WTO or abuse their rights of access to decision makers) continue to have the opportunity to participate in the WTO decision processes, but nothing more extensive would be required.

There is a further level of concern about the kinds of groups that might choose to participate in the WTO process. In particular, some Southern governments are worried that Northern NGOs would be more likely to join the WTO debate and further aggravate the political imbalance that already exists between the North and the South.[43] This fear is also misplaced. Although a significant number of the NGOs that would participate in WTO decision processes would be from developed countries, most of them would not be supporting the positions taken by Northern governments. Indeed, recent experience suggests that Northern NGOs at the WTO would more often support Southern governments' perspectives than those of their own governments. Furthermore, as the cost of information and international communications falls, it will be ever easier for NGOs, wherever they might be located, to participate in WTO debates. And, increasingly, it is not physical presence that matters but rather the quality of the arguments that one advances. Solid logic presented by e-mail will almost always prevail over the loudest shouts of an on-the-scene lobbyist. In the Information Age, Southern NGOs will have no trouble being heard alongside their more established Northern counterparts.

Practicalities

Some of the worries about the role of NGOs at the WTO centre on the practical difficulties of accrediting and organizing NGO participation. How would the WTO determine which groups actually qualify as NGOs? Who would allocate the right to speak in particular meetings? Would not the already limited time available to government participants in open meetings be further diluted? Would the presence of NGOs reduce the candour of those who speak at WTO meetings? Some of these concerns do represent real issues, but none of the practicalities of NGO participation in the WTO decision-making processes represents a serious obstacle to outreach to civil society.

NGOs are already participating in a great number of international organizations and decision processes.[44] They have been accredited within the United Nations in New York for many years. Similarly, NGOs have played a role in all of the recent major international environmental negotiations.[45] And the Organization for Economic Cooperation and Development in Paris has increasingly found NGO participation in its deliberations to be constructive and not especially burdensome.

Whatever the expense of reaching out to NGOs, the WTO would find that the costs are more than justified by the benefits. With a relatively small staff devoted to outreach and a few simple procedural reforms, the WTO could easily make itself accessible to NGOs under most conditions. The link to civil society would quickly prove to be invaluable.

5. Differentiated WTO roles

It may make sense to vary the privileges extended to NGOs depending on the particular WTO activity involved. For instance, the arguments for allowing NGO observers to participate in WTO dispute settlement procedures are overwhelming. Having NGOs watch the proceedings when parties give evidence to dispute panels and providing them access to written submissions would go a great distance towards dispelling fears about who is making decisions at the WTO and on what basis.

The Uruguay Round Dispute Settlement Understanding moves the WTO dispute resolution process solidly in the direction of more formal adjudication (GATT 1994). Opening the proceedings to non-governmental observers would be a useful additional step, at no risk to the integrity of the process. Indeed, it is hard to imagine how the presence of NGOs would distort the outcome of the panel process, except that governments could not say one thing to the panellists and something else publicly. To the extent that governments want to negotiate solutions to disputes privately, they would, of course, continue to be free to do so. That the WTO dispute resolution process would no longer be available as a forum for such discussions is of little consequence. All of the governments at the WTO know how to set up private intergovernmental meetings.

The practicalities of assigning seats in the audience for panel hearings represent an inconsequential administrative burden. Limited space might be allocated by lottery or given in turn to accredited NGOs. I would envision an accreditation process that gives WTO access to all non-governmental groups that agreed to abide by the WTO's rules and procedures. Any group that created a disruption could be, and should be, barred from future WTO access.

Allowing NGOs to make submissions to the panels would also be constructive. In many cases, WTO dispute panels would benefit from having outside views available. In cases where the scope of a case goes beyond the boundaries of trade law, when environmental questions or other scientific and technical issues are at play, for example, non-governmental viewpoints may be especially illuminating. Not only would NGO submissions thus be available to provide competing data, science, risk or cost–benefit analyses, and policy conclusions that would broaden the information base on which the panel could rely, but the NGO participation in the decision process would also help to legitimize the panel's decision and broaden public acceptance of the outcome.

If rules prohibiting *ex parte* contacts with panel members were in place and all submissions were required to be in writing and open to scrutiny and rebuttal, the risk of manipulation by special interests is virtually non-existent. WTO decisions would rely on NGO submissions only to the extent that the arguments and information presented assisted the members of the dispute panel with their analyses. The administrative burden would be easy to manage through page limits, form requirements, and the provision of legal assistants to the panellists in any case in which the outside submissions were large in number.[46]

Defining the bounds of NGO participation in WTO policy development, review, and rule-making activities would require a somewhat more complicated structure. With respect to formal meetings such as the General Council or to the sessions of subgroups such as the Committee on Trade and Environment, allowing NGO observers might broaden public understanding of the work of the WTO. If NGOs were permitted to watch the proceedings, they could, with their networks of contacts, help to disseminate information on policy issues under discussion. If they were given (carefully circumscribed) opportunities to present material, they could also add to the knowledge base of the WTO Secretariat and of governmental officials participating in the work of the WTO.

The risk of outcome manipulation by special interests is not especially serious in the course of *formal* meetings. The fact that information must be presented publicly, that records are kept on what is said, and that any material offered is open to scrutiny and debate minimizes the risk of inappropriate influence being exerted. The real danger of special interest distortion comes from *informal* contacts and private meetings. Of course, lobbying of the WTO staff or national representatives by special interests occurs today. Establishing formal roles for NGO participation in WTO activities would not add to, and might even diminish, the risk of inappropriate pressure in informal settings. In particular, if formal procedures for the airing of NGO views were in place, WTO officials could steer those seeking to meet with them privately toward these public sessions where attempts to win special favours would be more difficult.

The opening of formal WTO meetings to NGOs also might present an opportunity to introduce lobbying disclosure requirements that mandate public reporting of all informal contacts between NGOs (including business as well as public interest groups) and WTO officials.[47] At the same time, rules on gifts to officials might be put in place. As the WTO matures into a more important element of our global governance structure, it is reasonable to expect that it will have to adopt operating procedures that improve the transparency and perceived fairness of its decision processes.

In any case, the salient fact is that excluding NGOs from the WTO does not shelter the organization from special interest manipulation. Likewise, establishing a formal role for NGOs within the WTO creates no *additional* risk of protectionist results. Thus, the argument that excluding NGOs from formal meetings creates a useful "buffer" between decision makers and special interest groups has no foundation whatsoever.[48]

Actual trade negotiations remain a fundamentally government-to-government bargaining process and thus present the strongest case for a measure of secrecy and exclusion of NGOs. Given the complexity of making trade deals and the added degree of difficulty that open negotiations would entail, WTO mandates on NGO involvement in negotiating sessions would be misguided. Whether national authorities want to share their negotiating positions and strategies with non-governmental entities must be left to each country individually. Although many countries have found it useful to consult with interested parties in the course of negotiations,[49] whether and how such discussions take place should remain a matter of national policy.

6. Conclusion

The WTO is emerging as a critical element of the world's governance structure. As the international body charged with managing economic interdependence, the WTO cannot help but make decisions that affect a great many other policy realms. In doing so, the WTO must show sensitivity to the concerns and values that are reflected by these other domains. To win ongoing public support, the WTO must attend scrupulously to its representativeness, authoritativeness, and reputation for fairness. At stake is nothing less than the organization's legitimacy. Broadening the base of its connections to the citizens of the world through NGOs represents an important step forward for the organization. Indeed, the future of the WTO can hardly be envisioned without a broader set of connections to civil society.

Acknowledgements

This article builds upon and draws on Daniel C. Esty, "Non-Governmental Organizations at the World Trade Organization: Cooperation, Competition, or Exclusion," *Journal of International Economic Law* 1, 1998, 123–147.

Notes

1. John H. Jackson, *The World Trading System: Law and Policy of International Economic Relations,* Cambridge: MIT Press, 1997; Robert Gilpin, *The Political Economy of International Relations,* Princeton, NJ: Princeton University Press, 1987.

2. Daniel C. Esty, *Greening the GATT: Trade, Environment and the Future,* Washington, DC: Institute for International Economics, 1994.

3. Daniel C. Esty, "Economic Integration and Environmental Protection: Synergies, Opportunities, and Challenges," speech presented at the World Trade Organization, Geneva, Switzerland, 5 March 1999.

4. Daniel C. Esty, "Non-Governmental Organizations at the World Trade Organization: Cooperation, Competition or Exclusion," *Journal of International Economic Law* 1, 1998, 123–147; and John H. Jackson, *World Trade and the Law of the GATT,* Indianapolis: Bobbs-Merrill, 1994.

5. Robert Litan, Robert Lawrence, and Charles Schultze, eds., *American Living Standards: Threats and Challenges,* Washington, DC: Brookings Institute, 1998; and Dani Rodrick, *The New Global Economy and Developing Countries: Making Openness Work,* Washington, DC: Johns Hopkins University Press, 1999.

6. Esty, "Non-Governmental Organizations," op. cit.; W. Michael Reisman, "Myres S. McDougal: Architect of a Jurisprudence for a Free Society," *Mississippi Law Journal* 66, 1996, 15–26.

7. Paul Wapner, "Governance in Global Civil Society," in Oran Young, ed., *Global Governance: Drawing Insights from the Environmental Experience,* Cambridge, MA: MIT Press, 1997, pp. 133–167.

8. Many NGOs are ideally situated to play this dissemination role insofar as they produce regular newsletters and devote significant resources to outreach. They thus have direct connections to millions of individuals with whom government officials have no easy method of contact.

9. Ralph Nader, ed., *The Case Against Free Trade: GATT, NAFTA and the Globalization of World Power,* Berkeley, CA: North Atlantic, 1993; Walter R. Mead, "Bushism Found," *Harpers,* September 1992, 285–287.

10. See John Vidal, "Eco Soundings," *Guardian* (United Kingdom), 28 July 1999.

11. Daniel C. Esty and Robert Mendelsohn, "Moving from National to International Environmental Policy," *Policy Sciences* 8, 1998, 1–30; Peter S. Menell, "Institutional Fantasylands: From Scientific Management to Free Market Environmentalism," *Harvard Journal of Law and Public Policy* 15, 1992, 489–510; and Maxwell L. Stearns, "The Misguided Renaissance of Social Choice," *Yale Law Journal* 103, 1994, 1219–1293.

12. Naomi Roht-Arriaza, "The Committee on Regions and the Role of Regional Governments in the European Union," *Hastings International and Comparative Law Review* 20, 1997, 413–436; Sol Picciotto, "Networks in International Economic Integration: Fragmented States and the Dilemmas of Neo-Liberalism," *Northwestern Journal of International Law and Business* 17, 1996–97, 1014–1056.

13. Esty, "Non-Governmental Organizations," op. cit.

14. There is a small WTO staff or secretariat. But these international civil servants almost always bring a trade background to their service in Geneva and thus cannot be counted upon to enrich the WTO's field of political vision.

15. Anthony Downs, *An Economic Theory of Democracy,* New York: Harper, 1957; Mancur Olson, *The Logic of Collective Action: Public Goods and the Theory of Groups,* Cambridge, MA: Harvard University Press, 1965; James M. Buchanan and Gordon Tullock, *The Calculus of Consent,* Ann Arbor: University of Michigan Press, 1971.

16. Herbert Hovenkamp, "Legislation, Well-Being and Public Choice," *University of Chicago Law Review* 57, 1990, 63–116.

17. Paul Wapner, *Environmental Activism and World Civic Politics,* Albany: State University of New York Press, 1995; Wendy Schoener, "Nongovernmental Organizations and Global Activism: Legal and Informal Approaches," *Indiana Journal of Global Legal Studies* 4, 1997, 537–564.

18. Cass R. Sunstein, "Interest Groups in American Public Law," *Stanford Law Review* 38, 1985, 29–87; Cass R. Sunstein, "Beyond the Republican Revival," *Yale Law Journal* 97, 1988, 1539–1590.

19. E. U. Petersmann, *Constitutional Functions and Constitutional Problems of International Economic Law,* Boulder, CO: Westview, 1991; E. U. Petersmann, "National Constitutions, Foreign Trade Policy, and European Community Law," *Aussenwirtschaft* 46, 1991, 197–225; Frieder Roessler, "The Constitutional Function of the Multilateral Trade Order," in M. Hilf and E. U. Petersmann, eds., *National Constitutions and International Economic Law,* Boston: Kluwer, 1992, pp. 114–142; Michael Smith and Guy de Jonquieres, "EU Farm Chief Rebuked over Swipe at WTO," *Financial Times,* 5 September 1997, 4.

20. In at least some circumstances, I might be better understood as an environmental law professor than as a resident of Connecticut.

21. Anthony Giddens, *Beyond Left and Right: The Future of Radical Politics,* Cambridge: Polity, 1994.

22. Marvin S. Soros, *Beyond Sovereignty: The Challenge of Global Policy,* Columbia: University of South Carolina Press, 1986; Thomas J. Biersteker and Cynthia Weber, eds., *State Sovereignty as Social Construct,* New York: Cambridge University Press, 1996; Harold H. Koh, "Why Do Nations Obey International Law?" *Yale Law Journal* 106, 1997, 2599–2659.

23. Barbara J. Bramble and Gareth Porter, "Nongovernmental Organizations and the Making of US International Environmental Policy," in Andrew Hurrell and Benedict Kingsbury, eds., *The International Politics of the Environment,* New York: Oxford University Press, 1992, pp. 31–66.

24. G. Richard Shell, "The Trade Stakeholders' Model and Participation by Nonstate Parties in the World Trade Organization," *University of Pennsylvania Journal of International Economic Law* 17, 1996, 359–380; Thomas G. Weiss and Leon Gor-

denker, eds., *NGOs, the UN and Global Governance,* Boulder, CO: Lynne Rienner, 1996.

25. Daniel C. Esty, "Environmentalists and Trade Policymaking," in Alan Deardorff and Robert Stern, eds., *Constituent Interests in US Trade Policies,* Ann Arbor: University of Michigan Press, 1997.

26. Fredrick M. Abbott, "Foundation-Building for Western Hemispheric Integration," *Northwestern Journal of International Law and Business* 17, 1997, 900–947; John Audley, *Green Politics and Global Trade,* Washington, DC: Georgetown University Press, 1997; Esty, *Greening the GATT,* op. cit.

27. Robert Hudec, *Enforcing International Trade Law,* Salem, NH: Butterworth, 1995; Pierre Pescatore, William J. Davey, and Andreas F. Lowenfeld, *Handbook of WTO/ GATT Dispute Settlement,* The Hague: Kluwer, 1996; E. U. Petersmann, *The GATT/ WTO Dispute Settlement System: International Law, International Organizations and Dispute Settlement,* Boston: Kluwer, 1997.

28. Jeffrey L. Dunoff, "Trade And: Recent Developments in Trade Policy Scholarship and Their Surprising Political Implications," *Northwestern Journal of International Law and Business* 17, 1996–97, 759–774.

29. Richard Revesz, "Rehabilitating Interstate Competition: Rethinking the 'Race to the Bottom' Rationale for Federal Environmental Regulation," *New York University Law Review* 67, 1992, 1210–1254; Paul A. Samuelson and William D. Nordhaus, *Economics,* Boston: Irwin/McGraw-Hill, 1995.

30. Daniel C. Esty, "Stepping up to the Global Environmental Challenge," *Fordham Environmental Law Journal* 8, 1996, 103–129; Kirsten A. Engel, "State Environmental Standard-Setting: Is There a Race and Is It to the Bottom?" *Hastings Law Journal* 48, 1997, 271–376; Joshua D. Sarnoff, "Cooperative Federalism, the Delegation of Federal Authority, and the Constitution," *Arizona Law Review* 39, 1997, 205–281.

31. Daniel C. Esty, "Greening World Trade," in Jeffrey Scott, ed., *The World Trading System: Challenges Ahead,* Washington, DC: Institute for International Economics, 1996, pp. 69–86; Steve Charnovitz and Elizabeth Dowdeswell, "Globalization, Trade and Interdependence," in Marian Chertow and Daniel Esty, eds., *Thinking Ecologically: The Next Generation of Environmental Policy,* New Haven, CT: Yale University Press, 1997, pp. 91–124.

32. Abram Chayes and Antonia Chayes, *The New Sovereignty: Compliance with International Regulatory Agreements,* Cambridge, MA: Harvard University Press, 1995; Edith Brown Weiss and Harold Jacobson, eds., *Engaging Countries: Strengthening Compliance with International Accords,* Cambridge, MA: MIT Press, 1998; Robert Housman, "Democratizing International Trade Decision Making," *Cornell International Law Journal* 23, 1994, 699–747.

33. Peter J. Spiro, "New Global Communities: Nongovernmental Organizations in International Decisionmaking Institutions," *Washington Quarterly* 18, 1994, 45–56.

34. Arvind Subramanian, "Trade Measures for Environment: A Nearly Empty Box," *World Economy* 15, 1992, 135–167.

35. William M. Reichert, "Resolving the Trade and Environment Conflict: The WTO and NGO Consultative Relations," *Minnesota Journal of Global Trade* 2, 1996, 219–246.

36. Peter J. Spiro, "New Global Potentates: Nongovernmental Organizations and the Unregulated Marketplace," *Cardozo Law Review* 18, 1996, 957–969; Kevin Stair

and Peter Taylor, "Nongovernmental Organizations and the Legal Protection of the Ocean: A Case Study," in Andrew Hurell and Benedict Kingsbury, eds., *The International Politics of the Environment,* New York: Oxford University Press, 1992, pp. 110–133.

37. James Bovard, *The Fair Trade Fraud,* New York: St. Martins Press, 1991; Steve Charnovitz, "Participation of Non-Governmental Parties in the World Trade Organization," *University of Pennsylvania Journal of International Economic Law* 17, 1996, 331–357.

38. Esty, "Non-Governmental Organizations," op. cit.

39. J. Oloka-Onyango, "Beyond the Rhetoric: Reinvigorating the Struggle for Economic and Social Rights in Africa," *California Western International Law Journal* 26, 1995, 1–73.

40. Philip Nichols, "Extension of Standing in WTO Disputes to Nongovernmental Parties," *University of Pennsylvania Journal of International Economic Law* 17, 1996, 295–329.

41. Philip Nichols, "Realism, Liberalism, Values, and the World Trade Organization," *University of Pennsylvania Journal of International Economic Law* 17, 1996, 851–882; Esty, "Stepping up to the Global Environmental Challenge," op. cit.; Anne Marie Slaughter, "Liberal International Relations Theory and International Economic Law," *American University Journal of International Law and Policy* 10, 1995, 717–743; Kenneth Waltz, *Theory of International Politics,* Reading, MA: Addison-Wesley, 1979.

42. W. Michael Reisman, "Sovereignty and Human Rights in Contemporary International Law," *American Journal of International Law* 84, 1990, 866–876; Anne Marie Slaughter, "The Real New World Order," *Foreign Affairs* 76, 1997, 183–197; Soros, *Beyond Sovereignty,* op. cit.; Koh, "Why Do Nations Obey International Law?", op. cit.

43. Steve Charnovitz, "Two Centuries of Participation: NGOs and International Governance," *Michigan Journal of International Law* 18, 1997, 183–286.

44. Ibid.

45. Daniel Bodansky, "The United Nations Framework Convention on Climate Change: A Commentary," *Yale Journal of International Law* 18, 1993, 451–558.

46. Many models exist for such submissions, including the *amicus curiae* (friend of the court) procedures under US law. See Sup. Ct. R. 37.

47. The recent leadership problems within the European Union show what happens when governance procedures are not supported by an adequate structure of administrative law and conflict-of-interest rules.

48. Nichols, "Extension of Standing," op. cit.; Nichols, "Realism," op. cit.

49. US Trade Act 1974; Jonathan I. Miller, "Prospects for Satisfactory Dispute Resolution of Private Commercial Disputes under the North American Free Trade Agreement," *Pepperdine Law Review* 21, 1994, 1313–1389.

5

The WTO Dispute Settlement System

William J. Davey

It would make little sense to spend years negotiating the detailed rules in international trade agreements if those rules could be ignored. Therefore, a system of rule enforcement is necessary. In the World Trade Organization (WTO), that function is performed by the Understanding on Rules and Procedures Governing the Settlement of Disputes (usually called the "Dispute Settlement Understanding," or simply the "DSU"). As stated in Article 3.2 of the DSU, "[t]he dispute settlement system of the WTO is a central element in providing security and predictability to the multilateral trading system." In the commercial world, such security and predictability are viewed as fundamental prerequisites to conducting business internationally.

In this chapter, I will first describe the WTO dispute settlement process by outlining its four basic phases: consultations, the panel process, the appellate process, and the surveillance of implementation. Secondly, the actual performance of the system from 1 January 1995 to date will be evaluated.[1] Finally, a number of important issues currently facing the system will be discussed. Among those issues are whether or not the system adequately takes into account the special needs of developing countries and whether or not the system's transparency should be increased through, for example, allowing greater access for the public to the various elements of the process. These two concerns have been particularly important in WTO cases that have touched on environmental issues.

At the outset, it is important to recall that the WTO dispute settlement system is an elaboration of the General Agreement on Tariffs and Trade (GATT) system that preceded it. The GATT system was relatively successful as an international dispute settlement mechanism. It produced 100 or so formal decisions (more than the International Court of Justice during the comparable period). One extensive academic study of the GATT dispute settlement system concluded that countries with legitimate complaints achieved complete satisfaction in some 60 per cent of the cases and partial satisfaction in most of the rest.[2] However, the system was criticized because the GATT consensus decision-making rules meant that a party could prevent the dispute settlement process from starting and, even if the process was allowed to go forward, a losing party could prevent formal adoption of a decision against it (and losing parties did so more frequently over time).[3] Without adoption, the report remained in limbo; it expressed the view of three experts but had no status in GATT. Thus, the dispute remained unresolved. As a result, there was a perception that the GATT system was not adequate. Moreover, it was believed that cases that should have been resolved in the system were never even brought to it because of this perceived shortcoming.

In the Uruguay Round trade negotiations, the United States in particular wanted to improve and strengthen the dispute settlement system. Traditionally, the United States had supported a more judicial-like system in GATT, whereas major powers such as the European Communities and Japan preferred a system that stressed the negotiated settlement of disputes.[4] However, one of their major concerns in international trade was what they viewed as inappropriate US unilateralism and they became convinced during the course of the Uruguay Round that one way to restrain US unilateralism would be to strengthen the GATT dispute settlement system and persuade the United States to commit to use the improved system in lieu of taking unilateral action.

As a result and as will be seen below, compared with the GATT system, the WTO system operates with more efficiency and within defined time-frames. Its increased automaticity is highlighted by the fact that in the WTO dispute settlement reports must be adopted unless there is a consensus to the contrary, in contrast to the GATT system where a positive consensus was needed to adopt reports. Moreover, in the WTO, there is a new appellate process and a much more effective system for surveillance of the implementation of the conclusions of the reports.

1. WTO dispute settlement: An outline of the process[5]

The settlement of disputes in the World Trade Organization is governed by the Dispute Settlement Understanding (DSU), which is in effect an interpretation and elaboration of Articles XXII and XXIII of GATT 1994.[6] Article XXII provides for consultations generally with respect to any matter affecting the operation of the agreement. Article XXIII provides for consultations and dispute settlement procedures where one member considers that another member is failing to carry out its obligations under the agreement.[7] The other agreements annexed to the WTO Agreement also rely on GATT Articles XXII and XXIII, or very similar provisions, as a basis for dispute settlement.[8]

There are essentially four phases in the WTO dispute settlement process: consultations, the panel process, the appellate process, and surveillance of implementation. Each is discussed in turn.

Consultations

Under the WTO dispute settlement system, a member may ask for consultations with another WTO member if the complaining member believes that the other member has violated a WTO agreement or otherwise nullified or impaired benefits accruing to it. The goal of the consultation stage is to enable the disputing parties to understand better the factual situation and the legal claims in respect of the dispute and to resolve the matter without further proceedings. The DSU provides that "[t]he aim of the dispute settlement mechanism is to secure a positive solution to a dispute. A solution mutually acceptable to the parties to a dispute and consistent with the [WTO] agreements is clearly to be preferred."[9] At this stage, as well as at later stages in the process, there is a possibility of utilizing the good offices of the WTO Director-General or mediation to settle a dispute.[10]

If consultations are requested under Article XXII of GATT 1994 or the equivalent provision of another WTO agreement,[11] WTO members with a substantial trade interest may request to be joined in the consultations as third parties.[12] If the member asked to consult agrees that the claim of substantial interest is well founded, the request to join will be honoured. If, however, consultations are requested under Article XXIII (or its equivalent), there is no provision for third parties to join in the consultations.

The manner in which the consultations are conducted is up to the parties. The DSU has no rules on consultations beyond that they are to be entered into in good faith and are to be held with 30 days of a request.[13] Typically, they are held in Geneva and involve capital-based officials, as well as local delegates. During the consultations, both parties are likely to try and learn more about the facts and the legal arguments of the other party. Written questions may be exchanged and written answers requested. Despite the fact that the structure of consultations is undefined and there are no rules for conducting them, consultations lead to settlements (or at least the apparent abandonment of a case) in respect of a significant number of consultation requests. For example, of the 138 consultation requests made prior to 30 June 1998 (i.e. requests that are over one year old as of the date of this chapter), slightly more than one-half (72) have not been brought before a panel. Although some of these may eventually end up before a panel, this statistic suggests that the consultation process disposes of roughly one-half of the cases brought.

The panel process

Panel establishment

If consultations fail to resolve the dispute within 60 days of the request, the complaining WTO member may request the WTO Dispute Settlement Body (DSB) to establish a panel to rule on the dispute.[14] The DSB is composed of all WTO members and is charged with administering the rules and procedures of the DSU and overseeing the operation of the WTO dispute settlement system.[15] Technically, the DSB is the WTO General Council, performing its dispute settlement role under a separate chairperson. Under the DSU, if requested, the DSB is required to establish a panel no later than the second meeting at which the request for a panel appears on the agenda,[16] unless there is a consensus in the DSB to the contrary.[17] Thus, unless the member requesting the establishment of a panel consents to delay, a panel will be established within approximately 90 days of the initial request for consultations.[18] It should be stressed, however, that parties are not required to request a panel at any point in time and that, in most cases, a panel is not requested 60 days after the start of consultations. Rather, consultations continue for some time thereafter.

Panellist selection

After the panel is established by the DSB, it is necessary to select the three individuals who will serve as panellists.[19] To accomplish this, the WTO Secretariat suggests the names of possible panellists to the disputing parties. The DSU allows the parties to reject a Secretariat proposal only for "compelling reasons,"[20] but in practice the parties have rather free rein to object since their agreement to the composition of the panel is necessary, unless the Director-General of the WTO is requested to appoint the panel. The practice of frequent objections means that the panel selection process is often rather slow. The median time for selection is seven weeks.[21]

If the parties cannot agree on the identity of the panellists within 20 days of the panel's establishment, any party to the dispute may request the WTO Director-General to appoint the panel, which he is required to do within 10 days of the request.[22] Over time, it has become more common for the Director-General to appoint panels. To date, he has appointed 16 of the 45 panels that have been composed. It should be noted, however, that it is common for the parties to have agreed upon one or two of the panellists on the panels appointed by the Director-General.

The DSU provides that panels shall be composed of "well-qualified governmental and/or non-governmental individuals, including persons who have served on or presented a case to a panel, served as a representative of a Member or of a contracting party to GATT 1947 or as a representative to the Council or Committee of any covered agreement or its predecessor agreement, or in the Secretariat, taught or published on international trade law or policy, or served as a senior trade policy official of a Member."[23] These criteria could be roughly summarized as establishing three categories of panellists: government officials (current or former), former Secretariat officials, and academics. It is specifically provided that panellists shall not be nationals of parties or third parties, absent agreement of the parties.[24] It is also specified that, in a case involving a developing country, one panellist must be from a developing country (if requested).[25] The 135 WTO panellist positions filled through 30 June 1999 were filled by 93 different individuals, with four individuals having served on four panels and nine individuals having served on three panels. Most of these positions were filled by government officials (114), one-third of whom were Geneva based; 29 positions were filled by academics; and 8 positions were filled by former Secretariat officials.[26] The DSU provides for the creation of an indicative list of individuals qualified for panel service. Members have followed varying practices in respect of nominations to the list—most nominate non-governmental individuals, but many also nominate non-Geneva governmental individuals and some even nominate Geneva-based officials. Most members do not nominate anyone. To date, about one-third of the panel positions have been filled with persons on the indicative list.

The 135 panellist positions have been filled with persons from a wide range of countries (38 in all), with Switzerland, New Zealand, Australia, Hong Kong/China, and European Union countries supplying the most.[27] More than one-half of the WTO panellists selected to date had served on a previous GATT or WTO panel at the time of their selection.

Rules of conduct for panellists and Secretariat staff

The DSU provides that panellists serve in their individual capacities and that members should not give them instructions or seek to influence them.[28] In addition, in December 1996, the DSB adopted rules of conduct applicable to participants in the WTO dispute settlement system.[29] There were no such rules in the past. The rules require that Appellate Body members, panellists, arbitrators, experts, and Secretariat staff assigned to assist in the dispute settlement process "shall be independent and impartial, shall avoid direct or indirect conflicts of interest and shall respect the confidentiality of proceedings."[30] To ensure compliance with the rules, such persons are to disclose "the existence or development of any interest, relationship or matter that person could reasonably be expected to know and that is likely to affect, or give rise to justifiable doubts as to, that person's independence or impartiality."[31] Disputing parties have the right to raise an alleged material violation of the rules, which, if upheld, would lead to the replacement of the challenged individual.

The panel's functions and terms of reference

A panel's terms of reference are normally determined by the complaining party's request for a panel, unless the parties agree upon special terms of reference. The normal terms of reference provide that the panel shall examine, in light of the relevant WTO agreements, the matter referred to the DSB by the complainant and make such findings as will assist the DSB in making the recommendations or in giving the rulings provided for in those agreements.[32] More specifically, the DSU provides that a panel shall make an objective assessment of the matter before it, including an objective assessment of the facts of the case and the applicability of and conformity with the relevant WTO agreements.[33] The "matter" referred to a panel is typically that contained in the complaining party's request for the establishment of a panel. The DSU requires that such a request be in writing and identify the specific measures at issue and provide a brief summary of the legal basis of the complaint.[34]

Panel proceedings

A panel normally meets with the parties shortly after its selection to set its working procedures and time schedule.[35] The standard proposed timetable for panels makes provision for two meetings between the panel and the parties to discuss the substantive issues in the case.[36] Each meeting is preceded by the filing of written submissions. In the case of the first meeting, the complainant files first and the respondent is expected to file two or three weeks thereafter. Rebuttal submissions filed after the first meeting are typically filed simultaneously. Panels normally ask oral and written questions to which the parties are expected to respond. If it deems it appropriate, a panel may either consult individual experts or form an expert review group to advise it on technical and scientific issues.[37]

After completing the fact-gathering and argument phase, the panel issues a draft of the "descriptive part" of its report, which summarizes the arguments of the parties and on which the parties may submit comments.[38] Following receipt of comments, the panel issues its "interim report," which contains the descriptive part as revised, as well as the panel's findings and recommendations. The interim report becomes the final report unless one of the parties requests the panel to review "precise aspects" of the report.[39] If requested, the panel is required to hold an additional meeting with the parties to hear their views on those aspects of the interim report. With one exception, parties have always commented on some aspects of the interim report. However, it is not uncommon for parties to forgo an additional meeting with the panel and to make their comments in written form only. The extent of those comments varies widely. Some parties comment only on factual issues, saving their legal arguments for appeal. Others treat the interim review process as a mini-appeal in which they raise a multitude of factual and legal issues. The prevailing party typically suggests ways to strengthen the panel's reasoning. In light of the comments received, the panel then issues its final report. To date, no final report has reached a different result than an interim report, although some significant changes in wording have been made from time to time.

Non-party WTO members may participate in the dispute settlement process to a limited degree as third parties if they have a substantial interest in the matter.[40] Otherwise panel proceedings are not open to non-parties. Parties may make their own submissions to a panel public and, if a party does not do so, it may be requested to provide a non-confidential summary of its submissions that can be made public.[41] As discussed below, there is interest in expanding access to the system, particularly for other members, but also for interested non-governmental entities (i.e. NGOs and the public at large).

The DSB sets as a goal that the final report should be issued to the parties within six months of the panel's composition[42] and that, at the latest, the report should be circulated to all members within nine months of the panel's establishment.[43] To date, 27 WTO panels have issued reports, and the median time elapsed between establishment and circulation has been 11.1 months. The failures to meet the nine-month target have often involved cases where the panel felt it necessary to have recourse to outside experts, where there were translation delays, and where the cases were extraordinarily complex. The current median time of 11.1 months is, however, an increase in median time of one month since August 1998, suggesting that the timely performance of panels has been declining, perhaps because of inadequate resources in the system, an issue discussed below.

Adoption of the panel report

After its circulation to WTO members, the final report is referred to the DSB for formal adoption, which is to take place within 60 days unless there is either a consensus not to adopt the report or an appeal of the report to the WTO Appellate Body. This so-called negative consensus rule is a fundamental change from the GATT dispute settlement system, where a positive consensus was needed to adopt a panel report, thus permitting a dissatisfied losing party to block any action on the report. Now, as long as one member wants the report adopted, it will be adopted. Although the power to block adoption of reports was used relatively infrequently, its use was increasing over time, as noted above. Moreover, it was used in a number of high-profile cases and had led to significant complaints about the effectiveness of the GATT system. Observers found it hard to accept that the losing party could exercise such control. Now, however, the losing party cannot block adoption but, in part to compensate for the loss of that power, there is a right of appeal. If a panel report is appealed, after completion of the appeal it is adopted as affirmed, modified, or reversed by the Appellate Body.

The appellate process

The possibility of an appeal is a new feature of the WTO dispute settlement system. The Appellate Body[44] consists of seven individuals, appointed by the DSB for four-year terms.[45] The Appellate Body hears appeals of panel reports in divisions of three, although its rules provide for the division hearing a case to exchange views with the other four Appellate Body members before the division finalizes its report.[46] The members of the division that hears a particular appeal are selected by a secret procedure that is based on randomness, unpredictability, and the opportunity for all members to serve without regard to national origin.[47]

The Appellate Body's review is limited to issues of law and legal interpretation developed by the panel.[48] However, the Appellate Body has taken a broad view of its power to review panel decisions. It has the express power to reverse, modify, or affirm panel decisions,[49] but the DSU does not discuss the possibility of a remand to a panel. Partly as a consequence, the Appellate Body has adopted the practice, where possible, of completing the analysis of particular issues in order to resolve cases where it has significantly modified a panel's reasoning. This avoids requiring a party to start the whole proceeding over as a result of those modifications.[50]

The Appellate Body is required to issue its report within 60 (at most 90) days from the date of the appeal,[51] and its report is to be adopted automatically by the DSB within 30 days, absent consensus to the contrary. There have been 17 Appellate Body reports adopted to date. In three cases, the panel was affirmed; in one case, it was reversed. In the remaining 13 cases, the Appellate Body has modified, sometimes extensively, the panel's findings. In all but two cases, however, the basic result reached by the panel has been upheld, albeit sometimes to a different degree and/or on the basis of different reasoning.

It is probably much too early to judge an institution that has been in operation for fewer than four years. None the less, to date there seems to be general satisfaction with the overall performance of the Appellate Body and none of the proposals in the ongoing review of the DSU (discussed below) suggest any fundamental change to the Appellate Body or the way it would work, except for the possibility of extending the scope of its review powers and permitting it to remand cases to the original panel for reconsideration in light of its decision.

Surveillance of implementation

The final phase of the WTO dispute settlement process is the surveillance stage. This is designed to ensure that DSB recommendations (based on adopted panel/Appellate Body reports) are implemented. If a panel finds that an agreement has been violated, it typically recommends that the member concerned bring the offending measure into conformity with its WTO obligations.[52] Although a panel may suggest means of implementation, it is left to members to determine how to implement.[53]

Under the surveillance function, the offending member is required to state its intentions with respect to implementation within 30 days of the adoption of the applicable report(s) by the DSB. If immediate implementation is impractical, a member is to be afforded a reasonable period of time for implementation.[54] Absent agreement, that period of time may be set by arbitration. The DSU provides that, as a guideline for the arbitrator, the period should not exceed 15 months.[55] In the first six cases, the reasonable periods of time, whether set by arbitration or by agreement, happened to be 15 months. In the next nine cases, the times ranged from 7 to 13 months, with a median of 8.3 months. Starting six months after the determination of the reasonable period of time, the offending member is required to report to each regular DSB meeting as to its progress in implementation.[56]

If a party fails to implement the report within the reasonable period of time, the prevailing party may request compensation.[57] If that is not forthcoming, it may request the DSB to authorize it to suspend concessions (i.e. retaliate) owed to the non-implementing party.[58] DSB authorization is automatic, absent consensus to the contrary, subject to arbitration of the level of suspension if requested by the non-implementing member.[59] To date, suspension of concessions has been authorized in two cases—at the request of the United States vis-à-vis the European Union in respect of the *Bananas* case; at the request of Canada and the United States vis-à-vis the European Union in respect of the *Hormones* case. In each case, the level of suspension was set by arbitration.[60] Suspension of concessions is viewed as a last resort and the preference is for the non-implementing member to bring its measure into conformity with its obligations.[61]

The above-described rules on suspension of concessions work without problem when it is agreed that there has been no implementation. However, if there is a disagreement over whether or not there has been satisfactory implementation, the provisions of the DSU do not work harmoniously.

On the one hand, Article 21.5 of the DSU provides that such a disagreement shall be referred to the original panel, where available, which shall issue its report in 90 days. It is unclear whether there is a requirement for consultations prior to such referral and whether the DSB must make the referral. Likewise it is not clear whether there is a right of appeal. Article 21.5 refers to using "these dispute settlement procedures," which arguably suggests that all of these steps may be necessary (although, unlike the case of the panel process, Article 21.5 does not provide that these other steps should be expedited).

At the same time, Article 22.2 of the DSU provides that, on request, the DSB must authorize suspension of concessions, absent consensus to the contrary, within 30 days of the expiration of the reasonable period of time. An Article 21.5 proceeding would normally not be completed within 30 days of the expiration of the reasonable period of time. As a consequence, a number of questions arise. Can the procedures be followed simultaneously or must the Article 21.5 procedure precede the Article 22 procedure? Can the deadline for DSB authorization of suspension pursuant to the negative consensus rule be suspended until completion of an Article 21.5 proceeding? Would the right to a decision absent negative consensus still apply? These issues are not clearly dealt with in the DSU and became quite controversial in the *Bananas* case. As a result, as explained below, the ongoing review of the DSU has focused on these issues.

2. The operation to date of the WTO dispute settlement system

Generally speaking, the WTO dispute settlement system has operated well since the founding of the WTO on 1 January 1995. WTO members have made extensive use of the system. To date, there have been 175 requests for consultations, involving over 130 distinct matters.[62] Consultation requests since 1995 have been on the order of 40–50 a year. This extensive use of the system suggests that WTO members have confidence in it.

As noted above, a significant number of consultation requests seem to have been resolved by the parties without the need for recourse to the panel process.[63] It appears that roughly one-half of the cases are resolved in this manner.

To date, there have been panels established in respect of 54 matters (involving some 70 total consultation requests). Of those 54 matters, 6 were later settled or abandoned. Of the remaining 48 matters, the DSB has adopted reports of panels and/or the Appellate Body in 23 matters (17 after appeal). The remaining 25 matters are at various stages in the dispute settlement process: 1 awaiting adoption by the DSB; 3 on appeal; 5 panel reports pending adoption or appeal; 8 in the panel process; 3 suspended for the moment; 5 in the panel composition process.

So far the record of implementation of panel results has been good. To date, all parties found not to be in compliance with their WTO obligations have indicated that they intend to comply with the DSB's recommendations within a reasonable period of time. In respect of the 23 completed cases, implementation has occurred in 8 cases and no implementation was required in 4 other cases.[64] Of the remaining 11 cases, the reasonable period of time for implementation has not expired in 7 cases.[65] The remaining four cases are *EC–Bananas* (two cases), *EC–Hormones,* and *EC–Poultry.* In the *Bananas* case, the original panel was asked to consider the EU's implementing measures under Article 21.5 of the DSU and found that they were WTO inconsistent. Serving as arbitrators under Article 22.6 of the DSU, the original panel concluded that retaliation by the United States of US$191.4 million would be equivalent to the level of nullification and impairment suffered by the United States. In the *Hormones* case, the EU conceded that it had not implemented the DSB's recommendations. The original panel, acting as arbitrators under Article 22.6 of the DSU, concluded that the level of nullification and impairment suffered by the United States was US$116.8 million and the level suffered by Canada was Can$11.3 million. Negotiations in the *Poultry* case were ongoing as of 30 June 1999, the reasonable period of time for implementation having expired on 31 March 1999.

Although the volume of cases submitted to the WTO has far exceeded the volume during comparable periods under GATT, the WTO dispute settlement system has coped reasonably well in meeting the tight time-periods established by the DSU.

3. The review of the WTO Dispute Settlement Understanding

At the time that the Uruguay Round negotiations were concluded on 15 December 1993, ministers decided to "[i]nvite the WTO Ministerial Conference to complete a full review of dispute settlement rules and procedures under the [WTO] within four years of the entry into force of the [WTO Agreement], and to take a decision on the occasion of its first meeting after the completion of the review, whether to continue, modify or terminate such dispute settlement rules and procedures."[66] The DSB did not complete the review by the end of 1998 but currently hopes to complete the review by the end of July 1999. It is possible, however, that the DSU review will become part of the Seattle Ministerial process.

It is too early to know whether and how the DSU may be changed as a result of the review. However, among the issues raised that are particularly important are the following: (a) the operation of the surveillance function, and in particular the need to define more precisely the relationship of Articles 21, 22, and 23 of the DSU; (b) the adequacy of the WTO's resources for processing disputes; (c) the professionalization of panels; (d) transparency and access issues; and (e) the problems of developing country member participation in the system. So far, the focus of discussion has been on the first issue. The second issue has been ignored, while the other three have only been introduced. It is not likely that the 1999 review will produce major action, except perhaps in respect of the first issue.

Before examining the five issues specified, it should be mentioned that there are a number of proposals to improve various phases of the panel and Appellate Body process. For example, there are proposals to formalize the consultation process and to make it more of a discovery procedure, to eliminate the interim review of panel reports, and to grant remand authority to the Appellate Body. By and large, however, most members seem to believe that the system works in a mechanical sense and that only some tinkering with the details of the procedures is appropriate, with the exception of the first issue discussed below.

Operation of the surveillance function: Articles 21, 22, and 23 of the DSU

As noted above, the time-frames specified in Articles 21.5 and 22 of the DSU do not seem to have been appropriately coordinated. For the sake of clarity and to avoid week-long DSB meetings such as occurred in the *Bananas* case, members have committed themselves to clarify this stage of the process. It is generally agreed that if there is no dispute over whether or not implementation has occurred at the end of the reasonable period of time, then the prevailing party should be entitled to seek compensation or authorization to suspend concessions. It is also agreed in principle that, if there is a dispute over whether or not implementation has occurred (for example, there is a claim that the new measures are inconsistent with WTO agreements), it is first necessary to determine whether or not there has been implementation before moving to the issues of compensation and suspension of concessions. It is also agreed that the determination of WTO consistency must be done in the WTO system and not unilaterally.

The sticking point in the negotiations appears to be over the amount of time that this determination should take, which in turn depends on the procedures to be followed in making it. For example, are consultations after the expiration of the reasonable period of time needed (and, if so, for how long), must the DSB meet (how many times?) to refer the matter for determination, should the determination be made by the panel followed by a possibility of appeal or only by the last instance (i.e. the Appellate Body if the original matter had been appealed; the panel if it had not), must the DSB adopt the determination, how quickly can authority to suspend concessions be requested, and, if the amount of suspension is challenged, how long should the arbitration take? Some members do not want to add to the overall time of WTO dispute settlement, which means that, if more time is devoted to this last phase of the process, they want the time allocated to some other part of the overall process to be reduced. Others argue that this part of the process is no less important than the initial proceedings and therefore deserves a similar amount of time. It seems that an agreement should be possible, but it may be difficult to reach if the issue becomes part of a larger negotiation over a new round of trade negotiations.

WTO resources for processing disputes

The increase in dispute settlement activity in the WTO system compared with the GATT system can be seen from the following statistics on pages of panel findings:[67]

1986–1995 (GATT)	855 pages, or 86 pages/year
1996–1998 (WTO)	1,379 pages, or 394 pages/year
1999 to date (WTO)	563 pages in 6 months[68]

This increase is explained by an increase not so much in the number of disputes (although that has taken place as well) but in their complexity. Claims under more than one agreement were not possible in the GATT system; in the WTO system, one-third of the cases involve three or more agreements, while another one-third involve two agreements. Moreover, the existence of the Appellate Body has tended to make panel reports longer and more analytical and to give panels an impetus to consider more of the claims made, lest a modification of the panel report by the Appellate Body result in the need to start the case over.

Although there has been an increase in Secretariat resources devoted to dispute settlement (from panel secretaries to legal officers to translators), that increase has not kept pace with the increase in the workload. For example, the staff of the WTO Legal Affairs Division, which has the principal responsibility for providing legal advice to panels, has doubled since 1991, but the panel workload has increased much more. More significantly, the burden placed on panellists has significantly increased in terms of the time that they must devote to cases. Although the system has continued to function, it is clear that problems of inadequate resources are leading to delays and that WTO members may soon be forced to confront the reality that, if more resources are not devoted to the system, its effectiveness may decline significantly. To date, they have not done so.

Professionalization of panels

One of the proposals made in the review is to form a permanent panel body, like the Appellate Body, from which all panellists would be drawn. Although this idea is not ready for action in the near future, it seems inevitable that the WTO system will have to move in this direction. Currently, most panellists serve only once or twice. Yet, as cases become more complex, particularly in respect of procedural aspects and the evaluation of evidence, experience is ever more necessary. A standing panel body would have a host of advantages: it would speed the process because the time now taken for panellist selection would be avoided and scheduling delays would be less common; panellists would likely know each other and be able to establish an effective working relationship immediately; panellists would have greater expertise on procedural issues and could more easily meet at short notice to deal with preliminary issues; consistency of approach and results would be more easily achievable.

There are, of course, a few disadvantages. From the members' perspective, there would be more expense. Nowadays most panellists are not paid (except to reimburse travel and living expenses). The choice of the members of the panel body would be difficult, given the importance of their role. Depending on how members handled the selection process and the importance given to nationality, there could be a politicization of the system. Moreover, the use of professional panellists would mean that delegates and government officials would be much less involved in the process than at the moment, which would mean there would be less contact with the realities of governments and trade negotiations. In the end, however, these disadvantages do not seem so great, especially given that the same concerns exist in respect of the Appellate Body. Yet, in its case, they do not seem to have prevented its emergence as an effective institution.

Transparency and access to the WTO dispute settlement system

There have been complaints, particularly by non-governmental organizations, that the WTO dispute settlement system lacks transparency and does not permit sufficient access for non-members. In this regard, it is worth noting that panel and Appellate Body reports (and all other WTO documents relating to specific disputes) are issued as unrestricted documents and placed on the WTO website immediately after their distribution to members.[69]

The United States has proposed that dispute settlement proceedings be open to the public, that submissions be made public, and that non-parties be permitted to file "friend-of-the-court" submissions to panels. These matters are currently under discussion; it is unclear whether or not the proposals will be accepted. Some members view the WTO system as exclusively intergovernmental in nature and hesitate to open it to non-governments. In their view, if a non-governmental organization wants to make an argument to a panel, it should convince one of the parties to make it and, if no party makes the argument, those members would view that as evidence that the argument is not meritorious.

Other members argue that the credibility of the system would be much enhanced if it were more open and that openness would have no significant disadvantages. Given popular fears of globalization and the WTO's connection therewith, such increased credibility is viewed as essential to ensure the future effectiveness of the WTO itself, as well as of the dispute settlement system.

In this regard, it is noteworthy that the Appellate Body recently ruled that panels have the right to accept non-requested submissions from non-parties (such as NGOs).[70] It remains to be seen to what extent panels will exercise this right since the Appellate Body also ruled that a panel could appropriately call such submissions to the attention of the parties and ask if the parties wished to adopt all or part of them.

Developing countries and dispute settlement

Developing countries have made greater use of the WTO dispute settlement system than they made of the GATT system. In some cases, they are bringing claims that would not have been cognizable under GATT, such as claims based on the Agreement on Textiles and Clothing. Even allowing for this, they seem to be more active users of the system than they were, as they have made some 40 consultation requests. It is also noteworthy that they have become more frequent targets of complaints (by both developed and developing countries). Their greater involvement is undoubtedly good for the system in the long run.

The DSU provides special treatment for developing countries in a number of respects. For example, it provides the possibility (used only once under GATT) of an expedited process (Article 3.12), that special consideration should be given to developing countries in consultations (Articles 4.10 and 12.10) and in the panel process (Articles 8.10, 12.10, and 12.11), and that account should be taken of developing country interests in the surveillance phase (Article 21.2, 21.7, and 21.8). There are also special provisions for least developed countries (Article 24), although none of those countries has been involved in the dispute settlement proceedings to date. By and large, none of these provisions has been of great importance in dispute settlement proceedings, mainly because they relate to procedures. There have been proposals for additional such provisions considered in the DSU review, but they are not under very active discussion at the moment.

The principal issue of interest to developing countries in the DSU review has concerned the resource difficulty that many developing countries face when they participate in the dispute settlement system. For the moment, the DSU addresses this problem by requiring the WTO Secretariat to provide legal assistance to such countries,[71] which it does through two staff lawyers in the Technical Cooperation Division and through the use of lawyers (typically ex-Secretariat employees) who are hired on a consultancy basis to provide assistance on a regular (e.g. one day a week) or case-specific basis. The Secretariat also conducts a number of training courses that either include or are exclusively focused on dispute settlement. Earlier in 1999, a group of developed and developing countries announced plans for an Advisory Centre on WTO law, which would be an international intergovernmental organization providing legal assistance to developing countries in respect of WTO matters. It is not known whether or not sufficient funding for the Centre will be forthcoming, but a number of substantial pledges have been made. The Centre seems to offer the best hope for a significant improvement in dealing with inadequate developing country resources.

4. Conclusion

I noted in the spring of 1996 that there were five difficult cases on the horizon that would severely test the WTO dispute settlement system: *Bananas, Hormones, Helms-Burton, Shrimp-Turtle,* and *Japan–Film.* The EU suspended its action against the US Helms-Burton law, so no report was issued. A panel rejected the US complaint in the *Japan–Film* case and the United States did not appeal. The resolution of the *Bananas* and *Hormones* cases is described above, while the reasonable period of time for implementation in the *Shrimp-Turtle* case has not expired. Although the results in the four decided cases were very controversial, so far the system seems to have survived relatively unscathed, no mean feat given that these severe tests were imposed on it at the very beginning of its existence.

One must not be complacent, however. The solutions in *Bananas* and *Hormones* are temporary in that the EU measures found to be WTO inconsistent are still in place. Yet the possibility of retaliation has acted as a sort of pressure relief valve for the moment. However, long-term non-compliance could undermine the system if other less powerful members ask themselves why they should accept adverse decisions if the major trading partners are unwilling to do so. Moreover, even if these cases have been processed successfully, a number of other difficult cases are now wending their way through the system. Many of them will not receive the media attention of those mentioned above, but they may pose difficult implementation problems if violations are found.

Outside of these five cases, the record of implementation of panel/ Appellate Body decisions has been quite good. But members continue to bring difficult and potentially controversial cases. In the end, the most difficult challenge facing the WTO dispute settlement system is to promote and maintain an image of impartiality and competence, so as to give the decisions of the panels and Appellate Body a degree of legitimacy and ensure their acceptability by WTO members and, in the long run, by their citizens. At a minimum that will require greater resources, increased professionalization, and increased openness to the world at large.

Acknowledgements

The author would like to thank Werner Zdouc for comments on an earlier draft.

Notes

1. The cut-off date for statistics in this paper was 30 June 1999.
2. Robert E. Hudec, *Enforcing International Trade Law,* Salem, NH: Butterworth Legal Publishers, 1993.
3. Of the 25 panel reports circulated in the five-year period from 1986 to 1990, only 3 were not adopted. Of the 24 reports circulated in the five-year period from 1991 to 1995, 11 were not adopted.
4. William J. Davey, "Dispute Settlement in GATT," *Fordham Journal of International al Law* 11(1), 1987, 51.
5. See, generally, David Palmeter and Petros C. Mavroidis, *Dispute Settlement in the World Trade Organization: Practice and Procedure,* The Hague: Kluwer Law International, 1999.

6. One of the annexes to the Marrakesh Agreement Establishing the World Trade Organization ("WTO Agreement") is the General Agreement on Tariffs and Trade 1994 ("GATT 1994"), the basic provisions of which are essentially identical to the General Agreement on Tariffs and Trade of 1947, although GATT 1994 also includes several understandings on GATT 1947 provisions and incorporates various past acts of the GATT 1947 contracting parties. GATT 1994 does not change the text of GATT 1947 Articles XXII and XXIII, which were the basis for dispute settlement in the GATT system and are the basis of the WTO system. The DSU, which is also an annex to the WTO Agreement, extensively elaborates the procedures to be followed in WTO dispute settlement. Article 3.1 of the DSU provides: "Members affirm their adherence to the principles for the management of disputes heretofore applied under Articles XXII and XXIII of GATT 1947, and the rules and procedures as further elaborated and modified herein."

7. This is an oversimplification of the provisions of Article XXIII. In fact, it covers either of two situations—where benefits accruing to a member under the agreement have been nullified or impaired or where attainment of the objectives of the agreement has been impeded—that arise as a result of one of three reasons: the failure of a member to carry out its obligations, the application by a member of any measure (whether or not it conflicts with the agreement), or the existence of any other situation. Of the six possible combinations, the vast majority of cases involve allegations of nullification or impairment arising from a failure of a member to carry out its obligations. A few cases—referred to as non-violation cases—involve allegations of nullification or impairment by a measure not in conflict with the agreement. No panel reports have been based on an impedance of the objectives of the agreement or on the existence of any other situation, although allegations thereof have occasionally been made.

8. See General Agreement on Trade in Services, Articles XXII and XXIII; Agreement on Trade-Related Aspects of Intellectual Property Rights, Article 64; Agreement on Agriculture, Article 19; Agreement on the Application of Sanitary and Phytosanitary Measures, Article 11; Agreement on Technical Barriers to Trade, Article 14; Agreement on Trade-Related Investment Measures, Article 8; Agreement on Implementation of Article VI of the GATT 1994 (Antidumping Agreement), Article 17; Agreement on Implementation of Article VII of the GATT 1994 (Customs Valuation Agreement), Article 19; Agreement on Preshipment Inspection, Article 8; Agreement on Rules of Origin, Articles 7–8; Agreement on Import Licensing Procedures, Article 6; Agreement on Subsidies and Countervailing Measures, Article 30; Agreement on Safeguards, Article 14. The DSU may also be applied by plurilateral agreements. See Agreement on Government Procurement, Article XXII. Appendix 2 of the DSU contains a list of special or additional dispute settlement rules in WTO agreements that prevail over DSU rules (DSU, Article 1.2). For an interpretation of the relationship of these special and additional rules to the DSU rules, see *Guatemala–Anti-Dumping Investigation Regarding Imports of Portland Cement from Mexico,* Appellate Body Report, adopted on 25 November 1998, WT/DS60/AB/R. For a discussion of dispute settlement in respect of textile products and in particular the role of the Textiles Monitoring Body vis-à-vis that of dispute settlement panels, see *United States–Measures Affecting Imports of Woven Wool Shirts and Blouses,* Panel Report, adopted on 23 May 1997, WT/DS33/R, paras. 7.18–7.21.

9. Understanding on Rules and Procedures Governing the Settlement of Disputes (DSU), Article 3.7.

10. DSU, Article 5. In fact, I am aware of no cases where this provision was invoked. The DSU also provides for ad hoc arbitration on agreement of the parties (Article 25).

11. The equivalent provisions are listed in a footnote to DSU, Article 4.11.

12. DSU, Article 4.11.

13. DSU, Article 4.3. If a member does not respond to a request within 10 days or does not enter into consultations within 30 days, the requesting member may proceed directly to request the establishment of a panel. In cases of urgency, consultations are to be held within 10 days of a request.

14. DSU, Article 4.7. In cases of urgency, a panel may be requested after 20 days.

15. WTO Agreement, Article IV:3. See also DSU, Article 2.1.

16. The wording of the relevant DSU provision is: "the DSB meeting following that at which the request first appears as an item on the DSB's agenda" (Article 6.1). This has led some members to argue that the second request must be made at the next DSB meeting. If the requests are not consecutive, these members argue that the panel need not be established by the DSB. So far, this view is shared by only a few members.

17. DSU, Article 6.1.

18. The DSB's Rules of Procedure in effect require that a request for an item to appear on the agenda must be made 11 days in advance of the meeting because the agenda is circulated 10 days in advance of the meeting. Although the matter is disputed, the practice seems to be developing that it is not appropriate to put a request for the establishment of a panel on the agenda until the 60-day consultation period has expired. Thus, in practice at the moment, the first panel request will not be considered at a DSB meeting until 71 days after the request for consultations. Thereafter, the DSU provides that the complaining party may request a second meeting within 15 days of the first. Thus, even with the possible inconvenient interference of weekends and other non-working days, a determined complainant should be able to ensure that a panel is established within 90 days of its request for consultations.

19. The DSU provides for the possibility of using five panellists (Article 8.5). Such panels were used in the early years of GATT. All of the WTO panels to date have consisted of three panellists.

20. DSU, Article 8.6.

21. Based on the 45 panels selected to date. The range was from 12 to 140 days.

22. DSU, Article 8.7.

23. DSU, Article 8.1.

24. DSU, Article 8.3.

25. DSU, Article 8.10.

26. Some individuals are counted in more than one category in light of their experience.

27. Switzerland—18; Australia—12; New Zealand—12; Hong Kong/China—9; Brazil—7; South Africa—6; Canada—5; Czech Republic—5; Norway—5; Egypt—4; Germany—4; Sweden—4; Belgium—3; Colombia—3; Finland—3; Israel—3; Mexico—3; Poland—3; Thailand—3; Chile—2; India—2; Japan—2; Singapore—2; United States—2; and one each from Argentina, Austria, Bulgaria, Costa Rica, France, Hungary, Iceland, Korea, the Netherlands, the Philippines, Slovenia, Uruguay, and Venezuela.

28. DSU, Article 8.9.

29. WT/DSB/RC/1, 11 December 1996. See, generally, Gabrielle Marceau, "Rules on Ethics for the New World Trade Organization Dispute Settlement Mechanism," *Journal of World Trade* 32(3), June 1998, 57. The Appellate Body had previously adopted similar rules on the basis of an earlier draft. It modified its rules in light of the final text adopted by the DSB—WT/AB/WP/1; WT/AB/WP/2.

30. WT/DSB/RC/1, Article II, "Governing Principle," para. 1.

31. Ibid., Article III, "Observance of the Governing Principle," para. 1.

32. DSU, Article 7.1. Article 7.3 allows the DSB to authorize its chairperson to draw up terms of reference in consultation with the parties. Such authorization was granted in one case (WT/DSB/M/12) and the chair's designee brokered an agreement between the parties on non-standard terms of reference. See WT/DS22/6.

33. DSU, Article 11.

34. DSU, Article 6.2. This provision is interpreted in *European Communities–Regime for the Importation, Sale and Distribution of Bananas,* Appellate Body Report, adopted on 25 September 1997, WT/DS27/AB/R.

35. Panels have relatively broad discretion to craft their own working procedures. For example, they can revise the standard working procedures listed in DSU Appendix 3 after consulting the parties (DSU, Article 12.1).

36. DSU, Appendix 3.

37. DSU, Article 13.

38. DSU, Article 15.1.

39. DSU, Article 15.2.

40. DSU, Article 10.

41. DSU, Articles 14 and 19.

42. DSU, Article 12.8. The goal is three months in case of urgency.

43. DSU, Article 12.9.

44. The Appellate Body is established and regulated by Article 17 of the DSU. Its working procedures, which it is authorized to draw up itself in consultation with the chairperson of the DSB and the Director-General, are contained in WT/AB/WP/1.

45. The first seven members of the Appellate Body were James Bacchus (USA), Christopher Beeby (New Zealand), Claus-Dieter Ehlermann (Germany), Florentino Feliciano (the Philippines), Said El Naggar (Egypt), Julio Lacarte-Muro (Uruguay), and Mitsuo Matsushita (Japan). Ehlermann, Feliciano, and Lacarte-Muro were deemed to have initial two-year terms and were reappointed to four-year terms on expiration of those initial terms. Only one reappointment is permitted (DSU, Article 17.2).

46. Appellate Body Working Procedures, rule 4(3).

47. Appellate Body Working Procedures, rule 6(2).

48. DSU, Article 17.6.

49. DSU, Article 17.13.

50. See, e.g., *Canada–Certain Measures Affecting Periodicals,* Appellate Body Report, adopted on 30 July 1997, WT/DS31/AB/R.

51. DSU, Article 17.5. In recent cases, 90 days has been the standard.

52. As a consequence, WTO remedies are typically viewed as prospective in nature. No reparation of past damage is awarded.

53. DSU, Article 19.1.

54. DSU, Article 21.3.

55. DSU, Article 21.3.

56. DSU, Article 21.6.

57. DSU, Article 22.2.

58. DSU, Article 22.2 and 22.6.

59. DSU, Article 22.6 and 22.7.

60. In the *Bananas* case, the level of suspension requested was US$520 million and the amount authorized was US$191.4 million (WT/DS27/AB/R, op. cit.). In the *Hormones* case, the amounts requested were US$202 million and Can$75 million. The amounts authorized were US$116.8 million and Can$11.3 million (WT/DS26/AB/R; WT/DS48/AB/R).

61. DSU, Articles 3.7 and 22.1.

62. Since consultation requests involving a single measure may be made by several members, the number of consultation requests may overstate the number of disputes. Although there may be some imprecision in counting "matters," the concept is a useful one for approximating the true number of disputes.

63. It is not possible to give a precise number of settlements. Although members are supposed to notify mutually agreed solutions to the DSB (DSU, Article 3.6), it appears that this requirement is often not respected. Moreover, a fair number of cases are simply not pursued, presumably because it is felt that there is no valid claim.

64. The eight cases are *US–Gasoline, Japan–Alcohol Taxes* (compensation provided for delayed implementation of one measure), *US–Underwear, US–Shirts & Blouses, Canada–Periodicals, India–Patents* (two cases), and *Argentina–Textiles.* The four cases where the complainant lost were *Brazil–Desiccated Coconut, Japan–Film, EC–LAN Computer Equipment,* and *Guatemala–Cement.*

65. In one of the seven cases, *Australia–Salmon,* implementation was due by 6 July 1999 and did not occur. However, in another, *Indonesia–Autos,* implementation was announced prior to expiration of the reasonable period of time.

66. Decision on the Application and Review of the Understanding on the Rules and Procedures Governing the Settlement of Disputes, in the Agreement Establishing the World Trade Organization, signed Marrakesh, 15 April 1994, Annex 4.

67. The date of circulation to members is used to assign reports to specific years. The page totals focus only on the pages of panel findings, because most of the rest of the report is a detailed summary of the parties' arguments and, although its preparation is sometimes time consuming, it is largely a question of editing existing texts, whereas panel findings are the analytical part of the report and must be drafted from scratch.

68. This statistic may be somewhat misleading because 13 reports were circulated in the first half of 1999 and it is likely that far fewer will be circulated in the second half. Although at least eight reports are scheduled to go to the parties in the second half of 1999, translation delays may mean that a smaller number of reports are circulated to members.

69. A party may request that a panel report be restricted for up to 10 days after its issuance, but no party has ever done so.

70. *United States–Import Prohibition of Certain Shrimp and Shrimp Products,* Appellate Body Report, adopted on 6 November 1998, WT/DS58/AB/R, paras. 99–110.

71. DSU, Article 27.2.

6

Fishery Subsidies and the WTO

David K. Schorr

In July of 1999, as this book was going to press, momentum was building among members of the World Trade Organization (WTO) to include the issue of environmentally harmful fishery subsidies on the negotiating agenda for a new round of WTO talks. If the issue is included in the next round, it will constitute a potential watershed for the WTO, representing the first time the WTO has acted in serious pursuit of "win–win" outcomes for trade and sustainable development.

The economic and environmental illogic of many fishery subsidies should make addressing them within the WTO seem an obvious proposition. But the issue has been controversial from a variety of perspectives. Remaining questions range from lingering doubts professed in some quarters about the need for international action on fisheries subsidies at all, to more serious questions about the need for action within the context of the multilateral trade system.

This chapter provides some basic background on this rapidly evolving issue, beginning with an overview of the nature of the fishery subsidies problem, then moving through a brief critical examination of existing international disciplines on fishery subsidies, and closing with some preliminary thoughts about the potential for future WTO fishery subsidies disciplines.

1. The nature of the problem

Fish caught in the oceans of the world provide a vital food source to billions of people, and an essential livelihood to fishermen and fishing communities on every inhabited coastline. But the world's fisheries are in trouble. In 1996, the UN Food and Agriculture Organization (FAO) estimated that 60 per cent of the world's fisheries are overexploited or already exploited at maximum rates.[1] One major factor contributing to this fisheries crisis is the simple fact that there are too many fishing boats chasing too few fish. In fact, some experts have estimated that the world's fishing fleets have nearly two and a half times the fishing capacity needed to harvest fish stocks in an economically optimal and environmentally sustainable manner.[2] What keeps so many fishing boats afloat, even as fish stocks shrink? In many cases, the answer is huge government payments that promote excess harvesting capacity and reward unsustainable fishing practices. These subsidies, many of which are administered in open violation of existing international trade rules, constitute a profound failure of both economic and environmental policy.

The range and scale of subsidization

The practice of providing governmental support to the fishery sector is widespread among major fishing nations. Although precise data remain elusive—obscured by a universal lack of transparency in subsidy regimes—the basic facts are not much in doubt. Governments around the world are providing billions of dollars in subsidies annually to the fishery sector, for a wide variety of purposes, and in many different forms. Although smaller in absolute amounts than, for example, subsidies to the agricultural sector, these payments are conservatively estimated to be roughly 20–25 per cent of the annual revenues of the commercial fishing industry.[3]

Subsidies commonly granted to the fishery sector include:[4]

- grants, low-cost loans, loan guarantees, or tax incentives to promote vessel construction or repair, or the acquisition or modernization of fishing gear;
- price supports for fish and fish products;

- grants, low-cost loans, or other financial benefits to support the transportation or processing of fish or fish products;
- income or wage supports, or unemployment or other social benefits for fishermen and their families;
- export promotion programmes;
- provision of discounted or free marine insurance;
- governmental promises to reimburse vessel owners for fines or impoundments imposed by foreign authorities;
- construction or maintenance of port facilities;
- construction or maintenance of housing or other community infrastructure specifically for fishermen;
- provision of fuel or of tax credits or other rebates to offset the cost of fuel;
- provision of access rights to domestic fisheries, or payment or subsidization of payments for access to foreign fisheries;[5]
- government campaigns to promote consumption of fish and fish products;
- grants to support research and development of fishery technology;
- grants to support fisheries management;
- vessel buy-back programmes;
- worker retraining.

Naturally, not all of these subsidies should be considered harmful or illegitimate. The key distinction is between those subsidies that promote unsustainable fishing (especially by encouraging overcapacity or excess effort) and those that promote a transition to sustainable fisheries (especially by encouraging reductions in capacity and effort, by encouraging environmentally responsible fishing techniques, or by promoting sustainable community development).[6] This distinction is not always easy to apply. Is an income support programme helping a depressed fishing community adjust to new limits on the available resource, or is it artificially maintaining the workforce for an oversized national fleet? Is a vessel buy-back programme truly reducing total effective capacity, or is it just a shell game that moves boats around while promoting additional investments in fishing capital? Is a gear modernization programme helping fleets adopt cleaner fishing practices, or is it just underwriting operating costs? Questions of this kind will have to be confronted in detail by any serious scheme to reduce harmful fishery subsidies. But in assessing the adequacy of current international rules, it is enough to begin with the widely accepted fact that "capacity-enhancing" subsidies greatly outweigh "capacity-reducing" or "conservation" subsidies in the fishery sector.[7]

Lack of transparency in the administration of fishery subsidies has also made it difficult to discover exactly how much subsidization is going on. Different estimates have been offered by a variety of experts. One commonly cited figure—based on data published by the FAO in 1992—puts annual fishery subsidies in the range of US$54 billion.[8] But this FAO figure was not a direct estimate of known subsidies. Rather, the FAO calculated the difference between the gross revenue to the worldwide commercial fishing fleets (value of landed catch) and their total estimated annual operating and capital costs. The result was a "deficit" of US$54 billion. The portion of this deficit met through government support has been speculated to range from half to all.[9] Another observer has argued that the US$54 billion figure "could be off in either direction, depending upon how one resolves uncertainties both in data and in definition."[10] The WTO Secretariat has succinctly concluded: "Even if these figures are not universally accepted, they cannot be ignored."[11]

A more direct effort to calculate fishery subsidies—perhaps the most comprehensive effort to date—is found in a 1998 World Bank technical paper by Mateo Milazzo, an official of the United States National Marine Fisheries Service.[12] Milazzo analysed public data about the budgets and practices of fisheries agencies from selected fishing countries, and concluded that worldwide fishery subsidies total between US$14.5 and US$20.5 billion annually.[13] Milazzo's bottom line excludes subsidies aimed at reducing overcapacity, and Milazzo admits he omitted potentially significant sources of governmental support from the scope of his review. He concludes that his estimates "probably err on the low side, perhaps by a considerable margin."[14]

These and other efforts to examine fishery subsidization are all necessarily general and imprecise. Exercises are now under way in various forums—including the FAO, the Organization for Economic Cooperation and Development (OECD), the Asia-Pacific Economic Cooperation Conference (APEC), and domestically within several countries—that may add substantially to the available data. For the moment, it is safe to assume that subsidies to the fisheries sector amount to many billions—and perhaps tens of billions—of dollars per year. This is a staggering level in an industry whose total revenues are in the range of US$70–80 billion.[15]

The links to fisheries depletion and trade distortion

Subsidization on the scale described above unavoidably raises the level of industry-wide capitalization and fishing effort, with consequent pressures on the resource base.[16] A stark fact suggests that subsidies are playing a significant role in fisheries depletion: the world's most depleted fisheries are often those that are dominated by fleets from countries with the largest fishery subsidy programmes. Despite occasional voices to the contrary, the conclusion that subsidies help drive fishing overcapacity pervades the literature from both official and non-governmental sources.[17] Those who argue otherwise have generally failed to explain how such massive infusions of income could do otherwise than encourage the growth or maintenance of capacity. And the historical fact remains that subsidies to the fishery sector have gone hand in hand with a dramatic expansion of fishing capacity and with the collapse or threatened collapse of many of the world's principal commercial fisheries.[18]

Still, in the debate over how best to address the world's fisheries crisis, there are some who argue that subsidies should not be considered a problem in themselves. Rather, they hold, the fundamental cause of both overcapacity and overfishing is the failure of governments to impose proper limits on permissible catches of fish. According to this view, if you limit legal takes of fish, excess levels of capacity and subsidization become the financial problems of businesses and governments, but not the cause of overfishing. This argument merely begs the question, however. Even if the fundamental cause of overfishing is the failure to manage fishing effort, this hardly means that subsidies on the order of 20–25 per cent of industry revenues ought to be ignored. The scope of the fisheries crisis requires the use of every tool reasonably available to reduce unsustainable fishing effort. Fisheries management regimes will not reach their full potential overnight. And even the best management regimes will be subject to problems of compliance and long-term political stability. Capacity-enhancing subsidies will serve only to maintain special interest constituencies that may not always favour the rapid development, smooth functioning, or longevity of effective management regimes.

Besides, a serious effort to address fisheries subsidies would necessarily include increased attention to fisheries management issues. Clarification of the economic issues surrounding subsidies would contribute to more transparent and rational approaches to management, and would help highlight the need for husbandry of marine resources. Similarly, the subsidies discussion could help bring a new level of political attention to fisheries issues more generally. Meanwhile, at the international level, agreeing new management regimes will depend in part on the ability of fishing nations to negotiate the allocation of fishing rights. A shared view of the legitimate levels of government support for fishing fleets and communities would help establish the proper context for such allocations. This last point is especially relevant where the evolution of developing-country fisheries is concerned. And finally, environmentally positive subsidies will likely be required to assist in the transition to sustainability. International cooperation on the definition, provision, and administration of those subsidies would be a useful input into discussions about improved management.

The trade impacts of fishery subsidies have also been the focus of increasing attention. Although the fishery sector is not especially large in comparison with the global economy, its economic and social importance is not slight. Fish trade represents a significant source of foreign currency earnings for many developing countries—a dependency that is increasing steadily.[19] Unfortunately, current empirical knowledge about the trade consequences of fishery subsidies is thin. But it has been broadly accepted that subsidies as large as those now granted to various national fishing industries must have significant impacts on the international market.[20] In any case, concern with the trade implications of fishery subsidies has been rising.[21] A recent commitment by Pacific Rim nations gathered under the auspices of APEC to address fishery subsidies as a priority trade issue is further evidence of this growing consensus. As the WTO Secretariat has put it:

Although the precise identification and quantification of subsidies in the fisheries sector has not yet been fully undertaken, consensus exists that fisheries subsidies are widespread, trade distorting and undermine the sustainable use of fish resources.[22]

2. Existing disciplines on fishery subsidies

Many subsidies to the fishery sector make such little economic or environmental sense that it is easy to wonder why governments do not simply reduce them without the need for external disciplines. But fishery subsidies have tended to prove the basic rule that government economic supports are politically much easier to initiate than to terminate. This does not mean that governments always prove unable to make hard choices. Countries such as Iceland, New Zealand, and Norway have already demonstrated that, with sufficient national will, harmful fishery subsidies can indeed be eliminated one country at a time. But the fact remains that—as in other sectors such as agriculture—fishery subsidies will likely need to be reduced in the context of concerted international action to do so. Despite the arguments of many classical economists—who would urge governments to reduce subsidies simply out of prudent national policy—governments and industry participants alike often believe that the reduction of their own subsidies will leave them at a competitive disadvantage, unless other countries do the same. "No unilateral disarmament!" is thus a war cry frequently heard.

Currently, the only international disciplines directly applicable to fishery subsidies are those contained in a new non-binding "plan of action" recently adopted by the FAO, and the binding but more general rules about subsidies maintained by the WTO system.[23] Each of these is discussed briefly below.

The FAO International Plan of Action

In February 1999, the FAO's Committee on Fisheries adopted the first international instrument specifically aimed at reducing overcapacity in the fishing industry. The International Plan of Action for the Management of Fishing Capacity (IPOA) is a non-binding agreement under which FAO members volunteer to assess levels of capacity in their national fishing fleets, and then to come forward with plans for the management of that capacity. The IPOA singles out subsidies as a potentially negative factor and calls on countries to assess the impacts of their own subsidies and to "reduce and progressively eliminate" those that contribute to overcapacity.[24] The IPOA also instructs the FAO Secretariat to collect "all relevant information and data" about such subsidies.[25]

The FAO IPOA represents a significant step for the international community. If fully implemented, the IPOA could go a long way towards resolving the fishery subsidies problem. There are, however, several reasons most observers have been cautious in their hopes that the IPOA will fully deliver.

First, the voluntary nature of the IPOA is explicitly stated in its leading paragraphs,[26] and is repeatedly emphasized in the hortatory language of its key provisions. In the absence of binding obligations (and of any enforcement mechanism), it is reasonable to fear that implementation of the IPOA may suffer the very imperfect fate of so many other hortatory international agreements.

Second, although the IPOA will offer a forum for developing international consensus on the definition and measurement of fishing capacity,[27] it is unclear to what extent this will prove a fruitful opportunity for dealing with a number of the difficult technical and political details specific to the subsidies problem.

Third, even if the IPOA produces increased consensus about the nature of the problem, it is poorly designed to produce strong international solutions to the subsidies issue—particularly where competitive interactions among national fleets are perceived. The IPOA relies on a model of simultaneous but unilateral actions by fishing nations to manage capacity. No provision is made for ensuring the mutuality of subsidies reductions.

Fourth, the IPOA is relatively weak in dealing with the export of fishing capacity[28] and with the impacts of distant water fleets[29]—both areas in which fishery subsidies can play a particularly negative role.

Finally, rational management of the fishery subsidies issue will require attention to their trade impacts. The IPOA does not deal with this dimension of the issue, and several governments were adamant during the IPOA negotiations that such questions be left to the exclusive jurisdiction of the WTO.

In short, with some FAO members still quite resistant to any serious conversation about subsidies—even in the relatively safe context of efforts to manage capacity—the voluntary and often vague provisions of the IPOA may simply prove too narrow and too weak to impose real disciplines on fishery subsidies in the near term. This does not mean governments or advocates should relax their interest in full implementation of the IPOA, but only that the IPOA alone may prove an insufficient instrument.

Current WTO rules

Currently, the only binding international legal disciplines on fishery subsidies are those administered by the WTO. The multilateral trading system has long considered subsidies as potential non-tariff barriers to trade. Although initial limits on subsidies under the General Agreement on Tariffs and Trade (GATT) (1947 version) were relatively weak, the rules have undergone steady evolution, particularly since the 1970s. At present the core multilateral subsidies disciplines are set forth in the WTO's Agreement on Subsidies and Countervailing Duties ("Subsidies Agreement"), except for agricultural subsidies, which are covered by the Uruguay Round Agreement on Agriculture ("Agriculture Agreement").[30] Despite some obvious similarities between agricultural and fisheries subsidies, fisheries products were specifically excluded from the terms of the Agriculture Agreement.[31] Thus, since 1994, fishery subsidies have been subject to the general limits of the Subsidies Agreement.

The right to challenge

Unlike the Agriculture Agreement—which provides a framework for the specific control and phased reduction of agricultural subsidies—the WTO Subsidies Agreement provides only a set of general rules and an adversarial form of control. Under the Subsidies Agreement, a narrow class of subsidies is "prohibited" (so-called "red light" subsidies), while another narrow class is explicitly permitted ("non-actionable" or "green light" subsidies). The majority of subsidies fall into a middle category of "actionable" ("amber light") subsidies, which can be subject to challenge if they cause certain kinds of harm to the complaining party.

The "red light" and "green light" categories appear to have only limited applicability in the fishery sector. The only subsidies prohibited outright by the "red light" are those directly promoting either export performance or import avoidance (i.e., the inclusion of domestic parts or labour). Only a fraction of fishery subsidies likely fall within this prohibited category.[32] On the flip side, the "green light" permits subsidies for certain research activities, for general assistance to disadvantaged geographic regions, and for adapting existing facilities to new environmental regulatory requirements. Oddly, the environmental category (the "green light for green subsidies") may be the least applicable of all. It appears to apply mainly to subsidies for retrofitting industrial plants with pollution abatement equipment. Subsidies for fishing capacity reductions (such as vessel buy-back and worker retraining programmes) would not qualify. Even subsidies for environmentally motivated fishing gear modifications may fall outside the "green for green" box, which applies only to technology adopted specifically to meet new legal requirements, and which may be limited to equipment designed to reduce "pollution" (rather than, for example, to reduce bycatch).[33] The non-actionable categories for research and regional development, on the other hand, may have broader application to some fishery subsidy programmes.

Thus, for most fishery subsidies, the question is whether they can be successfully challenged under the "amber light" rules. The stakes are relatively high—a successful challenge can lead to a WTO recommendation calling for the removal of the challenged subsidy or, alternatively, to the imposition of countervailing duties against the offending member. In order to prevail, a complainant must show two things: first, that a given government support meets the Agreement's definition of a "subsidy"; and, second, that the subsidy is actionable and causes one of several kinds of harm described by the Agreement.

Is it a "subsidy"?

Article 1 of the Subsidies Agreement defines "subsidy" as any *benefit* conferred on an industry as a result of:

- a *direct transfer* of government funds (e.g. grants, loans, equity in-fusions) or potential direct transfers (e.g. loan guarantees);
- *forgone government revenues* (e.g. tax credits or rebates);
- the provision of *goods or services* other than "general infrastructure" (e.g. a fishing net, not a navigational buoy);
- payments to any *private funding mechanism* by which any of the fore-going is accomplished;
- *price or income supports* generally.

To be covered by the Subsidies Agreement, a subsidy must also be "specific to an enterprise or industry or group of enterprises" (as opposed to available to or for the benefit of a broad class of actors), as set forth in Article 2 of the Agreement.

This broad definition would appear to cover many or even most types of fishery subsidies.[34] However, a few important categories of fishery subsidies may fall outside this definition. For example, payments of fishery access fees by one national government to another, or the provision of port facilities, may not be captured by the WTO definition. Income support programmes and subsidies that benefit foreign fisher-men (for example, payments to support the export of fishing capacity) also raise tough definitional issues. Still, the WTO definition is broad enough to encompass a substantial portion of existing subsidies.

Does it cause a cognizable harm?

A party complaining against an actionable subsidy must also generally show that it has suffered some kind of trade-related harm (such as international market displacement or price undercutting). The rapid depletion of the world's fisheries obviously causes international economic injuries. However, these may not be expressed in classic distortions of international trade, for two reasons. First, the fisheries game is more of a race for access to resources than a race for access to markets. If subsidies in country X prevent fishermen from country Y ever having access to a particular breed of fish, it will be difficult to discuss the problem in terms of the underpricing of product from country Y. Secondly, the multilateral trading system has traditionally focused on creating and enforcing trade obligations that run between national governments. But, in the case of fishery subsidies, the interests run more fundamentally between individual nations and the shared interests of the international community. Harms to such common interests are not likely to be cognizable by traditional WTO rules, even if they are precipitated in part by the kind of irrational governmental market meddling that the WTO was designed to help prevent.

So if the WTO "amber light" category were fully restricted to addressing proven "trade" harms, the applicability of the Subsidies Agreement to fishery subsidies would be greatly reduced. However, there exists (at least through the end of 1999) an exception to the general "prove a trade harm" rule—something called (if the reader will permit one more traffic signal) the "dark amber" category. The dark amber category is created by language in Article 6.1 of the Agreement that shifts the burden of proof from the complainant to the defendant if:

- the value of the subsidy exceeds 5 per cent ad valorem;
- the subsidy covers operating losses sustained by an industry or (when not a "one-time" measure) by an enterprise; or
- the subsidy is a direct or indirect forgiveness of government-held debt.

This device—which forces the defendant to prove the negative (absence of harm)—is of special relevance to the discussion of fishery subsidies, for two reasons. First, many fishery subsidies may qualify for the "dark amber" treatment. Aggregate subsidies totalling 20–25 per cent of sectoral revenues suggest that the 5 per cent ad valorem test may not be difficult to meet.[35] Similarly, many fishery subsidies arguably cover operating losses sustained by the fishing industry. Secondly, as discussed below, the presumptions raised by Article 6.1 are evidence of an important trend in the development of the GATT/WTO rule system that bears on whether the WTO's mandate properly extends beyond responding to provable trade distortions.

It is worth noting that the "dark amber" language of Article 6.1 was enacted only on an experimental basis. Under Article 31 of the Subsidies Agreement, the provisions of Article 6.1 apply for only five years after the entry into force of the WTO Agreement (i.e. until 31 December 1999), unless they are extended by the WTO members.[36]

Table 6.1 gives a very rough first cut at how various kinds of subsidies to the fishery sector might be treated under WTO rules.[37] Apart from a

Table 6.1.   Whether certain classes of fishery subsidies would be "actionable" under the WTO Subsidies Agreement

"Unlikely"	"Uncertain/possibly"	"Likely"
Payments for port facilities	Support for general shipbuilding (where only effect on fishermen is challenged)	Grants/loans/guarantees to fishermen for:
Reduced fees for access to domestic waters (for some foreign nationals, in comparison with others)[a]		—vessel/gear construction —vessel/gear purchase —vessel/gear repair
	Support for fish processing industry (where only effect on fishermen is challenged)	—vessel/gear decommission —fisheries management
Granting trade benefits to foreign coastal states in return for access rights for grantor's nationals	Purchase of access rights to foreign coastal waters	Price supports for fish products
		Wage supports for fishermen (if "specific")
Relaxed regulatory requirements (other than forgoing fees)	or	
	Reduced fees for access to domestic waters (for own nationals, in comparison to fees for foreign nationals)[b]	Discounted marine insurance, or a policy to absorb liabilities
		Grants or tax breaks to cover fuel costs (if "specific" to fishery sector)
	Income supports/worker retraining for fisherman leaving industry	

Notes:

[a]This is the case of a foreign government in effect subsidizing nationals of another country. The Subsidies Agreement does not contemplate actions against such subsidies, although nothing on the face of Article 1 rules out such an interpretation.

[b]The purchasing or granting of access rights is listed here as merely "possibly" actionable in deference to the analyses of both Stone and Porter. I would otherwise have placed these important classes of fishery subsidy in the "likely" to be actionable column. Gareth Porter (*Fishing Subsidies, Overfishing and Trade,* UNEP/WWF workshop on the role of trade policies in the fishing sector, Geneva, 4–5 June 1997, 37) assumes that a "transfer of funds" or a "revenue forgone" within the meaning of Article 1.1(a)(1)(i)–(ii) requires a transfer to or non-collection from the producer whom the subsidy allegedly benefits. He concludes that such subsidies are not covered by the Subsidies Agreement. Christopher Stone ("Too Many Fishing Boats, Too Few Fish: Can Trade Laws Trim Subsidies and Restore the Balance in Global Fisheries?" *Ecology Law Quarterly* 24(3), 1997, 525) appears to make the same assumption, but considers that the subsidy might still qualify as a "good or service" provided to the producer within the meaning of Article 1.1(a)(1)(iii). However, there is nothing on the face of either Articles 1 or 2 requiring that the transfer or forgone revenue be granted to the producer, and GATT/WTO jurisprudence sometimes recognizes actions against subsidies paid to parties other than the ultimate beneficiary (e.g. in "upstream" subsidies).

subsidy's qualifications for "green light" or "red light" treatment, the main sticking points appear likely to be whether a subsidy is specific,[38] whether the benefit is a "good" or a "service,"[39] and whether the "benefit" conferred is to the fishermen.

In sum, the Subsidies Agreement appears to create significant opportunities for challenges to fishery subsidies, although substantial questions about the legal limits on such challenges remain. At the same time, it is clear that several classes of important fishery subsidies appear "unlikely" to be disciplined under these rules, while some environmentally beneficial subsidies remain subject to attack. In any case, the effectiveness of disciplines under the foregoing rules depends on the willingness—so far unproven—of WTO members to litigate them.

The notification obligation

Apart from the direct constraints on subsidies discussed above, the WTO Subsidies Agreement has one other major requirement with potential application to fishery subsidies: under Article 25, each WTO member must notify the WTO formally of every subsidy granted by it, whether the subsidy is prohibited, actionable, or non-actionable.

This broad notification requirement is much more than a clerical procedure. It is a fundamental substantive obligation, which the inaugural chair of the WTO Subsidies Committee called "of critical importance to the effective operation of the Agreement."[40] Not only is transparency in national subsidy policies necessary to allow affected WTO members to know about the subsidies they may wish to challenge, it also helps impose self-discipline on subsidy policies themselves. Market-distorting subsidies are often maintained (sometimes long after their originally intended life) as a result of political pressures raised by local constituencies. In the face of these pressures, mandatory transparency in national policy-making can help generate a context for more rational outcomes. At present, Article 25 notifications constitute one of the richest sources of public information about particular subsidies granted to the fishery sector, and to this extent the notification requirement has begun to prove its potential worth.

In light of the importance of Article 25, it is especially disturbing to note that compliance with it remains profoundly unsatisfactory. A juxtaposition of Article 25 notifications for the year 1996 with the data reported in the 1998 World Bank technical paper by Mateo Milazzo suggests that only a fraction of current fishery subsidies have been duly notified. Milazzo's paper provides a good frame of reference because his numbers are quite conservative and because—with one exception (what he calls "resource rent" subsidies)—he includes only subsidies that meet the definitions of the Subsidies Agreement. For the period including 1996, Milazzo calculates subsidies of the kind that should be reported to the WTO to be approximately US$10.0–12.5 billion.[41] But a review of WTO Article 25 notifications for the same period reveals a total of only about US$792 million in monetized subsidies to the fishery sector.[42]

Putting these figures together, the best evidence currently available suggests that something on the order of 7–8 per cent of global fishery subsidies granted in 1996 that should have been notified to the WTO actually were notified. Put another way, less than 1 fishery subsidy dollar in 10 was reported. If Milazzo's very conservative numbers are low by even 12 per cent, the number would be less than 1 in 20.

A few country cases also illustrate the problem. Japan has one of the world's most heavily subsidized fishing fleets—Milazzo finds a minimum of US$885 million annually in Japanese subsidies[43]—and a history of heavy governmental participation in industrial policies. Yet, for the period including 1996, Japan reported only two particular subsidies to its fishing industry: one modest grant to support "pre-commercial" research and development for ship construction (totalling approximately US$7 million in 1996); and one law granting vessel owners an additional 20 per cent depreciation on their boats for tax purposes (Japan's notification offers no estimate of the taxes forgone).[44] For the United States, Milazzo estimates up to US$69 million annually in some years[45]—a figure that may be low by a substantial amount—and the United States Congress thinks fishery subsidies are high enough to have warranted a federally appointed task force to investigate them. But the United States notified only a single fishery subsidy for 1996 (a tax exemption on fuel), for which it reported no amounts.[46] The European Union (EU), which appears to be more fully in compliance with Article 25 than most WTO members, still appears to have failed to notify hundreds of millions of dollars in annual fishery subsidies.[47]

Additionally, the majority of WTO notifications that have been submitted provide only the barest of responses to the WTO's standard questionnaire. In most cases, it is essentially impossible to know what actual use was made of the subsidy, under what precise legal authority it was granted, or what likely market impact (not to mention impact on fisheries) the grant may have. Here again, EU member states have generally done better than average, but are still far from satisfactory. The information given by the EU for subsidies granted at the EU level itself is remarkably scant.

On a worldwide basis, all of this is evidence of a stunning disregard for the Subsidies Agreement's transparency requirements. The bottom line is that the vast majority of current fishery subsidies are maintained in outright violation of one of the WTO's central rules for disciplining them.

Gaps in the current system

The discussion above suggests that current WTO rules could provide some significant disciplines on harmful fishery subsidies. But even if the current rules were more fully implemented, they would not provide a complete response to the fishery subsidies problem. Several short-comings of the status quo suggest the need for new norms and new mechanisms for their implementation:[48]

- *The current definition of "subsidy" is too narrow.* As noted above, the WTO Subsidies Agreement appears to exclude several classes of subsidy that may make an important contribution to overcapacity and excess fishing effort, such as payments for access to foreign fisheries, infrastructure supports, and capacity exports.
- *Current distinctions between legitimate and illegitimate subsidies are inapt.* Current definitions focus too closely on narrow definitions that equate economic harms only with trade distortions. New definitions need to be supplied for classifying fishery subsidies in terms of effect on capacity, effort, and sustainability.
- *The current system lacks an affirmative obligation to discipline harmful subsidies.* WTO members at present are required only to halt the narrow class of "prohibited" or "red light" subsidies.
- *The current system lacks a mechanism for phasing out harmful subsidies.* Given the political difficulties of removing some of the most harmful

fishery subsidies, governments should consider adopting planned phase-outs of particular subsidies (e.g. with national schedules identifying subsidies in some detail) or classes of subsidies (no schedules, but fairly detailed obligations, with target dates).

- *The current system relies too heavily on national rights and adversarial process.* As noted earlier, the current system tends to ignore harms to the commons, and is implemented principally through an adversarial process between individual nations. Norms recognizing harms to the commons, and mechanisms for organic action (joint monitoring and enforcement), should be thoroughly explored.

- *Current notification and transparency rules are inadequate.* Transparency rules should require information about the impacts of particular fishery subsidies on fishing capacity and effort. Transparency rules should also extend certain rights of participation to foreigners in domestic rule-making processes (cf. the WTO Agreement on Technical Barriers to Trade). Failure to comply with transparency requirements should be punishable through the disciplinary mechanisms, including sanctions.

3. A call for WTO action

Two basic facts emerge from the foregoing: fishery subsidies are a significant contributing cause of global overfishing; and binding international norms are currently not adequate to reform them. The urgency of the worldwide fisheries crisis makes this an unacceptable situation. With proposals for WTO action on fishery subsidies now receiving preliminary consideration by the international community, it may be helpful to review some of the arguments in favour of a stronger WTO role.

Is the WTO a proper forum for new fishery subsidies rules?

It is difficult to imagine a solution to the fishery subsidies problem that does not include at least some significant role for the WTO. At a minimum, that role should include full implementation of existing notification obligations, judicious handling of any fishery subsidy cases brought before it under the Subsidies Agreement, and some level of participation in negotiations over new rules and mechanisms that may develop outside the WTO.

Indeed, even if new fishery subsidy rules are located wholly outside the WTO, certain adjustments to WTO rules and practice will be needed. The current tensions between the WTO and multilateral environmental agreements would likely be brought to the fore by an environmental regime focused on subsidies, especially if such a regime were not universally adopted, and had recourse to trade measures as a tool of enforcement. A healthy fishery subsidies regime outside the WTO, therefore, would require clarification of the WTO rules. The formation of such a regime would be an excellent opportunity for a first experiment in forging institutional links between the WTO and a multilateral environmental agreement system—to avoid redundancy, to cooperate as useful, and to give careful definition to the mutual limits of their dispute resolution mechanisms.

But the broader question is whether such a minimal WTO role would be optimal. It is true that the concerns driving international attention to fishery subsidies are presently focused more on the environmental dimensions of the issue than on trade. Moreover, many of the international policy and market failures associated with overfishing (including irrational subsidies) are of a kind appropriately addressed through environmental treaties. Even so, there are good reasons to contemplate a more direct role for the WTO on the fishery subsidies issue. First, fishery subsidies do cause trade distortions, and so the WTO may already have substantial work to do on the issue. Secondly, some aspects of a new fishery subsidy regime would be similar to familiar WTO turf. The WTO has experience with handling subsidies-related disputes and with negotiating subsidies disciplines (e.g. the Agriculture Agreement). The operations of the WTO Subsidies Committee (including oversight of the notification process) could also provide the seed of a structure for a fuller notification and monitoring system on fishery subsidies. Finally, the WTO system offers a ready-made process for binding dispute resolution and a plausible context for negotiations to forge new fishery subsidies rules.

All of these points, however, beg a fundamental question: would broader involvement in the fishery subsidies issue entangle the WTO in environmental matters beyond its appropriate mandate? This question can be broken into two parts. First, would deeper involvement in the issue inevitably require the WTO to make judgements of environmental policy? Secondly, would it be appropriate for the WTO to take cognizance of issues other than of environmental policy that lie beyond a traditional concern with "trade" distortions?

There is wide agreement in both the environmental and trade communities that the WTO should not be engaged in making environmental policy (although there is, of course, some difference of views regarding whether the WTO might already be so engaged). But would new fishery subsidies rules necessarily invite the WTO to stray beyond its competence? The answer depends on what boundaries are set to the WTO's involvement in the issue, and on the precise nature of the legal questions with which the WTO might have to grapple. For example, whether a subsidy detracts from sustainability obviously calls for an environmental judgement. But whether a subsidy causes "excess fishing capacity" seems more like the kind of straightforward (i.e. impossibly complex) economic issue with which trade institutions must deal every day. Given proper definitions of "capacity" and "effort," and of how much capacity is "over" and how much effort "excess," the question begins to sound more like one the WTO is well equipped to handle.

Two problems, however, suggest that this platonic separation between fisheries economics and environmental policy may be difficult to achieve in practice. First, as will doubtless become apparent during implementation of the FAO IPOA on fishing capacity, measuring "overcapacity" will likely require reference to facts about the condition of particular fisheries or about the optimal measures for managing them. Secondly, even where definitions can be held independent of environmental judgements, the complex effects of policies may frustrate that independence. What happens, for example, if a subsidy designed to promote technological alternatives to driftnets turns out to enhance capacity in an already overcrowded fishery? Whether, on balance, such a subsidy is good or bad policy would be a consummately environmental judgement. As discussed below, issues of this kind strongly suggest that the WTO could not—or certainly should not—craft fishery subsidies disciplines that work in isolation from intergovernmental bodies expert in fisheries management (such as the FAO).

The second question posed above—regarding the scope of the WTO's trade-oriented mission—arises not because of the "environmental" character of the fishery subsidies problem, but because, as previously noted, redressing many of the economic harms caused by fisheries subsidies would require moving beyond a preoccupation with classic distortions of international trade. Can or should the WTO head down this path?

The short answer is that it already has. The evolutionary direction of the multilateral trading system suggests that the system has been growing steadily away from being a simple arbiter of national rights, towards being a guardian of a well-functioning international market per se. Perhaps the best example of this trend is the Uruguay Round Agreement on Trade-Related Aspects of Intellectual Property Rights (the TRIPS Agreement), which creates obligations running far deeper than necessary simply to avoid measurable injuries to individual trade interests.[49] Article 6.1 of the WTO Subsidies Agreement (the "dark amber," burden-shifting category discussed above) is also an example of this trend insofar as it seeks to discipline certain subsidies in the absence of a provable harm to an individual nation's trade interests. The Preamble to the WTO Charter itself similarly reflects this evolution from "arbiter" to "guardian,"[50] and specifically notes the communal interest in "allowing for the optimal use of the world's resources in accordance with the objective of sustainable development." If it is possible to insulate the WTO from entanglement in environmental policy-making, its evolutionary path suggests it may not be out of character for the WTO to address the kind of economic injuries associated with fishery subsidies.

In sum, the significant advantages to locating at least some new fishery subsidy rules within the WTO system—along with the expertise and evolving mission of the WTO—suggest that a stronger WTO role makes sense. But real dangers and pitfalls lurk, and must be successfully avoided. Some preliminary thoughts on how the form and content of new WTO rules might accomplish this conclude this chapter.

Parameters to the form and content of new WTO rules

If the WTO is to craft new rules to discipline fishery subsidies, three questions seem especially relevant:

- What should be the objective of the new rules? How far from a focus on pure "trade distortions" should they stray?
- What legal form should the new rules take? Where should new rules (and, perhaps more importantly, negotiations over new rules) be located within the WTO system?
- Should new institutional mechanisms be created alongside new fishery subsidies rules? To what degree should other intergovernmental organizations with relevant competence (e.g. FAO, UNEP) play a role in these mechanisms?

No definitive views on these interrelated questions will be offered here. However, a few preliminary thoughts—providing more questions than answers—may help provoke constructive debate.

First, there would appear to be a direct relationship between the degree to which new WTO rules seek to redress harms falling beyond classic trade distortions and the degree of institutional integration given to the mechanisms adopted for implementing the new rules. Simply put, the further the new rules move away from a focus on traditional trade distortions, the greater the need for institutional integration with environmental and development intergovernmental organizations. But where the best balance should be struck is harder to say. For example, should the rules focus on "subsidies that contribute to overcapacity" or simply on "subsidies that enhance capacity" (without judgements of what is "over" or not)? What kinds of judgements would each of these formulas require? What would be the implications for the form of the desion-making mechanism? Similarly, what difference would it make whether the new rules included an actual schedule of subsidies phase-outs, or only a new categorization of prohibited subsidies? From an advocate's perspective, specific and time-bound subsidy reductions sound most likely to be effective. This option may also tend to reduce the need for downstream judgements of a hybrid character, since its implementation would theoretically require less textual interpretation.

Second, the options for the legal form of the new rules (which may also be tantamount to the institutional format of the negotiations over them) include, at a minimum: (i) modifications to the Subsidies Agreement, (ii) incorporation of fishery subsidies into an expanded Agreement on Agriculture, or (iii) negotiation of a new WTO sectoral agreement. Given the nature of the issues, the negotiation of a new WTO sectoral agreement appears the most attractive. A simple effort to amend the Subsidies Agreement would likely remain too focused on correcting only traditional and provable trade distortions. The notion of integrating fishery subsidies into the WTO Agriculture Agreement would tend to confuse what are in some ways very different technical issues, and clearly would run a high risk of ensnaring fishery subsidies disciplines in the politics of the agricultural subsidies issue.

Finally, none of the foregoing is meant to suggest the WTO take charge of fishery subsidies on its own. Just as a regime located outside the WTO would require active participation by the trade system, a fishery subsidies regime within the WTO would have to be crafted and administered with the direct participation of key environmental bodies. The relationship between any new WTO rules and the recently concluded FAO IPOA on fishing capacity, for example, would have to be specifically considered. But it would be a squandered opportunity to view new WTO rules as simply providing the "trade" complement to the IPOA. More imaginative and significant solutions might include establishing direct legal relationships between the regimes, such as recognition by the WTO of key definitions or standards established within the FAO process.

In the end, the goal should be for the WTO to play a meaningful and effective role in addressing the fishery subsidies problem. This will necessarily require the WTO to move, in effect, beyond a narrow focus on trade distortions (classically understood), and beyond the WTO's current tendency to eschew real working relationships with environmental intergovernmental organizations. Both of these will entail certain institutional risks—risks of the unknown if nothing else. But those risks should be easily manageable, and the potential benefits for the world's fisheries, as well as for the maturation of our system of global governance, make it a risk well worth taking.

Acknowledgements

This chapter is based on a discussion paper issued by the World Wildlife Fund as part of its report entitled *The Footprint of Distant Water Fleets on*

World Fisheries (Gland, Switzerland: WWF, 1998; http://www.panda. org/resources/publications/water/footprint/download.html). The chapter is indebted to work previously brought forward by Gareth Porter and Mateo Milazzo, among others. The advice of Scott Burns, Charlie Arden-Clarke, Konrad von Moltke, and Aaron McLoughlin, as well as the valuable input of Ronald Steenblik and the research assistance of Prabhu Patel, are gratefully acknowledged.

Notes

1. FAO Fisheries Department, *The State of World Fisheries and Aquaculture (SOFIA) - 1996 Summary,* Rome: FAO, 1996.
2. See, e.g., Gareth Porter, *Estimating Overcapacity in the Global Fishing Fleet,* Gland, Switzerland: WWF, 1998.
3. Based on estimated total annual subsidies of US$15–20 billion and annual revenue (based on FAO figures for "first sale" of landed fish) of US$80 billion. See Mateo Milazzo, *Subsidies in World Fisheries: A Reexamination,* World Bank Technical Paper No. 406, April 1998, pp. 16 and 74.
4. See, generally, FAO Fisheries Department, "Marine Fisheries and the Law of the Sea: A Decade of Change," Special chapter (revised) of *The State of Food and Agriculture 1992,* FAO Fisheries Circular No. 853, Rome: FAO, 1993, p. 23; Christopher Stone, "Too Many Fishing Boats, Too Few Fish: Can Trade Laws Trim Subsidies and Restore the Balance in Global Fisheries?" *Ecology Law Quarterly* 24(3), 1997, 515; Gareth Porter, *Fishing Subsidies, Overfishing and Trade,* UNEP/WWF workshop on the role of trade policies in the fishing sector, Geneva, 4–5 June 1997, pp. 15–20; Milazzo, *Subsidies in World Fisheries,* op. cit., 18–35; WTO Committee on Trade and Environment (CTE), "Note by the Secretariat," in *GATT/WTO Rules on Subsidies and Aids Granted in the Fishing Industry,* WT/CTE/W/80, 9 March 1998, paras. 30–33 (including list of subsidies) and Annex II, para. 4. The types of subsidies listed here are often conferred in addition to tariff and other border measures designed to protect domestic fishing industries from import competition.
5. The provision of fishery access rights constitutes a subsidy if access fees are set lower than necessary to cover the costs of resource extraction not otherwise borne by the fishermen. See, FAO Fisheries Department, "Marine Fisheries," op. cit., 23; Milazzo, *Subsidies in World Fisheries,* op. cit., 56–57; Stone, "Too Many Fishing Boats," op. cit., 526. These subsidies can be provided through low fees charged by a domestic government to its own nationals, or by a coastal state government to foreign nationals, or through payment of access fees by governments to coastal states on behalf of their nationals. For an in-depth study of how reduced access fees have functioned as subsidies to European fishing fleets operating off the coasts of Africa, see Gareth Porter, "Euro-African Fishing Agreements: Subsidizing Overfishing in African Waters," in *Subsidies and Depletion of World Fisheries: Case Studies,* Gland, Switzerland: WWF, 1997.

6. For more sophisticated efforts to divide fishery subsidies into distinct analytic categories, see, e.g., FAO Fisheries Department, "Marine Fisheries," op. cit., 23–24; Stone, "Too Many Fishing Boats," op. cit., 523–529; Milazzo, *Subsidies in World Fisheries,* op. cit., 9–14.

7. See, e.g., Milazzo, *Subsidies in World Fisheries,* op. cit., 74 (estimating that "environmental" fishery subsidies are roughly 5 per cent of the total).

8. FAO Fisheries Department, "Marine Fisheries," op. cit., 32, 50–53. The figures cited refer to the period circa 1988–1989.

9. See, e.g., Porter, *Fishing Subsidies,* op. cit., 21 ("more than half"); Hope Shand, *Human Nature: Agricultural Biodiversity and Farm-based Food Security,* an independent study prepared for the FAO (http://www.fao.org/sd/edpir), Winnipeg: Rural Advancement Foundation International, 1977, fn 27 and accompanying text (citing full US$54 billion as representing subsidies).

10. Stone, "Too Many Fishing Boats," op. cit., 518. Stone accepts the FAO's formulation that "most" of the US$54 billion deficit is likely covered by subsidies: "Too Many Fishing Boats," op. cit., 517 and notes 48–49. Porter, *Fishing Subsidies,* op. cit., 21, similarly finds the FAO numbers may be off in either direction, but concludes that worldwide fishery subsidies are likely in the US$16–20 billion range.

11. WTO CTE, "Note by the Secretariat," op. cit., Annex II, para. 5.

12. Milazzo, *Subsidies in World Fisheries,* op. cit.

13. Ibid., 73.

14. Specifically, in most cases Milazzo reviewed only government budgets for departments responsible for fisheries—ignoring other government agencies that might provide subsidies to the fishery sector—and, with occasional exceptions, did not include subsidies provided by governmental entities at the subnational (or sub-EU) level. Milazzo also reports that he exercised "prudence and caution" in his overall approach (ibid.).

15. Ibid., 16 and 74 (citing FAO figures).

16. Porter (*Fishing Subsidies,* op. cit., 7–9) has surveyed a number of ways in which subsidizing the extraction of natural resources can degrade the environment, including through: (1) overcapitalizing the productive sector; (2) altering incentives away from environmentally friendly technologies; (3) misallocating resources by under-pricing natural inputs; (4) making it profitable to harvest even at very low or negative unsubsidized marginal returns; (5) encouraging overconsumption; and (6) reducing public revenues available for proper management of a resource (especially to the extent that revenues generated by the resource are a significant source of funding for its management).

17. See, e.g., WTO CTE, "Note by the Secretariat," op. cit., Annex II, para. 3 (quoting the FAO's conclusion that "as the opportunities for an increased catch from fishery resources have declined considerably, a continuation of the high subsidies can only lead to greater and greater economic distress as well as further depletion of stocks"); WTO Committee on Trade and Environment, *Environmental and Trade Benefits of Removing Subsidies in the Fisheries Sector (Submission by the United States), WT/CTE/W/51,* 19 May 1997, paras. 8–9 ("Subsidies tend to exacerbate the over fishing [*sic*] and overcapitalization common in the world's commercial fisheries . . . most subsidies in fisheries have a negative impact from a conservation standpoint") (see also paras. 18–19); WTO Committee on Trade and Environment, Item 6: *The*

Fisheries Sector (Submission by New Zealand), WT/CTE/W/52, 21 May 1997, para. 7 ("By providing additional revenue or reducing costs, the returns from fisheries are inflated beyond normal economic levels of exploitation. In the case of a fisheries resources [*sic*], the normal economic rate of exploitation will often be above the long term sustainable biological rates of yield"); Asian Development Bank, *Draft Working Paper on the Bank's Policy on Fisheries,* 18 January 1996, para. 55 ("Incentives in the form of subsidies and protection can lead to overexploitation of fishery resources, lower harvest, and economic inefficiency"); United Nations Commission on Sustainable Development, *Protection of the Oceans, All Kinds of Seas, Including Enclosed and Semi-enclosed Seas, and Coastal Areas and the Protection, Rational Use and Development of their Living Resources,* Report of the Secretary-General, E/CN.17/1996/3, 12 February 1996, para. 21(c) ("Governments are urged to reduce subsidies to the fishing industry and abolish incentives leading to over-fishing").

18. See Milazzo, *Subsidies in World Fisheries,* op. cit., 4–8; Ronald P. Steenblik and Paul Wallis, *The OECD's Program of Work in the Area of Fishery Policies,* Paris: OECD, 1998, Sec. 2.2.

19. FAO Fisheries Department, *The State of World Fisheries and Aquaculture (1996),* Rome: FAO, 1997, 7. Nearly a quarter of the developing countries that rely on single-commodity exports depend on seafood for 40–80 per cent of their export earnings; WTO CTE, *Environmental and Trade Benefits . . . (Submission by the United States),* op. cit., para. 15.

20. Milazzo, *Subsidies in World Fisheries,* op. cit., 74–75, notes the equivalence of fishery subsidies, in relative terms, to agricultural subsidies that are commonly decried as serious market distortions and barriers to trade.

21. See, e.g., WTO CTE, *Environmental and Trade Benefits . . . (Submission by the United States),* op. cit., paras. 13 and 18; *The Fisheries Sector (Submission by New Zealand),* op. cit., paras. 7, 10–12.

22. WTO Committee on Trade and Environment, *Environmental Benefits of Removing Trade Restrictions and Distortions (Note by the Secretariat),* WT/CTE/W/67, 7 November 1997, para. 93.

23. Various international environmental instruments may also have a bearing on the legitimacy of environmentally harmful fishery subsidies. See, e.g., the Convention on Biological Diversity, the UN Convention on the Law of the Sea (including the related Agreement on the Conservation and Management of Straddling Fish Stocks and Highly Migratory Fish Stocks), the FAO Code of Conduct for Responsible Fisheries, the Convention on International Trade in Endangered Species of Wild Fauna and Flora (CITES), and Agenda 21. Although a number of these speak directly to the overcapacity issue, none contains specific binding obligations to reduce environmentally harmful fishery subsidies, and this chapter will not deal further with them. They may, however, contribute to a body of emerging international environmental norms constraining national fisheries policies generally, including the use of subsidies. In addition to these international rules, national "countervailing duty" laws provide another avenue for disciplining fishery subsidies. Since these "CVD" laws rely on a controversial and adversarial approach to subsidy reduction that is not likely to prove sufficient to deal with the fishery subsidies problem, this chapter does not consider them further.

24. FAO, The International Plan of Action for the Management of Fishing Capacity Adopted by the 23rd Session of the FAO Committee on Fisheries, Rome, 15–19 February 1999, paras. 25 & 26.

25. Ibid., para. 45.

26. Ibid., para. 4.

27. The IPOA calls for a "technical consultation" in 1999 to examine this theme, and to kick off development of "technical guidelines for data collection and analysis." Ibid., para. 12.

28. Para. 37 of the IPOA calls only for capacity exports to be done with the express consent of the importing country, and so does nothing to reduce the significant international pressures to import capacity that subsidies to capacity exports can engender.

29. The mechanisms under the IPOA for the management of capacity in high seas fisheries are far less clear than those provided for the management of capacity within domestic fisheries. See, e.g., paras. 31, 38, and 39.

30. Also applicable to subsidies is Article XVI of GATT. Since, for present purposes, the obligations of the Subsidies Agreement are both broader and stricter, the legal relevance of GATT Article XVI will not be analysed here.

31. Uruguay Round Agreement on Agriculture, Annex I (Product Coverage), 1.(i) (excluding "fish and fish products"). One observer has reported that the exclusion was intended to allow major fish importing nations to maintain tariff-quotas on fish imports. Rory McCleod, *Market Access Issues for the New Zealand Seafood Trade,* New Zealand Fishing Industry Board, 1996, 73 (cited in Porter, *Fishing Subsidies,* op. cit., 36).

32. See Porter, *Fishing Subsidies,* op. cit., 37 (such subsidies are "not significant in the fisheries sector"). But see Stone, "Too Many Fishing Boats," op. cit., 529 and notes 109–110 ("such practices have certainly taken place in the fisheries context"). Article 27 of the Subsidies Agreement exempts developing countries from Article 3 prohibitions, although with time limits on the exemption in some cases. Some developing countries have notified otherwise prohibited fishery subsidies in accordance with that rule. See, e.g., G/SCM/N/6, Notification of Singapore, 8 May 1995 (tax relief for fish exports, conditioned on certain minimum export sales).

33. WTO, Agreement on Subsidies and Countervailing Duties, Article 8.2(c)(iv), refers to the "reduction of nuisances and pollution." Bycatch reduction would strain this definition, and clearly was not in the minds of the drafters. Still, the general spirit of the "green for green" box should allow such an expansion of its meaning. Otherwise, this might be better called the "green for brown" box.

34. On the coverage of Articles 5–6 in the fishery context, see, generally, Stone, "Too Many Fishing Boats," op. cit., 523–537; Porter, *Fishing Subsidies,* op. cit., 35–39.

35. The Subsidies Agreement provides that multiple subsidy programmes can be aggregated in calculating the overall rate of subsidization to a given product. Subsidies Agreement, Annex IV, 6. Porter and Stone agree that the 5 per cent ad valorem rule is the most interesting of the Article 6.1 clauses (Porter, *Fishing Subsidies,* op. cit., 39; Stone, "Too Many Fishing Boats," op. cit., 530).

36. The Article 31 sunset provision also applies to the "green light" subsidies category.

37. The categorizations in table 6.1 are roughly based on Stone, "Too Many Fishing Boats," op. cit., and Porter, *Fishing Subsidies,* op. cit., as well as on my own knowledge. No rigorous defence of them will be provided.

38. E.g. if a fuel subsidy is granted to more than just the fishery sector (see Porter, *Fishing Subsidies,* op. cit., 37 and note 148); or if a port facility is for use by more than just fishermen (see Stone, "Too Many Fishing Boats," op. cit., 524, who also considers that such facilities might be "infrastructure" within the meaning of Article 1.1(a)(1)(iii)).

39. Stone raises this question with regard to payment of access fees ("Too Many Fishing Boats," op. cit., 525).

40. WTO Committee on Subsidies and Countervailing Measures, "Minutes of the Meeting Held on 22 February 1995," G/SCMM/1, 5 May 1995, para. L.

41. This figure reflects what Milazzo reports as a global total for non "resource rent" subsidies, adjusted by deducting US$1 billion to account for the fact that Russia and China are not WTO members. This US$1 billion is my conservative overestimate, based on Milazzo's figures for the European Union and Japan (the two largest subsidizers).

42. This figure was derived by reviewing all of the notifications collected and reported in WTO CTE, "Note by the Secretariat," op. cit. In the case of the EEC Notification, information in a more recent comprehensive notification (G/SCM/N/25/EEC, 12 March 1998) was also reviewed. Several of these notifications failed to provide any monetized amount for the subsidy; see, e.g., *Notification by the Philippines,* G/SCM/N/3/PHL, 15 April 1996; *Notification by Japan,* G/SCM/N/25/JPN, 17 November 1997, 32 ("Additional Depreciation on Fishing Boats"); *Notification of the United States,* G/SCM/N/16/USA, 26 September 1997 ("Commercial Fishing Exemption from Deficit Reduction Rate Component of Excise Tax on Motor Fuels"). The inadequacy of these notices makes it appropriate not to count them in the total. For consistency with Milazzo, the total does include a portion of subsidies identified for general shipbuilding in the relevant period. Again relying on notices listed in WTO CTE, "Note by the Secretariat," op. cit., there were roughly US$2.7 billion of such subsidies notified for 1996. Following Milazzo, *Subsidies in World Fisheries,* op. cit., 52, 10 per cent (US$27 million) have been counted towards the total for subsidies to the fishery sector.

43. Milazzo, *Subsidies in World Fisheries,* op. cit., 19, 39, 68. These figures do not include significant "unbudgeted" or "cross-sectoral" subsidies, for which precise numbers are hard to extract from Milazzo's analysis.

44. *Notification by Japan,* op. cit., 22, 32.

45. Milazzo, *Subsidies in World Fisheries,* op. cit., 25, 30, and 41.

46. *Notification of the United States,* op. cit.

47. Milazzo reports at least US$895 million in EU subsidies at the EEC level, not including two large categories of subsidy that Milazzo finds difficult to quantify: *Subsidies in World Fisheries,* op. cit., 22, 38, 67. The EU Notification for the period 1996, above, totals approximately US$592 million.

48. In referring to the "shortcomings" of the present system, it is not intended to criticize the drafters of the WTO accords for failing to do what they manifestly did not consider doing. These "shortcomings" arise from a comparison of the WTO rules with what is needed in the future, not with what might have been wished in the past. The discussion that follows draws in part on Stone, "Too Many Fishing Boats," op. cit., 523 et seq.; Milazzo, *Subsidies in World Fisheries,* op. cit., 75–81; and Porter, *Fishing Subsidies,* op. cit., 40–44.

49. The TRIPS Agreement creates broad obligations to maintain certain aspects of an open and well-functioning intellectual property rights regime at the national level. The terms of the TRIPS Agreement can be enforced for "nullification or impairment" arising from breach of these obligations—claims of a kind that receive presumptions of injury under traditional GATT law (much like those created under Subsidies Agreement Article 6.1); see above. It is interesting to note that TRIPS Article 64.2 disallows cases under the broader "non-breach" type of nullification or impairment for the first five years of the Agreement—again paralleling the experimental character of Subsidies Agreement Article 6.1.

50. The Preamble's repeated references to the multilateral trading "system" are interesting in this regard.

7

Improving the Agreement on Sanitary and Phytosanitary Standards

Steve Charnovitz[1]

One of the most significant achievements of the Uruguay Round was securing the Agreement on the Application of Sanitary and Phyto-sanitary Measures (known as SPS). This Agreement imposes controls on the use of national laws and regulations to protect humans, animals, or plants from pests, disease, and harmful food additives. During its first five years, SPS has had some favourable impact. In some arenas, however, SPS is criticized for violating national autonomy. The Seattle Ministerial Conference in December 1999 will provide an opportunity for governments to take stock of SPS implementation and to consider whether the Agreement needs to be renegotiated. At a time when food safety concerns are paramount,[2] everyone interested in the linkages between trade, health, and biotechnology has a stake in the ongoing debate about SPS. This chapter seeks to inform the consideration of SPS in Seattle.

Although the SPS Agreement can serve to improve public health, the main motivation for this treaty was to prevent the use of unnecessary health measures that impede foreign exporters. SPS has proven to be controversial because it puts the World Trade Organization (WTO) in a position of telling a government regulator to remove measures that the regulator claims are needed for health reasons. The idea behind SPS is that food safety and related disputes should be settled by science-based rules. But although scientists may be able to answer some scientific questions, they cannot bridge differences in values that often underlie health-related conflicts between countries.[3]

As of mid-1999, three judgments pertaining to the SPS Agreement have been handed down by WTO panels and the Appellate Body. In all three cases, the defendant government employing the health measure lost. Two of the disputes involved "sanitary" measures focusing on food safety or fishery disease. One dispute involved "phytosanitary" measures focusing on agricultural disease. The cases were also split between old-style disputes that might have occurred 50 years ago and a modern dispute involving biotechnology.

The first case was *EC–Measures Concerning Meat and Meat Products (Hormones)*.[4] The United States and Canada complained against a European Commission ban (begun in 1989) on the importation of meat produced with growth hormones. The Commission had banned the use of six growth hormones in Europe to promote food safety and sought to keep out foreign meat produced with such hormones. The rationale for the ban was that the hormones might be carcinogenic. The WTO Appellate Body ruled against the European Union in January 1998 and an arbitrator gave the Commission 15 months to bring its law into conformity with SPS rules. As of mid-1999, the Commission had not yet removed the ban and the United States and Canada are threatening trade retaliation.[5]

The second case was *Australia–Measures Affecting the Importation of Salmon*.[6] In this dispute Canada complained against an Australian ban (begun in 1975) on the importation of uncooked salmon. Australia had enacted this ban to prevent the introduction of exotic pathogens not present in Australia. (This was a fishery health measure, not a food safety measure.) The Appellate Body ruled against Australia in October 1998 and an arbitrator gave Australia eight months to bring its regulation into conformity with SPS rules. As of mid-1999, Australia has not yet removed the ban and Canada is threatening trade retaliation.

The third case was *Japan–Measures Affecting Agricultural Products*.[7] Here the United States complained about a Japanese phytosanitary measure (begun in 1950) that banned imports of apples, cherries, nectarines, and walnuts potentially infested with coddling moth. In 1987, Japan had provided for lifting this ban subject to certain quarantine and fumigation requirements, which called for each variety of fruit to be individually tested. It was this separate testing requirement that provoked the WTO dispute. The Appellate Body ruled against Japan in February 1999. Thereafter, Japan agreed to bring its regulation into conformity with SPS rules by the end of 1999.

The victory by plaintiffs in these three disputes will surely lead to more such cases in the future.[8] Already in the WTO pipeline are cases regarding a French ban on asbestos and a US subnational import ban on Canadian cattle and grain. Disputes may also be looming on issues such as the overuse of antibiotics in animals and the use of genetically modified organisms (GMOs).[9] Even when the substance being regulated is unquestionably harmful (e.g. dioxin), disputes can occur over whether or not the regulatory response is broader or longer lasting than necessary.

This chapter contains five sections. The first section provides a brief discussion of the historical context for international negotiations on sanitary standards. The second section explains the SPS rules and the interpretations given by the WTO Appellate Body. The third section appraises SPS dispute settlement. The fourth section appraises the WTO role on food safety. The fifth section discusses a few key issues that may be considered in Seattle.

1. The historical context of SPS

Concerns about the trade effects of unjustified sanitary measures go back many years. This problem was extensively examined in the League of Nations with a view to using science to determine the validity of trade bans. But no multilateral discipline was created until 1947, with the General Agreement on Tariffs and Trade (GATT). Although GATT rules were intended to prohibit trade measures for sanitary purposes that were not "necessary" for health or that were really disguised trade barriers, these rules were hardly ever tested. Instead, a GATT Standards Code was written in 1979 and, when that proved inadequate, a new effort to draft a separate SPS Agreement was begun in the late 1980s.

Although SPS builds on GATT in many ways, perhaps the most important addition is the discipline on domestic measures. Under GATT, a domestic health standard impeding an import was held only to the principle of "national treatment." So long as the import was treated no less favourably than the domestic product, it did not matter how flimsy the justification was for the domestic standard. As will be explained below, SPS subjects domestic standards to supervision whenever they directly or indirectly affect trade. Because SPS has more stringent disciplines than GATT, the health exception in GATT Article XX(b) is not available to a government as a defence in an SPS lawsuit.

It should be noted that the SPS Agreement pertains only to health standards applied to imports. Thus, it would not be an SPS violation for a country to impose an unscientific ban on the use of hormones in food production so long as it did not apply that standard to imports. Yet this retained sovereignty right is unlikely to prevent trade conflict. It would be rare indeed for a government to impose a health standard on domestic products and yet allow in imports that do not meet that standard.

Although a review of trade history shows a long-time concern about unjustified non-tariff barriers, that is not the only historical development relevant to appreciating SPS. Another is the way that trade concerns contributed to raising food safety and sanitary standards. As Percy Bidwell explains, "The first [US] federal legislation regarding meat inspection was directed, not toward protecting American consumers . . . but toward improving the healthfulness of American products destined for foreign markets."[10] This initiative in the early 1890s arose in response to import bans against American imports throughout Europe. Since inspectors were to be hired to examine meat exports, they were also ordered to examine domestic meat trade. Another interesting interplay between health and trade occurred in the 1929 Convention for the Protection of Plants. On health, the Convention committed governments to prevent and control plant disease. On trade, the Convention provided that disputes about phytosanitary measures could be brought to the International Institute of Agriculture, which would appoint a committee of experts to investigate and issue a report.[11]

These historical episodes are suggestive of how SPS might become a broader agreement aimed not only at promoting trade but also at promoting food safety and public health. It is not that these concerns are absent from SPS. After all, its Preamble notes the desire "to improve the human health, animal health and phytosanitary situation in all Members." But the food safety goal has not been developed. Greater cooperation by governments to improve food safety and sanitation, especially in developing countries, could prevent trade conflicts and ultimately lead to greater economic growth and trade.

2. SPS rules and case-law

The SPS rules apply only to sanitary and phytosanitary measures as defined in the Agreement.[12] In broad terms, SPS pertains to laws or regulations to protect against exposure to pests (i.e. insects), to micro-organisms, and to additives, contaminants, and toxins in food for humans and feedstuffs for animals. For example, protection against insecticide in fruit is covered by SPS because that is a contaminant. But protection against bio-engineering in fruit might not be covered by SPS because genetic modification is not a risk listed in the above categories. The applicability of SPS to GMOs is a complex issue that will no doubt be determined by a future WTO panel.[13]

The SPS Agreement interrelates with other WTO agreements.[14] If a measure is governed by SPS, then it is excluded from coverage under the WTO Agreement on Technical Barriers to Trade (TBT). All measures governed by SPS will also be governed by GATT, but the SPS rules are much stricter. It remains unclear how the WTO will deal with a measure that has dual purposes—for example, to protect both food safety and biodiversity.[15]

Before discussing SPS rules, it will be helpful to provide a brief background on WTO dispute settlement. If a WTO member government believes that another WTO member government is utilizing a health measure in violation of SPS rules, it can lodge a complaint to the WTO. A panel will be appointed to hear testimony from the plaintiff and defendant governments and then render a decision. After the panel hands down its decision, it may be appealed to the WTO Appellate Body (as were the first three SPS cases). The Appellate Body then delivers a final decision within 60 days. If the defendant government loses the case, it is asked by the WTO Council to bring its SPS measure into conformity with whatever SPS rule it was found to violate. If the government does not do so within a specified period of time, the WTO Council may authorize the complaining country to impose trade retaliation on the scofflaw government. In all three SPS cases, the panels availed themselves of the provision in SPS enabling them to consult experts. Instead of setting up the advisory technical experts group provided for in SPS Article 11.2, the panels brought in several experts in their individual capacities.

The SPS rules apply only between WTO member governments. Thus, a populous country such as China, which has not been permitted to join the WTO, has no rights or obligations under SPS. For example, the US government now bars certain wood crates from China that might harbour a destructive beetle. But China cannot ask the WTO to evaluate the scientific evidence for this ban.

Before explaining SPS rules, this chapter should discuss the burden of proof and the standard of review. As in most WTO disputes, the initial burden lies with the government lodging the complaint, which must establish a clear (i.e. *prima facie*) case of inconsistency with SPS rules. Once that occurs, the defendant government utilizing the health measure has the burden to bring forward evidence and arguments to refute the allegation that it is violating a WTO rule.

The standard of review dictates whether the panel should be deferential to the regulatory authorities of the country imposing the health measure. In *Hormones,* the Appellate Body rejected the arguments of the European Union (EU) for deference and instead stated that the role of the panel is to make an "objective assessment of the facts," relying on the evidence as presented by governments and outside experts.[16] Some analysts continue to argue that WTO panels should show deference to governments.[17] It should be noted that SPS rules seem to apply identically to national laws both where regulators require applicants to show that a product is safe and where regulators have the burden to show that a product is unsafe.

The complex SPS rules can be abridged into seven disciplines and one exemption.

The science requirement

The first SPS discipline is the science requirement. SPS Article 2.2 states that governments "shall ensure that any sanitary or phytosanitary measure is applied only to the extent necessary to protect human, animal or plant life or health, is based on scientific principles, and is not maintained without sufficient scientific evidence."[18] In *Agricultural Products,* the Appellate Body interpreted this provision to require "a rational or objective relationship between the SPS measure and the scientific evidence."[19] The panel and the Appellate Body concluded that Article 2.2 was being violated because Japan could not show that the quarantine and fumigation used for one variety of fruit or nut would be inadequate for other varieties.

Although it is often averred that the SPS Agreement requires governments to use "sound science," it should be noted that this term does not appear anywhere in the SPS Agreement. This point is significant because it is unclear to what extent panels may discount scientific findings presented by a government. So far, no panel has been faced with such a decision. But a dispute will surely arise where a government presents a scientific study for an SPS measure that is then challenged by other scientists as being a poorly conducted study. It seems likely that future WTO panels will seek to weigh such competing positions in the manner that many national courts do.

Risk assessment requirement

SPS Article 5.1 requires governments to ensure that their sanitary and phytosanitary measures are "based on an assessment, as appropriate to the circumstances, of the risks to human, animal or plant life or health." This requirement has proven to be of central importance in enforcing the SPS Agreement. It was litigated in all three WTO disputes and thus there is a small body of case-law on it. In all three disputes, the defendant government was found to be in violation of Article 5.1.

What is a risk assessment? The SPS Agreement explains that a risk assessment can be either (1) the evaluation of the likelihood of entry, establishment, or spread of a pest or disease, or (2) the evaluation of the potential for adverse effects on human or animal health arising from the presence of additives, contaminants, toxins, or disease-causing organisms in food, beverages, or feedstuffs (SPS Annex A, para. 4). In interpreting this provision, the Appellate Body seems to be saying that, although an adequate assessment must evaluate the probability of risk, it does not have to make a monolithic finding.[20] Thus, a risk assessment that presented both a "mainstream" and a "divergent" scientific view could be an adequate assessment.[21] Moreover, there is no requirement that a risk assessment be expressed as a quantitative conclusion.[22]

According to the Appellate Body, a risk assessment must find evidence of an "ascertainable" risk.[23] This seems to mean that a tangible risk must be found. The Appellate Body has stated that it will not be sufficient for governments to impose regulations simply on the basis of the "theoretical" risk that underlies all scientific uncertainty.[24] For example, in *Salmon,* the Appellate Body agreed with the panel that the analysis conducted by the Australian government was not a proper risk assessment because it lent too much weight to "unknown and uncertain elements."[25] On the other hand, there is no minimally sufficient magnitude of risk that regulators must find.[26] Adding this up, the Appellate Body appears to be saying that a risk assessment can still be acceptable even if it points to an extremely small risk.

Although there is no requirement that the defendant government actually do the risk assessment itself, there must be a risk assessment in order to comply with SPS Article 5.1. A government can use a risk assessment conducted by another government or by anyone. But an adequate assessment must be in place. This requirement was first implemented in the *Hormones* dispute. There was considerable evidence on the record that the use of hormones as a growth promoter was safe. Yet most of this evidence assumed that the hormones would be used in accordance with "good veterinary practice."[27] Thus, if hormones were overused or misused in fattening animals, the available evidence did not demonstrate the safety of eating such meat.

Even while admitting that hormone abuse could constitute a health risk, the Appellate Body faulted the European Commission for not conducting a risk assessment of this prospect. Therefore, the Appellate Body found a violation of Article 5.1.[28] Although many commentators suggest that SPS prohibits import bans only of products that have been proven safe, this episode shows that SPS disciplines can disallow health regulations aimed at genuinely unsafe practices.

Once the existence of an adequate risk assessment is shown, the panel must then consider whether the health measure in dispute is "based on" this assessment. The Appellate Body reads "based on" as a substantive requirement. In the first SPS case (*Hormones*), the panel sought to impose a procedural requirement that the defendant government actually rely upon the risk assessment. The panel undertook an administrative law analysis of the EU's decision-making process. This approach also had the effect of excluding new scientific evidence that arose during the course of WTO review. In an important ruling, the Appellate Body rejected this attempt to incorporate minimum procedural obligations into SPS.[29]

The Appellate Body has been a bit unclear on how this "based on" test operates. Within the same decision, it said that the risk assessment must "sufficiently warrant," "sufficiently support," "reasonably warrant," "reasonably support," or "rationally support" using the health measure, and that there must be an "objective relationship" or a "rational relationship" between the risk and the measure.[30] This test was first implemented in the *Hormones* case, where the panel and the Appellate Body found that the thin EU risk assessment did not rationally support banning the importation of meat produced with growth hormones. The Appellate Body admitted that one expert consulted by the panel had testified that one out of every million women would get breast cancer from eating meat produced with growth hormones.[31] But the Appellate Body discounted this testimony from Dr. George Lucier of the US National Institute of Environmental Health Sciences, noting that Lucier's opinion was not based on studies that he had conducted and that his views were "divergent" from the other views received by the panel. It is unclear whether the Appellate Body dismissed Dr. Lucier's opinion as speculative, or adjudged a one-in-a-million risk to be unimportant.

Whenever a government violates SPS Article 5.1, there will perforce also be a violation of the science requirement in SPS Article 2.2. Although this conclusion is not at all obvious, the *Salmon* panel made this contention, which was upheld by the Appellate Body.[32] The issue is sure to arise in the future.

The SPS Agreement does not direct panels to apply benefit–cost analysis.[33] Thus, so long as a governmental measure is based on an adequate risk assessment, restricting the use of a chemical whose benefit exceeds its harm should not constitute a violation of SPS. Still, there will be continuing pressure by litigant governments to impose an economic test on defendant governments via Article 2.2. Even in its first SPS decision, the Appellate Body noted that promoting international trade and protecting human health were "sometimes competing" interests.[34]

The requirement for national regulatory consistency

Article 5.5 states that, "[w]ith the objective of achieving consistency" in levels of protection against health risks, a government "shall avoid arbitrary or unjustifiable distinctions in the levels it considers to be appropriate in different situations, if such distinctions result in discrimination or a disguised restriction on international trade." This is the most controversial SPS rule and the one most intrusive into national decision-making processes because it focuses on the "levels" of health protection.[35] Although the SPS Agreement calls on the WTO Committee on Sanitary and Phytosanitary Measures to develop guidelines for the practical implementation of this provision, neither of the first two SPS panels was willing to await those guidelines before enforcing Article 5.5.

The Appellate Body has pointed out that there are three elements to an Article 5.5 violation. First, the defendant government must be seeking different levels of health protection in "comparable" situations. In *Salmon,* the Appellate Body explained that situations are "comparable" when there is a common risk of entry or spread of one disease of concern.[36] For example, health regulations on salmon may be compared to regulations on herring for bait because both salmon and herring can impose the same health risk. The second element is that the differences in the government's intended level of protection must be "arbitrary or unjustifiable." This can be found if the risks are similar but the level of protection is different. The third element is that the health measure embodying these differences results in discrimination or a disguised restriction on international trade. In the cases so far, the first two elements have been easily shown, while the third element has received the greatest attention by the panels and the Appellate Body.

In *Salmon,* the Appellate Body offers five arguments for concluding that the Australian health measure constituted discrimination or a disguised restriction on trade. It will be useful to examine the Appellate Body's analytical approach because the five arguments do not prove much. The first two arguments are mere bootstrapping: the Appellate

Body points to the lack of a risk assessment and to the different levels of health protection being sought (both discussed above). The third argument is that there was a "substantial" difference in the level of health protection being sought. The fourth argument is that an Australian government draft report in 1995, which would have been tolerant of salmon imports, was revised in the final report of 1996. The fifth argument is that Australia lacks strict internal controls on salmon equivalent to those it imposes at the border against foreign diseases. According to the Appellate Body, whereas no single one of these arguments might be conclusive, together they add up to a trade law violation.

This judicial approach is confounding in its analytical weakness and in its potential for mischief. Accusing a government of trade discrimination or a disguised restriction is a serious charge that should not be hurled lightly. As the Australian representative explained to the Appellate Body, it cannot possibly be a violation of the WTO for a government to change a recommendation between a draft and a final report. Similarly, it cannot possibly be a violation of the WTO for a government to lack internal controls on commerce equivalent to border controls. Yet, according to the Appellate Body, such innocent acts can aggregate into a WTO violation. It is unclear why the Appellate Body did not realize that an island nation might need stricter health controls at the perimeter than internally. According to the Australian government, there are at least 20 diseases of salmon not currently found in Australia.

A government convicted of violating Article 5.5 has two choices if it wants to comply. It can upwardly harmonize its chosen level of health protection or it can downwardly harmonize. Thus, although it would not be correct to say that Article 5.5 promotes downward harmonization, there is that potential, and therefore the implementation of dispute reports should be closely monitored. The WTO will certainly not gain in the public's esteem if it is blamed for lowering public health goals.

The requirement of least trade restrictiveness

Article 5.6 states that governments shall ensure that their sanitary and phytosanitary measures "are not more trade-restrictive than required to achieve their appropriate level" of protection. To prove a violation, there must be an alternative measure, reasonably available, that is significantly less restrictive to trade. So far, the WTO has found no Article 5.6 violations. In two cases, the panels held that Article 5.6 was being violated, but both decisions were reversed on appeal. Nevertheless, these Appellate Body rulings contain some important interpretations of Article 5.6, which will be noted briefly. One is that governments are obligated to determine and reveal their chosen level of protection to WTO panels so that SPS rules can be applied. Another is that, in analysing an alternative measure, panels will consider whether it matches the intended level of protection, not the level of protection actually achieved by the SPS measure that is the target of the WTO lawsuit. Another is that the complaining country must show that the alternative measure exists. In other words, a panel may not posit the alternative based on the advice of experts.

The requirement to use international standards

Article 3.1 states that governments "shall base" their SPS measures on international standards, where they exist, except as otherwise provided. As this provision links with others in a very confusing skein of obligations and exceptions, this chapter will seek only to give a summary of this part of the SPS Agreement. International standards are the standards drafted by organizations such as the Codex Alimentarius Commission for food safety, the International Office of Epizootics for animal health, and the International Plant Protection Convention for plant health. When such standards do not exist, then Article 3.1 has no effect.

When international standards do exist, a government has three choices. It can use a higher standard in order to pursue a higher level of health protection. It can use a lower standard. Or it can conform its SPS measure to the international standard. By so conforming, a government would gain a presumption in the WTO that its measure complies with SPS rules. This presumption would be rebuttable, however, and so it is unclear how much of a "safe harbour" using international standards will be. Some analysts have suggested that governments would have a greater incentive to use international standards if they were truly a "safe harbour" from being challenged as SPS violations.

If a government chooses to pursue a level of health protection higher than the international standard, then it must meet all the SPS requirements, including the four disciplines discussed above. The existence of the international standard does not put a government in a worse position for not having followed it. Thus, a government does not have to justify the deviation from international standards. This point was litigated in the *Hormones* case, where the panel, surprisingly, had sought to shift the burden of proof to a government choosing not to use an international standard. The Appellate Body quickly reversed this ruling.[37]

If a government chooses to pursue a level of health protection lower than the international standard, then it too must meet all other SPS requirements. It would not have to justify the deviation from international standards, even for its exports. The government need only assert that the lower standard results from its chosen level of protection. There are unlikely to be WTO complaints about standards being too low.

The recognition of equivalence

Article 4.1 requires an importing country (or a government refusing to import) to accept an SPS measure by an exporting country as equivalent to its own, if the exporting government can objectively demonstrate that its health measure achieves the level of protection chosen by the importing government. This provides a valuable opportunity for exporting countries that often face impenetrable regulatory systems in importing countries.[38]

The transparency requirement

SPS Annex B requires governments imposing a regulation to notify the WTO and to allow time for affected governments to make comments and for the regulators to take such comments into account. In addition, governments are required (except in urgent circumstances) to allow a reasonable interval between the publication of a regulation and its enforcement date.

In focusing on these seven core SPS disciplines, this chapter does not cover numerous other SPS rules. There is too much to explain in one short chapter. But there is one other SPS provision—regarding provisional measures—that needs to be discussed. Article 5.7 provides that, "in cases where relevant scientific evidence is insufficient," a government may "provisionally adopt sanitary or phytosanitary measures on the basis of available pertinent information." In such circumstances, the government is required to obtain additional information necessary for a more objective assessment of risk and to review the SPS measure within a reasonable period of time. This provision is a qualified exemption from Articles 2.2 and 5.1.

The first country to invoke Article 5.7 was Japan in the *Agricultural Products* case. The panel rejected this claim and was upheld by the Appellate Body. The Appellate Body stated that Japan had not obtained information on the key point of whether or not different varieties experience dissimilar quarantine effects. It is interesting to note that the panel suggested that it was up to the United States (the plaintiff) to establish that Japan had not complied with Article 5.7.[39]

A discussion of Article 5.7 provides a good window for introducing the Precautionary Principle, which is central to this provision and perhaps also relevant to SPS as a whole. The precautionary principle is a key tenet of modern environmental policy. As articulated in the Rio Declaration on Environment and Development (Principle 15), it states that, "where there are threats of serious or irreversible damage, lack of full scientific certainty shall not be used as a reason for postponing cost-effective measures to prevent environmental degradation." In the *Hormones* dispute, the EU defended its failure to follow Article 5.1 by calling attention to the precautionary principle, which it characterized as a rule of customary international law. The panel responded that, even if it were part of customary international law, the precautionary principle would not override Article 5.1, particularly since the precautionary principle had been incorporated into Article 5.7.[40] The Appellate Body agreed with this conclusion and offered some additional observations about the precautionary principle. First, it found that it was not clear that the precautionary principle had crystallized into a general principle of customary international law. Secondly, it found that, outside of environmental law, the status of the precautionary principle awaits more authoritative formulation. Thirdly, it stated that the precautionary principle had not been written into the SPS Agreement as a ground for justifying a measure that otherwise violates SPS. Fourthly, it found that the precautionary principle "finds reflection" in SPS Article 5.7, but that this provision does not exhaust the relevance of the precautionary principle for SPS.[41] Fifthly, the Appellate Body counsels panels considering whether or not "sufficient scientific evidence" exists to bear in mind that responsible, representative governments commonly act from perspectives of prudence and precaution where risks are irreversible. The Appellate Body counterbalances this point, however, by stating that the precautionary principle does not by itself relieve a panel from applying principles of treaty interpretation. What all these dicta add up to must await clarification in a future case.

3. Appraisal of SPS dispute settlement

SPS dispute settlement is providing good results for producers in exporting countries. Three long-time complaints have been brought to the WTO and been adjudicated in favour of the exporter. Additional exports have not yet ensued, but could within a year or two. Of course, the impact of SPS is seen not only in the cases that go to panels, but also in actions taken by importing countries to avoid panels.[42] Even in disputes where the losing defendant fails to change its import ban (e.g. hormones), there is still benefit in having the WTO issue a ruling.

Consumers are also gaining from SPS. When unjustified import bans are removed, consumers secure greater access to meat, salmon, fruit, etc. that they are now being denied. This will presumptively result in lower prices and/or more choices. It may be true, as some consumer groups allege, that SPS rules can hurt consumers and citizens by reducing their sense of self-government. Yet, although SPS can be anti-democratic in this way, it can be pro-democratic in vindicating the volitions of uninformed consumers who can be politically overpowered by special interests seeking an unjustified SPS measure. SPS could also be pro-democratic in mandating risk assessments that will give citizens greater opportunity to participate in reasoned decision-making.[43]

In mandating science-based analysis, the WTO will promote global economic welfare. So it is unfortunate that this respect for science does not permeate other areas of WTO law. Aside from the SPS Agreement and the review of environmental measures under GATT Article XX, the scientific basis for government regulations is not being scrutinized elsewhere in the WTO system. For example, is there a scientific justification for the WTO to condemn "dumping" in a broad definition that includes the practice of selling a product at less than its cost of production when that prevents price increases in the country of importation? Is there a scientific basis for the WTO to require governments to issue patents for at least 20 years?

Champions of SPS say that no health interests have been sacrificed because the overruled import bans were unjustified. But, until new imports enter, no one can know for sure. Suppose that Australia complies with the WTO ruling, allows in Canadian salmon, and then suffers a huge loss from foreign salmon disease. Who would bear the cost of the WTO panel being wrong about the danger of alien pathogens? Not the panel surely. Not the Canadian exporter. Not the WTO. No, it would be Australia that would suffer that cost. In pointing this out, this chapter is not suggesting that three WTO judges sitting in Geneva are less competent to weigh the risk of salmon disease than Tasmanian salmon fishers. Rather, the point here is that resolving the legal dispute is not equivalent to resolving the health dispute.

The health dispute gets resolved by a real world experiment that has financial liability for Australia but none for the WTO. One wonders whether the WTO dispute system might be rounded out by providing some financial insurance for Australia. If Australia were violating SPS Article 2.2, then insurers presumably would recognize the insignificant sanitary threat from imports and would agree to insure the Australian salmon industry. It would be an interesting market test of WTO dispute settlement to see how costly such disease insurance would be.

The process used by SPS panels is reasonable except for one flaw—its secretive, closed nature. It seems contradictory for governments to make sanitary decisions with open, transparent procedures and then have them reviewed at the WTO behind closed doors. Although this problem is common to all WTO dispute settlement, it is perhaps most acute in the area of health and environment. Not only are panel sessions closed, but panels so far have been unwilling to entertain *amicus curiae* briefs submitted by non-governmental organizations (NGOs). For example, when an NGO submitted an *amicus* brief to the *Hormones* panel, it was rejected by the WTO Secretariat. This may change as a result of the Appellate Body's decision in the *Turtle* case that panels may consider unsolicited NGO briefs.[44] A willingness to consider *amicus* briefs is one of many procedural changes needed before the public will accept the WTO as a food safety tribunal.

Another process problem is that, once a panel rules against a defendant government, there are no procedures for that government to introduce new scientific evidence. An inadequate risk assessment or a risk assessment that does not demonstrate risk are both deficiencies that are potentially curable. But a government that believes that re-doing the risk assessment achieves compliance may find it difficult to present this new evidence to the Appellate Body or the WTO Dispute Settlement Body.[45]

So far, no SPS litigation has involved a developing country.[46] In part, this may be due to the provision in SPS Article 14 giving the least developed countries until the year 2000 to comply.[47] A bit harder to explain is the lack of developing country plaintiffs. Surely there are numerous questionable SPS barriers that impede exports to industrial countries? One answer is that it is very difficult to lodge an SPS case against a rich country. Because SPS dispute settlement is so complicated, countries with large governmental legal staffs that are repeat litigants will have the advantage in SPS adjudication. (The new Advisory Centre on WTO law could redress this imbalance.)

In noting this situation, this chapter is not suggesting that developing countries begin filing SPS lawsuits. The economic harm from unjustified SPS measures is surely small compared with the economic harm from unabashedly protectionist barriers such as tariffs, quotas, and subsidies. Thus, looking at the position of developing countries, they can gain more from demanding better compliance with the WTO Agreement on Textiles and Clothing than from better compliance with SPS.

4. Appraisal of WTO activities on food safety

The biggest barrier to greater trade in food is not unjustified government regulation. Rather, it is unsafe food. The government in the exporting country should take greater responsibility for assuring the salubrious condition of its food exports. With its legal sovereignty over the process of food production, the exporting government is the lowest-cost avoider.

So far, the WTO has conceived its role narrowly as facilitating world food trade (which is about 9 per cent of total world merchandise trade). In this frame, food safety is the responsibility of the importing country. But the WTO could broaden its role by better coordination with other international organizations. For example, the Codex Alimentarius Commission has promulgated a Code of Ethics for International Trade in Food. Among its principles is that "[n]o food should be in international trade" that has in it any substance "which renders it poisonous, harmful or otherwise injurious to health."[48]

The WTO needs to address the popular misperception that it may undermine consumer health. To do so, the WTO should reposition itself to promote the safety of food in international trade. The legal bases for doing so already exist. SPS Article 3.1 directs governments to base their SPS measures on international standards. SPS Article 3.5 directs the WTO's SPS Committee to coordinate efforts on harmonization with relevant international organizations. SPS Article 10.4 calls on governments to facilitate the active participation of developing countries in relevant international organizations (among the relevant organizations are the World Health Organization and the Food and Agriculture Organization[49]). SPS Article 9 memorializes a commitment by governments to consider providing technical assistance to developing countries to enable producers to meet the health standards in export markets. SPS Article 12.2 directs the SPS Committee to sponsor technical consultations with the objective of increasing coordination in the use of food additives or establishing tolerances for contaminants in foods, beverages, and feedstuffs.

The SPS Committee is the proper institution for expanding the WTO role. In its March 1999 report, the Committee stressed the need for enhanced technical assistance to developing countries, particularly with regard to human resource development, national capacity-building, and the transfer of technology and information.[50] But the Committee itself has accomplished very little along these lines. In Seattle, the Committee could be invigorated by giving it a broader mandate and authorizing more coordination with external agencies. Although several intergovernmental organizations have sought closer cooperation with the Committee—for example, the Latin American Economic System—the Committee has been very slow to approve applications for observer status.[51] Equally disturbing is the Committee's unwillingness to approve observer status for NGOs. At least two NGOs have already sought such status: the International Meat Secretariat and the International Seed Federation. Many food and biosafety NGOs would apply if they thought that the WTO would cooperate with them.

Higher food safety standards could strengthen the WTO through win–win solutions. Although such standards are needed throughout the world, it is in developing countries that the regulatory regimes are weakest.[52] By working with those countries to implement international food safety standards, the WTO could reduce potential barriers to food exports by those countries.

5. Further issues for Seattle

Although everything in this chapter is an issue for Seattle, this final section discusses three controversial issues in the current worldwide debate about SPS. They are: SPS Article 5.5 on regulatory consistency, product labelling, and the precautionary principle.

Regulatory consistency

Article 5.5 is more likely to hurt the trading system than to help it. The idea behind scrutinizing regulatory consistency might have been a good one. But both panels enforcing Article 5.5 used flimsy grounds to find violations. Whereas the first decision (*Hormones*) was overturned by the Appellate Body, the second (*Salmon*) was not. Yet, even if the panels had acted on good evidence, one wonders whether the game is worth the candle. In conducting an intrusive examination into national regulatory consistency, an SPS panel is bound to provoke public concern about the loss in regulatory autonomy. And to what end? Is inconsistency in sanitary policy so bad that the WTO must come down hard on it? If the WTO is to become a policy consistency policeman, surely there are many self-contradictory trade policies that deserve greater attention than whether Australia tolerates more risk in herring than it does for salmon.

Actually, there is an easy way out of this problem. As noted above, Article 5.5 directs the Committee to develop guidelines to further the practical implementation of Article 5.5. Since the SPS Committee has not yet been able to develop such guidelines, the Seattle Ministerial Conference should consider calling a moratorium on any further Article 5.5 lawsuits.

Product labelling

It is unclear how SPS regulates product labelling. In its definition of SPS measures, the Agreement includes "packaging and labelling requirements directly related to food safety." The implication is that other labelling requirements are unregulated by SPS. For example, labelling for animal safety or for general consumer information would seem to be regulated, if at all, by other WTO agreements such as TBT and GATT. But no panel has yet clarified this point.

For food safety labels, there is a difference of opinion as to what the SPS requires. The US government's position seems to be that "[r]equiring labeling when there is no health or safety risk discriminates against products produced through biotechnology and suggests a health risk when there is none."[53] Other governments have a more tolerant attitude toward requirements for factual labels and consider a GMO labelling requirement to be WTO legal.

In general, product labels are a market-friendly measure. Providing consumers with additional information empowers them to make decisions according to their own self-interest. Although a labelling requirement is coercive when the manufacturer would prefer not to disclose the information, there is far less coercion from labelling than from banning a product. Recently, the Codex Alimentarius Commission has been trying to reach agreement on a GMO labelling standard.[54] One roadblock is the uncertainty about what WTO rules require.

It may be true that gratifying consumer inquisitiveness with unnecessary information can be counterproductive because consumers will make poor choices with that information. But, even so, it is hard to see how the WTO can take a stand against any food-labelling requirement when it allows governments to require labels disclosing the country of origin. Such national origin labels can lead to consumer discrimination against imports.

The precautionary principle

As noted above, the Appellate Body held that the precautionary principle finds reflection in SPS Article 5.7, which states that, where scientific evidence is insufficient, governments may provisionally adopt sanitary measures based on pertinent information. This article provides leeway to an interventionist-minded government worried about risk. At this early stage of SPS adjudication, there is no reason to conclude that the existing language in Article 5.7 is inadequate. Thus, proposals either to tighten this article by requiring more science or to loosen it by deleting the word "provisionally" are premature.

More problematic are proposals explicitly to incorporate the precautionary principle into Article 5.7. As articulated in the Rio Convention, the precautionary principle contemplates a consideration of cost-effectiveness in justifying precautionary measures. Indeed, the European Commission acknowledges that "[m]easures based on the Precautionary Principle must include a cost/benefit assessment."[55] But one of the distinctive features of SPS is that it does not mandate the use of cost–benefit analysis.[56] One wonders if the consumer groups demanding SPS recognition of the precautionary principle have reflected on the fact that, because bio-engineered foods provide clear benefits, a proposal to bar their entry might fail a cost-effectiveness test. The excessive attention to an SPS precautionary principle is lamentable because it distracts attention from actions needed to address real food safety threats that have already been demonstrated through science.

In view of the conflicting policy currents, there is doubt about whether or not the SPS Agreement will be "reopened" in Seattle. Although many governments are unhappy with particular aspects of SPS, there may be insufficient consensus on any specific change. Moreover, there are generalized fears that a rewrite of SPS might make things "worse." So the governments could well agree in Seattle to make no decisions about SPS and to consider only minor changes to SPS in the forthcoming round.

6. Conclusion

In adjudicating SPS complaints, the WTO may gain a reputation as a naysayer to food safety regulation. Every time it declares an SPS measure to be WTO illegal, there will be consumers who lament a perceived loss in health security. Already there are many NGOs around the world that oppose the WTO because they believe that it privileges trade over a healthy environment.

Inattention to SPS in Seattle would be a missed opportunity. The benefits of science-based standards need to be better explained to the public. The SPS Committee should conduct its work more openly and with greater participation by interested stakeholders. The WTO should expand the cooperative aspects of SPS so that people can buy foreign food and eat it safely.

Notes

1. The views expressed are those of the author only.
2. For example, on 3 July 1999, US President Bill Clinton gave an address to the nation announcing new actions to keep out unsafe foreign food. The President noted that "some importers are sidestepping our laws and getting contaminated food across our borders and onto our kitchen tables."
3. See David A. Wirth, "The Role of Science in the Uruguay Round and NAFTA Trade Disciplines," *Cornell International Law Journal* 27, 1994, 817, 835–836, 845.
4. *EC–Measures Concerning Meat and Meat Products (Hormones),* Report of the Panel, WT/DS26 and WT/DS48; modified by Report of the Appellate Body, AB-1997-4, 16 January 1998 (hereinafter Appellate Body *Hormones* Decision).
5. "EU Panel Finds Beef Hormones Harmful; U.S. Sees Ploy to Avoid WTO Deadline," *World Food Regulation Review* 9(1), June 1999, 3.
6. *Australia–Measures Affecting the Importation of Salmon,* Report of the Panel, WT/DS18; modified by Report of the Appellate Body, AB-1998-5, 20 October 1998 (hereinafter Appellate Body *Salmon* Decision).
7. *Japan–Measures Affecting Agricultural Products,* Report of the Panel, WT/DS76; modified by Report of the Appellate Body, AB-1998-8, 22 February 1999 (hereinafter Appellate Body *Agricultural Products* Decision).
8. See Terence P. Stewart and David S. Johanson, "The SPS Agreement of the World Trade Organization and the International Trade of Dairy Products," *Food and Drug Journal* 54, 1999, 55, 68–70.
9. "U.S. Considers Filing WTO Complaint over EU Barriers to GMO Trade, USTR Says," *BNA Daily Report for Executives,* 25 June 1999, p. A-2.
10. Percy W. Bidwell, *The Invisible Tariff,* New York: Council on Foreign Relations, 1939, pp. 169–170.
11. Convention for the Protection of Plants, 16 April 1929, 126 L.N.T.S. 305, Arts. 4, 16.

12. Agreement on the Application of Sanitary and Phytosanitary Measures (SPS), in the Agreement Establishing the World Trade Organization, signed Marrakesh, 15 April 1994, Annex A.1.

13. Analysts suggesting that SPS regulates genetically modified organisms point to the SPS Annex A.1 definition, which states that SPS measures include processes and production methods. But it seems likely that this is meant to describe the range of SPS measures "relevant" to the covered risks, not to add additional risks.

14. The WTO Secretariat has devised a good flowchart showing how trade issues are split between SPS and TBT, and how some issues are unregulated by either. See World Trade Organization, *Sanitary and Phytosanitary Measures (WTO Agreement Series 4)*, Geneva: WTO, 1998, pp. 15–16.

15. Joost Pauwelyn, "The WTO Agreement on Sanitary and Phytosanitary (SPS) Measures as Applied in the First Three SPS Disputes," *Journal of International Economic Law* 2, 1999 (forthcoming).

16. Appellate Body *Hormones* Decision, paras. 113–118.

17. For example, see Vern R. Walker, "Keeping the WTO from Becoming the World Trans-science Organization: Scientific Uncertainty, Science Policy, and Fact-finding in the Growth Hormones Dispute," *Cornell International Law Journal* 31, 1998, 251, 283, and 286.

18. SPS Agreement, op. cit., Annex C, para. 1(a) strengthens this discipline by requiring that SPS approval and inspection measures be "completed without undue delay." This provision has not yet been applied by a WTO panel.

19. Appellate Body *Agricultural Products* Decision, para. 84.

20. Appellate Body *Hormones* Decision, para. 187; Appellate Body *Salmon* Decision, para. 124.

21. Appellate Body *Hormones* Decision, para. 194.

22. Appellate Body *Salmon* Decision, para. 124.

23. Appellate Body *Hormones* Decision, para. 187; Appellate Body *Salmon* Decision, para. 125.

24. Appellate Body *Hormones* Decision, para. 186.

25. Appellate Body *Salmon* Decision, para. 129.

26. Appellate Body *Hormones* Decision, para. 186; Appellate Body *Salmon* Decision, para. 124.

27. Appellate Body *Hormones* Decision, para. 206.

28. Ibid., paras. 206–208.

29. For a good discussion of the issues, written by the chairman of the *Hormones* panel, see Thomas Cottier, "SPS Risk Assessment and Risk Management in WTO Dispute Settlement: Experience and Lessons," 1999, unpublished draft.

30. Appellate Body *Hormones* Decision, paras. 186, 189, 193, 197, 253(L).

31. Ibid., para. 198 (and notes therein).

32. Appellate Body *Salmon* Decision, para. 138.

33. Alan O. Sykes, "Regulatory Protectionism and the Law of International Trade," *University of Chicago Law Review* 66, 1999, 1, 31–33.

34. Appellate Body *Hormones* Decision, para. 177.

35. Steve Charnovitz, "The World Trade Organization, Meat Hormones, and Food Safety," *International Trade Reporter* 14, 15 October 1997, 1781–1787.

36. Appellate Body *Salmon* Decision, para. 152.

37. Some commentators have criticized the Appellate Body for making it so easy for governments to use a more stringent regulation than an international standard. For example, see Ryan David Thomas, "Where's the Beef? Mad Cows and the Blight of the SPS Agreement," *Vanderbilt Journal of Transnational Law* 32, March 1999, 487, 507–516.

38. "27 Nations Seek Equivalence Status to Open U.S. Doors to Meat, Poultry," *World Food Regulation Review* 8(12), May 1999, 13.

39. *Japan–Measures Affecting Agricultural Products,* Report of the Panel, op. cit., para. 8.58.

40. *EC–Measures Concerning Meat and Meat Products (Hormones),* Report of the Panel, op cit., para. 8.157.

41. Appellate Body *Hormones* Decision, para. 124.

42. For example, see "Fearing Trade Disputes, EU Suspends Deadline on Salmonellosis Programs," *World Food Regulation Review* 8, May 1999, 5.

43. Robert Howse, "Democracy, Science, and Free Trade: Risk Regulation on Trial at the World Trade Organization," 1999, unpublished draft.

44. *United States–Import Prohibition of Certain Shrimp and Shrimp Products,* Report of the Appellate Body, AB-1998-4, 12 October 1998, para. 110.

45. The WTO Dispute Settlement Understanding, Articles 21.5, 21.6, 22.2, and 22.8, contains the available rules, but there are no specific procedures for a declaratory judgment that a new risk assessment puts a government into compliance with SPS.

46. Two cases were lodged against Korea, but were settled early in the panel process. The cases involved shelf-life requirements and bottled water.

47. India has asked that this deadline be extended. Note that SPS Article 10 calls for Special and Differential Treatment to developing countries.

48. Code of Ethics for International Trade in Food, CAC/RCP 20-1979, Rev. 1 (1985), Art. 4.2(a).

49. SPS Agreement, op. cit., p. 27.

50. World Trade Organization, *Review of the Operation and Implementation of the Agreement on the Application of Sanitary and Phytosanitary Measures, Report of the Committee on Sanitary and Phytosanitary Measures,* G/SPS/12, 11 March 1999, para. 9.

51. World Trade Organization, *Report (1998) on the Activities of the Committee on Sanitary and Phytosanitary Measures,* G/L/274, 16 November 1998, para. 2.

52. Linda R. Horton, "Food from Developing Countries: Steps to Improve Compliance," *Food and Drug Law Journal* 53, 1998, 139–171.

53. US Trade Representative, *National Trade Estimate Report on Foreign Trade Barriers,* Washington, DC: Office of the US Trade Representative, 1999, pp. 225–226.

54. "Codex Alimentarius: Setting Food Safety Standards for Global Trade," *Bridges* 3(4), May 1999, 1.

55. European Commission, "Guidelines on the Application of the Precautionary Principle," 17 October 1998, p. 9. It is interesting to note that, in the context of food safety, the government of Sweden has presented a formulation of the precautionary principle that does not include cost–benefit analysis, but does call for a "proportionate" response. Codex Alimentarius Commission, *Report of the 14th Session of the Codex Committee on General Principles,* ALINORM 99/33A, April 1999, para. 28.

56. See Wayne Jones, "Weigh up the Costs and Benefits," *OECD Observer,* No. 216, March 1999, 30.

8

Environmental Labelling Schemes: WTO Law and Developing Country Implications

Arthur E. Appleton

1. Introduction

Product labelling schemes are rapidly becoming more common. Traditionally labels have been employed to alert consumers to health and safety considerations. Increasingly labels are also being employed to provide information reflecting social policy concerns, for example environmental or labour characteristics associated with a particular product. This chapter explores the developing country implications of environmental labelling schemes. Labour-related labelling issues are also touched upon when relevant.

Environmental labelling schemes alert consumers to particular environmental issues and serve to popularize environmental issues among producers, consumers, and government officials. Examples include eco-labelling schemes (labels reflecting environmental characteristics associated with various stages in a product's life cycle) and single-issue labels (labels that relate to one aspect in a product's life cycle), e.g. that a can of tuna is "dolphin safe" or a product recyclable.

The proliferation of environmental labelling schemes has raised economic concerns among developing countries. There is fear that meeting the norms furthered by foreign labelling schemes will be technically difficult. There is also concern that it will be financially costly—particularly if labelling standards differ among importers. Finally, there is a preoccupation that the labelling of certain products will result in consumer discrimination against unlabelled products, and that many of these products will be from countries in the developing world that have not met certain environmental or labour standards strongly supported by the developed world. This is expected to have adverse economic implications for developing countries. Indeed, the purpose of many labelling schemes is to make it easier for consumers to discriminate against products that do not meet selected environmental or labour norms. Because such norms, or higher norms, are often more likely to be found in the developed world, manufacturers of products in the developing world, as well as their government officials, are inclined to view such measures as potentially protectionist. Opinions are therefore split, frequently along North–South lines, concerning the acceptability of labelling schemes for social policy purposes.

For some time there has been a growing likelihood of a trade dispute wherein the legality under the Marrakesh Agreement Establishing the World Trade Organization ("WTO Agreement")[1] of an eco-labelling scheme will be tested. The battle lines in the WTO are generally drawn along economic lines. A preliminary legal analysis of the problem has been undertaken by the WTO's Committee on Trade and Environment. Now it is only a matter of time before a WTO member launches an attack on an eco-labelling programme that it views as discriminatory. Such a dispute would pose risks to the WTO as an institution, pitting developing country growth, consumer rights, environmental and social norms, free speech considerations, and trade rules against one another. Regardless of the outcome, respect for the WTO will diminish, either among developing countries or in the environmental and labour communities of the developed world. The alternative is that the members negotiate a solution to labelling questions before the Appellate Body is asked to find one.

In this chapter, relevant terms are defined, policy issues examined, applicable WTO rules discussed, and suggestions offered on how labelling questions might be addressed in future multilateral trade negotiations. In order to prevent the discussion from becoming too technical, legal issues are simplified. Nevertheless, certain important trade law concepts are addressed.

2. Terminology

Labelling terminology

There is no agreed terminology applicable to environmental labelling schemes. Recent experience with environmental labelling schemes and studies of such schemes by various organizations have however begun to yield some accord on the use of terms.[2] Environmental labelling schemes, whether voluntary or mandatory, are often divided into three groups: single-issue labels, negative labels, and eco-labels. These terms are explained below.

1. *Single-issue labels:* alert consumers about a particular issue, for example whether a product is recyclable, biodegradable, or "dolphin safe." They can also inform consumers about a particular performance-related characteristic; for example, automobile gas mileage, emissions, or electricity consumption.

2. *Negative labels:* alert consumers about dangerous or other negative characteristics; for example, "cigarettes are dangerous to your health," "drinking during pregnancy can cause foetal damage," "poison," or "do not inhale fumes."

3. *Eco-labels:* are granted by a public or private body to particular products based on a life-cycle analysis.[3] Eco-labels are awarded to what a granting authority deems to be environmentally superior products in a particular category (usually not more than 10–15 per cent of the products in a category). In theory, eco-labels rely on market forces (consumers) to promote products determined to be environmentally friendlier. Participation in eco-labelling schemes is assumed to be voluntary. The first eco-labelling scheme, the "Blue Angel," was created in Germany in 1977. Eco-labelling programmes, in various forms, are now prevalent throughout the developed world and increasingly in the developing world.[4] They remain controversial, in part because domestic schemes have the potential to influence foreign production practices.

The above terminology, although frequently repeated in the literature, is not entirely satisfactory. First, there is potential for overlap between single-issue and negative labels. Should a label reading "Made from genetically modified organisms" or "Cattle fed natural hormones" be classified as a single-issue or a negative label? The answer to this question may depend on scientific analyses that are not yet conclusive. Secondly, there is a growing realization that the term "environment" is now being applied very broadly. Growth in scientific understanding has led to an expansion of what is considered to be environmental in nature. The result is an increase in what is perceived scientifically to relate to the environment and what might be reflected on a label. Thirdly, there is no guarantee that the life-cycle analysis used in a given eco-labelling scheme will take into consideration only social factors that are strictly environmental in nature; for example, certain labour issues (perhaps with distant environmental implications) might be assessed. It is easy to imagine a labelling authority examining production-related working conditions (e.g. employee exposure to hazardous chemicals or child labour issues) when deciding whether to award an eco-label. One reason certain developing countries oppose eco-labelling schemes is fear that the continued growth in the popularity of eco-labelling schemes will open the door wider for other forms of labelling, in particular labels that reflect labour-related issues. This fear is reinforced by the realization that certain child labour practices are already the subject of labelling campaigns. This point will be returned to when policy issues are discussed.

PPM terminology

Among the most controversial trade issues is whether a WTO member should be permitted to apply its trade policy to influence the selection of manufacturing processes in other countries—so-called foreign "processes and production methods" (PPMs). Certain environmental labelling schemes provide a means of discriminating between products based on how they are made by informing consumers when production methods do not meet particular environmental, labour, or other criteria. Changes in demand for a product may influence the selection of production methods.

From the trade law perspective, this issue is intertwined with the "like product" distinction made, among other places, in Articles I:1 and III:4 of the 1947 General Agreement on Tariffs and Trade (GATT 1947).[5] The concept of "like products" is critical for an understanding of the PPM question because the GATT Agreement restricts the right to discriminate between and among foreign and domestic like products, and past GATT/WTO practice has generally relied upon an examination of a product itself (as opposed to how it is made) in determining whether two products are alike ("like products").[6] The result has been that "processes and production methods" that cannot be detected in the final product are generally not examined in the like product determination.

If a PPM causes a change detectable in the product itself, trade experts classify the PPM as "product related" or "incorporated." If a PPM cannot be found in the product itself, it is said to be "non product related" (NPR-PPM) or "unincorporated." PPM questions must be seen against the fact that, with a few notable exceptions (e.g. intellectual property matters and products made by prison labour), goods have not generally been distinguished for purposes of the WTO Agreement based on PPMs unless the PPMs are detectable in the final product ("product related"). In other words, a widget is a widget regardless of how it is made, unless the manufacture of the widget changes some important characteristic detectable in the widget itself. More specifically, for WTO purposes trade lawyers would distinguish automobiles based on fuel efficiency or exhaust emissions, but not based on the sulphur dioxide emissions used to make the steel in a given vehicle.

Whereas from an environmental or labour perspective the disregard for non-product-related PPMs in the like product determination may be subject to criticism, from the trade perspective it is justified on the grounds that differentiating between goods based on NPR-PPMs would increase trade barriers and result in increased trade discrimination. Treating a car differently based on how it is made, as opposed to how efficiently it operates, would provide a new basis for trade discrimination. Developing countries have been particularly adamant in opposing trade restrictions based on NPR-PPMs out of fear that they would lose economically. In part this is because the technical capacity and capital to meet the stringent production standards that exist in certain developed countries may be lacking. This opposition is also based on the realization that, if standards for NPR-PPMs differed greatly among countries, economies of scale would diminish. If Countries A and B establish different production-related environmental standards for widgets, a widget producer in Country C might have to build two separate factories in order to export to both Country A and Country B.

WTO members have little problem with the idea that a particular state can regulate production processes within its own jurisdiction, or that a member can establish performance-related environmental standards applicable to products within its own jurisdiction. Controversies arise when a member seeks to apply its laws to influence production processes and methods outside its jurisdiction. These problems tend to be more serious when the member seeking to apply its standards abroad is a major market for the product in question.

Eco-labelling schemes (schemes based on a life-cycle analysis) have aroused particular concern among developing countries because they provide a means of permitting consumers to discriminate against goods based on NPR-PPMs. This issue will be returned to in the discussion of policy issues that follows.

3. Policy issues

Several important policy issues have already been noted. It should be evident by now that, in theory, eco-labelling schemes rely on market forces (changes in consumption patterns) to influence production practices. Products are labelled to affect consumer purchasing habits, i.e. demand. By affecting demand, changes may occur relative to supply—producers and suppliers may choose to become more environmentally "responsible" when consumers become environmentally more discerning. Thus viewed, one goal of eco-labelling schemes is demand-side discrimination against certain products in order to alter the supply side of the economic equation.

Most evidence on the effectiveness of eco-labelling schemes is anecdotal in nature. Nevertheless, developing countries fear the potential discriminatory implications of labelling schemes. Providing consumers with the ability to discriminate against products perceived to be less environmentally sound is a source of worry for developing countries for the technical and financial reasons alluded to above. Producers in developing countries may also lack the resources and political expertise to influence the development of foreign labelling criteria, and may find it difficult from a linguistic and cultural perspective to inform themselves about the requirements of foreign labelling schemes and to participate in these schemes.[7] In other words, information asymmetries may influence participation in particular schemes. Local manufacturers are more likely to be aware of the criteria being applied in a particular scheme, and are often better positioned politically to influence the selection of applicable criteria.

Developing countries are also concerned because of the perceived tendency of developed countries to formulate eco-labelling criteria based on conditions in the developed world, or only in the labelling state.[8] Flexibility is necessary to assure that labelling criteria also reflect the conditions prevailing in developing countries. This flexibility may be lacking in certain developed country programmes, particularly when protectionist interests influence the drafting of labelling criteria.

Complicating the problem are questions of comparative advantage. Wage considerations, regulatory requirements, and the enforcement of regulations are often viewed as sources of comparative advantage. Labelling schemes that alert consumers to serious discrepancies in the above may disadvantage certain developing countries.

Another potential problem is that eco-labelling schemes are likely to be of greater interest to the residents of developed countries—from the perspective of both demand and supply. From the demand perspective, increased discretionary income brings the luxury of selecting products based on factors other than price, including social and moral considerations. Assuming that many labelled products are more expensive to produce, and that they may command a premium price, it is probable that labelled products will be more expensive than competing unlabelled products, and as a result less likely to attract consumer interest in developing countries that have labelling schemes. On the supply side, to the extent that products labelled by a developed country are of interest to a developing country (often not the case because primary goods and agricultural products are frequently not labelled), for reasons mentioned above it may be difficult for developing countries to participate in foreign labelling schemes.

From the developing country perspective, eco-labelling schemes are particularly problematic. This is because, by definition, eco-labelling programmes evaluate environmental aspects of production processes—an area of potential weakness in some developing countries. Although the overall goal of such labelling schemes (using market forces to improve the environment) is laudable, certain risks exist for producers arising from what can be very subjective factors. For example:

- What should receive a greater weighting in a life-cycle analysis—factors associated with a product's production, use, or disposal?
- Should one evaluate transport-related criteria, given that this would seem to discriminate against many imports?
- How do you evaluate products produced using dirty or dangerous sources of energy?
- How do you evaluate foreign production processes that may be more suitable given a particular country's geographical, climatic, and other circumstances?
- More specifically, how do you evaluate products coming from countries at different levels of development and with different levels of technology?

Concern about the implications of single-issue labelling schemes is also present in certain special interest communities in the developed world, particularly those in industrial sectors, such as agribusiness, which fear labelling schemes will be used to discriminate against products in which they have invested heavily. For example, the labelling of foodstuffs produced with the aid of hormones or genetic engineering has those in the agribusiness, chemical, and biotechnology sectors worried. More generally, products with health risks, in particular tobacco and alcohol, have long been affected by various single-issue labelling schemes.

The policy considerations presented above are serious, but at this point there is little evidence to suggest that eco-labelling schemes have significantly altered consumer buying habits or manufacturing practices. Instead, fears concerning labelling schemes currently appear exaggerated. From the developing country perspective, the strong opposition in many quarters to labelling schemes may be a strategic decision. By keeping the attention of the trade community focused on eco-labelling, other more important issues, such as the internalization of environmental externalities and labour-related labelling, have been kept off the agenda.

Government officials and businessmen in the developing world and certain constituencies in the developed world may be preoccupied with the trade effects of environmental labelling schemes, but this is not to suggest that labelling schemes have received universal opposition, or that there are not important arguments in support of these schemes. Many in the environmental, labour, and consumer advocacy communities strongly support labelling schemes. The potential environmental advantages seem clear. To the extent that labelling informs consumers, influences consumption habits, and changes production processes in favour of environmentally superior products, labelling can play a beneficial role. The success of such schemes will, however, depend on many variables, including consumer acceptance, the willingness of manufacturers to change production processes, the availability of reasonably priced products of sufficient quality, adequate publicity, and effective developing country participation.

The potential benefits of eco-labelling programmes have led environmentalists to question uncertainties that arise pursuant to the WTO Agreement concerning the legal treatment of these schemes, in particular with respect to the treatment of NPR-PPMs. Environmentalists, as well as labour activists, would like states to have the freedom to use trade as a means of influencing foreign environmental and labour practices. They do not see why a consumer should be forced to buy a product manufactured in a manner that he or she would find objectionable if the PPMs were revealed through labelling.

Environmentalists have a second concern that is also rooted in a criticism of the WTO Agreement. They recognize that many environmental problems are trans-boundary or global in nature. This is because resources such as air and water are migratory, and production processes in one state may affect resources in another state. For example, forest resources, animal resources, and coastal and marine resources can be affected by environmental decisions taken in other countries. Environmentalists tend not to accept what they view as a jurisdictional limitation present in interpretations of the GATT/WTO Agreement (even if from the WTO perspective the limitation is framed otherwise) restricting a state's use of trade measures to protect the environment.

Consumer sentiment also favours environmental labelling programmes. From the consumer perspective, labelling furthers consumer awareness, empowers consumers to make better-informed choices, satisfies certain moral, political, and social convictions, and provides economic and social pressure, which may compel manufacturers to change production processes. Furthermore, some consumers view labelling as a form of advertising supported by freedom of speech considerations.

To what extent should those in one state be able to influence production methods in another state? From the perspectives of state sovereignty and trade policy, one might be inclined to take a restrictive view. Trade policy remains an essentially state-centric system. From an environmental or consumer perspective, however, the scope for action is arguably broader. Environmental issues, like human rights issues, challenge fundamental notions of state sovereignty and jurisdiction, owing in part to their cross-border implications. The intersection between trade and environmental issues is, from a strictly legal perspective, an instance of two cultures colliding. Environmental labelling, or more correctly the questions of international trade and environmental law that lie beneath labelling questions, is not necessarily clear or logical when viewed from the perspective of the other system or culture. The WTO perspective, including the uncertainties that have arisen in the application of international trade law to labelling, is examined below.

4. Legal issues—The WTO Agreement

No eco-labelling scheme has ever been challenged before the GATT or the WTO, although a single-issue labelling scheme was challenged in the first *Tuna-Dolphin* dispute,[9] and labelling did arise as an issue in the *Malt Beverages* panel.[10] In light of the limited GATT/WTO practice concerning labelling, the comments that follow are somewhat speculative in nature but should offer insight into various potential challenges and possible results. They are meant to provide an overview of the applicable law and the points left to be resolved, either through dispute settlement proceedings or, preferably, through future negotiations.

One starting point in an analysis of the legality of eco-labelling schemes is the Report of the WTO Committee on Trade and Environment (CTE) produced for the 1996 Singapore Ministerial Meeting. Paragraph 183 of this report (containing Conclusions and Recommendations applicable to labelling programmes) reads in part: "Well-designed eco-labelling schemes/programmes can be effective instruments of environmental policy to encourage the development of an environmentally-conscious consumer public."[11] This statement is both non-binding and carefully drafted. Not only does it say nothing about the WTO-legality of eco-labelling schemes, but paragraph 185 of the same report reveals the discord in the CTE with respect to the treatment of the NPR-PPM component of eco-labelling schemes.

Three other points of departure offer better starting points for an analysis of the legality of eco-labelling schemes: the Preamble to the WTO Agreement,[12] the relevant provisions of GATT 1947, which is now a part of GATT 1994,[13] and the Agreement on Technical Barriers to Trade (TBT Agreement).[14] The Preamble will be discussed first. Then the legality of labelling schemes will be addressed first from the perspective of GATT (where many of the principles found in the TBT Agreement originate), and then from the perspective of the TBT Agreement. This mirrors the approach of recent WTO dispute settlement reports, which have avoided examining TBT issues despite the fact that the TBT Agreement enjoys a higher legal precedence than GATT 1994 in the event of a conflict between the two.

Preamble

The Preamble of the WTO Agreement acknowledges the need to allow "for the optimal use of the world's resources in accordance with the objective of sustainable development, seeking both to protect and preserve the environment."[15] In an earlier work, I concluded that the inclusion of environmental language in the Preamble was probably not intended to alter the fundamental balance of rights and obligations that existed pursuant to GATT 1947, in particular with respect to developing country members.[16] This conclusion must now be re-examined in light of the Appellate Body's decision in the *Shrimp-Turtle* dispute.[17] In *Shrimp-Turtle,* the Appellate Body found that the Preamble's environmental language "reflects the intentions of negotiators of the WTO Agreement" and "must add colour, texture and shading to our interpretation of the agreements annexed to the WTO Agreement, in this case, the GATT 1994."[18] It then took account of the Preamble's language as part of the context of GATT Article XX's chapeau.[19]

It is difficult to second guess to what extent the Appellate Body will be influenced by the Preamble's language when confronted with a challenge to an environmental labelling scheme. Suffice it to say that the Appellate Body is now on record as having recognized the importance of the Preamble when interpreting the rights and obligations of members under the WTO Agreement (which includes the TBT Agreement) and under GATT 1994 (which includes GATT 1947). This would suggest that, in borderline situations, environmental labelling schemes may receive the benefit of the doubt.

GATT Article I ("General Most-Favoured-Nation Treatment")

GATT Article I, which provides for most-favoured-nation (MFN) treatment, ensures that a trade privilege extended to one member is extended to all members. Article I:1 prohibits a member from using financial and regulatory measures as a means of discriminating against "like products" from one member in favour of like products from another member. With respect to mandatory labelling requirements, the effect of Article I:1 is to assure that labelling requirements applicable to the imports of one member are applicable to like products imported from all members. Likewise, a voluntary labelling programme open to one member must generally be open to like products from all members on similar terms.[20]

A voluntary environmental labelling scheme reflecting an NPR-PPM (whether or not tuna was "dolphin safe") withstood a challenge based on Article I:1 in the 1991 *Tuna-Dolphin* report.[21] The panel found that the voluntary US scheme at issue, which was promulgated by federal law, did not prevent tuna products from being sold freely with or without the "dolphin-safe" label; nor did the scheme establish requirements that had to be met to obtain an advantage from the US government. Any advantage that occurred was due to consumer choice.[22]

The 1991 *Tuna-Dolphin* report was never adopted by the GATT contracting parties. Unadopted GATT panel reports have been found by the Appellate Body to have "no legal status in the GATT or WTO system," but the Appellate Body has found that a panel "could nevertheless find useful guidance in the reasoning of an unadopted panel report that it considered to be relevant."[23]

GATT Article III ("National Treatment on Internal Taxation and Regulation")

GATT Article III contains the "national treatment" obligation. This provision is intended to ensure that imported like products are treated no less favourably than like domestic products with respect to the application of internal taxes, charges, "laws, regulations and requirements affecting the internal sale, offering for sale, purchase, transportation, distribution or use of products." The goal is to prevent internal measures from being applied so as to afford protection to domestic production.[24] The Appellate Body noted in the *Alcoholic Beverages* report that:

> The broad and fundamental purpose of Article III is to avoid protectionism in the application of internal tax and regulatory measures. More specifically, the purpose of Article III "is to ensure that internal measures 'not be applied to imported or domestic products so as to afford protection to domestic production.'" Toward this end, Article III obliges Members of the WTO to provide equality of competitive conditions for imported products in relation to domestic products. "[T]he intention of the drafters of the Agreement was clearly to treat the imported products in the same way as the like domestic products once they had been cleared through customs. Otherwise indirect protection could be given." . . . Article III protects expectations not of any particular trade volume but rather of the equal competitive relationship between imported and domestic products. Members of the WTO are free to pursue their own domestic goals through internal taxation or regulation so long as they do not do so in a way that violates Article III or any of the other commitments they have made in the WTO Agreement.[25]

Article III:4 has particular relevance for mandatory labelling schemes. This provision assures that laws, regulations, and requirements affecting the internal sale, offering for sale, purchase, transportation, distribution, or use are not applied so as to accord less favourable treatment to imported over domestic like products. The concepts of "like products" and "treatment no less favourable" are essential elements of Article III:4, and are also found in the TBT Agreement.

Like products

In determining whether two products are like products, the test set forth by the Working Party on Border Tax Adjustments[26] regained favour in the *Alcoholic Beverages* report. This test consists of determining likeness based on a case-by-case examination of factors such as a "product's end-uses in a given market; consumers' tastes and habits, which change from country-to-country; [and] the product's properties, nature and quality."[27] The like products test applied in the *Alcoholic Beverages* report leaves panels with less discretion to use the likeness determination as a means of protecting a member's domestic policy autonomy. Although the Appellate Body found in the *Alcoholic Beverages* report that the likeness standard "stretches and squeezes" like an "accordion" in different places in the WTO Agreement,[28] there is little reason to believe that this test, which was applied in conjunction with Article III:2 (taxes), would not be applied in an Article III:4 case (regulations), particularly in light of what appears to have been a conscious decision on the part of the Appellate Body to distance itself from the "aim and effect" approach taken by the *Malt Beverages*[29] and *Automobiles*[30] panels.

Article III:4 is applicable to product-related labelling requirements. Many in the environmental community would also like to see NPR-PPMs included in an Article III:4 assessment of "likeness." Past and recent GATT/WTO practice suggests that this is not a realistic expectation. This conclusion is supported by the findings of the unadopted 1991 and 1994 *Tuna-Dolphin* panels,[31] whose reasoning is at best a source of "useful guidance." Nevertheless, the reasoning of these panels appears to have won some acceptance from the United States, as evidenced by its decision not to argue at the panel stage that Article III:4 was applicable in the *Shrimp-Turtle* dispute.[32]

Excluding NPR-PPMs from the Article III:4 determination of likeness prevents members from arguing that a mandatory or voluntary labelling scheme reflecting NPR-PPMs that is applied equally to domestic and foreign products ("like products") would be in conformity with the national treatment obligation (and would not instead be subject to the requirements of GATT Article XI). From the perspective of international trade, this is a prudent outcome. If all products could be differentiated for likeness purposes based on NPR-PPMs, the WTO would become an international arbitrator of a broad range of "trade-related" social and political differences, be they environmental, labour, religious, or political in nature. This could rapidly undermine the effectiveness of the international trading system.

Treatment no less favourable

Assume we are dealing with a product-related labelling requirement applicable to two like products, one domestic and one imported; for example, the mandatory labelling of domestic and imported automobiles based on fuel consumed or emissions produced. Pursuant to Article III:4, there is an obligation to assure that the imported product is accorded "treatment no less favourable" than the like domestic product. This requires an examination of the conditions of competition—whether imported products are afforded "effective equality of opportunity" (treatment at least equal to that accorded like domestic products).[33]

Do labelling requirements affect the conditions of competition and have implications for the maintenance of effective equality of opportunity? This problem can be viewed from two perspectives: in terms of the general labelling requirements, and in terms of the specific information yielded by these requirements. Strictly speaking, mandatory product-related labelling requirements designed to reveal information, if applied in a fair, open, non-discriminatory, and transparent manner, do not *directly* affect the conditions of competition, nor do they have *direct* implications for the maintenance of effective equality of opportunity. This is because they do not prevent the sale of the good in question provided that it is labelled. They also do not have a *direct* effect on price, as would a tax. Furthermore, they do not impose less favourable regulatory treatment on imported products. All products, whether domestic or imported, would be subject to the same regulatory regime—they would each be required to bear a label revealing the same product-related characteristics.

Questions arise only when the analysis is taken one step further and the contents of the label are examined. Mandatory product-related labelling requirements are likely to reveal information that could result in consumer discrimination against a particular product (domestic or imported) based on performance-related characteristics. Viewed in this light, labelling schemes can have an *indirect* effect on price and competitiveness, and might *indirectly* affect the conditions of competition. Developing countries might find it particularly difficult to compete in such an environment if they lack the necessary financial and technical resources to manufacture products that meet the environmental expectations of consumers in the developed world.

Such a labelling requirement would not prevent products from being sold freely, nor would it establish requirements needed to procure a government-accorded advantage. It would only further the ability of consumers to make an informed decision based on product-related characteristics, and to discriminate against products based on this information. Successfully challenging such a scheme could be difficult. One approach might be to prove that a particular labelling requirement was purposefully designed by a government to reveal environmental deficiencies in foreign like products, with the expectation that consumers would accord these products less favourable treatment. This might require a showing of intentional abuse, in the form of a government attempt to protect or actively promote domestic production based on environmental superiority.

This is not necessarily a surprising result. WTO members have historically recognized the need to retain a certain degree of domestic policy autonomy. For example, there is acceptance among members that states must be able to apply domestic regulations to preserve natural resources and to protect the health and safety of their citizens.[34] In the *Malt Beverages* and *Automobiles* reports, this autonomy was assured by ruling that certain goods, distinguished on the basis of product-related characteristics for reasons other than protectionism, were not like products (therefore Article III did not apply). As a result of the Appellate Body decision in the *Alcoholic Beverages* dispute, this line of argument now appears to be closed,[35] but the need to retain a degree of domestic policy autonomy still exists, and it is possible that such autonomy may be preserved in the interpretation and application of the "treatment no less favourable" test.[36]

The GATT Article III legality of voluntary product-related labelling schemes, including the product-related portion of eco-labelling schemes, has been treated to some extent above, but requires a few additional comments. It has been argued that, like mandatory labelling requirements, voluntary labelling can discriminate against members with fewer technical and financial capabilities and thus affect the conditions of competition.[37] Although certain developing countries will find this argument attractive, it would probably be difficult to sustain before a panel or the Appellate Body.

First, it would need to be proven that voluntary labelling schemes constitute regulations or requirements for the purposes of Article III:4. This has not been established. Secondly, for the reasons noted above, it seems unlikely that a panel or the Appellate Body would find that likeness can be dependent on an NPR-PPM. This would suggest that NPR-PPMs in eco-labelling schemes would not be considered for Article III purposes in the event that the regulations or requirements establishing a voluntary eco-labelling scheme were deemed to fall within Article III. Thirdly, if certain mandatory labelling schemes are GATT consistent, it is probable that even more voluntary schemes would also be GATT consistent. Voluntary labelling programmes do not prevent products from being sold freely, nor do they establish requirements needed to procure a government-accorded advantage. They are designed to further the ability of consumers to make informed decisions. They are therefore less likely to affect the conditions of competition than mandatory schemes are.

In conclusion, without a showing of purposeful abuse of a voluntary labelling scheme, in particular purposeful government abuse, a finding by a dispute settlement body against such a scheme based on Article III:4 is unlikely. Given the large number of eco-labelling schemes already in existence, and the reputation of the WTO concerning environmental issues, ruling against an eco-labelling scheme based on Article III could pose political risks for the WTO system. In light of the above, a member that chooses to oppose a voluntary labelling scheme should instead be prepared to give greater emphasis to arguments arising under the TBT Agreement, particularly technical arguments concerning necessity, harmonization, notice, and transparency (discussed below), as opposed to broad policy arguments that are likely to raise controversial political issues.

GATT Article XI ("General Elimination of Quantitative Restrictions")

GATT Article XI sets forth a general prohibition on import and export restrictions other than duties, tariffs, and other charges. The intent of Article XI is to limit import restrictions to tariff-based measures, and to prohibit "most non-tariff measures from being applied against imports at the point of importation."[38] GATT Articles III and Article XI are mutually exclusive. Article III governs internal measures, including internal measures applied against imports at the point of importation,[39] whereas Article XI governs the importation of products. Article XI is generally deemed to be comprehensive, and is even applicable to non-mandatory measures where sufficient government incentives exist to encourage implementation.[40]

As noted in the discussion of Article III, it is probable that it is GATT Article XI and not GATT Article III that is applicable to non-product-related environmental labelling requirements. If this is the case, import restrictions, such as a requirement that NPR-PPMs be labelled as a prerequisite to import, would violate Article XI. Prohibiting the import of products that do not bear an eco-label would also violate Article XI to the extent that NPR-PPMs are part of the labelling criteria.

Voluntary labelling schemes, including the NPR-PPM component of eco-labelling schemes, are unlikely to violate Article XI. The only conceivable exception would be when there are sufficient government incentives to discourage the import of goods that do not bear the label in question—perhaps in the form of a government programme that stigmatizes the import of unlabelled goods.

GATT Article XX ("General Exceptions")

Much has already been written about Article XX, so it will be only briefly mentioned here. Assuming that a labelling scheme has been alleged to violate one of the Articles discussed above, the scheme would probably be defended on the basis of GATT Article XX (b) or (g), two of the general exceptions to the GATT Agreement.

GATT Article XX(b)[41] has never been successfully invoked and panel reports have cast doubt on its viability. The interpretation of the term "necessary" is so strict that it is virtually impossible to satisfy.[42] Article XX(g)[43] has instead been the focus of recent attention.

Two recent Appellate Body reports, *Shrimp-Turtle* and *Reformulated Gasoline,* have demonstrated the viability of Article XX(g),[44] but in each case the environmental measure at issue was found not to satisfy the conditions present in Article XX's chapeau. The fact that the *Shrimp-Turtle* case concerned NPR-PPMs was not an express barrier to the application of Article XX(g) or the chapeau. Were an Article XX(g) labelling case to arise, it is likely that the decision would rest on the application of the chapeau. This makes the Appellate Body's decisions in *Shrimp-Turtle* and *Reformulated Gasoline,* each of which interprets the chapeau, important for the "application" of labelling schemes that take NPR-PPMs into consideration. Both reports stress the need for a co-operative resolution to international environmental problems, suggesting that labelling schemes that conform with international standards might be more acceptable.

The Agreement on Technical Barriers to Trade

The TBT Agreement is the most important instrument applicable to environmental labelling in the WTO Agreement. The TBT Agreement was drafted with labelling regulations and standards in mind. There has been a general reluctance on the part of both panels and the Appellate Body to rule based on the TBT Agreement when confronted with the possibility of basing a decision on the GATT Agreement. Given the unanswered questions arising from the GATT Agreement with respect to labelling schemes, a developing country seeking to challenge a labelling scheme would be better served by basing its challenge on both the GATT and the TBT Agreements. This being said, there is also a degree of uncertainty concerning the application of the TBT Agreement to labelling schemes.

The principal uncertainty concerns the treatment of labels reflecting NPR-PPMs.[45] This point is of particular importance for voluntary eco-labelling schemes and for other voluntary schemes that reflect environmental and labour-related considerations. This confusion arises from the definitions of "technical regulation" and "standard" provided in

Annex 1 of the Agreement. The generally accepted rule is that only product-related PPMs are covered by the TBT Agreement, but this point remains open to debate. Some developing countries have taken the view that the TBT Agreement prohibits the labelling of NPR-PPMs, and therefore eco-labels, whereas other members have taken the view that eco-labels fall within the TBT Agreement.[46] A middle position— that only the product-related portion of an eco-label falls within the TBT Agreement—is tenable, but from a practical viewpoint unworkable.

The TBT Agreement is important and complex, and because of its potential "rigidity" a politically sensitive instrument. Much of the foundation required for an understanding of this agreement has been set forth in the above discussion of GATT Articles I, III, and XI. It is not possible to undertake a thorough analysis of the TBT Agreement in a short chapter of this nature, but the provisions of greatest interest for developing countries are outlined below.

The TBT Agreement differentiates between technical regulations (mandatory provisions) and standards (voluntary provisions) and establishes provisions applicable to both. Environmental labelling programmes can fall into either category depending upon whether or not a label is mandatory or voluntary. The distinction between mandatory and voluntary labelling requirements is important for ascertaining which provisions of the TBT Agreement apply.

Article 2 of the TBT Agreement is applicable to mandatory labelling requirements. Many important GATT principles that have already been discussed are incorporated into this provision. Article 2.1 provides for MFN and national treatment (treatment no less favourable for like products). Article 2.2 requires that technical regulations do not create "unnecessary" obstacles to international trade, and that such regulations are not more trade restrictive than necessary to fulfil legitimate objectives, taking account of the risks that non-fulfilment would create. Certain legitimate objectives are identified, including the protection of human, animal, and plant life or health and the environment. Article 2.4 requires the use of relevant international standards as a basis for technical regulations, unless they would be ineffective or inappropriate for the fulfilment of a legitimate objective. Article 2.5 provides that technical regulations that are in conformity with the international standards mentioned in Article 2.4 are "rebuttably presumed not to create unnecessary obstacles to international trade." Other portions of Article 2 set forth important notice and transparency requirements. In Article 3, rules for the application of these provisions by local governments and non-governmental bodies are set forth.

Article 2 recognizes the protection of human, animal, and plant life and health as legitimate objectives that might justify technical regulations, but trade measures to protect such legitimate objectives may not constitute "unnecessary" obstacles to international trade. This parallels the necessary test applied in conjunction with GATT Article XX(b), as evidenced by the fact that Article 2.2 incorporates a "least trade-restrictive measures" provision.[47] This provision is designed to minimize the burden to technical regulations and to prevent the abuse of technical regulations for protectionist purposes. The earlier characterization of the TBT Agreement as "rigid" is due to the incorporation of this "necessary" test. Past GATT/WTO experience with this standard suggests that certain non-protectionist measures may not satisfy this test owing to the frequent availability of a less trade-restrictive alternative.

This raises the question of whether or not mandatory labelling requirements are particularly trade restrictive. By their very nature, labelling requirements that simply provide product-related information, even if mandatory, are not a particularly trade-restrictive measure. Instead, product-related labelling tends to play an informative role. Despite the fact that labelling may result in consumers choosing not to purchase certain products based on the information provided, as noted above, such product discrimination is indirect and, for many people (particularly those in the developed world), well within what they would view as necessary for informed decision-making and consumer choice.

From the developing country perspective, one point should be noted. Article 2 places considerable emphasis on the promulgation of technical regulations in accordance with international standards. Although this provision is intended to encourage international harmonization, developing country interests will be served only if they participate actively in the harmonization process. If they do not, it is conceivable that harmonized standards may be promulgated that are significantly more difficult for developing countries to meet. This means the capacity of developing countries to participate in the international harmonization process must be enhanced, and developing country resources must be directed toward participation in such activities. This will mean participation in certain international harmonization activities that may have no immediate benefit for certain developing countries.

With respect to voluntary labelling schemes, including eco-labelling schemes, the situation is somewhat less straightforward. These schemes fall under Article 4 of the TBT Agreement, which incorporates the "Code of Good Practice for the Preparation, Adoption and Application of Standards" (Annex 3 of the TBT Agreement). The Code of Good Practice contains the principal TBT obligations applicable to voluntary labelling schemes. Pursuant to Article 4.1, *only* central government standardizing bodies are bound by the provisions contained in the Code. Other standardizing bodies have the option to accept and apply the Code. However, members are obligated to take "reasonable measures" to assure that local and non-governmental standardizing bodies do indeed accept and comply with the Code. This leaves a risk that labelling standards that do not comply with the Code will be promulgated by various subnational governmental authorities (or non-governmental bodies), particularly in countries with decentralized political systems. If the intent of the members is to widen the application of the Code, a goal that is probably in the interest of developing countries, attention should be given to defining what constitutes the "reasonable measures" required by a member to assure that subnational governmental and non-governmental bodies accept and comply with the Code.

With respect to voluntary labelling schemes, the obligations set forth in the Code generally parallel those of Article 2 of the TBT Agreement: MFN and national treatment provisions exist, standards are not permitted to create unnecessary obstacles to international trade, deference is given to international standards,[48] harmonization is encouraged, and notice and transparency obligations receive considerable attention.

As already noted, the treatment of NPR-PPMs for the purposes of the Code is a point of contention that the members have not been able to resolve. The area of greatest preoccupation for developing countries has, not surprisingly, been the labelling of non-product-related environmental criteria, particularly the criteria found in eco-labelling schemes. Although the problem is not serious yet, if eco-labelling schemes become a well-accepted marketing tool, and if eco-labelling schemes attribute particular importance to NPR-PPMs, labelling could eventually undermine what some perceive to be a comparative advantage in certain countries. This means that the concern of developing countries with respect to the NPR-PPM question is legitimate, but that present fears are overstated given the paucity of data demonstrating the effectiveness of eco-labelling schemes in increasing a product's market share.

Other concerns revolve around the fact that few products from developing countries are currently labelled, and that the industries that tend to be found in the least developed countries are frequently not those that will benefit, at least for now, from labelling schemes. This again suggests that much of the fear that developing countries have about eco-labelling schemes is not warranted. Yet, the vigorous opposition to eco-labelling programmes on the part of some developing country members is not without purpose. Opposition to voluntary eco-labelling schemes has slowed down progress in the WTO's Committee on Trade and Environment (CTE), preventing more controversial issues (such as internalization) from receiving serious consideration. It has also made members realize that environmental issues are a stalking horse for labour-related issues, in particular "core labour standards." By blocking the resolution of the environmental questions now on the CTE's agenda, some countries are hoping that they are also blocking the advancement of labour issues up the WTO's agenda.

5. Concluding comments

Environmental issues transcend national borders and are not solely a developed country concern. Developing countries are beginning to experience serious environmental difficulties, and these problems will grow. The continued deterioration of environmental conditions world-wide means that eco-labelling and other product-related labelling programmes are not going to disappear from the international trade agenda. Yet the polarized manner in which environmental issues are being addressed in the CTE has left little hope for progress in this forum. Although this may be in accord with certain developing country interests, it is inevitable that pressure will increase on developing countries during the next round of trade talks to reach a compromise, particularly with respect to less controversial environmental issues, such as eco-labelling.

For many developing countries, environmental issues remain a luxury, and green protectionism is a legitimate concern. They realize that environmental agreements are possible only if all sides are willing to make concessions, and they are waiting for movement from the members in the developed world. If, as is likely, certain environmental issues are going to be on the agenda of the next round of trade talks, it may be time for the developing countries to take advantage of this fact, and to begin to line up concessions from the developed country members, perhaps in areas such as agriculture and textiles, in exchange for movement on environmental issues such as eco-labelling.[49] Despite opposition among many developing countries to eco-labelling programmes, negotiating a solution where trade concessions are won for developing countries may be preferable to "rolling the dice" and letting the Appellate Body resolve the unanswered GATT Article III and TBT questions.

Uncertainty concerning the treatment of NPR-PPMs in the TBT Agreement will remain the focus of attention for the developing world. This is not because eco-labelling poses an economic threat, but instead because of the "slippery slope" argument. Authorizing an evaluation of foreign NPR-PPMs for labelling purposes could open the door to other more effective means of influencing foreign NPR-PPMs. Going further down the "slippery slope," it could even open the WTO's doors to labour-related issues, human rights issues, and other sensitive social and political concerns. This is something most members want to avoid. Neither the use of trade as an economic lever to compel social change nor the use of the WTO's dispute settlement mechanism as a means of resisting social change is perceived as being in the best interests of the WTO, or of most of its members.[50]

Returning to voluntary eco-labelling programmes, with the exception of some uncertainty regarding the treatment of NPR-PPMs, the TBT Agreement seems adequate to prevent most cases of "green protectionism." There are nevertheless improvements, already discussed at length in the CTE, that could lead to broader support for eco-labelling schemes. For example, assuming that they are permissible, voluntary eco-labelling schemes that reflect NPR-PPMs should take local geographic, environmental, economic, and developmental conditions into consideration. Furthermore, the need for developing country input in the drafting of criteria for labelling schemes is important. Lastly, maximum transparency in all stages of the labelling process must be assured. Progress on labelling issues is possible only if all sides recognize that legitimate aspirations and concerns are at stake and are prepared to work together towards a compromise that reflects these mutual interests.

Notes

1. Marrakesh Agreement Establishing the World Trade Organization, 15 April 1994 (hereinafter WTO Agreement); reprinted in GATT, *The Results of the Uruguay Round of Multilateral Trade Negotiations: The Legal Texts,* 5, 1994.
2. The International Standards Organization (ISO) has a system of classification that utilizes a different nomenclature. "Type I" labels are voluntary life-cycle labels based on pre-set criteria established by third parties. "Type II" labels are based on manufacturers' claims concerning individual environmental characteristics. "Type III" labels do not imply a product preference. They are based on an independent scientific assessment of environmental information. Arthur E. Appleton, *Environmental Labelling Programmes: International Trade Law Implications,* London: Kluwer Law International, 1997, p. 4.
3. A life-cycle analysis ("LCA" or "cradle-to-grave analysis") is an assessment of environmental factors present in the production, use, and disposal of a product. By definition it includes the production processes used to make a product, use of the product (emissions, noise, etc.), and disposal (recyclability, biodegradability, etc.). From an environmental perspective the concept of life-cycle analysis is of considerable importance, given that every stage in a product's life can have environmental consequences.
4. Schemes exist or have existed in Austria, Canada, Croatia, the Czech Republic, the European Union, Finland, France, Germany, Iceland, India, Israel, Japan, the Netherlands, New Zealand, Norway, Republic of Korea, Singapore, Spain, Sweden, and the United States. Schemes were under consideration (and may have now been implemented) in Brazil, Chile, Colombia, Indonesia, Poland, and Thailand. An attempt to implement a scheme failed in Australia. Appleton, *Environmental Labelling Programmes,* op. cit., p. 6. The most famous schemes are probably the Nordic White Swan and the German Blue Angel.
5. The General Agreement on Tariffs and Trade, opened for signature 30 October 1947, 55 *UNTS* 187, entered into force 12 January 1948; reprinted in GATT, *Basic Instruments and Selected Documents [BISD]* 4/1, 1969.
6. GATT Article I provides for most-favoured-nation (MFN) treatment. GATT Article III provides for national treatment. Together these provisions make up GATT's "non-discrimination" obligation.
7. This being said, certain developing country products may qualify for a label based on their naturalness, lack of chemical processing, etc. Stores such as the Body Shop and Magasins du Monde and certain "fair trade" organizations are capitalizing on the marketing potential of developing country products.
8. Depending on geological or climatic considerations, certain production or disposal techniques may be adequate in one state but not in another. For example, the

suitable use of hydrological power and the safe disposal of hazardous chemical substances may require geological or climatic considerations that can vary region by region.

9. *United States–Restrictions on Imports of Tuna,* Report of the Panel, GATT Document DS21/R, 3 September 1991 (unadopted), *BISD* 40S/155 (hereinafter *Tuna* Panel Report); reprinted in 30 *ILM* 1594 (1991), paras. 5.41–5.44.

10. *United States–Measures Affecting Alcoholic and Malt Beverages,* Report of the Panel, GATT Document DS23/R, adopted 19 June 1992, *BISD* 39S/206 (hereinafter *Malt Beverages* Panel Report), paras. 5.70–5.76.

11. WTO Document Press/TE 014, 14 November 1996.

12. WTO Agreement, op. cit., p. 6.

13. Ibid., p. 485.

14. Ibid., p. 138.

15. Ibid., p. 6.

16. Appleton, *Environmental Labelling Programmes,* op. cit., p. 91.

17. *United States–Import Prohibition of Certain Shrimp and Shrimp Products,* AB-1998-4, WT/DS58/AB/R, 12 October 1998 (hereinafter *Shrimp-Turtle* Appellate Body Report).

18. Ibid., para. 153.

19. Ibid., para. 155.

20. Appleton, *Environmental Labelling Programmes,* op. cit., pp. 141–142.

21. *Tuna* Panel Report, op. cit., paras. 5.41–5.44. See also Appleton, *Environmental Labelling Programmes,* op. cit., pp. 142–145.

22. *Tuna* Panel Report, op. cit., para. 5.42.

23. *Japan–Taxes on Alcoholic Beverages,* AB-1996-2, WT/DS8, 10 & 11/AB/R, 4 October 1996 (hereinafter *Alcoholic Beverages* Appellate Body Report), §E.

24. Appleton, *Environmental Labelling Programmes,* op. cit., p. 147. GATT Articles III and XI ("General Elimination of Quantitative Restrictions") are mutually exclusive. Article III applies even if the internal measures at issue are applied at the point of importation against like imported products. See GATT Annex I, "Notes and Supplementary Provisions," ad Article III.

25. *Alcoholic Beverages* Appellate Body Report, op. cit., §F (footnotes omitted).

26. *Border Tax Adjustments, Report of the Working Party,* GATT Doc. L/3464, adopted 2 December 1970, *BISD* 18S/97, para. 18.

27. *Alcoholic Beverages* Appellate Body Report, op. cit., §H(1)(a), quoting *Border Tax Adjustments,* op. cit., para. 18. This test differs from the approach set forth in the *Malt Beverages* Panel Report wherein the panel analysed the purpose (aim and effect) of the trade measure at issue.

28. *Alcoholic Beverages* Appellate Body Report, op. cit., §H(1)(a).

29. *Malt Beverages* Panel Report, op. cit.

30. *United States–Taxes on Automobiles,* Report of the Panel, GATT Doc. DS31/R, 11 October 1994 (unadopted), reprinted in 33 *ILM* 1399, 1994.

31. *Tuna* Panel Report, op. cit., para. 5.14; and *United States–Restrictions on Imports of Tuna,* Report of the Panel, GATT Doc. DS29/R, 16 June 1994 (unadopted), reprinted in 33 *ILM* 842, 1994, paras. 5.8–5.9. Both reports found that Article XI would be applicable because Article III (Note ad Article III) does not permit an assessment (in the determination of like products) at the point of importation of

policies and practices that do not have an effect on a product's physical characteristics (NPR-PPMs).

32. *United States–Import Prohibition of Certain Shrimp and Shrimp Products,* Report of the Panel, WT/DS58/R, 15 May 1998, para. 3.143.

33. Appleton, *Environmental Labelling Programmes,* op. cit., pp. 105 and 149.

34. See e.g. Agreement on Technical Barriers to Trade (hereinafter TBT Agreement), in Agreement Establishing the World Trade Organization, Marrakesh, 15 April 1994, Annex 1a, Article 2.

35. Mr. Lacarte signed both the *Malt Beverages* and *Alcoholic Beverages* reports. This change in practice is therefore somewhat surprising.

36. The Appellate Body recognized the right of members to pursue certain domestic goals in a WTO-consistent manner in the *Alcoholic Beverages* report (*Alcoholic Beverages* Appellate Body Report, op. cit., §F). In making such an evaluation, it is possible that considerations of domestic policy autonomy, in such areas as health, safety, and the environment, will enter into the analysis.

37. C. Tietje, "Voluntary Eco-labelling Programmes and Questions of State Responsibility in the WTO/GATT Legal System," *Journal of World Trade* 29(123), October 1995, 139–141.

38. Appleton, *Environmental Labelling Programmes,* op. cit., p. 159.

39. See GATT, Annex I, "Notes and Supplementary Provisions," ad Article III.

40. Appleton, *Environmental Labelling Programmes,* op. cit., pp. 159–160.

41. Article XX(b) provides an exception for measures "necessary to protect human, animal or plant life or health."

42. A measure is not "necessary" for GATT purposes if a GATT-consistent measure can be applied or if a trade measure that is less trade restrictive can be implemented.

43. Article XX(g) provides an exception for measures "relating to the conservation of exhaustible natural resources if such measures are made effective in conjunction with restrictions on domestic production or consumption."

44. See *Shrimp-Turtle* Appellate Body Report, op. cit.; and *United States–Standards for Reformulated and Conventional Gasoline,* AB-1996-1, WT/DS2/AB/R, 29 April 1996.

45. See, generally, Doaa Abdel Motaal, "Eco-labelling and the World Trade Organisation," paper prepared for the International Conference Green Goods V: Eco-labelling for a Sustainable Future, Berlin, Germany, 26–28 October 1998 (on file with the author).

46. Ibid., p. 5.

47. TBT Agreement, Article 2.2, reads in part "technical regulations shall not be more trade-restrictive than necessary to fulfil a legitimate objective."

48. Unlike TBT Agreement, Article 2.5, no rebuttable presumption of validity is created in the Code for national and subnational standards based on international standards, nor are legitimate objectives for standardization set forth as in Article 2.2.

49. To this list can be added the treatment of multilateral environmental agreements that incorporate trade measures.

50. A preferable solution would be to strengthen international and regional agreements governing areas such as environment, labour, and human rights, and to create effective enforcement mechanisms. There is, however, no consensus on such a step.

9

The Agreement on Technical Barriers to Trade, the Committee on Trade and Environment, and Eco-labelling

Doaa Abdel Motaal[1]

1. Introduction: Context of discussions on eco-labelling in the World Trade Organization

Eco-labelling has been discussed in the World Trade Organization (WTO) in the Committee on Trade and Environment (CTE) and the Committee on Technical Barriers to Trade (CTBT). In the CTE it has been examined within the broader context of all product-related environmental requirements, and in the CTBT within the context of the Agreement on Technical Barriers to Trade (TBT Agreement). At issue in the WTO is the extent to which eco-labelling schemes are covered by and are consistent with the provisions of the TBT Agreement. From an environmental perspective, it is important to establish the WTO consistency of these schemes in order to provide environmental policy makers with the security that their policies do not run counter to international trade rules and cannot be reversed by WTO member governments. From a trade perspective, ensuring their WTO consistency is needed to prevent them from becoming barriers to trade.

In its conclusions and recommendations to the 1996 Singapore Ministerial Conference, the CTE stated that "[w]ell-designed eco-labelling schemes/programmes can be effective instruments of environmental policy to encourage the development of an environmentally conscious consumer public."[2] However, a number of concerns were expressed regarding the employment in these schemes of criteria related to processes of production that do not affect the final product; the extent to which they discriminate between imported and domestically produced products, as well as between various imported products; and their transparency.

Two main questions have been raised by WTO members (quite different ones) with respect to eco-labelling schemes. The first relates to the coverage of the TBT Agreement, where some members have questioned the extent to which the Agreement covers measures such as eco-labelling schemes. The second relates to the consistency of eco-labels with the provisions of the TBT Agreement, where other members have argued that they are inconsistent and that the issue is not one of "coverage" at all. The extent to which such schemes differentiate between products on grounds that are accepted by the WTO has been discussed with respect to both these viewpoints. Because this is an issue of fundamental importance to the international trading system, it has proved to be extremely controversial.

So far, no firm decision on the WTO coverage and consistency of eco-labels has been taken. However, the extensive discussions undertaken in both the CTE and the CTBT on this subject have served to flush out the links between international trade rules and eco-labels, and have raised awareness of the need to make trade and environmental policies both compatible and mutually supportive.

2. Overview of the Agreement on Technical Barriers to Trade

The TBT Agreement has been at the heart of eco-labelling discussions in the WTO. To understand these discussions, it is important to understand the Agreement itself—why it was created, what problems it attempts to resolve, and how. The TBT Agreement was developed in response to a realization by the contracting parties to the General Agreement on Tariffs and Trade (GATT) that non-tariff barriers, in particular product technical requirements, were creating new obstacles to trade. Although originally a Tokyo Round agreement, it was revised during the Uruguay Round, and its revised version entered into force in 1995.

The TBT Agreement is premised on an acknowledgement of the right of WTO members to develop product requirements as well as procedures to assess compliance with those requirements. However, it attempts to ensure that these measures do not create *unnecessary* obstacles to trade during their preparation, adoption, and application. The Agreement covers product requirements that are both voluntary (known as "standards") and mandatory (known as "technical regulations"). It also covers all testing, inspection, and certification procedures designed to assess compliance (known as "conformity assessment procedures").

While technical regulations and conformity assessment procedures are covered through the main body of the Agreement, standards are covered through a "Code of Good Practice for the Preparation, Adoption and Application of Standards" (Annex 3 of the Agreement). Most of the principles applied by the Agreement to technical regulations also apply to standards through the Code. All governmental as well as non-governmental standardizing bodies, at the national and regional levels, are invited to accept the Code and to abide by its provisions.[3]

To ensure that product requirements and conformity assessment procedures do not create unnecessary obstacles to trade, the Agreement begins by delineating the "legitimate objectives" for which technical regulations may be developed. These include ensuring national security, preventing deceptive practices (such as false product labelling), protecting animal, human, or plant life or health, or the environment, etc. The Agreement then sets out a number of key principles to be adhered to by standardizing bodies.

The first principle is non-discrimination. Originally incorporated under GATT, the principle constitutes the backbone of the international trading system and is mirrored in the TBT Agreement. It outlaws discrimination between imported and domestically produced like goods (which is GATT's National Treatment clause), and between like goods imported from different sources (GATT's Most-Favoured-Nation or MFN clause). Within the context of the TBT Agreement, it means that WTO members must not subject some goods to more stringent requirements or stricter tests than others that are alike.

The second principle of the Agreement is the avoidance of unnecessary obstacles to trade. With respect to technical regulations and conformity assessment procedures, this means that members must design their regulations and procedures in the least trade-restrictive way possible, making them proportional to the objectives that they are trying to achieve (i.e. they must reflect on the impact of their measures on trade). The Agreement also encourages members to base their technical regulations and standards on performance rather than on design criteria (for instance, to say that all doors should have a burn-through time of at least 30 minutes, instead of requiring that all doors be made of steel and have a certain thickness). Such criteria provide producers with greater leeway in meeting the objectives of product requirements.

The third principle is harmonization. Members are called upon to base their technical regulations, standards, and conformity assessment procedures on international standards, guides, and recommendations. The call for harmonization is designed to avoid the emergence of undue layers of product requirements and assessment procedures, and to encourage the use of ones that have been developed with the approval of the international community.

The fourth principle concerns equivalence and mutual recognition. The Agreement stipulates that WTO members give positive consideration to recognizing other members' technical regulations as equivalent to their own, even when they differ from theirs, provided they are satisfied that they adequately fulfil their objectives. This reduces obstacles to trade until full-fledged international harmonization becomes possible. With respect to conformity assessment procedures, it also calls upon members to ensure, whenever possible, that the results of the assessment procedures of other members are accepted as equivalent, even when they differ from theirs, provided the procedures give the same level of confidence. This avoids multiple product testing (in both exporting and importing countries) and its associated costs. Members are also encouraged to conclude mutual recognition agreements (MRAs) to achieve equivalence in the area of conformity assessment (MRAs usually cover defined product groups).

The fifth and final principle of the Agreement is transparency, which is a central feature of the TBT Agreement. It includes notification obligations and the establishment of enquiry points. Under the TBT Agreement, members must notify other members of, among other things, their draft technical regulations, standards, and conformity assessments and must provide them with sufficient time to comment on them (with the obligation of taking their comments into account). They must also establish enquiry points to respond to all questions their trading partners may have on issues relating to the TBT Agreement.

3. Analysis under the Agreement on Technical Barriers to Trade

Legal analysis of the WTO consistency of eco-labelling schemes, which has taken place within the framework of the TBT Agreement, has involved discussion of the meaning of "standards" under the Agreement, and of the concept of "like products" incorporated in its non-discrimination principle.

Because most eco-labelling schemes are voluntary, discussions have focused on the rules of the WTO in relation to voluntary measures. As stated in the previous section, voluntary product requirements under the TBT Agreement are known as standards. Annex 1 of the Agreement defines a standard as follows:

> Document approved by a recognized body, that provides for common and repeated use, rules, guidelines or characteristics, for products or related processes and production methods, with which compliance is not mandatory. It may also include or deal exclusively with terminology, symbols, packaging, marking or labelling requirements as they apply to a product, process or production method.[4]

Concerns raised under the TBT Agreement

The first issue addressed within the context of the TBT Agreement has been the extent to which eco-labels fall under the purview of the Agreement by meeting its definition of a standard (i.e. the Agreement's coverage).

It would seem logical that eco-labels, as voluntary product environmental requirements, be considered "standards" under the TBT Agreement. However, disagreement has arisen on this issue in the WTO because of the fact that most eco-labelling schemes are based on product life-cycle analysis (LCA). LCA is a tool that examines the environmental impact of products during the sourcing of raw materials, production, consumption, and disposal. Particularly controversial in the WTO has been the fact that LCAs extend their assessment of environmental impacts to the production stage. Although WTO members agree that processes and production methods (PPMs) that have an impact on the final product (referred to as incorporated PPMs) are allowed by the TBT Agreement, there is disagreement over whether or not PPMs with no effect on the final product (unincorporated PPMs) are allowed.[5]

According to the Agreement, a standard is a document that sets out rules for products or *related* processes and production methods, and it is the term "related" that has been interpreted by some WTO members to exclude unincorporated PPMs. Those who believe that unincorporated PPMs (such as in LCAs) are not covered argue that eco-labels are neither consistent nor inconsistent with the Agreement; they simply fall outside its scope. Questions have also been raised about the extent to which eco-labels are approved by "recognized bodies" (i.e. on how eco-labelling organizations themselves are to be considered), which are the words used in the Agreement's definition of a standard.

The second, and quite different, issue raised in the context of the TBT Agreement has been the compatibility (and consistency) of life-cycle analysis with the concept of "like products," a concept that forms the backbone of the WTO's non-discrimination principle. Under GATT's MFN clause, WTO members must accord treatment that is no less favourable to *like* imported products. Under the national treatment clause, they must accord treatment that is no less favourable to imported products than to *like* domestically produced products. As previously stated, the principle of non-discrimination is itself incorporated in the TBT Agreement. Some WTO members have questioned the extent to which the trading system (particularly the TBT Agreement) allows for the likeness of "products" to be extended to cover the likeness of "PPMs" (i.e. the extent to which products may be differentiated based on production criteria that do not affect their characteristics). Those who have argued that it does not allow for such a distinction between products have stated that eco-labels based on LCA are inconsistent with the TBT Agreement.

Examined in a number of different disputes under both GATT and the WTO, the concept of "like products" has been assessed on the basis of product physical characteristics, end-use, tariff classification, competitiveness, substitutability, and so on. However, there is disagreement as to whether or not the "likeness" of products can be stretched to factor in unincorporated PPMs. Thus, whereas eco-labelling schemes that do not address PPMs or that are based on incorporated PPMs are clearly allowed by the TBT Agreement, the situation is much less certain with respect to schemes based on unincorporated PPMs.

A number of other concerns were raised in the WTO with respect to eco-labelling schemes. For example, concerns were expressed regarding the ability of eco-labelling schemes to discriminate between products from different sources and to be developed in an untransparent (opaque) fashion. If eco-labelling schemes were deemed to fall under the purview of the TBT Agreement, they would have to comply with its provisions and that, in and of itself, would serve to ensure that they were prepared, adopted, and applied in a non-discriminatory and transparent way. However, this issue has not yet been resolved.

The concerns raised with respect to discrimination have included the fact that eco-labels may discriminate between imported and domestically produced goods if local industry influences the choice of products they cover as well as the selection of criteria on which they are based. Criteria could, for example, be selected that foreign producers could not reasonably meet. Eco-labels may also discriminate against foreign producers in the process of conformity assessment by, for instance, placing undue restrictions on the conformity assessment bodies to be used. In short, they could become the subject of protectionist abuse.

The concerns raised with respect to transparency have included that a lack of transparency could prevent foreigners from participating in product selection and criteria development—a situation that could result in exporters being faced with "surprise" standards and, thus, "surprise" adaptation costs. Discussion has also taken place on the extent to which the transparency provisions of the TBT Agreement would need to be modified to deal with eco-labels, if it was to be decided that they fall within its scope. For instance, although the TBT Agreement calls for the notification of standards at a draft stage to allow WTO members to comment on them and to have these comments taken into account, one WTO member argued that this would not work for instruments based on LCA, because the expenses involved in conducting

LCAs (even when still at a draft stage) would make their revision economically unrealistic.

"Like products" and life-cycle analysis

As is clear from the above presentation, the issue of how to distinguish between products—and the methods that are and are not accepted by the WTO—has been at the heart of the eco-labelling debate. The issue of LCA and its coverage by the TBT Agreement is reflective of how products are defined differently for different purposes. From an environmental perspective, LCA is an important environmental policy-making instrument. In the context of eco-labelling, it provides consumers with information about, amongst other things, PPMs, so they may distinguish products that have harmed the environment during their production from those that have not.

However, a number of arguments may also be made to support the prevention of product differentiation on the basis of unincorporated PPMs. The first of these is a political one, and has to do with the need to preserve territorial sovereignty. To prevent discrimination between products on the basis of unincorporated PPMs is to prevent external intervention in rule-setting within national boundaries. It is precisely because the WTO is able to offer such security to its members that its membership has expanded to the size it is today. Had this principle been put into question, the benefits brought by the 50-year existence of the multilateral trading system might not have been reaped.

The second argument is an economic one. The prevention of product differentiation based on unincorporated PPMs allows countries to set standards (environmental or otherwise) that are appropriate for their level of development, rather than having inappropriate ones imposed on them from the outside (with respect to the environment, this is an argument that environmental economists themselves make). In other words, it allows countries to trade their developmental needs against their needs for environmental protection in a manner that is consistent with how they themselves value these needs (and not on the basis of how others value them for them).

The third and final argument is an environmental one. By preventing the imposition of one country's environmental standards on another, differences in environmental absorptive capacities, priorities, and problems in different parts of the world can be taken into account.

4. Viewpoints expressed in the Committee on Trade and Environment

Most of the substantial discussions on eco-labelling in the CTE took place prior to the 1996 Singapore Ministerial Conference. This section presents the main views expressed in these discussions.[6]

It is often stated that a North–South divide characterizes trade and environment discussions in the WTO, but this assertion is frequently a misrepresentation. Numerous standpoints have been taken in the CTE on the extent to which eco-labels are covered by and are consistent with WTO rules, and several proposals have been put forward on how to accommodate the trade concerns that they raise. Although it may be argued that there is a distinctly Southern perspective in the CTE on this issue, it cannot be stated that a distinctly Northern viewpoint has emerged. It is important to note that, during the CTE's discussion of this issue, a number of delegations stressed the utility of eco-labelling schemes as instruments of environmental policy.

The different positions on eco-labelling taken in the CTE have included the following:

(a) Eco-labels are both covered by and consistent with the TBT Agreement.

(b) Eco-labels are not covered by the TBT Agreement, but scope needs to be created for them.

(c) Eco-labels are not covered by the TBT Agreement, and creating scope for them could endanger the trading system. Tremendous care should be exercised in addressing this issue in future. A combination of increased transparency, equivalence, and mutual recognition could help alleviate their effects on trade.[7]

(d) Eco-labels are inconsistent with the TBT Agreement, and should not find any accommodation within the WTO system. A combination of increased transparency, equivalence, and mutual recognition could help alleviate their effects on trade.

The first three positions (a–c) were advocated by developed countries.

The principal advocate of position (a) argued that, despite the WTO Secretariat's finding that the negotiating history of the TBT Agreement upholds the view that unincorporated PPMs are not covered by the Agreement,[8] all standards (whether based on incorporated or unincorporated PPMs) fall under the scope of the Code of Good Practice, including eco-labels. However, the proponent of this view stated that there is a need to amplify existing transparency provisions with respect to: (i) the design of eco-labelling programmes, their statutory or regulatory basis, and procedures for input from interested parties, (ii) the selection of products being considered for an eco-label, (iii) the LCA used to develop criteria, (iv) draft criteria for new or revised product groups, and (v) documentation on how the criteria are to be implemented. Although the existing transparency provisions of the TBT Agreement could adequately address these different stages, it argued that they also need to be tailored to the specifics of eco-labelling schemes. For instance, whereas standards under the Agreement must be notified at a draft stage to provide an opportunity for comments, it questioned whether this would work with eco-labels based on LCA.

A position that falls between (a) and (b) is that the TBT Agreement could be interpreted to cover the use of certain standards based on unincorporated PPMs in voluntary eco-labelling programmes, provided that these programmes are developed according to multilaterally agreed guidelines consistent with the basic obligations of GATT and the TBT Agreement. Guidelines developed by the International Standards Organization (ISO) on environmental labelling could for instance be used. In reaction to this proposal, concerns were expressed (particularly by developing countries) about the use of ISO guides on the grounds that not all WTO members participate in ISO and that its decision-making process is not consensus based.

The position in line with (b) argues that, on the basis of the WTO Secretariat's document on the negotiating history of the TBT Agreement, unincorporated PPMs do not appear to be covered by the Agreement. Two related proposals have been put forward for addressing the issue: (i) seeking full coverage by the TBT Agreement of voluntary eco-labelling schemes based on LCA, or (ii) negotiating a Code of Conduct specifically targeted at eco-labelling schemes. The advantage of the latter would be that it would allow WTO members to tailor a new instrument to suit eco-labels.

With respect to (c), one argument was that, whereas eco-labels addressing incorporated PPMs are clearly covered by the TBT Agreement, a broad interpretation of the Agreement to cover unincorporated PPMs raises concerns. Expanding the scope of the TBT Agreement to cover such PPMs could have far-reaching ramifications for the entire WTO system, extending beyond the issue of eco-labelling. However, it was argued that information is the most important issue in relation to voluntary labelling, and the CTE was requested to increase the transparency of voluntary eco-labelling schemes, including those that are based on unincorporated PPMs.

Another view expressed with respect to (c) was that eco-labels based on unincorporated PPMs raise significant trade concerns. When based on the environmental conditions and priorities of importing countries, they risk being ineffective and irrelevant to the environmental protection needs of exporting countries. The schemes may be based on criteria that foreign producers could not reasonably satisfy. Therefore, unincorporated PPMs can affect the competitive opportunities of foreign producers and can mislead consumers into rejecting products that are environmentally equal or superior to domestic products. Thus, work is needed on the transparency and mutual recognition of labelling schemes.

Most developing countries adopted position (d), arguing that the TBT Agreement prohibits the use of standards based on unincorporated PPMs. This is because its definition of standards does not embrace those that are based on such PPMs, and because GATT/WTO jurisprudence on the term "like products" does not allow for product differentiation on these grounds. They argued that it is unacceptable for products to be judged on the basis of environmental impacts that might be limited to exporting countries alone. Accommodating unincorporated PPMs under the TBT Agreement would amount to creating scope for the extra-territorial imposition of national standards, and this would have significant consequences for the trading system as a whole. A need to provide developing countries with technical assistance to meet the requirements of eco-labelling schemes was also mentioned.

Several developing countries stressed the importance of the role that equivalence and mutual recognition could play in helping them more easily meet the requirements of foreign schemes. One delegation pointed to the proliferation of different schemes for the same products based on conflicting criteria, and the dangers that such a situation could pose.

5. The Triennial Review of the Agreement on Technical Barriers to Trade

At the end of 1997, the CTBT conducted its first Triennial Review of the TBT Agreement. A number of issues emerged from the Review that may be important to future discussions on eco-labelling in the WTO.

Improving international standardization

One WTO member argued that improvements could be made to the process of international standards development. Although the TBT Agreement contains transparency provisions for standards, technical regulations, and conformity assessment procedures, for instance, it does not contain similar provisions for international standards. This member stated that greater transparency is necessary, and that attempts must also be made to ensure that the international standardization process represents the interests of all parties concerned. Although international standards are rebuttably presumed in the TBT Agreement not to create unnecessary obstacles to international trade, there is a need to examine the difficulties and trade effects that they create.

The proposal was supported by a large number of delegations, and the considerations it raised were included in the results of the Triennial Review.[9]

This proposal could have interesting consequences with respect to eco-labelling. ISO Technical Committee 207 on Environmental Management has been working on, amongst other issues, the development of international standards in the field of eco-labelling. These have ranged from general principles that eco-labelling schemes may follow, to principles on how to conduct life-cycle analysis. Whereas a developed country had argued in the CTE that the TBT Agreement should be interpreted as creating scope for eco-labels based on multilaterally agreed guidelines (such as ISO standards), numerous countries (particularly developing countries) rejected the proposal on the grounds that the process of international standardization was not sufficiently representative and was not consensus based. If the process of international standardization were to be re-examined, however, it is possible that agreement on the use of international eco-labelling standards could in future be obtained. Nevertheless, although this is a very significant development, it does not promise to deliver short-run solutions.

Providing for the equivalence of standards

Another WTO member argued that, whereas the TBT Agreement calls upon WTO members to give positive consideration to accepting as equivalent the technical regulations of other members, the Code of Good Practice does not contain a similar provision with respect to standards. It urged the CTBT to examine this issue further, and its concerns were expressed in the results of the Triennial Review. Once again, this is likely to be a significant development for eco-labelling schemes because a number of delegations emphasized that equivalence and mutual recognition could be key to alleviating their trade effects.

Improving transparency

With respect to the transparency of eco-labelling schemes, the CTBT (within the context of the Triennial Review) concluded that:

> In order to improve the transparency, acceptance of, and compliance with the Code [of Good Practice], the Committee agreed to the following:
>
> . . . without prejudice to the views of Members concerning the coverage and application of the [TBT] Agreement, the obligation to publish notices of draft standards containing voluntary labelling requirements under paragraph L of the Code is not dependent upon the kind of information provided on the label.[10]

The exact meaning of this decision can, of course, be interpreted only by WTO members themselves. However, it represents an attempt by the CTBT to address the transparency concerns that had been raised with respect to eco-labelling schemes, without prejudging whether or not they are allowed or covered by the TBT Agreement.

6. Moving forward

In its conclusions and recommendations to the Singapore Ministerial Conference, the CTE stated that the starting point for addressing eco-labels in the WTO should be to increase their transparency. To some extent this appears to have been achieved by the CTBT in its above-mentioned decision on notification. However, although concerns were voiced in the CTE on the extent to which existing transparency provisions were suited to the set-up of eco-labelling schemes, these have yet to be addressed.

A number of delegations indicated the importance of equivalence and mutual recognition in addressing the trade concerns raised by eco-labelling schemes. The United Nations Conference on Trade and Development (UNCTAD) has conducted important work in this area, which may eventually contribute to resolving the issue.[11]

With respect to eco-labelling criteria based on unincorporated PPMs, UNCTAD argues that, when these PPMs result in intrinsically local environmental problems in the producing country, the eco-labelling programmes of importing countries could accept PPMs that are friendly to the domestic environment of the exporting (producing) country as equivalent. These would be more suited to the producing country's environmental and developmental conditions. In addition, UNCTAD argues that, in LCA, equivalencies may also be considered between product and process-related criteria. For example, it states that, with respect to waste generation, the volume and type of waste generated during production could be weighed against the recyclability and biodegradability of the product after disposal.

The framework laid down by UNCTAD for establishing equivalence could be extremely useful in addressing unincorporated PPMs that create local environmental problems. On the basis of equivalent criteria, mutual recognition agreements between existing eco-labelling schemes could also be negotiated. The development of international guidelines on equivalence and mutual recognition would be extremely useful in this regard.

With respect to unincorporated PPMs that create trans-boundary or global environmental problems, UNCTAD states that these would best be addressed through multilateral environmental agreements (MEAs). MEAs allow for the cooperative design of multilateral solutions to problems of international concern. They would be much more likely to achieve better and more coordinated results than a series of unilateral attempts through a diversity of eco-labelling schemes.

A large number of options, therefore, remain to be explored for the successful resolution of eco-labelling discussions in the WTO. Regardless of which option is chosen, however, it is clear that greater national coordination between trade and environment policy makers is needed. Only through such coordination can problems be addressed at an early stage and trade and environment policies come to complement each other.

Notes

1. This document is my sole responsibility, and has not been written on behalf of WTO members.
2. CTE, *Report (1996) of the Committee on Trade and Environment*, WT/CTE/1, November 1996.
3. Because most of the bodies that develop standards are non-governmental, the Code was created to bring their work under the purview of the Agreement. Through their acceptance of the Code, private standardizing bodies are able to generate greater confidence in the standards that they prepare (because they are seen to comply with the rules of international trade) and to gain their wider acceptance and use.
4. Annex 1 of the Agreement on Technical Barriers to Trade, "Terms and Their Definitions for the Purpose of this Agreement."
5. An example of an incorporated PPM would be cotton grown using certain pesticides and that itself contains pesticide residues. An example of an unincorporated PPM would be cotton grown using certain pesticides but that does not itself contain any pesticide residues.
6. These have been extrapolated from the following summary records of CTE meetings: WT/CTE/M/5, 30 November 1995; WT/CTE/M/6, 17 January 1996; WT/CTE/M/7, 22 March 1996; WT/CTE/M/8, 11 April 1996; WT/CTE/M/10, 12 July 1996; WT/CTE/M/11, 22 August 1996; and WT/CTE/M/12, 21 October 1996.
7. Equivalence means the acceptance by a country of another country's standards or regulations as equivalent to its own, even if they are different, provided that they adequately fulfil its objectives. Mutual recognition in the context of eco-labelling schemes generally means that, if certain conditions are met, qualifying for the

eco-label of an exporting country becomes an acceptable basis for the award of the eco-label used in the importing country.

8. CTE/CTBT, *Negotiating History of the Coverage of the Agreement on Technical Barriers to Trade with Regard to Labelling Requirements, Voluntary Standards, and Processes and Production Methods Unrelated to Product Characteristics,* WT/CTE/W/10, August 1995.

9. CTBT, *First Triennial Review of the Operation and Implementation of the Agreement on Technical Barriers to Trade,* G/TBT/5, November 1997.

10. Ibid.

11. UNCTAD, *Trade, Environment and Development: Aspects of Establishing and Operating Eco-labelling Programmes,* TD/B/WG.6/5, 28 March 1995; *Eco-labelling and Market Opportunities for Environmentally Friendly Products,* TD/B/WG.6/2, 6 October 1994.

10

The Precautionary Principle

James Cameron

In order to achieve sustainable development, policies must be based on the precautionary principle. Environmental measures must anticipate, prevent, and attack the causes of environmental degradation. Where there are threats of serious or irreversible damage, lack of full scientific certainty should not be used as a reason for postponing measures to prevent environmental degradation.[1]

[We must] recognize that much more progress is needed in the WTO Committee on Trade and the Environment. Its work must be revitalised if the trade and environmental agendas are to advance in a mutually supportive way . . . Other areas where we need to clarify the relationship between both policy objectives—trade liberalization and environmental protection—include, among others . . . the so-called precautionary principle.[2]

Questions involving the environment are particularly prone to uncertainty. Technological man has altered his world [the effects of which] are often unknown . . . commonly, "reasonable medical concerns" and theory long precede certainty. Yet the statutes—and common sense—demand regulatory action to prevent harm, even if the regulator is less than certain that the harm is otherwise inevitable.[3]

The precautionary principle is part of a system of rules designed to guide human behaviour towards the ideal of an environmentally sustainable economy.[4] Fundamentally, it provides the philosophical authority to take public policy or regulatory decisions in the face of scientific uncertainty.[5] The precautionary principle began to appear in international legal instruments only in the 1980s, but it has since experienced what has been called a meteoric rise in international law.[6]

It has been said that the "Precautionary Principle is a statement of commonsense"[7] and it certainly has utility in balancing the competing concerns of economic development against limited environmental resources. The economics of globalization continue to place ever-increasing demands on resources while increasing the efficiency of their use. This essential paradox, together with well-organized opposition to trade liberalization from the environment lobby, has informed the search for balance between trade and environment policy.[8] As Renato Ruggiero, former Director-General of the World Trade Organization (WTO), has stated, "we plainly need a balance, and an integrated approach to policy-making."[9] Furthermore, the precautionary principle has now entered the jurisprudence of the WTO's Dispute Settlement Body.[10] It is no longer a remote concept exclusively located in the environmental law sphere.

This chapter first sets out a brief history of the principle, as evidenced in the usage of explicit precautionary language in law. It then seeks to identify the core concepts of the precautionary principle and define what exactly it is, and examines the principle's status in international law; finally it looks at the precautionary principle in trade in the context of the WTO. The first three parts lead to the fourth and in part respond to those in the trade community who ask straightforwardly: What is the precautionary principle?

1. History of the precautionary principle

The first treaty to make explicit reference to precaution is the 1985 Vienna Convention on Ozone Depleting Substances, wherein the parties recognize "precautionary measures" taken at the national and international levels.[11] The most commonly referenced form of the principle comes from the Bergen Declaration of 1990, quoted above.

Though there have been critics along the way,[12] the principle was finally embraced at the United Nations Conference on Environment and

Development (UNCED) in Rio de Janeiro in 1992.[13] Five environmental instruments, two binding (the United Nations Framework Convention on Climate Change and the Convention on Biological Diversity) and three non-binding (Agenda 21, the Rio Declaration on Environment and Development, and Statement of Forest Principles), were signed and acceded to by virtually all heads of state. Though the full acceptance of the principle as universal can be seen as coinciding with this conference, the precautionary principle has since been reaffirmed in virtually every international agreement on the environment and as the lead principle in the European Union's environmental law, and has been applied by tribunals at all levels to determine disputes and as the basis of domestic regulation relating to the environment.

A more detailed tracking of the precautionary language can be found elsewhere, but there is no doubt that the principle, through general international law, "seeps through the pores"[14] into the legal order of the WTO.

2. The conceptual core of the precautionary principle

Some critics have argued that the principle is an "elusive concept,"[15] and therefore has questionable status in international law, or "at present . . . is not a term of art."[16] However, the precautionary principle does have a conceptual core, and, though its legal status is often contested, its essence should not be.[17]

Much of the confusion surrounding the principle's interpretation stems from confusion between precautionary and preventative measures.[18] Preventative standards may be precautionary or non-precautionary in certain degrees, but precautionary standards, although able to vary the degree of prevention, cannot be non-preventative. This is because, regardless of the particular language used by an instrument, a key element in defining the core of precaution is a lack of certainty about the cause-and-effect relationships or the possible extent of a particular environmental harm. If there is no uncertainty about the environmental risks of a situation, then the measure is preventative, not precautionary. In the face of uncertainty, however, the precautionary principle, like the

Vorsorgeprinzip, allows for the state to act in an effort to mitigate the risks. Put best, *"the precautionary principle stipulates that where the environmental risks being run by regulatory inaction are in some way uncertain but non-negligible, regulatory inaction is unjustified."*[19]

This definition of the conceptual core of the precautionary principle does leave three issues undecided, though it must be stressed that these questions centre around distinctions in kind and do not detract from the essence of the principle.[20] The three issues prompted by the core principle are the meaning and extent of non-negligible risk, the regulatory action that is justified by the principle, and the thresholds and responses to uncertainty.[21] It is important to point out that the third issue, of thresholds, is really addressing the question of how to determine answers to the first two issues, an exercise that ultimately relies on politics and incorporation.

The notion of non-negligible risk is the first issue raised by the well-defined core of the precautionary principle. Gundling, in augmenting his definition of the precautionary principle as "more than the prevention of risk," elaborates that it requires "prevention of environmental impacts irrespective of the existence of risks,"[22] meaning that non-negligible risk arises in all cases of environmental impact. This must be too broad, because all human activity carries with it environmental impacts, and human pollution is unavoidable.[23] What is essential here is the recognition that not all environmental risks are non-negligible and that the scope of precaution must be reasonable in defining this threshold, otherwise an unsustainable utopian element enters into the discourse of the precautionary principle.[24]

Like the confusion between prevention and precaution mentioned above, there is a possible arena of confusion here in the distinction between risk and uncertainty.[25] Risk is the amalgam of the probability of an event occurring and the seriousness of the event's consequences.[26] Thus, if either the likeliness or the seriousness of the event is high, the strategy is high risk. As a starting point, then, the threshold of risk must incorporate the notion that, in order to be non-negligible, a given risk must, in theory, have both of its aspects, on balance, meet this threshold. In the most common form of precaution adopted to date, there is a minimum risk severity before precaution is triggered, that of "serious or irreversible harm."[27] But risk obviates itself altogether from the precautionary principle when its likeliness and severity are known. If both the probability and the magnitude of risks are known, precaution is not a factor because the level of uncertainty involved is relatively low.[28] Risk is inseparable from uncertainty,[29] then, but is not the same as uncertainty.

Assuming the threshold of non-negligible risk is surpassed, the question of what are justifiable regulatory actions comes into play. Regulation seeks the advancement of particular social ends through law.[30] An instrument is designed through a political process to change behaviour for the public good. The ends sought through precautionary means range from avoidance of irreversible environmental harm[31] to protecting biodiversity "regardless of its worth to man."[32] This range of ends provides a further scaling of the precautionary aspect of any environmental regime, with the degree of precaution increasing as more emphasis is placed on environmental ends in their own right and decreasing as qualifying ends (perhaps economics) are incorporated.[33] Thus, in cost–benefit terms, the precautionary principle attributes a high cost to regulatory inactivity in the face of uncertainty while recognizing the inherent benefit of action in such cases.[34]

Though the notion of justified regulatory action was bifurcated into ends and means, the points of note in regard to each are quite similar. This is because means in such international environmental regimes are in essence intermediate ends rather than specific procedures, such as the use of best available technology (BAT).[35] One key is that, because it deals in matters of degree, limiting language on such subsidiary or final ends of any precautionary device does not preclude those ends from being precautionary or imply non-recognition of the doctrine. In fact, there are inherent dangers in being too precautionary, such as economic waste, political embarrassment, or a reduction in later precautionary measures owing to the waste and embarrassment.[36] Thus, such limiting of degree is necessary in mitigating these dangers. Some analyses suggest that, for this reason, cost assessment procedures should be applied in precautionary principle situations,[37] while others, arguing on an insurance analogy, point out that the value obtained by any disaster aversion policy is not undermined by the non-occurrence of the disaster insured against.[38] "Precaution accepts that uncertainty in both outcome and practical response is a precondition of action and devises techniques to plan always for the worst outcome."[39]

After entertaining the notions of thresholds of risk and action on a general level, the question of thresholds becomes, more specifically, one of how the thresholds of (a) non-negligible risk and (b) costs of regulatory inaction should be set. A general precautionary answer to this question stipulates that the thresholds should be (a) low and (b) high, though that, in turn, again begs the question of degree.[40] Since the scientific evidence is uncertain, this determination must be made in a more overtly judgemental forum, namely that of politics, because such institutions are where one must regulate public affairs absent recourse to pure science.[41] Thus, by explicitly noting the limits of scientific determination, the precautionary principle legitimates public political determination of these issues, in some sense democratizing international environmental law.[42]

The question remains as to how much such political processes can be superimposed on scientific evidence. Again, the examples from international law vary in degree, from "no scientific evidence to prove a causal link"[43] to "before a causal link has been established by absolutely clear scientific evidence."[44] Science cannot be divorced from the precautionary principle because a scientific view of the risk is an essential component of the evaluation of risk that the principle anticipates.

The following observations can be made. First, the precautionary principle can attribute much of its rise, nationally and abroad, to a public perception of scientific inadequacy in addressing environmental regulation. Secondly, the fact that science is uncertain at its most basic level[45] throws doubt on its adequacy, in theory, at addressing environmental concerns.[46] As well, science has little ability to answer the questions of law and policy, which ask science to provide answers in yes or no terms, a task it is uniquely designed to avoid. Finally, all scientific assessments of environmental damage are dependent on subjective assumptions of what constitutes harm, especially in degrees, and therefore necessarily involve judgements that have cultural, economic, and political bases.[47]

Once it is established that the thresholds of non-negligible risk and justified regulatory action in response to uncertainty necessarily boil down to a judgemental political question, two other points of interest become apparent. The first of these is the phenomenon of changing uncertainties and precaution due to a change in physical circumstances and geographic locale.[48] This notion of understanding differing ecological, cultural, political, and economic needs of differing places and physical circumstances, often found under the rubric of "equity" in international environmental discourse, has many impacts on the implementation of the precautionary principle. Different states will define non-negligible risk and justified regulatory acts differently based on differing probability and severity of risk and differing capabilities to regulate. For instance, just looking at the risk side of the equation, one can see that the magnitude of global climate change, which might be low for some countries, could be potentially devastating or fatal for low-lying small islands. In such a case, not only may degrees of precaution change, but a regime may even switch between being preventative or being precautionary.[49] One point that cannot be overstated, however, is that environmental interdependence and the nature of uncertainty dictate that the successful implementation of a vital preventative standard in one part of the planet is contingent upon the adoption of, at a minimum, precautionary standards elsewhere.[50]

Finally, a commonality of all precautionary measures is a shifting of the burden of proof away from traditional legal standards, which have said that parties accused of environmental degradation must be "proven wrong" before they are required to stop the activity in question.[51] The precautionary principle, via determining what the thresholds are for both risks and justifiable regulation, can ease the required burden for what exactly constitutes a likely harm, making it less than scientific proof.[52] In fact, this burden of what must be proven can shift completely, requiring that there be proof of no harm prior to action, rather than proof of harm prior to halting action. But what must be proven is only one facet of the burden of proof. The party bearing the burden is of legal concern as well, and it has been pointed out that the burden of proof should rest with the party seeking to change the status quo. Of note is that the "status quo" refers to the unaltered state of the environment in this instance, because in some contexts in international law "status quo" will refer to development and its current pace, a completely opposite framing of the issue.[53]

3. The precautionary principle as international law

I feel confident in making the argument that the precautionary principle is part of the body of international environmental law. It is possible reasonably to argue the contrary. Experience reveals that it is very easy to challenge an argument for a customary law rule in a court of law, especially a domestic court or a specialist international tribunal used to applying technical rules. Judges of one kind or another generally prefer to interpret rules written in an agreement rather than construct a rule from widely differing sources of evidence and *then* interpret it.

None the less, the starting point of the argument for the principle, being a principle of law, must be to list the sources of international law.[54] Treaties apply only to signatories to the treaty, and only within its scope. Customary law, however, has the potential to bind all states, if the specific conditions for custom are met. General principles of law are evidenced, for the most part, through the specific national legal practices of various states, and will often derive from judicial decisions and even the writings of leading individual authorities, as pointed out by the Statute of the International Court of Justice (ICJ) and evidenced in example by the ALI Restatement on International Law.

Where the precautionary principle is part of a treaty such as the UN Framework Convention on Climate Change, it is binding on the parties that sign and ratify the treaty. It is binding in the terms expressed in writing as interpreted by the parties themselves in the practice of the organization, by the Secretariat if and when asked to contribute an opinion, by any compliance procedure internal to the treaty, or by any other international tribunal called upon to decide on a particular case where a party argues for its relevance. In this way, at one level, there is simply no doubt that the principle is part of international environmental law. It is there in writing in multilateral environmental agreements. But in order to judge whether the principle is relevant to another international agreement, on trade, we must look at the other sources of international law as well as WTO agreements.

Customary law is developed over time in the international arena as states exhibit a pattern or practice of behaviour arising from a perceived legal duty. These two requirements of customary law are called state practice and *opinio juris,* respectively. Historically, little environmental law reached the level of custom. Respecting the exercise of high seas freedoms, cooperating in the use of shared resources, and preventing trans-boundary pollution are items on the shortlist of what constitutes customary environmental obligations binding on all states.[55]

There are several who argue that the precautionary principle is not, or not yet, customary law. Some claim there are problems with its variety of interpretations, leading to difficulty in deciding when to apply it and opening the floodgates for far-reaching effects.[56] Others cite its vagueness, and urge the conundrum that one use precaution when applying precaution.[57] Both of these arguments, essentially the same, speak not to custom but rather to the principle itself, and can be answered by the core meaning discussion above.

The precautionary principle has been included in virtually every recently adopted treaty and policy document related to the protection and preservation of the environment.[58] The Convention on Biological Diversity places no direct precautionary obligation on the parties. This is because the language of the principle—"full scientific certainty should not be used as a reason"[59]—is contained in the preamble, a non-binding statement of general principles in international documents. However, obligations under the Convention will be interpreted in light of such preambular statements.[60] Another of the UNCED documents, the Rio Declaration, more fully embraces the wide application of the precautionary principle, stating, "the precautionary approach shall be widely applied," and "lack of full scientific certainty shall not be used as a reason for postponing cost-effective measures."[61] The Framework Convention on Climate Change from Rio requires "precautionary measures," forbids scientific uncertainty as an excuse for inaction in the face of irreversible damage,[62] and outlines ways to achieve precaution.[63] Agenda 21 employs precautionary language tied to specific measures to enhance sustainable development policy.[64]

The OSPAR Convention[65] makes the principle a mandatory obligation of the parties ("shall apply") and establishes a threshold for precautionary action ("reasonable grounds for concern").[66] The Second Protocol to the 1979 Convention on Long-Range Transboundary Air Pollution incorporates "precautionary measures" in the preamble,[67] and further reflects the approach in its targets and monitoring programme. Signatories to the Second North Sea Conference saw the "precautionary approach [as] necessary"[68] as well, and signatories to the Baltic Sea Declaration state their "firm intention" to "apply the precautionary principle."[69] In addition to multilateral documents, the precautionary principle also appears in regional international documents, such as the African Bamako Convention[70] and European Directives on genetically modified organisms (GMOs).[71] These international legal instruments evidence state practice and, within their spheres, *opinio juris*. Where states make arguments in international tribunals as to the state of the law, evidence can be derived of *opinio juris*. For example, Hungary, in its application to the ICJ on the Diversion of the Danube River, referred to the obligation in international law to apply the precautionary principle to protect a trans-boundary resource.[72] The parties to the 1992 Trans-boundary Watercourses and International Lakes Convention agreed to be bound by the precautionary principle "by virtue of which action to avoid the *potential transboundary impact* of the release of hazardous substances shall not be postponed on the ground that scientific research has *not fully proved a causal link* between those substances, on the one hand, and the potential transboundary impact, on the other hand."[73]

A fairly recent statement of the principle is found in the 1995 UN Straddling Stocks Agreement, which has specified how states should apply the principle:

> States shall apply the *precautionary approach widely to conservation, management and exploitation* of straddling fish stocks and highly migratory fish stocks in order to *protect* the living marine resources and *preserve* the marine environment.

> States shall be *more cautious* when the information is uncertain, unreliable or inadequate. The absence of adequate scientific information shall *not* be used as a reason for postponing or failing to take conservation and management measures.[74]

The expression "precautionary principle" formally entered the language of environmental policy in the European Communities (EC) only with the Dublin Declaration of 1990, followed in 1992 by the Fifth Action Programme on Environment. The Fifth Action Programme, which refers to the Dublin Declaration, states in Chapter 2 that: "the guiding principles for policy decisions under this Programme derive from the PRECAUTIONARY APPROACH and the concept of SHARED RESPONSIBILITY, including effective implementation of the Polluter Pays Principle."[75] In 1992, the Maastricht Treaty amended Article 130R, inserting the precautionary principle among the other principles of EC environmental law (the principle of prevention, the principle of rectifying damage at source, and the polluter-pays principle). Article 130R(2) now provides that: "Community policy on the environment . . . *shall* be based on the precautionary principle."

The earliest example of an explicit reference to a precautionary measure in legislation of the European Communities is to be found in the EC Council Decision of April 1980 on chlorofluorocarbons (CFCs), which provides that "a significant reduction should, as a *precautionary measure,* be achieved in the next few years in the use of chlorofluorocarbons giving rise to emissions." Other examples of the precautionary principle being embodied in EC legislation are Directive 79/831 on the testing of new chemicals before they are marketed, Directive 80/778 of July 1980 on maximum admissible concentrations of pesticides in drinking water, Directives 90/219 and 90/220 concerning genetically modified organisms, and Directive 91/271 on urban waste water.

The precautionary principle can also be seen in the domestic regulation of states, which in turn can be taken as evidence of *opinio juris.* It is also possible, although it is a more exacting task, to show that these national laws displaying precaution count as evidence of the third type of international law: "general principles common to the major legal systems."[76]

In Germany, as detailed above, the *Vorsorgeprinzip* demands that damage to the environment be avoided in advance and provides for action absent conclusive science, buttressing governmental precautionary action.[77] The *Vorsorgeprinzip* also encourages immediate investment into existing cleaner technology, requires the use of best available technology, and promotes economic measures meant to internalize the pollution externalities.[78] The United Kingdom incorporated precaution in, *inter alia,* the White Papers, dating back to the 1990 *This Common Inheritance: Britain's Environmental Strategy,* which states the government "will be prepared to take precautionary action . . . even where scientific knowledge is not conclusive, if the balance of likely costs and benefits justifies it."[79] An interesting version appeared in the National Report of what was then the Czech and Slovak Federal Republic prepared for UNCED: "Environmental policy should be based on the following principles [among them] preliminary prudence and caution."[80]

The precautionary principle has seen extensive implementation not only in Europe, but on other continents as well. In North America, Canada incorporated the principle in the Environmental Protection Chapter of the Agreement on International Trade, aimed at interprovincial barriers to trade. Article 1502.3 permits the use of the precautionary principle as a rationale for environmental measures even if these might have a negative impact on international trade.[81] And, although not explicitly referred to, Alberta's Environmental Protection and Enhancement Act implicitly supports the precautionary principle in that standards can be set without full scientific proof.[82] There is currently a Bill, C-32, going through the Canadian parliament to amend the Environmental Protection Act to include the precautionary principle.

Ironically, however, given the ambivalent position of the United States at the international level, no country has so fully adopted the essence of the precautionary principle in domestic law as the United States. Although not described as such, the principle underlay the first wave of US federal environmental statutes in the 1970s, with the most striking characteristic being the unwillingness to wait for definitive proof.[83] The 1970 Clean Air Act (CAA) called on the Environmental Protection Agency (EPA) to apply "an ample margin of safety" in setting emissions limits for hazardous pollutants.[84] The Clean Water Act of 1972 (CWA) adopted a zero emissions goal on water pollution.[85] In fact, though the United States has often questioned the precautionary principle in international forums, its domestic law has been surprisingly precautionary.[86]

The United States' first true environmental law, the National Environmental Policy Act (NEPA) of 1969, substantively required the Environmental Protection Agency, which it created, to "use all practicable means . . . consistent with other considerations" in "considering" the environment, an act necessitated by any major federal action significantly affecting the quality of the human environment.[87] NEPA is an example, more than anything, of the use of procedural duties in an effort to act in precaution. Though the substantive duty listed above is quite discretionary for the Agency, the preparation of an Environmental Impact Statement (an analogue of the environmental impact assessment) is required by any federal action unless the environment will not be affected. In order to determine this, an environmental assessment must be done and, if there is no need for an Environmental Impact Statement, a Finding of No Significant Impact (FONSI) must still be filed.[88] Further, in *Sierra Club v. Siegler,* the Court found that NEPA requires a worst-case analysis, saying it is necessary "to assist decision making in the face of scientific uncertainty and as furthering the mandate of NEPA."[89]

Being exhaustive here is not possible. The US environmental regulations embracing precaution abound, with many statutes shifting the burden of proof (e.g. Federal Food, Drug, and Cosmetics Act and the Federal Insecticide, Fungicide, and Rodenticide Act), some creating strict liability for destroying biodiversity (e.g. Endangered Species Act, Marine Mammal Protection Act, and Bald and Gold Eagle Protection Act), and still others requiring the best available technology (e.g. CAA and CWA).[90] Congress has even chosen to be specific on this issue, saying of the 1977 CAA Amendments that the EPA's duty was to "assess risks rather than wait for proof of actual harm."[91]

There are now several judicial decisions concerning the precautionary principle. In the second nuclear test case (*New Zealand v. France*) in the International Court of Justice, the precautionary principle was argued. Although the case never proceeded to the merits, and the order of the ICJ of 22 September 1995 does not rule upon the status of the principle in international law, there is ample material to be derived from the case that advances the argument that the principle is custom. Judges Weeramantry and Palmer, having reviewed all the international treaties applying the precautionary principle, arrived at the conclusion that this principle had developed sufficiently to be considered "a principle of custom international law relating to the environment."[92] It is worth noting that in addition to New Zealand all the other intervening governments from the South Pacific region (Australia, Samoa, Solomon Islands, Marshall Islands, and the Federated States of Micronesia) argued that France was bound by custom international law to respect the precautionary principle and to carry out environmental impact assessment before conducting the nuclear tests.

In 1996 the International Court of Justice heard two requests for an advisory opinion from the World Health Organization and the United

Nations General Assembly on the legality of the threat or use of nuclear weapons. Again the precautionary principle was argued and, although incidental to the ultimate decision of the tribunal, the Court did refer to the principle in a brief section on the general principles of international environmental law.[93] In the *Gabcikovo–Nagymaros* case, also before the ICJ, Vice President Weeramantry in a separate opinion ruled that, in the case of a potential significant impact on the environment, there was a duty upon states to carry out "continuing environmental impact assessment." He stated that the environmental impact assessment was "a specific application of the larger general principle of caution."[94]

In the European Court of Justice (ECJ) there has been no definitive ruling on the status of the precautionary principle. The issue might have been determined if the plaintiffs in *Danielsson & Others v. The Commission*[95] had been granted standing to bring their case. However, the *Danish Bees* case[96] indirectly applies the precautionary principle to justify a measure having equivalent affect to a quantitative restriction in EC law. In the *Danish Bees* case the ECJ ruled in favour of a decision by the Danish Minister for Agriculture prohibiting the keeping of nectar-gathering bees, other than those of the sub-species *Apis Mellifera Mellifera* (Laeso Brown Bee), on the island of Laeso. Even in the absence of conclusive scientific evidence establishing both the particular character of that sub-species of bee in relation to others and the risk of extinction, the Court concluded that:

> Measures to preserve an indigenous animal population with distinct characteristics contribute to the maintenance of biodiversity by ensuring the survival of the population concerned. By so doing, they are aimed at protecting the life of those animals and are capable of being justified under Article 36 of the Treaty.

Here, in the context of a trade principle such as the free movement of goods, the public policy exceptions in Article 36 are being interpreted in a precautionary manner.

In an Australian decision, the Land and Environment Court of New South Wales noted that Australia was a signatory to international conventions containing the principle and had incorporated it into state regulatory strategies.[97] Stein J. said of the debate over the legal status of the principle, "It seems to me unnecessary to enter into this debate . . .

the precautionary principle is a statement of commonsense prior to the principle."[98] This reasoning was followed in the *Friends of Hinchinbrook Society* case. This was a case involving the World Heritage Convention, the Great Barrier Reef, and ministerial decisions taken under Australia's implementing legislation, the 1983 World Heritage Properties Conservation Act. The Federal Court found in favour of the ministerial decision but only on the basis that the minister had in fact exercised caution in the face of scientific uncertainty:

> It is true that the Minister did not expressly refer to the precautionary principle or some variation of it, in his reasons. But it is equally clear that before making a final decision he took steps to put in place arrangements designed to address the matters of concern identified in the scientific reports and other material available to him. The implementation of these arrangements . . . indicates that the Minister accepted that he should act cautiously in assessing and addressing the risks to World Heritage values . . . he took into account the commonsense principle that caution should be exercised where scientific opinion is divided or scientific information is incomplete.[99]

Barton points to this and other instances in Australia to support the statement that, in Australia, the principle is "a valid policy means of achieving improved environmental protection."[100]

In the United Kingdom, the Court held that Article 130R of the EC Treaty, as amended by the Maastricht Treaty, did not impose the duty on the Secretary of State to implement the principle in relation to trade. However, the important fact is that the principle was accepted as a principle of law by the tribunal, with the debate being limited to whether Article 130R created direct obligations on a Minister of the Crown.[101] Along with the cases mentioned above, the US courts have also said, "[w]here a statute is precautionary in nature, the evidence difficult to come by [or] uncertain . . . the regulations designed to protect the public health, and the decision that of an expert administrator, we will not demand rigorous step-by-step proof of cause and effect."[102] Further, national judicial decisions supporting the constitutional right to a balanced ecology for both present and future generations have been found in Costa Rica, Argentina, Ecuador, Peru, India, and Pakistan.[103]

There are common elements in all instruments implementing pre-caution. These common elements constitute the core meaning. Regard-less of the differences in wording, all of these precautionary examples share three common elements: (1) regulatory inaction threatens a non-negligible harm; (2) there exists a lack of certainty as to the cause-and-effect relationships; and (3) in such circumstances, regulatory inaction is unjustified.[104]

International law can readily absorb these elements in the principle of good neighbourliness, which, for environmental protection purposes, is expressed in Principle 21 of the Stockholm Declaration.[105] The duty to take state action to prevent harm is embedded in the customary duty to prevent trans-boundary pollution, dating back to the *Trail Smelter Arbitration* early in the twentieth century.[106] The precautionary principle on the international plane can attach itself to Principle 21, which is an established customary law rule.[107]

The precautionary principle is no less legal because it is general—the lack of definitive understandings for the terms "property rights" and "public utility" would not keep the international legal system from hearing an expropriation and compensation case.[108] In short, the sup-port for the principle is steadily becoming broader, perhaps even to the degree that it reflects a principle of customary law.

4. The precautionary principle and international trade

The precautionary principle is now implicated in the trade and environ-ment debate. It will be on the agenda, in the loosest sense of that word, for the third Ministerial Conference of the WTO in Seattle in December 1999. The European Union (EU) has "clarification of the application of the precautionary principle" on its official proposal for negotiations in the new round.[109] Specifically, the EU argues for a review if a clarifica-tion of the relationship between multilateral trade rules and core en-vironmental principles, notably the precautionary principle, is needed. It is necessary to ensure the right balance between prompt, proportional action, where justified, and the avoidance of unjustified precaution, bearing in mind that the basic concept of the precautionary principle is already present in the WTO in several key provisions, such as the Agreement on the Application of Sanitary and Phytosanitary Measures (SPS) and the Agreement on Technical Barriers to Trade (TBT).

The context for this proposal is well expressed by Renato Ruggiero:

[E]conomic integration can turn what were once domestic issues into global concerns. And all represent legitimate and important policy goals that the international trading system is being asked in one way or another to address . . . "No one is being asked to choose one over the other and no one should."[110] None of us can ignore the reality of these global concerns—whether they be environmental, development, social, or ethical issues. To describe the WTO—as sometimes happens at present—as an institution which is only focused on free trade and is insensitive to broader human concerns and values is a false representation.[111]

The EU makes its proposal having attempted to use the principle to prevent imports of US hormone-raised beef. Policy makers with complex environmental problems to address have a range of instruments at their disposal. The precautionary principle is designed to assist in changing behaviour in order to reduce risk to society. It is a controversial policy because it makes a difference. In these circumstances it is unsurprising that conflicts with economic interests emerge. Sir Leon Brittan stated recently: "There is of course a dilemma for policy makers when partial but not complete evidence becomes available that products may be harmful to the consumer, or damaging to the environment, or both. I accept the legitimacy of the concept of precaution in the field of environment and health."[112]

The WTO has already adopted sustainable development as an orientation for trade liberalization. The Preamble to the Agreement Establishing the WTO states:

Recognizing that their relations in the field of trade and economic endeavour should be conducted with a view to raising standards of living, ensuring full employment and a large and steadily growing volume of real income and effective demand, and expanding the production of and trade in goods and services, while allowing for the optimal use of the world's resources in accordance with the objective of sustainable development, seeking both to protect and preserve the environment and to enhance the means for doing so in a manner consistent with their respective needs and concerns at different levels of economic development. . .[113]

President Clinton referred to this at the Ministerial Conference of 1998, saying the Preamble "explicitly adopts sustainable development as an objective of open trade, including a commitment to preserve the environment."[114] This view is clearly expressed in the US communication to the General Council that contains its proposals for the 1999 Ministerial Conference.[115] Preambular provisions are not binding in themselves but they do guide interpretation of rules. It is possible therefore that precaution, allied to sustainable development, could be a guiding factor in determining where exactly the balance lies between free trade and environmental and health protection. This is consistent with good faith interpretation in accordance with stated objectives and purposes.[116] It is also possible that the precautionary principle will assist in interpreting unclear rules when environment or public health values are at risk, providing guidance to panels or the Appellate Body where the WTO rules have not.[117] Both the SPS Agreement and the TBT Agreement, together with the General Agreement on Tariffs and Trade (GATT), Article XX, can be informed by the principle.

The TBT Agreement applies to national regulations that use technical rules to protect health and the environment, such as packaging, marketing, and labelling requirements. The TBT Agreement is intended to ensure that members do not use technical regulations as disguised economic protectionism, and attempts to do this by encouraging harmonization.[118] The TBT Agreement places obligations on two types of measures: regulations and standards.[119] A regulation establishes mandatory product requirements based on processes and production methods (PPMs), whereas a standard establishes voluntary requirements for products or related PPMs.[120] Harmonization is promoted by requiring international standards to be used as the basis for such national requirements, unless the member can demonstrate such a standard is inappropriate to fulfil a legitimate objective.[121] Furthermore, there must be no other available means less restrictive to trade in addressing the issue.[122] The TBT Agreement does not explicitly incorporate the precautionary principle in its text. The principle could however be relevant to the application of the TBT to domestic measures in two ways:

- it may be used as a general principle behind the adoption of a specific rule that is classified as a technical barrier;
- it may determine the level of protection a country chooses.

In both circumstances the traditional analysis of what constitutes a "like product" will be stretched. The scientific evidence required to justify the domestic standard under the TBT Agreement will, for those countries adopting precautionary measures, pass through a precautionary lens.

The Worldwide Fund for Nature (WWF) urged application of the precautionary principle before the WTO Dispute Settlement Body in the *Shrimp-Turtle* dispute. The WWF urged the panel that, in review of Article XX exceptions, the panel should bear in mind the precautionary principle, in that the subject matter of the dispute concerned an endangered resource threatened with extinction.[123] The Sanitary and Phytosanitary Agreement (SPS) 1994 adopts a form of precautionary approach[124] to safeguarding human or animal life, and since the threat of turtle extinction was both serious and irreversible there should be cost-effective measures taken to prevent such damage from occurring.[125]

On Appellate Body review of the decision, WWF again filed a supplementary *amicus curiae* brief, in which it alleged that the panel failed to consider customary law in not applying the precautionary principle. It claimed that the SPS Agreement required the treaty— GATT 1994 in this case—to be interpreted taking into account relevant rules of international law.[126] The Appellate Body had already indicated a willingness to have arguments regarding custom and the principle in the *Hormones* case, and there was an even stronger case for its application here.[127]

The *Hormones* case

The principle did not determine the *Shrimp-Turtle* case, but it was a significant part of the *Hormones* case. In that case, the Appellate Body spoke directly to the relevance of the principle in the interpretation of the SPS Agreement. Ultimately, the principle did not apply, they decided, because it could not override the explicit wording of Article 5.1 and 5.2 of the SPS Agreement, which provided that SPS measures be based on risk assessment, a duty the EU had failed to honour.[128] The Appellate Body pointed out, though, that the principle had, in essence, been incorporated into Article 5.7 of the SPS Agreement.[129]

The SPS Agreement provides a state with arguments for trade-restrictive measures to protect health or the environment. It supersedes the requirements of GATT Article XX(b), and it is expressly not subject to the TBT Agreement.[130] The SPS Agreement has two main requirements relevant to the precautionary principle. The first is that measures be based on risk assessment, and the second is the right to take provisional measures where science is insufficient.

At the panel stage the EU chose not to argue its case based on the grounds of 5.7. It reasoned that 5.7 provides for a temporary measure, subject to requirements of further research and later review, and the EU sought a more permanent rule. Ultimately the EU argued that the precautionary principle had become "a general customary rule of international law" or at least "a general principle," and should be applied to Articles 5.1 and 5.2.[131] This would entail reading the risk assessment requirement of the SPS Agreement to be flexible in the face of scientific uncertainty, particularly by allowing members to be cautious. The United States argued that it did not consider the principle to be part of international law but merely "an approach." The United States further argued that the SPS Agreement does recognize a precautionary approach; indeed, Article 5.7 permits the provisional adoption of SPS measures even where the relevant scientific evidence is insufficient. Thus it argued there was no need to invoke a "precautionary principle" in order to be risk averse since the SPS Agreement, by its terms, recognized the discretion of members to determine their own level of sanitary protection. Furthermore the EU's indication of a "precautionary principle" could not create a risk assessment where there was none, nor could a "principle" create "sufficient scientific evidence" where there was none.[132]

The Appellate Body recognized that one of the issues in the appeal was "whether, or to what extent, the precautionary principle is relevant in the interpretation of the SPS Agreement."[133] The Appellate Body decided that the principle was "the subject of debate among academics, law

practitioners, regulators, and judges," and that the status of the precautionary principle in international law was something they should not
rule on.[134] They decided that "*the precautionary principle cannot override our
finding . . . namely that the EC import ban . . .* in accordance with good
practice, is, from a substantive point of view, not based on risk assessment."[135] The Appellate Body did however agree with the European
Union "that there is no need to assume that Article 5.7 exhausts the
relevance of a precautionary principle."[136]

Although not taking a decision on the substantive application of the
principle in the case, the Appellate Body was able to "note some aspects
of the precautionary principle in the SPS Agreement."[137] Although not
in itself a ground for maintaining an otherwise incompatible measure, it
does find reflection in Article 5.7. Also, it is reflected in Article 3.3,
which explicitly recognizes the right of members to establish their own
appropriate level of sanitary protection, which may be higher, or more
cautious, than international standards and guidelines. In addition,
the panel should bear in mind that responsible governments act from
a perspective of prudence when they determine "sufficient scientific
evidence."[138]

Another important outcome of the *Hormones* decision is what it revealed about the burden of proof. It confirmed explicitly that the burden
is on the member challenging an SPS measure to establish *prima facie*
evidence that there is a lack of risk assessment. Once that burden has
been met, the burden then shifts to the defending party to counter the
inconsistency.[139] The Appellate Body also interpreted that the 5.1 and
5.2 requirements that measures be "based on" risk assessment were
determined by a "rational relationship" test between the measure and a
risk assessment, which can be established absent scientific certainty.[140]

Two conclusions relating to precaution and trade come from this
discussion. First, the principle *is* relevant to the trade regime. Secondly,
by avoiding ruling on its status as custom, the Appellate Body ensured
that it will have to revisit the issue in future cases.

Hormones was followed by *Australia—Measures Affecting Importation of
Salmon*[141] in which Canada challenged an Australian prohibition on the
import of uncooked salmon. The Appellate Body upheld a panel decision
that Australia was in violation, ruling that the ban failed to meet the
requirements of Article 5.1 because it was not based on a risk assess-

ment.[142] For the first time interpreting "risk assessment" in the environmental, rather than health, context, the Appellate Body defined the elements of a risk assessment to be: (1) identification of the pests or diseases sought to prevent as well as the biological and economic consequences of their entry, (2) evaluation of the likelihood of entry and the consequences absent the SPS measure, and (3) evaluation of the likelihood with the measure in place.[143] The body also noted that a member could determine "its own appropriate level of protection to be 'zero risk.' as long as [it was] more than theoretical."[144] In principle, this decision suggests that members have scope in taking precautionary measures, but how much scope remains to be seen in practice.

Article 5.7 provides that members may provisionally adopt SPS measures in the face of insufficient scientific evidence, and this was the focus of *Japan–Varietals*. In this case, the United States challenged Japan's fumigation and varietal testing requirements on eight orchard crops. The Appellate Body cited Article 2.2 of SPS, pointing out that only 5.7 allows access to SPS measures absent scientific evidence and risk assessment.[145] Japan had violated this by maintaining requirements for four of the crops absent "sufficient" scientific evidence. Being forced to address this "sufficiency" requirement, the Appellate Body noted it was a "relational concept. 'Sufficiency' requires the existence of a sufficient or adequate relationship between . . . the SPS measure and the scientific evidence,"[146] to be determined on a case-by-case basis.[147] They went on to say that this requirement of 2.2 also applied to Articles 5.1 (basis on risk assessment) and 5.7, citing and reaffirming *Hormones*.[148] Further, the Appellate Body outlined four requirements created by 5.7, saying a member could adopt a provisional measure if: (1) the situation was one of insufficient scientific information, (2) it was adopted based on pertinent available information, (3) the member sought to obtain the additional information for a risk assessment, and (4) the member reviews the measure within a reasonable period of time.[149] The Appellate Body dealt with Japan's precautionary principle in short order, quoting *Hormones* briefly before moving on.[150]

5. Conclusion

The precautionary principle has been adopted by the environmental movement as a kind of standard to bear arms against those who threaten environmental harm. One notable response from Public Citizen sets out several of the key arguments of the more radical environmental groups:

The Evisceration of the Precautionary Principle in the Beef-Hormone Case

The Beef Hormone Decision demonstrates how the SPS Agreement can undermine countries' health, safety and environmental standards when trade challenges are initiated . . . Indeed, many areas of U.S. law—such as our system for pharmaceutical approval—are based on the precautionary principle . . . The potential boomerang effect of this WTO determination on a range of U.S. laws is immense.

Second, the Beef-Hormone case demonstrates that the SPS Agreement exalts the role of science far beyond the point it is appropriate, attempting to eliminate all "non-science" factors from standard-setting . . . While science plays a valuable role in informing such policy decisions, it is ultimately Congress or a state legislature that must make the political decision about how much risk society will face under a food safety or other law . . . by requiring food safety standards to be based on a risk assessment, the SPS Agreement eliminates the possibility that a society's values . . . should outweigh the uncertain outcome of a risk assessment . . .

Moreover, risk assessments can be no better or more accurate than the data on which they are based. Yet, most of the data on emerging toxins, like E-coli H:157, is scanty; and therefore, the risk assessments are incomplete as well . . .

The Beef-Hormone ruling makes clear that despite promises to the contrary by the United States government, the SPS Agreement will result in diminishing the safety of our food and in reducing the level of health or environmental protection for Americans. The U.S. beef industry may be happy with the bottom line, but the jurisprudence established by this case threatens numerous U.S. laws.[151]

Regardless of whether this view is accepted, the precautionary principle will continue to be argued in the international trading scheme. Members will look to safeguard their rights to prohibit or regulate trade in the public interest. The value-rich precautionary principle provides an authority or justification for that desire to safeguard. Finally, we must avoid the futility of the "sound science vs. precaution" debate. The application of the precautionary principle involves scientific argument about risk or irreversibility in a political and legal context. The case against the application of the precautionary principle involves scientific argument about risk or irreversibility in a political or legal context.

Acknowledgements

This paper could not have been completed without the help of Jon P. Sanders, Juris Doctorate candidate, Vermont Law School, USA; Intern, Foundation for International Environmental Law and Development (FIELD). I am extremely grateful to him for his assistance. I have also been assisted by reading an early unpublished draft of "The Implications of the Precautionary Principle for Trade and Sustainable Development," UNEP Paper, June 1999. And finally, at the College of Europe, Matthia Pellegrini wrote an excellent paper entitled "Is the Precautionary Principle a Norm of Customary International Law?" which I have found very helpful.

Notes

1. United Nations Economic Commission for Europe (ECE), Ministerial Declaration on Sustainable Development in the ECE Region, Bergen, May 1990, para. 7.
2. "The Future of the World Trading System," Address by Renato Ruggiero, Director-General of the World Trade Organization, 15 April 1998, to the Institute for International Economics Conference, Washington, DC, reproduced at http://www.wto.org/speeches/bergen.htm.
3. *Ethyl Corp. v. EPA*, 541 F.2d 1, 24, 25 (D.C. Cir. 1976), cert. denied, 426 U.S. 941 (1976).
4. James Cameron and Juli Abouchar, "The Status of the Precautionary Principle in International Law," in David Freestone and Ellen Hey, eds., *The Precautionary Principle and International Law: The Challenge of Implementation*, London: Kluwer Law International, 1996, pp. 29–53, at p. 29.

5. James Cameron, "The Precautionary Principle—Core Meaning, Constitutional Framework, and Procedures for Implementation," Conference paper, Institute of Environmental Studies, University of New South Wales, 1994, p. 2.

6. Cameron and Abouchar, "The Status of the Precautionary Principle," op. cit., p. 80. See also James Cameron and Will Wade-Gery, "Addressing Uncertainty: Law, Policy, and the Development of the Precautionary Principle," CSERGE Working Paper, GEC 92-43, 1992, also in Bruno Dente, ed., *Environmental Policy in Search of New Instruments,* Dordrecht: Kluwer Academic Publishers, 1994.

7. *Leatch v. National Parks and Wildlife Service* (1993) 81 LGERA 270 (Stein J.), Australia.

8. James Cameron, Paul Demaret, and Damien Geradin, eds., *Trade and Environment: The Search for Balance,* vol. 1, London: Cameron & May, 1994.

9. Ruggiero, "The Future of the World Trading System," op. cit., p. 2.

10. See, generally, *EC Measures Concerning Meat and Meat Products (Hormones)—Complaint by the United States,* Panel Report, WT/DS26/R/USA, 18 August 1997; see also the Appellate Body Report, WT/DS26/AB/R, WT/DS48/AB/R, 16 January 1998.

11. Vienna Convention on Ozone Depleting Substances, 1985, Preamble, n. 179.

12. See below.

13. Cameron and Abouchar, "The Status of the Precautionary Principle," op. cit., p. 37.

14. Timothy O'Riordan and James Cameron, "The History and Contemporary Significance of the Precautionary Principle," in Timothy O'Riordan and James Cameron, eds., *Interpreting the Precautionary Principle,* London: Earthscan Books, 1994, p. 16.

15. L. Gundling, "The Status in International Law of the Precautionary Principle," *International Journal of Estuarine and Coastal Law* 5(3), 1990, 25.

16. G. Handl, "Environmental Security and Global Change: The Challenge of International Law," *Yearbook of International Environmental Law* 1, 1990, 23.

17. See Cameron, "The Precautionary Principle," op. cit., p. 6.

18. Ibid.

19. Ibid., pp. 7 and 8; see also Cameron and Wade-Gery, "Addressing Uncertainty," op. cit., pp. 7 and 8.

20. Cameron, "The Precautionary Principle," op. cit., p. 8.

21. Ibid.; see also, Cameron and Wade-Gery, "Addressing Uncertainty," op. cit.

22. Gundling, "The Status in International Law of the Precautionary Principle," op. cit., pp. 26 and 27.

23. J. Cameron and J. Abouchar, "The Precautionary Principle: A Fundamental Principle of Law and Policy for the Protection of the Global Environment," *Boston College International & Comparative Law Review* 14(1), Winter 1991, 3.

24. Cameron and Wade-Gery, "Addressing Uncertainty," op. cit., p. 9.

25. Ibid.

26. Ibid., pp. 9 and 10.

27. Bergen Declaration, op. cit.

28. Cameron and Wade-Gery, "Addressing Uncertainty," op. cit., p. 9.

29. Anthony Giddens, *Risk,* BBC Reith Lectures 1999, lecture 2, available at http://news.bbc.co.uk/hi/english/static/events/reith_99/week2/week2.htm. See also H. Cousy, "The Precautionary Principle: A Status Question," *Geneva Papers on Risk and Insurance* 21, 1996, 162.

30. Ibid., p. 12.

31. See statement to the GLOBE General Assembly by H.E. Mr. Renagi R. Lohia, OBE, Permanent Representative of Papua New Guinea to the United Nations, on behalf of AOSIS, Washington, DC, 3 February 1992.

32. World Charter for Nature, G.A. Res 37/7, GAOR, Thirty-Seventh Sess. Supp. No. 51 (A/37/51).

33. Cameron and Wade-Gery, "Addressing Uncertainty," op. cit., p. 13.

34. Ibid.

35. Ibid., p. 14.

36. Ibid., pp. 14 and 15, citing T. O'Riordan, "The Precaution Principle in Environmental Management," CSERGE paper, GEC 92-03, 1992, pp. 25 and 26.

37. Ibid., p. 15.

38. Ibid.

39. Cameron, "The Precautionary Principle," op. cit., p. 13.

40. Ibid., pp. 14 and 15.

41. O'Riordan, "The Precaution Principle," op. cit., p. 1.

42. Cameron, "The Precautionary Principle," op. cit., p. 15.

43. Final Ministerial Declaration of the Third International Conference on the Protection of the North Sea, The Hague, 8 March 1990, p. 4, reproduced in *Yearbook of International Environmental Law* 1, 1990, 658–691.

44. Second International Conference on the Protection of the North Sea, London, 24–25 November 1987, Ministerial Declaration, issued by the UK Department of the Environment, April 1988.

45. As demonstrated by "Hume's Problem," wherein it is found that, no matter how often a phenomenon is observed, we cannot be sure this represents a universal law, a problem biting at the heart of the hypothesis–falsification–new hypothesis nature of the scientific method. See John M. Stonehouse and John D. Mumford, *Science, Risk Analysis and Environmental Policy Decisions,* UNEP Environment and Trade Series No. 5, 1994, p. 2.

46. Cameron, "The Precautionary Principle," op. cit., pp. 15–17.

47. Ibid., p. 17, citing Greenpeace International, *Critical Review of GESAMP Reports and Studies: No. 45 on Global Strategies for Marine Environmental Protection,* 1991, LDC 14/INF.29, 22 November 1991, p. 2.

48. Cameron and Wade-Gery, "Addressing Uncertainty," op. cit., p. 10.

49. Ibid., pp. 10 and 11.

50. Ibid., p. 11.

51. Ibid., p. 19.

52. Ibid., p. 20.

53. See, *inter alia,* arguments in the Climate Change context based on projected climate change possibilities based on "business as usual" and the current status quo.

54. Article 38(1) of the Statute of the International Court of Justice:

> The Court, whose function is to decide in accordance with international law such disputes as are submitted to it, shall apply:
>> (a) international conventions, whether general or particular, establishing rules expressly recognized by the contesting states;
>> (b) international custom, as evidence of a general practice accepted as law;
>> (c) the general principles of law recognized by civilized nations;

(d) subject to the provisions of Article 59, judicial decisions and the teaching of the most highly qualified publicists of the various nations, as subsidiary means for the determination of rules.

The ALI Restatement on International Law (*The Restatement of the Law Third, Foreign Relations Law of the United States 3d*, vols. 1–2, American Law Institute, 1988), §102:

Sources of International Law

1) A rule of international law is one that has been accepted as such by the international community of states:

    (a) in the form of customary law;

    (b) by international agreement; or

    (c) by derivation from general principles common to the major legal systems of the world.

2) Customary international law results from a general and consistent practice of states followed by them from a sense of legal obligation.

3) International agreements create law for the state parties thereto and may lead to the creation of customary international law when such agreements are intended for adherence by states generally and are in fact widely accepted.

55. Patricia W. Birnie and Alan E. Boyle, *International Law and the Environment*, Oxford: Clarendon Press, 1992, p. 83.

56. Ibid., p. 98.

57. Daniel Bodansky, *Proceedings of the Annual Meeting—American Society of International Law*, Washington, DC: American Society of International Law, 1991, pp. 413–417, at p. 417.

58. Cameron and Abouchar, "The Status of the Precautionary Principle," op. cit., p. 40.

59. Convention on Biological Diversity, Preamble, para. 9.

60. Cameron and Abouchar, "The Status of the Precautionary Principle," op. cit., p. 42.

61. Ibid., citing Principle 15 of the Rio Declaration.

62. United Nations Framework Convention on Climate Change, Article 3.

63. Ibid., Article 3(3).

64. Cameron and Abouchar, "The Status of the Precautionary Principle," op. cit., p. 43.

65. Convention for the Protection of the Marine Environment of the North East Atlantic (OSPAR).

66. Cameron and Abouchar, "The Status of the Precautionary Principle," op. cit., p. 43, citing OSPAR, Chapter 17, para. 17.22.

67. Cameron and Abouchar, "The Status of the Precautionary Principle," op. cit., p. 44, citing Protocol to the 1979 Convention on Long-Range Transboundary Air Pollution on Further Reduction of Sulphur Emissions, 1994, United Nations Doc. GE.94.31969.

68. Second International Conference on the Protection of the North Sea, London, 24–25 November 1987, Ministerial Declaration, issued by the UK Department of the Environment, April 1988.

69. Cameron and Wade-Gery, "Addressing Uncertainty," op. cit., p. 3, citing Baltic Sea Declaration, adopted at Baltic Environment Conference held at Ronneby, Sweden, 2–3

September 1990, IMO Doc. MEPC 30/22/5, Annex, text reproduced in *Yearbook of International Environmental Law* 1, 1990, 423–429.

70. The Convention on the Ban of Import into Africa and the Control of Transboundary Movement and Management of Hazardous Wastes within Africa. Now ratified and in force; 51 developing countries have now committed to implement precaution in respect of the regulation of trade in waste.

71. Cameron, "The Precautionary Principle," op. cit., p. 3, citing Directive 90/219, Council Directive of 23 April 1990 on the continued use of genetically modified micro-organisms, O.J. L117/1 (1990), and Directive 90/220, Council Directive of 23 April 1990 on the deliberate release into the environment of genetically modified organisms, O.J. L117/15 (1990).

72. Ibid., p. 40, citing *Case Concerning the Gabcikovo-Nagymaros Project (Hungary/ Slovakia)*, International Court of Justice, 25 September 1997, General List, No. 92, 10.

73. Transboundary Watercourses and International Lakes Convention, Article 2(5)(a), emphasis added.

74. UN Straddling Stocks Agreement, Article 6(1)(2); UN Documents, A/CONF. 164/37.

75. Reproduced in Nigel Haigh, "The Introduction of the Precautionary Principle into the U.K.," in O'Riordan and Cameron, *Interpreting the Precautionary Principle,* op. cit., pp. 229–251, at p. 235.

76. ALI Restatement, op. cit. This was alluded to by Canada in the *Hormones* case—*EC Measures Affecting Meat and Meat Products (Hormones)—Complaint by Canada,* Appellate Body Report, WT/DS26/AB/R, WT/DS48/AB/R, 16 January 1998, para. 122.

77. Sonja Boehmer-Christiansen, "The Precautionary Principle in Germany— Enabling Government," in O'Riordan and Cameron, *Interpreting the Precautionary Principle,* op. cit., p. 30.

78. Ibid., p. 50.

79. Cameron and Abouchar, "The Status of the Precautionary Principle," op. cit., p. 39, citing Haigh, "The Introduction of the Precautionary Principle," op. cit., p. 246.

80. Cameron and Abouchar, "The Status of the Precautionary Principle," op. cit., p. 39, citing *National Report of the Czech and Slovak Federal Republic,* Czechoslovak Academy of Sciences and the Federal Committee for the Environment, March 1992, p. 117.

81. Cameron and Abouchar, "The Status of the Precautionary Principle," op. cit., p. 41, citing personal communication with Janet Bax, Director, Federal Provincial Relations, Environment Canada, letter at Foundation for International Environmental Law and Development (FIELD).

82. Cameron and Abouchar, "The Status of the Precautionary Principle," op. cit., citing personal communication with Ron Hicks, Assistant Deputy Minister, Alberta Environmental Protections, letter of 20 October 1994, on file at FIELD.

83. Daniel Bodansky, "The Precautionary Principle in US Environmental Law," in O'Riordan and Cameron, *Interpreting the Precautionary Principle,* op. cit., pp. 203–228, at p. 204.

84. Ibid., citing Clean Air Act (CAA), §112, 42 USC §7412.

85. Ibid., citing Clean Water Act (CWA), §101, 33 USC §1251.

86. Ibid.

87. National Environmental Policy Act (NEPA), §§ 101, 102.

88. NEPA, §102, argued in *Calvert Cliffs v. A.E.C.* (D.C. Cir. 1971).

89. *Sierra Club v. Siegler,* 695 F.2d 957, 974 (5th Cir. 1983).

90. Bodansky, "The Precautionary Principle," op. cit., pp. 209–221.

91. Ibid., p. 207, citing HR Rpt No. 294, 1977, 49.

92. Nuclear tests [1995] ICJ Reports, Weeramantry J dissenting opinion, p. 342, and Palmer J dissenting opinion, p. 412.

93. Advisory opinion of 8.7.1996, *Legality of Threat or Use of Nuclear Weapons* [1996] 35 ILM 809.

94. Judgment of 25.9.1997, *Case Concerning the Gabcikovo - Nagymaros Project* [1998] 37 ILM 162 at p. 212.

95. *Danielsson & Others -v- The Commission* [1996] ECR II-3051.

96. Judgment of 3.12.1998, Case 67/97 Bluhme.

97. Cameron and Abouchar, "The Status of the Precautionary Principle," op. cit., p. 46, citing *Leatch v. National Parks and Wildlife Service* (1993) 81 LGERA 270 (Stein J.)

98. Ibid., pp. 94 and 95.

99. *Friends of Hinchinbrook Society Inc -v- Minister for Environment & Others* [1997] 87 LGERA 10, p. 25.

100. Carmian Barton, "The Status of the Precautionary Principle in Australia: Its Emergence in Legislation and as a Common Law Doctrine," *Harvard Law Review* 22, 1998, 509, 523.

101. See *R. v. Secretary of State for Trade and Industry ex parte Duddridge et al.* (unreported judgment), 3 October 1994, Smith J.

102. *Ethyl Corp. v. EPA,* op. cit., p. 28.

103. Cameron and Abouchar, "The Status of the Precautionary Principle," op. cit., pp. 47–48, n.63–66.

104. Ibid., p. 45.

105. Ibid.

106. Ibid.

107. Ibid.

108. Ibid.

109. *EC Approach to Trade and Environment in the New WTO Round,* WT/GC/W/194, 1 June 1999.

110. Quoting Charlene Barshefsky.

111. Ruggiero, "The Future of the World Trading System," op. cit., pp. 1–2.

112. The Rt. Hon. Sir Leon Brittan QC, Vice-President of the European Commission, speech at the High Level Symposium on Trade and Environment, Geneva, 15 March 1999, SPEECH/99/47, reproduced at http://www.wto.org/wto/hlms/lbenv.htm.

113. Agreement Establishing the World Trade Organization, 1994, Preamble, para. 2.

114. Address by President William J. Clinton, Monday 18 May 1998, available at http://www.wto.org/wto/anniv/clinton.htm.

115. *Preparation for the 1999 Ministerial Conference, Trade and Sustainable Development: Communication from the United States,* WT/GC/W/30V, 6 August 1999.

116. Ibid., citing *United States—Standards for Reformulated and Conventional Gasoline*, AB-1996-1, Report of the Appellate Body, WT/DS2/AB/R, 29 April 1996, p. 17, which adopts this notion of treaty interpretation as an element of customary law.

117. Ibid., p. 34.

118. Ibid., p. 42.

119. Ibid.

120. Ibid., citing TBT Agreement, Annex I.

121. TBT Agreement, Articles 2.2–2.5 and Article 11 (providing for departing from international standards based on scientific justification).

122. TBT Agreement, Article 2.3.

123. Cameron and Werksman, Amicus Curiae Brief Submitted by WWF/FIELD, commissioned by and submitted on behalf of WWF International, Gland, Switzerland, para. 3.6.3, on file at FIELD.

124. Ibid., citing Articles 5–12 of the Sanitary and Phytosanitary Agreement 1994.

125. Ibid., paras. 3.5.4 and 3.6.5.

126. Cameron and Werksman, Supplementary Amicus Curiae Brief Submitted by WWF/ FIELD, commissioned by and submitted on behalf of WWF International, Gland, Switzerland, on file at FIELD, para. 9.4, citing Article 31(3)(c) of the Sanitary and Phytosanitary Agreement 1994.

127. Ibid., para. 9.3.

128. *EC Measures Concerning Meat and Meat Products (Hormones)—Complaint by the United States*, AB-1997-4, Report of the Appellate Body, WT/DS26/AB/R, WT/DS48/AB/R, 16 January 1998 (hereinafter *Hormones* Appellate Body Report), para. 44.

129. Ibid.

130. TBT Agreement, Article 1.5: "The provisions of this Agreement do not apply to sanitary and phytosanitary measures as defined in Annex A of the [SPS Agreement]."

131. *Hormones* Appellate Body Report, op. cit., para. 45, citing the EC's appellant's submission, para. 91.

132. Ibid., para. 43.

133. Ibid., para. 96(c).

134. Ibid., para. 123.

135. Ibid., para. 120.

136. Ibid., para. 124.

137. Ibid.

138. Ibid.

139. Ibid., para. 253(a).

140. Ibid., paras. 188–191, and *Japan—Measures Affecting Agricultural Products*, AB-1998-8, Appellate Body Report, WT/DS76/AB/R, 22 February 1999 (hereinafter *Japan-Varietals* Appellate Body Report), para. 84.

141. *Australia—Measures Affecting Importation of Salmon*, AB-1998-5, Appellate Body Report, WT/DS18/AB/R, 20 October 1998.

142. Ibid., para. 73.

143. Ibid.

144. Ibid., para. 74.

145. *Japan-Varietals* Appellate Body Report, p. 19, para. 72.

146. Ibid., para 73.
147. Ibid., p. 22, para. 84.
148. Ibid., para. 75.
149. Ibid., pp. 23–24, para. 89.
150. Ibid., p. 21, para. 81.
151. *Comments of Public Citizen Regarding U.S. Preparations for the World Trade Organi-zation's Ministerial Meeting,* Fourth Quarter 1999, 22 October 1998, reproduced at Public Citizen, Ralph Nader's NGO, website, www.citizen.org/public_citizen/pctrade/gattwto/1999.htm#intro.

11

Environmental Treaties and Trade: Multilateral Environmental Agreements and the Multilateral Trading System

Duncan Brack

One of the key issues in the debate over how best to reconcile the two objectives of environmental protection and trade liberalization revolves around the interrelationship between multilateral environmental agreements (MEAs)—environmental treaties—and the multilateral trading system (MTS), the complex of trade agreements centred around the General Agreement on Tariffs and Trade (GATT) and overseen by the World Trade Organization (WTO). This chapter summarizes the key issues at stake, examines various options for the resolution of the debate, and concludes that a new WTO Agreement on MEAs would provide the optimal solution.

1. Multilateral environmental agreements

As Principle 12 of the Rio Declaration states, international agreement is clearly preferable to unilateral action in tackling transboundary or global environmental problems. Nearly 200 MEAs now exist, with memberships varying from a relatively small group to about 170 countries—which means in effect the whole world. The main global MEAs include:

- Three that predate the Rio Earth Summit: the 1973 Convention on International Trade in Endangered Species (CITES), the 1987 Montreal Protocol on Substances that Deplete the Ozone Layer and the 1989 Basel Convention on the Control of Transboundary Movements of Hazardous Wastes.
- The 1992 Rio agreements: the Framework Convention on Climate Change, the Convention on Biological Diversity, and the Convention to Combat Desertification.
- Others agreed recently, but not yet in force, including the 1997 Kyoto Protocol on climate change and the 1998 Rotterdam Convention on hazardous chemicals in international trade; and draft MEAs still under negotiation, including the convention on the control of persistent organic pollutants, and the Biosafety Protocol to the Biodiversity Convention.

Over 20 of these MEAs incorporate restraints on the trade in particular substances or products, either between parties to the treaty and/or between parties and non-parties.[1] These include CITES, the Basel Convention, the Montreal Protocol, the Rotterdam Convention, and the draft Biosafety Protocol; the Kyoto Protocol will also interact with trade, but in more complex ways. Given the continued degradation of the global environment, the negotiation of further MEAs is almost bound to form an increasingly prominent part of the international agenda; and given the inescapable interaction of trade liberalization with environmental protection, and the shortage of policy instruments available with which to enforce MEAs, an increasing number of environmental treaties are likely to contain trade measures.

Trade provisions in MEAs have been designed to realize four major objectives:[2]

1. To control and restrict markets for environmentally hazardous products or goods produced unsustainably.

2. To increase the coverage of the agreement's provisions by encouraging governments to join and/or comply with the MEA.

3. To prevent free-riding (where non-participants enjoy the advantages of the MEA without incurring its costs) by encouraging governments to join and/or comply with the MEA.

4. To ensure the MEA's effectiveness by preventing leakage—the situation where non-participants increase their emissions, or other un-

sustainable behaviour, as a result of the control measures taken by signatories.

The trade measures incorporated in the five MEAs listed above are outlined briefly below.

The Convention on International Trade in Endangered Species of Wild Fauna and Flora (CITES)

CITES was agreed in 1973, and today includes 145 parties.[3] Parties are required to apply controls to trade in species according to the degree to which they are endangered by international trade:

- Species listed in *Appendix I* (600 animal and 170 plant species) are threatened with extinction and are or could be affected by trade.
- Species listed in *Appendix II* (2,700 animal and over 20,000 plant species) are not now threatened with extinction but may become so unless trade is subject to strict regulation; species that *look* like other listed species are also included in order to render the controls more effective.
- Species listed in *Appendix III* (200 animal and 46 plant species) are protected in individual countries that have requested the cooperation of other CITES parties in controlling trade.

Trade is regulated through the granting of permits, which may be issued only by CITES parties. *Export permits* are required for both Appendix I and Appendix II species; these may be granted only if the trade is not detrimental to the survival of the species, if the specimens have not been obtained in contravention of national laws, and if living specimens are shipped under conditions designed to guarantee their well-being. In addition, Appendix I species require *import permits,* and the export permit cannot be granted unless an import permit has already been obtained. Conditions for the grant of an import permit are similar to those for an export permit, but also include the requirement that the specimen must not be used for "primarily commercial purposes," a phrase that has generally been interpreted to prohibit trade in any instance where commercial considerations are present. Trade in Appendix III species requires an export permit from a country that has listed the species, or a certificate of origin from a country that has not listed it. Exceptions to the trade regulations have been allowed where specimens have been bred in captivity, artificially propagated, or ranched.

Parties may enter a reservation regarding any listing, in which case they are regarded, for purposes of trade in the species concerned, as a non-party. Trade with non-parties is not permitted except where documentation equivalent to CITES permits is provided; this has come to include a requirement for formal identification of competent scientific and management authorities, as required for CITES parties. In addition, trade with non-parties in Appendix I species is limited to special cases that benefit the conservation of the species.

In addition to the requirement for licences, total or partial bans on trade have also been employed as an enforcement mechanism.[4] In a number of cases where countries have been identified as being in persistent non-compliance, the Standing Committee of the CITES conference has recommended all parties to apply Article XIV(1) of the Convention, which allows parties to take stricter domestic measures than those provided by the treaty, including complete prohibitions of trade, collectively (albeit temporarily) against the offending countries. This has included the United Arab Emirates in 1985–1990, Thailand in 1991–1992, and Italy in 1992–1993. The procedure has also been used against states not party to the Convention, after persistent refusal to provide "comparable documents" to CITES licences; in the case of El Salvador (1986–1987) and Equatorial Guinea (1988–1992), the ban was lifted after the countries targeted became parties.

In other cases, countries have come into compliance with, or membership of, CITES after unilateral rather than collective action. Examples include a US ban on wildlife imports from Singapore in September 1986 (Singapore became a party in November 1986) and US unilateral trade sanctions against Taiwan from August 1994 (Taiwan amended its legislation in October 1994 along CITES lines, and the US embargo was lifted in June 1995)—the CITES Standing Committee had recommended stricter domestic measures in September 1993. Similarly, Indonesia's announcement of "voluntary" export quotas for several endangered species in 1994 may be attributed at least in part to a ban by the European Union (EU) on wildlife imports from Indonesia, imposed in 1991 and subsequently lifted in 1995.

Assessing the effectiveness of CITES is difficult, since the survival of a species generally depends on many more factors than the extent of international trade in it or its products. There have been some clear successes, including the spotted cats, the Nile crocodile, and the African elephant (where rapid population decline stabilized on its listing under Appendix I). Other species, however, remain threatened with extinction; the tiger is the classic example, where widespread illegal trade poses a serious problem. Although it is true to say that no species listed under CITES has become extinct since the treaty was signed, it should also be noted that almost three times as many species have been transferred from Appendix II to I (187 taxa, i.e. species, sub-species, and populations) as have been moved in the other direction (67 taxa).

The Montreal Protocol

The Montreal Protocol on Substances that Deplete the Ozone Layer (a protocol to the 1985 Vienna Convention on the Protection of the Ozone Layer) was negotiated in 1987 to control the production and consumption of ozone-depleting substances (ODS), of which the most common were the family of chlorofluorocarbons (CFCs).[5] Unlike CITES and the Basel and Rotterdam Conventions, the Montreal Protocol employs trade restrictions as one policy instrument among several. The trade aspects of the treaty fall into two categories: trade restrictions between parties, which are not mandated by the Protocol but are consequential on its control schedules; and trade restrictions between parties and non-parties, which are required under the terms of the Protocol.[6]

The Protocol requires parties to control both the consumption and the production of ODS. Since consumption is defined as production plus imports minus exports, parties must exercise control over trade if they are to satisfy their control schedules. A variety of trade restrictions have been employed, including voluntary industry agreements, product labelling requirements, requirements for import licences (sometimes incorporating a tradable permit system), excise taxes, quantitative restrictions on imports, and total or partial import bans. In addition, in response to concern over the growth of illegal trade in CFCs and halons, the Montreal Amendment to the Protocol (agreed in 1997 but not yet in force) will require parties to introduce a licensing system for all exports and imports of ODS (including used, reclaimed, and recycled substances).

The Protocol also imposes bans on trade between parties and non-parties to the treaty. These trade provisions cover restrictions on both imports from and exports to non-parties of ODS, products containing ODS (e.g. refrigerators), and products made with but not containing ODS (e.g. electronic components)—although to date the parties have decided that the introduction of the last category of trade bans is impracticable owing to difficulties in detection. Non-parties that are nevertheless in compliance with the control measures specified in the Protocol are treated as if they were parties with respect to the trade provisions.

These trade provisions had two aims. One was to maximize participation in the Protocol, by shutting off non-signatories from supplies of CFCs and providing a significant incentive to join. If completely effective this would in practice render the trade provisions redundant, because there would be no non-parties against which to apply them. The other goal, should participation not prove total, was to prevent industries from migrating to non-signatory countries to escape the phase-out schedules. In the absence of trade restrictions, not only could this fatally undermine the control measures, but it would help non-signatory countries to gain a competitive advantage over signatories, as the progressive phase-outs raised industrial production costs. If trade was forbidden, however, not only would non-signatories be unable to export ODS, but they would also be unable to enjoy fully the potential gains from cheaper production because exports of products containing, and eventually made with, ODS would also be restricted. (In fact, because industrial innovation proceeded far more quickly than expected, many of the CFC substitutes proved significantly cheaper than the original ODS—but this was not foreseen in 1987).

All the evidence suggests that the trade provisions achieved their objectives. All CFC-producing countries and all but a handful of consuming nations have adhered to the treaty (a total of 168 countries to date). Although it is difficult to determine states' precise motivations for joining—there are a variety of reasons, including the availability of financial support for developing countries—the trade restrictions do appear to have provided a powerful incentive, and at least some countries have cited them as the major justification (including China, and Korea, which initially expanded its domestic CFC production but then realized the disadvantages of being shut out of Western markets and acceded). The major CFC producers, mostly located in the United States and Western Europe and therefore subject to the controls from the start, were supporters of the trade restrictions, viewing them as a method of ensuring that the alternatives to CFCs that they produced were not undercut by cheaper competition from non-parties.

Trade restrictions have also played their part in the non-compliance procedures of the Montreal Protocol, which have been applied so far to a number of "transition economies" in central and eastern Europe and to the former Soviet Union, which have found it impossible to meet their phase-out target dates. The procedure is non-confrontational, conciliatory, and cooperative, encouraging and providing assistance to parties to come back into compliance, but the possibility of suspension from the Protocol, the withdrawal of financial assistance, and the application of trade measures (as to a non-party) provides an important underpinning to the procedure. So far, these more drastic measures have not had to be taken, though some non-parties in non-compliance have had trade restrictions imposed on their ability to export the ODS that they should not have been producing.

The Basel Convention

The Basel Convention on the Control of Transboundary Movements of Hazardous Wastes and their Disposal was negotiated in 1989 in response to concerns over the growth in volumes of hazardous waste and some high-profile cases of toxic waste dumping in developing countries.[7] The aim of the Convention is to protect human health and the environment against the adverse effects of the generation, trans-boundary movement, and management of hazardous waste, through minimizing generation, assisting developing countries in the environmentally sound management of waste, and reducing trans-boundary movements to a minimum consistent with their environmentally sound and efficient management.

The core of the agreement, however, deals with the control of trade. Movements of hazardous wastes across national boundaries can take place between parties to the Convention only via a "prior notification and consent" procedure involving the states of export, import, and transit; each shipment of waste subject to the Convention must be accompanied by a movement document from point of departure to point of disposal. Notwithstanding this procedure, the Convention also requires exporting states to prohibit shipments of hazardous or other wastes if there is reason to believe that the wastes will not be managed in an environmentally sound manner in the importing country. Any party also has the right to prohibit the import of hazardous wastes into its own territory. No category of wastes may be exported to states not party to the Convention unless the country in question is a signatory to another agreement—bilateral, regional, or multilateral. If the agreement was reached before the Basel Convention entered into force, it must be "compatible" with the aims of the Convention; if reached later, it must be "not less environmentally sound" than Basel.

The Basel Convention entered into force in May 1992 and there are currently 123 parties, the major exception being the United States (which has signed but not yet ratified). As far as can be ascertained, the Convention has had some success: the share of total hazardous waste exports destined for final disposal has declined in recent years and the worst forms of hazardous waste dumping on developing countries have largely ended. The rapid evolution of the regime, however, has outstripped the development of its technical and statistical support. Since basic data on the volumes and hazard characteristics of wastes generated and shipped across borders, and universal definitions of hazardous wastes, do not yet exist, a definitive conclusion is difficult to reach.

Even before the Convention was adopted there was pressure to go further than its provisions. African countries in particular argued for a total ban on the waste trade, and in 1991 agreed the Bamako Convention, which prohibited the import of all hazardous wastes into Africa from non-contracting parties and adopted a notification and consent system for trans-boundary movements within Africa. The Lomé Convention similarly bans all movements of hazardous wastes from the EU to the ACP (African, Caribbean, Pacific) developing countries. In 1995, an amendment to the Basel Convention was agreed requiring Annex VII countries (those in the Organization for Economic Cooperation and Development, the EU, and Liechtenstein) to prohibit the export to non-Annex VII countries of hazardous wastes for disposal, and, by the end of 1997, to end shipments to non-Annex VII states of hazardous wastes for recovery or recycling. The amendment (which has not yet entered into force) has proved controversial, however, with a number of countries—developing and industrialized—concerned over the potential negative economic impacts of the ban on exports for recycling.[8]

The Kyoto Protocol

The Kyoto Protocol to the United Nations Framework Convention on Climate Change (FCCC) was adopted in December 1997. The Protocol establishes a legally binding obligation on Annex I (developed) countries to reduce emissions of greenhouse gases on average by 5.2 per cent below 1990 levels by the period 2008–2012. These "quantified emission limitation and reduction commitments" are differentiated between countries and, relative to a business-as-usual scenario, imply real reductions of approximately 20–40 per cent.[9] As of July 1999, 84 countries had signed the Protocol and 12 had ratified it. It will enter into force when 55 parties, including Annex I parties accounting for at least 55 per cent of the Annex I carbon dioxide emissions in 1990, have ratified it.

Commitments are to be achieved in a number of ways. Article 2 of the Protocol commits each Annex I party to "implement and/or further elaborate policies and measures in accordance with its national circumstances," and then lists a wide range of potential areas for action, including energy efficiency, renewable energy sources (and advanced technologies in general), removal of market distortions such as subsidies, and transport. Although no further details are specified, it is not impossible that parties could claim justification from the Kyoto Protocol for measures that restrain greenhouse gas emissions from their own territories via methods that protect their own industries at the expense of importers. Although paragraph 3 of Article 2 states the principle of protection of countries from any adverse effects of any of the policies and measures that may be adopted, including effects on international trade, the wording is so general as to be fairly unhelpful for guidance in drawing up specific policies.

In addition to this framework of domestic measures, the Protocol contains a series of "flexibility mechanisms" designed to reduce emissions through international cooperation. These include international emissions trading, the clean development mechanism, and joint implementation, all of which are intended to optimize the cost-effectiveness of emissions-reduction initiatives and to lower the cost of complying with the respective emissions targets assumed under the Protocol. Together they have the potential to create an international market for greenhouse gas (and particularly carbon) emissions abatement, with profound implications for the international economy. This is another potential area for interaction with the MTS, both in the way in which emissions permits are allocated (which may have implications for the WTO Subsidies Agreement) and in the trade in permits themselves.

Several issues were left unresolved at Kyoto, including the details of the flexibility mechanisms and any non-compliance system (which could hypothetically contain Montreal Protocol-type trade measures, though this would be a highly contentious subject). These are to be settled by succeeding conferences of the parties to the FCCC.[10]

The Rotterdam Convention

The Rotterdam Convention on the application of the prior informed consent procedure for certain hazardous chemicals and pesticides in international trade was adopted in September 1998. The agreement has been signed by 61 states, and it will enter into force once 50 states have ratified it. The Convention builds on earlier work and agreements on the prior informed consent (PIC) procedure, including the Food and Agriculture Organization's International Code of Conduct for the Distribution and Use of Pesticides and the UN Environment Programme's London Guidelines for the Exchange of Information on Chemicals in International Trade. Both these instruments included procedures aimed at making information about hazardous chemicals more readily available, thereby permitting countries to assess the risks associated with their use. Both of them in due course came to include a voluntary PIC procedure, to provide a means for formally obtaining and disseminating the decisions of importing countries on whether or not they wished to receive future shipments of such chemicals. The procedure aimed to promote a shared responsibility between exporting and importing countries in protecting human health and the environment from the harmful effects of hazardous chemicals in international trade.

The Convention codifies the PIC procedure for a list of specified substances: currently 5 industrial chemicals (including PCBs and PBBs) and 22 pesticides (including aldane, chlordane, DDT, and lindane), though it is expected that many more chemicals will be added as its provisions are implemented. For each substance listed, parties are required to inform the Convention Secretariat whether they wish to permit or ban, or permit under particular conditions, its import, to ensure that exports of the substance from their jurisdictions take place in accordance with these decisions on import, and to provide export notifications where the substance is itself banned or severely restricted domestically. The Convention also encourages measures such as national registers and databases of the substances, information exchange on hazards and handling, and technical assistance from more advanced economies to other parties.

MEA trade measures

As can be seen, trade provisions in MEAs have in general been designed and used either to exercise control over trade itself, where this is perceived to be the source of the environmental damage, or as an enforcement mechanism, to ensure that the MEA is not undermined by the behaviour of non-parties. The second function is of particular importance. There are a limited number of means by which countries can affect the actions of other countries: political/diplomatic pressure, provision of financial and technological assistance, trade sanctions, and military force. The first two of these are clearly preferable, but they have obvious limits. One can assume that use of the military option is unlikely to be helpful. Trade measures are therefore likely to continue to play a role as one component of effective environmental agreements.

Can the use of trade measures in this way be regarded as an infringement of national sovereignty? The classical doctrines of sovereignty, originating in the seventeenth century, have little of use to say about relations between states or the "rights" of states to expect other states to engage in international trade with them. It is clear, however, that the unrestrained output of pollution that is trans-boundary or global in scope *does* constitute an infringement of sovereignty, in that it inflicts direct physical harm on the populations and/or territories of other states. The unrestrained depletion of the global commons—e.g. of non-territorial species—can, though more arguably, be regarded similarly. The responsibility of individual nations for the protection of the global environment and for the promotion of development that is environmentally sustainable has of course been accepted in many international agreements, most notably Agenda 21. Once again, the use of trade measures in MEAs must be contemplated if the global environment is to be protected effectively.

2. Interrelationship of MEAs with the multilateral trading system[11]

Disregarding these more general considerations, and accepting the value of MEA trade measures, can the use of them against WTO members be regarded as an infringement of their rights under the MTS? It seems fairly clear that there is a *potential* for conflict:

- GATT Articles I ("Most Favoured Nation Treatment") and III ("National Treatment") outlaw discrimination in trade: WTO members are not permitted to discriminate between traded "like products" produced by other WTO members, or between domestic and international "like products." Yet all the three major MEAs referred to above (CITES, the Montreal Protocol, and the Basel Convention) discriminate between countries on the basis of their environmental performance, requiring parties to restrict trade to a greater extent with non-parties than they do with parties; indeed, such discrimination is one of the points of these MEAs, since they are aimed to promote sustainable activities while punishing unsustainable behaviour.
- GATT Article XI ("Elimination of Quantitative Restrictions") forbids any restrictions other than duties, taxes, or other charges on imports from and exports to other WTO members; yet each of the three MEAs requires precisely such quantitative restrictions.
- Article III requires imported and domestic like products to be treated identically. The meaning of the term "like product" has become one

of the most difficult issues in the trade/environment arena. Originally incorporated into the GATT in order to prevent discrimination on the grounds of national origin, the term has usually been interpreted more broadly by GATT and WTO dispute panels to prevent discrimination in cases where process methods, rather than product characteristics, have been the distinguishing characteristic of the product and the justification for trade measures—for example, the US embargo on imports of shrimp caused by methods that kill sea turtles (the subject of a WTO dispute in 1998). Yet the Montreal Protocol envisages restrictions on trade in products made with but not containing ODS (originating from non-parties), whereas domestic products produced in this way are not subject to such regulation—although so far this provision has not been put into practice.

It is possible, of course, that an MEA trade measure could be "saved" by the General Exceptions clause of the GATT—Article XX—which states that:

> Subject to the requirement that such measures are not applied in a manner which would constitute a means of arbitrary or unjustifiable discrimination between countries where the same conditions prevail, or a disguised restriction on international trade, nothing in this Agreement shall be construed to prevent the adoption or enforcement by any contracting party of measures:
>
> . . .
>
> (b) necessary to protect human, animal or plant life or health; . . .
> (g) relating to the conservation of exhaustible natural resources if such measures are made effective in conjunction with restrictions on domestic production or consumption.

Unlike many MEAs, where terms tend to be defined in the treaty or in subsequent decisions of conferences of the parties, interpretation of the MTS usually proceeds through a case-law-type approach, relying on the findings of dispute panels in particular cases. Since a dispute case involving an MEA trade measure has never been brought before a GATT or WTO panel,[12] it is impossible to say for certain whether it would be found to be incompatible with the MTS.

It is possible, however, to extrapolate from the arguments and findings in a series of trade/environment disputes involving unilaterally imposed trade measures that were brought before panels.[13] In each of these cases, the panel found the environmental measures in question not to be justifiable, because either:

- the measures were not "necessary" (Article XX(b)) to the achievement of the environmental goal, because the panel believed that there were less trade-restrictive or GATT-inconsistent measures also available; or
- the measures were not "relating to the conservation of exhaustible natural resources" (Article XX(g)), because the policies in question were extra-jurisdictional—they attempted to modify the behaviour of other WTO members and could not therefore be considered to be primarily aimed at conserving the natural resources of the country applying the trade measures; or
- the measures represented "arbitrary or unjustifiable discrimination" (Article XX headnote) in that less discriminatory methods were available that could have been employed.

It is of course dangerous to extrapolate from arguments used in cases of trade measures imposed *unilaterally* to those involving the application of trade measures mandated by or in pursuance of the requirements of *multilateral* agreements. In any case, it is difficult, even from an environmental viewpoint, to defend most of the measures taken in the relevant disputes. The way in which the United States applied its embargo on shrimp imports from a number of South and South East Asian countries, for instance, does appear to be "arbitrary and unjustifiable discrimination" when compared with the much more gradual and participatory way in which it applied measures to protect sea turtles in the Caribbean region.

Furthermore, WTO dispute panels and its Appellate Body have become steadily more sophisticated in their arguments and more conscious of the environmental dimension of the arguments. The Appellate Body decision in the *Shrimp-Turtle* dispute, for example, used the reference in the Preamble of the Marrakesh Agreement Establishing the WTO to "allowing for the optimal use of the world's resources in accordance with the objective of sustainable development, seeking both to protect and preserve the environment and to enhance the means for doing so," to dispose of the argument that species protection was not a legitimate objective for trade measures. It also stressed, as have several panels before it, the desirability of multilateral agreement as opposed to unilateral measures (commenting approvingly on the US-inspired Inter-American Convention for the Protection and Conservation of Sea Turtles agreed in 1996).

Unsurprisingly, however, neither the panels nor the Appellate Body have ever speculated as to the acceptability to the MTS of *trade measures* implemented in order to fulfil such multilateral agreements—the point of the Inter-American Convention, for instance, being to avoid the need for recourse to such measures. It is still, therefore, not clear how panels, or the Appellate Body, would rule on MEA-mandated trade measures.

There is an important distinction to be made here between trade measures adopted between parties to an MEA (such as the import and export licences required under CITES) and trade measures adopted between parties and non-parties (such as the ban on trade in ODS, etc., with non-parties to the Montreal Protocol). The reasoning used by the Appellate Body in the *Shrimp-Turtle* decision suggests that the first category of trade measures (between parties) might now be found to be MTS compatible. Because all parties involved would have agreed to the trade restriction, it would be difficult to argue that it represented "arbitrary or unjustifiable discrimination."

In the case of the other main category (trade measures adopted between parties and non-parties), however, the non-parties have by definition not agreed to the measures. In the *Shrimp-Turtle* case, the reasoning used by the panel and Appellate Body suggests that they still might rule against this kind of MEA trade measure:

> In our view, if an interpretation of the chapeau of Article XX were to be followed which would allow a Member to adopt measures conditioning access to its market for a given product upon the adoption by the exporting Members of certain policies, including conservation policies, GATT 1994 and the WTO Agreement could no longer serve as a multilateral framework for trade among Members as security and predictability of trade relations under those agreements would be threatened.[14]

The panel quoted approvingly from the GATT panel findings in the 1994 *Tuna-Dolphin* case:

> If, however, Article XX were interpreted to permit contracting parties to take trade measures so as to force other contracting parties to change their policies within their jurisdiction, including their conservation policies, the balance of rights and obligations among contracting parties, in particular the right of access to markets, would be seriously impaired.[15]

> Perhaps the most conspicuous flaw in this measure's application relates to its intended and actual coercive effect on the specific policy decisions made by foreign governments, Members of the WTO.[16]

> However, it is not acceptable, in international trade relations, for one WTO Member to use an economic embargo to *require* other Members to adopt essentially the same comprehensive regulatory program, to achieve a certain policy goal, as that in force within that Member's territory.[17]

The entire point of the trade measures directed against non-parties to the Montreal Protocol is to compel them to change their policies, to phase out the production and consumption of ODS in the same way as parties—or, at least, to condition market access to parties on this phase-out policy. It is intentionally discriminatory between parties and non-parties, or, to be more accurate, between countries in compliance with the Protocol (whether formally parties or not) and those not in compliance. It is difficult to believe that the panel and Appellate Body could maintain their lines of reasoning and still find in favour of this kind of trade measure.

Regardless of this distinction, trade measures employed under the three main MEAs cited above are now unlikely to be challenged in the WTO, because of the wide international acceptability they enjoy— though this is less true of the Basel Convention, where the amendment banning trade in waste between Annex VII and non-Annex VII countries (not yet in force) has aroused hostility amongst some of the industries involved. The possible MTS-incompatibility of the amendment has been raised explicitly as an argument against adopting or ratifying it by those opposed to the principle.

This "political chill" argument has also surfaced in other MEAs. Attempts to include trade provisions in the International Convention for the Conservation of Atlantic Tuna and in agreements to control driftnet fishing were shelved because of the fear that they would be inconsistent with GATT rules.[18] The same issue was raised in the 1997 negotiations over the Kyoto Protocol, in discussions in 1998 over the Rotterdam Convention, and in 1999 in the unsuccessful negotiations on the Biosafety Protocol.

The continuation of this potential conflict between the MTS and MEAs is clearly undesirable. The fact that it is not known for certain how a dispute panel would rule on an MEA trade measure creates an unstable and uncertain situation. On the face of it, it does appear absurd that the operation of an important element of international law should be subject to a panel of three individuals deciding what they think 10 lines of printed text (the relevant sections of GATT Article XX) written 50 years ago could mean in a vastly changed international environment. In addition, it creates the spectre of a potential challenge to an existing MEA, bringing the two international regimes of trade liberalization and environmental protection directly into conflict; and it increases the likelihood of conflict over the negotiation of future MEAs with trade measures, potentially weakening their effectiveness—the "political chill" argument. Finally, the perception that the WTO threatens environmental sustainability, already widespread in some quarters, assists neither the growth of the MTS nor the further spread of trade liberalization, even where this would have environmental benefits.

3. Global systems in conflict

How can this clash be resolved? When two systems of law come into conflict, actually or potentially, there are three potential methods of dealing with the situation:

- create some superior balancing mechanism;
- determine that one legal system is superior to another, either wholly or in part;
- modify either or both legal systems to bring them into harmony.

The first option, the creation of a balancing mechanism, would be the most desirable solution in a perfect world. This is in effect the system that operates inside the European Union, where trade liberalization and environmental protection are both objectives of the Treaty of Rome. Any conflict between the two objectives can be resolved by the European Court of Justice, which has the power to rule on the appropriate balance between trade and environmental measures in any particular case. In the well-known *Danish bottles* dispute of 1986, for example, the Court upheld the core of the Danish law requiring a collection system for returnable drinks containers while striking down some of the details of the regulations as unnecessarily trade restrictive given the environmental objective in question.

The creation of an equivalent system at a global level would require substantial reform of the entire system of international institutions, however, and is not a realistic prospect in the short term. Having said that, there have been calls for such a reform, perhaps using the International Court of Justice as the superior body. Proposals for a new World Environmental Organization (for instance by Chancellor Kohl at the UN General Assembly Special Session, "Earth Summit 2," in June 1997) have had the objective of creating a balancing institution to the WTO at least partly in mind, though the interrelationship between such a new WEO and the WTO was not, and has not been, explored in any detail. It is interesting to note that the 1948 Charter for the International Trade Organization (the intended third leg of the Bretton Woods tripod, never adopted because of US opposition) did provide that a member prejudiced by an ITO decision could seek an advisory opinion from the ICJ, whose opinion would then bind the ITO.[19]

The second option, determining that one legal system is superior to the other, is *de facto,* even if not *de jure,* the position as it stands at present. As noted above, the validity of trade measures in MEAs could be challenged under the WTO, and a WTO dispute panel would then rule on their compatibility with the MTS. Although panels have become steadily more aware of and more open to environmental arguments (the decision of the Appellate Body in the *Shrimp-Turtle* case to accept "non-requested information from non-governmental sources" was a positive step forward), they are nevertheless composed of international trade experts who reach decisions in accordance with a body of international trade law—indeed, they cannot do otherwise, since this is the function of the WTO. The MTS has been constructed by trade negotiators with relatively little awareness of environmental requirements and policies, and, despite a number of references to environmental objectives in the WTO agreements, it is not well attuned to environmental imperatives even though it cannot avoid interacting with environmental regulation.

It could of course be argued that MEAs are constructed by environmental negotiators with little awareness of trade law and the desirability of liberalized trade. But that would be unfair. Many delegations to MEA negotiations routinely include trade department representatives, and, in a number of instances (including the Montreal Protocol), negotiators have sought advice from the GATT/WTO Secretariat in designing particular features of their treaties. Some MEAs, including the FCCC, borrow text directly from GATT.

More generally, national trade departments tend to wield greater political clout than do environment departments and agencies, environmental objectives are not well integrated into policy across the board, and at the international level the MTS and the WTO (and in particular its dispute settlement system) are considerably more powerful and influential than are MEAs and the various environmental institutions such as UN Environment Programme or the UN Commission on Sustainable Development. The trade implications of particular MEA requirements can in theory be subject to scrutiny by the institutions of the MTS, but there is no provision anywhere for the environmental implications of the MTS to be subjected to scrutiny by environmental institutions.

The existing hierarchy of international law therefore favours, in practice even if not in the letter, the MTS over MEAs. For the reasons rehearsed above, this is an undesirable situation if one accepts that the two objectives of trade liberalization and environmental protection are of equal validity. The conclusion reached, therefore, is that the third option—modification of one or both of the existing systems of international law, for which priority should be given to the modification of the MTS—is required.

4. Discussions in the WTO

The approach of the WTO Millennium Round, due to begin at the end of 1999, lends urgency to this analysis. Out of the very wide range of issues that could be considered under the "trade/environment" heading, resolution of the MEAs–MTS conflict has always been regarded as one of the most pressing, as evidenced by the concentration given to it by the WTO Committee on Trade and Environment (CTE) in its first two years of existence leading up to the Singapore WTO Ministerial Conference in December 1996. The Committee's discussions in 1995–1996 saw several countries put forward proposals for the resolution of the perceived conflict.[20]

The proposals tended to fall into three groups: "environment-minded," "trade-minded," and "development-minded"—though of course all participants in the debate claimed that they had the interests of trade, development, *and* the environment at heart.

The "environment-minded" group (represented by papers from the EU and Switzerland) broadly accepted the arguments for modification of the MTS, and much of the debate revolved around the EU proposal for an amendment of Article XX of the GATT to add trade measures taken pursuant to MEAs as a new qualifying subparagraph.

The "trade-minded" group (represented by papers from New Zealand, Japan, Korea, Hong Kong, and the Association of South East Asian Nations (ASEAN)) saw trade liberalization as the overriding aim of the WTO, and, although accepting the case for trade measures in MEAs, aimed to ensure that they were as tightly restricted as possible. Proponents of this standpoint often argued that no change to the MTS was necessary, an *ex post* waiver option (see further below) being all that was necessary to resolve any dispute; or perhaps some kind of "understanding" might be helpful to guide MEA negotiators in drawing up acceptable trade measures. Any amendment of Article XX was to be opposed as widening the scope for trade-restrictive measures and or disguised protectionism, and detracting from the rights of WTO members who were MEA non-parties. This group also frequently pointed out that only a small proportion of MEAs contained trade measures, and that there had never been a GATT or WTO dispute involving an MEA, thus questioning whether the discussion was really necessary.

The "development-minded" group (represented by papers from Egypt, India, and ASEAN, supported in debate by Nigeria and Mexico) regarded the concentration of debate on the use and definition of trade measures as at best unbalanced and at worst actively unhelpful. Trade measures should be seen in context as one component of, or one option for, a policy package also incorporating "positive measures" and improved market access (elimination of subsidies, reduction of tariffs and technical barriers to trade). Opinions differed on whether trade measures would be helpful in this context or whether they were straightforwardly undesirable, with other measures being able to achieve their objectives in a way that did not distort trade. The definition of an MEA was another much-stressed point, with the underlying concern being to avoid dealing with MEAs (and accompanying trade measures) that had been negotiated between a small group of countries without the participation of most, or all, developing countries.

The "environment-minded" group found itself more and more on the defensive, as the proposals put forward by other WTO members in response became more and more restrictive. Increasingly they aimed to limit the scope for trade measures in existing and future MEAs by specifying particular requirements for the trade measures under scrutiny. Any or all of "necessity," "effectiveness," "least trade-restrictiveness," "proportionality," or "sound scientific basis" were suggested as criteria that trade measures would have to fulfil, and that WTO panels would judge whether they satisfied. In practice this would have reinforced the existing international hierarchy, rendering MEAs more subject to WTO scrutiny and tilting the balance further towards the MTS and away from MEAs.

5. Options for resolution

It is to be hoped that any discussions in the Millennium Round will avoid a repeat of the CTE's long-drawn-out and ultimately inconclusive debate. Any solution to the conflict needs to satisfy the following criteria:

• There should be certainty about the MTS-compatibility of trade measures under existing MEAs, both those specifically mandated by the MEA in question ("specific measures") and those not specifically required by the MEA but taken in pursuance of its aims ("non-specific measures").[21]

- There should be certainty over the MTS-compatibility of trade measures that might be incorporated in future MEAs or those currently under negotiation.
- There should be flexibility for MEA negotiators to incorporate trade measures in future MEAs where they consider them necessary to the fulfilment of their objectives.
- If trade measures are required by MEA negotiators, they should be applied in as non-discriminatory a way as possible; i.e. they should employ only such trade discrimination as is required to fulfil the aims of the MEA, and should not provide an opportunity for trade protectionism unrelated to environmental objectives.
- If disputes arise, it should be clear in which forum they can be resolved.

There are three main possible routes to resolving the issue:

1. A waiver from the obligations of the existing MTS.

2. Modification of the MTS to create an "agreement-specific" exemption from MTS provisions.

3. Modification of the MTS to create a "criteria-specific" exemption from MTS provisions; this could be achieved either (a) through amendment of GATT itself and/or (b) through a new WTO Agreement on MEAs.

Waivers

The use of waivers has been referred to as the "*ex post*" approach. Article XXV of GATT provides for the granting of a waiver from other GATT obligations "in exceptional circumstances"; Article IX of the WTO Agreement extends this to the MTS as a whole. Such waivers, however, are usually time limited, can be considered only on a case-by-case basis, and require a three-quarters majority of WTO members. Once again, they reinforce the existing hierarchy, firmly placing the WTO in judgement over MEAs, cannot contribute to certainty about the relationship between MEAs and the MTS, and do not fulfil any of the criteria set out above.

The so-called *"ex ante"* approach, in contrast, implies modification of the MTS in some way.

"Agreement-specific" exemptions

One possible method is a "listing" of particular MEAs whose the provisions are deemed to be compatible with the MTS. This is similar to the approach taken by the North American Free Trade Agreement (NAFTA), which provides that, in the event of conflict between itself and CITES, the Montreal Protocol, or the Basel Convention (or other MEAs where all NAFTA parties agree), the provisions of the MEA should take precedence over the MTS—though it also adds that parties must use the means least inconsistent with the NAFTA in implementing the MEAs. Although more attractive than the waiver approach, this nevertheless involves the WTO reaching a decision over which MEAs it considers acceptable and which it does not; it still does not create any certainty over the relationship with MEAs in general.

"Criteria-specific" exemptions

A broader solution is preferred, dealing with MEAs as a category rather than one by one. This implies a "criteria-specific" modification of the MTS.

Amendment of GATT

The clearest political message would be to achieve modification of the MTS via amendment of GATT. The EU proposal in the CTE, for example, was for a new subparagraph of Article XX, covering measures "taken pursuant to specific provisions of an MEA complying with the 'Understanding on the relationship between measures taken pursuant to MEAs and the WTO rules'." The proposed Understanding included a simple definition of an MEA and stated that measures taken pursuant to the specific provisions of the MEA should be presumed to be "necessary" for the achievement of its environmental objectives, though they still remained subject to the requirements of the headnote to Article XX.

This particular approach now looks a little dated. Since the EU proposal was put together, a number of WTO panels have found trade measures in unilateral trade/environment cases to be justified under either para. (b) or para. (g) of Article XX, but then failed them under the headnote. If it is accepted that MEA trade measures would be likely to be treated similarly, then there is little point in adding a new paragraph; what would be required is amendment of the headnote itself. Since this would have implications for every category of exceptions to GATT, and for unilateral as well as multilateral trade measures, it would be exceptionally difficult—to put it mildly—to negotiate. In addition, the procedures for amendment of GATT are themselves quite stringent and time consuming.

A new WTO Agreement on MEAs

The alternative, and distinctly preferable, route for "criteria-specific" modification of the MTS is through a new WTO side agreement, similar in status to other WTO agreements such as those on Subsidies and Countervailing Measures, on Technical Barriers to Trade, or on Agriculture. The advantage of this approach is that: it avoids attempting to amend existing rules, with probable implications for a wide range of topics; it creates a very clear set of rules that would apply only to MEAs (i.e. that would not encourage further unilateral actions); and it is probably easier to negotiate.

What would the new Agreement need to cover? An outline of topics is provided here; further work would of course be necessary to develop detailed proposals:

- The definition of an "MEA," including criteria for its subject matter (possibilities include the promotion of sustainable development, the conservation of natural resources, the avoidance of trans-boundary pollution, and/or the protection of human, animal, or plant life or health) and for its openness to participation by all parties affected and concerned.
- The definition of trade measures and the treatment of different categories of measures. It would seem logical that specific measures—for example, the bans on trade with non-parties mandated by the Montreal Protocol, or the import and export licences required by

CITES—should fall within the scope of the Agreement and thereby be exempted completely from the other requirements of the MTS.

- Non-specific measures, on the other hand, such as the controls on trade with parties implemented by Montreal Protocol parties (including measures such as taxation, labelling requirements, and total or partial import bans) could be covered by the headnote to Article XX, as there seems little reason to think that they would need to be discriminatory to achieve their objectives. Conversely, if discriminatory measures *are* required, it seems reasonable to insist that they should be specific, i.e. included in the text of the MEA. What is decided here therefore has implications for the design of future MEAs.

- Linkage of burdens and offsets. Developing countries have tended, as a whole, to be most strongly opposed to any modification of the MTS for environmental purposes, including in the context of the MEA debate. Given the record of Western protectionism against developing country exports still enshrined in parts of the MTS, such as the Agreement on Textiles and Clothing, one can hardly blame them. It is important that trade measures are not used to force countries into implementing an agreement that unfairly retards their development— bearing in mind, of course, that in many cases the environmental harm at which the MEA is aimed may well retard their development anyway if it proceeds unchecked. The presence of trade measures *as one component* of a range of implementing measures in a particular MEA (including, for example, provisions for finance and technology transfer) is therefore an important feature of MEA design. To what extent this should be specified in a WTO Agreement is questionable, however; one would wish to avoid a situation in which a WTO panel found against the use of trade measures because the MEA's financial provisions were not working well.

- Dispute settlement. The Agreement would need to be clear about where disputes over the application of MEA trade measures should be resolved. In line with earlier CTE discussions, it seems logical for disputes between MEA parties to be resolved by the MEA, and for disputes between an MEA party and a non-party that is a WTO member to be resolved by the WTO. (This in turn has implications for WTO dispute settlement procedures and their ability adequately to consider environmental issues). There also needs to be some agreed procedure for cases where it is not completely clear whether a trade measure is MEA related or not; the US actions in the *Shrimp-Turtle* case, for example, could arguably be considered to be justified by a range of MEAs, including CITES, the Biodiversity Convention, and the Bonn Convention on the Conservation of Migratory Species of Wild Animals.

6. Conclusion

The WTO Millennium Round offers an opportunity for the resolution of the potential conflict between the MTS and MEAs with trade provisions. It creates the wider political and negotiating environment—notably lacking within the CTE discussions—within which trade-offs can be reached and all participants in the debate end up with perceived gains to offset perceived losses. It is the conclusion of this chapter that the opportunity should be taken to open negotiations on a new WTO Agreement on MEAs with Trade Provisions.

The biggest danger in this debate is that no political impetus will be given to it and nothing will in the end be resolved. It is entirely possible to argue, for example, that most MEAs do not contain trade provisions, that there has never been a WTO dispute involving an MEA, and that recent panel and Appellate Body findings have shown that the WTO is sensitive to the environmental imperative; therefore, no action is required. This would be a profound mistake. MEAs are growing in number, in scope, and in importance, matching the growing evidence of global environmental degradation. In some cases they will need to impact international trade if they are to be implemented effectively. There have already been too many instances of MTS-incompatibility arguments being used as weapons in MEA negotiations to retard their development.

Trade liberalization and environmental protection are both desirable objectives. But the legal regimes that govern them are developing largely in isolation. A failure to resolve the *potential* conflict between them can lead only to actual conflict, undermining both. The time to act is now.

Notes

1. The number is usually given as 17, following the GATT Secretariat's 1992 report on trade and environment (*International Trade 1990–91,* Geneva: GATT Secretariat, 1992), but some MEAs were omitted by this analysis (see Steve Charnovitz, "Multilateral Environmental Agreements and Trade Rules," *Environmental Policy and Law* 26(4), 1996, 164).

2. For a fuller consideration, see Steve Charnovitz, "The Role of Trade Measures in Treaties," in Agata Fijalkowski and James Cameron, eds., *Trade and the Environment: Bridging the Gap,* London: Cameron May, 1998.

3. For a good overview of CITES and its development, see Wilhelm Wijnstekers, *The Evolution of CITES,* Geneva: IUCN, 1995, 4th edition.

4. See Peter H. Sand, "Whither CITES? The Evolution of a Treaty Regime in the Borderland of Trade and Environment," *European Journal of International Law* 8, 1997, 29–58.

5. For a general overview of the Montreal Protocol and its evolution, see Richard Benedick, *Ozone Diplomacy: New Directions in Safeguarding the Planet,* Cambridge, MA: Harvard University Press, 1998 (enlarged edition).

6. For full descriptions of the evolution and operation of the trade provisions, see Duncan Brack, *International Trade and the Montreal Protocol,* London: Royal Institute of International Affairs, 1996.

7. For an overview of the hazardous wastes problem and the Basel Convention, see the Secretariat of the Basel Convention on the Transboundary Movements of Hazardous Wastes, *The Basel Convention: A Global Solution for Controlling Hazardous Wastes,* New York/Geneva: UN, 1997.

8. For a full analysis of the Basel Convention's interaction with trade, see Jonathan Krueger, *International Trade and the Basel Convention,* London: Royal Institute of International Affairs, 1999.

9. For an overview of the international climate change regime and the Kyoto Protocol, see Michael Grubb, Christiaan Vrolijk, and Duncan Brack, *The Kyoto Protocol: A Guide and Assessment,* London: Royal Institute of International Affairs, 1999.

10. For a discussion of the implications for trade of climate change policies in general, and the Kyoto Protocol in particular, see Duncan Brack, Michael Grubb, and Craig Windram, *International Trade and Climate Change Policies,* London: Royal Institute of International Affairs, 1999.

11. For a more detailed (but now rather dated) discussion of the interrelationship of MEAs with various parts of the MTS, see Robert Housman, Donald Goldberg, Brennan van Dyke, and Durwood Zaelke, eds., *The Use of Trade Measures in Select MEAs,* Geneva: UNEP, 1995.

12. In January 1997, Zimbabwe applied to the WTO for compensation for the loss of international ivory markets consequent upon the listing of the African elephant under Appendix I of CITES, but the case became irrelevant after the CITES Conference in June of that year decided to permit limited trade in ivory stockpiles.

13. Six dispute panel findings are generally considered to be the main trade/environment cases, though others are also relevant: *US–Restrictions on Imports of Tuna*

(1991); *US–Restrictions on Imports of Tuna* (1994); *US–Taxes on Automobiles* (1994); *US–Standards for Reformulated and Conventional Gasoline* (1996); *EC–Measures Concerning Meat and Meat Products (Hormones)* (1998); and *US–Import Prohibition of Certain Shrimp and Shrimp Products* (1998). The first three were GATT panel findings that were not adopted by the GATT Council; although the panel reports therefore have no legal status, they do tend to provide precedents. The others were WTO panel findings, which in each case were referred to the Appellate Body.

14. *United States–Import Prohibition of Certain Shrimp and Shrimp Products,* Report of Panel, WT/DS58/R, 15 May 1998, para. 7.4.

15. Ibid., para. 7.45, quoting *United States–Restrictions on Imports of Tuna,* GATT Doc. DS29/R, 16 June 1994 (unadopted), para 5.26. Reprinted in 1994, 33 ILM (International Legal Materials) 842.

16. *United States–Import Prohibition of Certain Shrimp and Shrimp Products,* Report of the Appellate Body, WT/DS58/AB/R, 12 October 1998, para. 161.

17. Ibid., para. 164.

18. See Steve Charnovitz, "GATT and the Environment: Examining the Issues," *International Environmental Affairs* 4(3), summer 1992, 216; and Grant Hewison, "Multilateral Efforts to Protect the Environment and International Trade: The Case of Driftnet Fishing," paper presented to the GATT symposium on trade, environment, and sustainable development, Geneva, July 1994.

19. See Steve Charnovitz, "Restraining the Use of Trade Measures in Multilateral Agreements: An Outline of the Issues," in T. M. C. Asser Instituut, Report of the Round Table Conference, "The Relationship between the Multilateral Trading System and the Use of Trade Measures in MEAs: Synergy or Friction?" 22–23 January 1996, The Hague.

20. For a summary and analysis of the discussions, see Duncan Brack, "Reconciling the GATT and MEAs with Trade Provisions: The Latest Debate," *Review of EC and International Environmental Law* 6(2), July 1997.

21. See the discussion above on the Montreal Protocol for the difference between the two. The Kyoto Protocol also seems likely to lead to a wide variety of non-specific measures.

Appendices

Appendix I

Trade and Environment in the GATT/WTO[1]

WTO Secretariat

I. INTRODUCTION

1. At the start of the seventies, GATT contracting parties recognized the need to address in the GATT environmental issues as they relate to trade. The Group on Environmental Measures and International Trade, set up in 1971, was the first institutional framework created to that effect within the GATT. Some twenty years later a group of countries, considering that it was important for contracting parties to gain a better understanding of the interrelationship between environmental policies and GATT rules, requested the activation of the 1971 Group. The work programme of the GATT also included the issue of domestically prohibited goods, which had been raised by some developing countries at the beginning of the eighties.

2. At the end of the Uruguay Round, Trade Ministers adopted the Decision on Trade and Environment which anchored environment and sustainable development issues in WTO work. They set up the Committee on Trade and Environment and assigned to it a broad mandate, covering virtually all aspects of the trade and environment interface. Work in the Committee has contributed to build up communication between trade and environment experts at both the national and international levels.

3. The environment was not, as such, a subject of negotiations during the Uruguay Round. At the beginning of the eighties, the need to

protect the environment was not as high on the political agenda of governments and no attempt was made to put this subject on the agenda of the Round. Environmental considerations were, nevertheless, not totally absent from the preoccupations of negotiators and are reflected in various WTO instruments. This Note also briefly summarizes trade disputes which concerned issues related to human or animal health, or the environment.

4. Over the past few years, steps have been taken to increase transparency of WTO activities. The derestriction of WTO documents has been facilitated and all derestricted documents are now readily available on the WTO homepage. Moreover, the Director-General and the Secretariat have taken various initiatives to improve the dialogue with civil society.

II. WORK IN THE GATT ON ENVIRONMENTAL ISSUES

A. Group on Environmental Measures and International Trade

1. Preparatory work for the 1972 Stockholm Conference

5. During the preparatory work for the Conference on the Human Environment, which took place in 1972 in Stockholm, the GATT Secretariat was requested by the Secretary-General of the Conference to make a contribution. In response to this request, the Secretariat prepared on its own responsibility a study entitled "Industrial Pollution Control and International Trade".[2]

6. The study focused on the implications which the introduction of measures for control of industrial pollution might have for international trade. Recognizing the need for governments to act to protect and improve the environment while at the same time avoiding introducing new barriers to trade, it explored some of the problems that would have to be solved in evolving guidelines for action that would permit effective pollution control without damage to the structure of international trade.

2. Establishment of the Group on Environmental Measures and International Trade

7. In October 1971 the Director-General, Mr. Olivier Long, suggested that contracting parties should follow the problems that could be created for

international trade by anti-pollution measures concerning industrial processes: "[i]n other words, to consider the implications of industrial pollution control on international trade, especially with regard to the application of the provisions of the General Agreement. Contracting parties carried a special responsibility in this area. They had to ensure that the efforts of governments to combat pollution did not result in the introduction of new barriers to trade or impede the removal of existing barriers. It was, therefore, perhaps worth considering whether it would not be useful for the CONTRACTING PARTIES to set up a flexible mechanism which could be used at the request of contracting parties if the need arose".[3]

8. In the discussion that followed, several representatives expressed agreement that the GATT had certain responsibilities in dealing with the implications of industrial pollution control on international trade. Many of them supported the idea of establishing a standing mechanism for the purpose. There was, however, some divergence of views on the nature and objectives of this mechanism and as to whether it should be set up in anticipation of the problems or whether one should await further developments. Some representatives suggested that a decision be made only after the Stockholm Conference had taken place; others thought it best to take up work on this matter before the issues had been settled there. Some representatives considered that the GATT was sufficiently equipped to deal with the matter and doubted the need for the establishment of a new mechanism.[4]

9. At the November 1971 Council meeting, the Council agreed to the establishment of a Group on Environmental Measures and International Trade and gave it the following mandate:

1. to examine upon request any specific matters relevant to the trade policy aspects of measures to control pollution and protect the human environment especially with regard to the application of the provisions of the General Agreement taking into account the particular problems of developing countries;
2. to report on its activities to the Council.[5]

10. In introducing the terms of reference, the Director-General stated that:

[t]he functions of the proposed group would be limited to the consideration of specific matters that were relevant to the applica-

tion of the provisions of the General Agreement. There was, thus, no danger of duplicating or encroaching on work going on in other bodies on this very large problem of environment. The Secretariat was not aware of any problem that could be placed before the group at present, were it established. One could, nevertheless, anticipate that concrete problems could well arise in this area. For this reason, it was better to equip oneself with the necessary machinery ahead of time rather than to wait until a particular problem had developed and then set up an appropriate organ, since its constitution would then be difficult and its nature strongly influenced by the particular case at hand.[6]

11. The Group was thus set up as a standby machinery which would be ready to act, at the request of a contracting party, when the need arose. It was agreed that Mr. Kaya (Japan) should be Chairman.[7] During nearly twenty years, however, no request was made to convene a meeting of the Group.

3. Activation of the Group on Environmental Measures and International Trade

12. At the Ministerial meeting in Brussels in December 1990, the countries from the European Free Trade Association (EFTA)[8] circulated a formal proposal for a statement on trade and environment to be made by Ministers. They declared that priority attention should be devoted to interlinkages between trade policy and environmental policy, and for that purpose required the CONTRACTING PARTIES to: (a) undertake a study on the relationships between environmental policies and the rules of the multilateral trading system; (b) consider the implications of preparatory work for the 1992 United Nations Conference on Environment and Development, and the possibility of submitting a GATT contribution to that Conference; (c) convene in 1991 the GATT Working Group on Environmental Measures and International Trade under an updated mandate, in order to provide contracting parties with a forum for these issues.[9] The Brussels Ministerial Meeting failed to conclude the Uruguay Round and no effect was given to the proposed statement.

13. The EFTA contracting parties followed this initiative by a statement at the 46th Session of the CONTRACTING PARTIES in which

they indicated that they believed it was important and urgent for contracting parties to gain a better understanding of the interrelationship between environmental policies and GATT rules in order to establish coherent multilateral cooperation in this field.[10] In February 1991 they requested the Director-General, Mr. Arthur Dunkel, to convene, at the earliest appropriate date, the Group on Environmental Measures and International Trade. Among the reasons they gave for their request, they explained that

> [t]he approach to environmental policy making varied considerably from country to country due to differing geographical settings, economic conditions, stages of development and environmental problems. Accordingly, governments' priorities on these problems differed as well. The important point here was that the resulting differences in actual policies could set the stage for trade disputes. The EFTA countries' prime concern was to ensure that GATT's framework of rules worked, provided clear guidance to both trade and environment policy makers and that its dispute settlement system was not faced with issues it was not equipped to tackle. . . .

> The EFTA countries were aware that one could not say with certainty exactly what the interlinkages between environmental and trade policies were. A great deal of technical work was therefore needed before drawing conclusions and beginning to strike a balance between different interests in this area. They believed that it was important to start studying the complex issues in this field soon, and had accordingly requested the Director-General to convene the 1971 Working Group at the earliest appropriate date. They considered the Group to be the appropriate forum to tackle the issues that have arisen and would arise in the context of environmental policies, so that the GATT can be maintained as a relevant body of rules in all respects. A careful study of the Group's mandate had led the EFTA countries to believe that it was sufficient in scope.

14. The EFTA countries also suggested that, like other international bodies, GATT might make a contribution to the 1992 United Nations Conference on Environment and Development (UNCED).[11]

15. Several delegations supported the proposal to convene the 1971 Group, considering the GATT could not remain outside the debate

which had commenced, but had to be part of it. Other delegations were
of the view that such an initiative was premature and that one should
await the outcome of the UNCED. Some also considered that priority
should be given to concluding the Uruguay Round. The appropriateness
of the mandate of the 1971 Group was also raised. While some agreed
that one should start pragmatically with the existing mandate, others
considered that this mandate did not encompass the general issue of the
interlinkages between trade and environment.

16. In view of the differences which existed on the proposal for the
convening of the Group, the Council decided to request the Chairman of
the CONTRACTING PARTIES, Ambassador R. Ricupero (Brazil), to
conduct informal consultations, in particular to reflect upon whether the
existing mandate of the group was the most appropriate.[12] In April
1991, Ambassador Ricupero reported that a consensus had emerged to
hold a so-called "structured debate" on the subject of trade and environment at the following Council meeting. With respect to the proposal for
reconvening the 1971 Group, informal consultations continued with the
aim of solving the problem of the terms of reference and deciding which
contribution the GATT might make to the UNCED process.[13]

17. To facilitate the structured debate, the Chairman went on to
circulate an "outline of points" that could be used by delegations
participating in the Council debate. According to this Note, "the
purpose of such a debate would be to identify measures taken on
environmental grounds which could affect trade and development in
the light of the provisions in GATT and Tokyo Round instruments".
This illustrative list of points was built around five broad themes: (i)
relationship between environmental policies, trade policies and
sustainable development, including further liberalization of trade,
(ii) identification of measures taken on environmental grounds that
directly or indirectly affect international trade, (iii) identification of
sectors of particular interest to developing countries, taking into
account their trade, financial and development needs, in which trade
may be affected as a result of environmental policy measures, (iv)
trade provisions in international environmental instruments; principles and concepts adopted or under discussion, (v) identification of
GATT articles and Tokyo Round instruments relevant to trade
measures taken for environmental purposes.[14]

18. Some thirty delegations participated in the structured debate.[15] A large number of issues were raised, ranging from: the need to ensure that GATT rules and environmental protection were mutually supportive; the relation between trade restrictions in international environmental instruments and GATT rules; the application of GATT rules and principles to trade-related environmental issues; the distinction to be made between legitimate environment-related measures and protectionist ones; the particular concerns of developing countries; poverty as the main source of environmental degradation in developing countries and economic growth brought by trade as a prerequisite for achieving sustainable development.

19. In the course of the debate, the ASEAN contracting parties proposed to request the GATT Secretariat to prepare a factual paper on trade and the environment. The ASEAN contracting parties suggested that the following elements be included: (i) historical background on circumstances which led to the establishment of the 1971 Working Party with its particular mandate; (ii) background information on any other GATT work in the past on environmental issues; (iii) describe how existing international arrangements on environmental protection, such as the Vienna Convention, Basel Convention, etc., affect GATT principles; (iv) listing of trade measures taken by countries for environmental protection, and environmental measures with trade implications. The proponents further specified that "the paper should not attempt an assessment of the broad question of the effects of environmental policies and measures on international trade".[16]

20. The structured debate, however, did not allow delegations to reach a consensus as to whether the 1971 Group should be activated and under which terms of reference. Consultations therefore continued and in July, Ambassador Ricupero had to note that "additional efforts were required to reach a consensus on how these issues should be dealt with in the GATT itself. . . . [M]ore time was required to allow delegations to develop ideas which could lead to an understanding on this matter . . . The best approach to develop the necessary mutual understanding and to allow a positive treatment of these issues in the GATT would be to identify specific issues which could properly be examined in the 1971 Group".[17]

21. Eventually, contracting parties agreed that the 1971 Group on Environmental Measures and International Trade ("EMIT Group", as it

would be called from now on) be convened to examine the following three items:

> (a) trade provisions contained in existing multilateral environmental agreements (e.g. the Montreal Protocol on Substances that Deplete the Ozone Layer, the Washington Convention on International Trade in Endangered Species and the Basle Convention on the Control of Transboundary Movements of Hazardous Wastes and Their Disposal) vis-à-vis GATT principles and provisions;
>
> (b) multilateral transparency of national environmental regulations likely to have trade effects; and
>
> (c) trade effects of new packaging and labelling requirements aimed at protecting the environment.

22. These three issues would be addressed within the Group's original mandate. The Group would be open-ended, i.e. open to any contracting party which wished to participate. Because of the burden on delegations arising from the Uruguay Round, until January 1992 it would limit the number of its meetings as much as possible.[18] Consultations led to the designation of Ambassador H. Ukawa (Japan) as Chairman of the Group.[19]

23. The EMIT Group met from November 1991 to January 1994.[20] As noted by the Chairman in assessing the results of two years of work, discussions in the EMIT Group resulted in delegations being better informed of, and more comfortable with, the subject matter of trade and environment. The exercise permitted the building of confidence and a spirit of mutual trust and cooperation. The Group had not been established as a negotiating forum and there was a widely shared view that it was premature to adopt a prescriptive approach until the dimensions of any problems that might exist were more clearly identified, particularly with respect to the significance of the trade effects that were involved. The Group had viewed therefore its role as one of examining and analysing the issues covered by its agenda.

24. The Chairman noted that there was agreement on a number of points. Discussions should remain within the mandate of the Group and GATT's competence, namely the trade-related aspects of environment policies which could result in significant trade effects for GATT contracting parties. GATT was not equipped to become involved in the

tasks of reviewing national environment priorities, setting environmental standards or developing global policies on the environment. For the Group, there was no policy contradiction between upholding the values of the multilateral trading system on the one hand, and acting individually or collectively for the protection of the environment and the acceleration of sustainable development on the other. If problems of policy coordination did occur, it was important to resolve them in a way that did not undermine internationally agreed rules and disciplines that governments reinforced through the Uruguay Round negotiations. The Chairman also stressed that it was important to ensure that the multilateral trade rules did not present an unjustified obstacle to environmental policy-making. An important point was the considerable extent to which the GATT rules already accommodated trade measures used to protect national environmental resources. He concluded that an open, secure and non-discriminatory trading system underwritten by the GATT rules and disciplines could facilitate environmental policy-making and environmental conservation and protection by helping to encourage more efficient resource allocation and to generate real income growth.[21]

4. GATT's contribution to the UNCED and follow-up to the UNCED

25. The issue of a GATT contribution to the Rio Conference had been addressed during the informal consultations held by the Chairman of the CONTRACTING PARTIES in the course of 1991. In September 1991, the GATT Secretariat circulated a Factual Note on Trade and Environment, which covered the elements outlined in the ASEAN proposal.[22] At the invitation of the Council, the Director-General sent this document, together with the section on trade and environment from the GATT Annual Report,[23] as the Secretariat's contribution to the UNCED.

26. The second question arising in relation with the UNCED was that of the follow-up action GATT contracting parties should undertake with respect to the Rio Declaration and *Agenda 21*. At the July 1992 Council meeting, the Director-General noted that *Agenda 21* contained a number of recommendations directly relevant to the work of the GATT in the field of trade, environment and sustainable development. He suggested that contracting parties should consider how to proceed on these recommendations.[24]

27. Reporting on this subject to the 48th Session of the CON-TRACTING PARTIES, Ambassador B. K. Zutshi (India), Chairman of the Council noted that

> it was clear that contracting parties warmly welcomed the UNCED Declaration and the progress that had been made by the UNCED in fostering further multilateral cooperation, and were determined that GATT should play its full part in ensuring that policies in the fields of trade, the environment and sustainable development were compatible and mutually reinforcing. It was also clear that the GATT's competence was limited to trade policies and those trade-related aspects of environmental policies which might result in significant trade effects for GATT contracting parties. In respect neither of its vocation nor of its competence was the GATT equipped to become involved in the tasks of reviewing national environmental priorities, setting environmental standards or developing global policies on the environment. Nevertheless, the multilateral trading system did have a central rôle to play in supporting an open international economic system and fostering economic growth and sustainable development, especially in the developing countries, to help address the problems of environmental degradation and the over-exploitation of natural resources.
>
> The importance attached by the UNCED to a successful outcome of the Uruguay Round negotiations had been welcomed, and remained the top priority for contracting parties. It held the key to the liberalization of trade and the maintenance of an open, non-discriminatory multilateral trading system, which were main elements of the framework for international cooperation that were being sought to protect the environment and to accelerate sustainable development in developing countries. Also, the special concerns that had been raised by the UNCED about the need to improve market access for developing countries' exports, particularly by reducing tariff and non-tariff impediments, including tariff escalation, and to improve the functioning of commodity markets were well recognized.[25]

28. The CONTRACTING PARTIES.further invited the Committee on Trade and Development and the EMIT Group to focus on the relevant

sections of *Agenda 21* and report to the Council on the progress they were making in that area.[26] The review took place in a special session of the Council in February 1994. Contracting parties generally considered the successful conclusion of the Uruguay Round to be an important step towards creating the conditions for sustainable development. They considered that trade liberalization and the maintenance of an open, non-discriminatory trading system were key elements of the follow-up to the UNCED. They noted that work that had already been undertaken in the GATT on trade and environment, both in the EMIT Group and the CTD, could be considered as follow-up to the UNCED. Contracting parties also agreed that further UNCED follow-up should await the decision of Ministers at their forthcoming meeting in Marrakesh on 12–15 April 1994 regarding the future work programme on trade and environment.[27]

B. The Issue of Domestically Prohibited Goods[28]

1. Historical background

29. The subject of exports of "domestically prohibited goods" ("DPGs") was included in the GATT's work programme at the 1982 Ministerial meeting as a result of concerns expressed by some developing countries regarding the export of products whose domestic sale was either prohibited or severely restricted in order to protect human health or safety, or the environment. The Ministerial Declaration adopted at the 38th Session of the CONTRACTING PARTIES held at Ministerial Level therefore encouraged contracting parties to notify GATT, "to the maximum extent feasible, of any goods produced and exported by them but banned by their national authorities for sale in their domestic markets on grounds of human health and safety".[29] Consultations held around that time with interested delegations made it possible in particular to shed light on the definition of "domestically prohibited" goods, or to identify DPG-related practices in exporting countries. They also pointed to the complexity of the issues involved and the practical problems of managing such trade.[30]

30. In 1986, as talks for launching the Uruguay Round were underway, the possible inclusion of the subject in the negotiations was raised. While several developing countries were in favour, others considered

that work in this area should be carried out under the regular GATT activities. The latter view prevailed.[31] At the Montreal Ministerial meeting ("Mid-Term Review") in December 1988, some delegations again proposed to include the subject of DPGs in the Uruguay Round. In his concluding remarks, the Chairman of the Ministerial Meeting, Mr. R. Zerbino, Minister of Economy and Finance of Uruguay, noting that the subject was covered by GATT's regular work programme, suggested that "the GATT Council be requested to take an early, appropriate decision for the examination of the complementary action that might be necessary in GATT, having regard to the work that was being done by other international organizations".[32]

31. In July 1989, the Council decided to establish the Working Group on Export of Domestically Prohibited Goods (hereinafter the "Working Group").[33] Ambassador J. Sankey (United Kingdom) was nominated as Chairman.

2. The Working Group on the Export of Domestically Prohibited Goods and Other Hazardous Substances

32. The terms of reference of the Working Group were the following:

[T]he Council agrees to establish a Working Group on the Export of Domestically Prohibited Goods and Other Hazardous Substances which, in the light of GATT obligations and principles and having regard to the work of other international organizations on these goods and substances, will examine trade-related aspects that may not be adequately addressed, and report to the Council.

The Working Group should take into account the specific characteristics of domestically prohibited goods and those of other hazardous substances, and the need to avoid duplicating the work of other international organizations.

The Working Group should complete its work by 30 September 1990, and submit a progress report to the Forty-Fifth Session of the CONTRACTING PARTIES in 1989.[34]

33. The Working Group met between September 1989 and June 1991.[35] At the first meeting, the Working Group, noting the request to have regard to the work of other international organizations, agreed to invite, as observers to its meetings, representatives from UNEP [the

United Nations Environment Programme], FAO [the Food and Agriculture Organization], WHO [the World Health Organization], the UN Secretariat, the ILO [International Labour Organization], the UN Centre for Transnational Corporations, the OECD [Organization for Economic Co-operation and Development], the ITC [International Trade Centre], and the International Atomic Energy Agency. Throughout the work of the Working Group, these representatives provided technical expertise and advice to delegations, to the Chairman and to the Secretariat.

34. Several contracting parties submitted proposals to the Working Group.[36] The Chairman subsequently presented a working paper containing a Draft Decision on Trade in Banned or Severely Restricted Products and Other Hazardous Substances, which was based on the two proposals presented by Cameroon and Nigeria on one hand, and by the European Community on the other, and took into account comments by other delegations. This Draft Decision was the subject of discussion in the Working Group, at both the technical and drafting level, and the text was revised to meet the requirements and advice of delegations and technical experts. Despite intensive efforts which continued into June 1991, a final version of the text could not be agreed.

35. At the July 1991 meeting of the Council, the Chairman of the Working Group submitted a report together with the text of a draft Decision on Products Banned or Severely Restricted in the Domestic Market, and explained that one country remained unable to accept it without amendments.[37] Although its mandate was extended, the Working Group never met again. At the end of the Uruguay Round, it was agreed in the Marrakesh Ministerial Decision on Trade and Environment to incorporate this issue into the work programme of the WTO Committee on Trade and Environment.

III. TRADE AND ENVIRONMENT IN THE WTO

A. The Committee on Trade and Environment

1. The Marrakesh Decision on Trade and Environment

36. Towards the end of the Uruguay Round, GATT contracting parties agreed that the Trade Negotiations Committee (TNC) should

adopt a work programme on trade and environment and present it, together with recommendations on an institutional structure for its execution, at the Marrakesh Ministerial Conference.[38] This led to the adoption, on 14 April 1994, of the Decision on Trade and Environment (hereinafter the "Marrakesh Decision")[39] in which Trade Ministers noted that it should not be contradictory to safeguard the multilateral trading system on the one hand, and act for the protection of the environment and the promotion of sustainable development on the other hand. Ministers further noted their desire to coordinate policies in the field of trade and environment, "but without exceeding the competence of the multilateral trading system, which is limited to trade policies and those trade-related aspects of environmental policies which may result in significant trade effects".

37. The Marrakesh Decision directed the first meeting of the General Council of the WTO to establish a Committee on Trade and Environment (CTE), whose tasks are: "to identify the relationship between trade measures and environmental measures, in order to promote sustainable development; (b) to make appropriate recommendations on whether any modifications of the provisions of the multilateral trading system are required, compatible with the open, equitable and non-discriminatory nature of the system".[40] The Marrakesh Decision lists ten items, encompassing all areas of the multilateral trading system: goods, services and intellectual property. These items are commonly referred to in the following order:

Item 1: "the relationship between the provisions of the multilateral trading system and trade measures for environmental purposes, including those pursuant to multilateral environmental agreements"

Item 2: "the relationship between environmental policies relevant to trade and environmental measures with significant trade effects and the provisions of the multilateral trading system"

Item 3: "the relationship between the provisions of the multilateral trading system and:

(a) charges and taxes for environmental purposes
(b) requirements for environmental purposes relating to products, including standards and technical regulations, packaging, labelling and recycling"

Item 4: "the provisions of the multilateral trading system with respect to the transparency of trade measures used for environmental purposes and environmental measures and requirements which have significant trade effects"

Item 5: "the relationship between the dispute settlement mechanisms in the multilateral trading system and those found in multilateral environmental agreements"

Item 6: "the effect of environmental measures on market access, especially in relation to developing countries, in particular to the least developed among them, and environmental benefits of removing trade restrictions and distortions"

Item 7: "the issue of exports of domestically prohibited goods"

Item 8: "TRIPS"

Item 9: "Services"

Item 10: "appropriate arrangements for relations with non-governmental organizations referred to in Article V of the WTO and transparency of documentation".

2. The Sub-Committee on Trade and Environment

38. Pending the establishment of the CTE, the Marrakesh Decision stipulated that work on trade and environment should be carried out by a Sub-Committee of the Preparatory Committee of the WTO. The Sub-Committee on Trade and Environment (SCTE) met in the course of 1994 under the chairmanship of Ambassador L. F. Lampreia (Brazil). It based its work on the terms of reference established by the Marrakesh Decision, while building on the work previously accomplished in GATT bodies, such as the EMIT Group or the Working Group on Domestically Prohibited Goods.[41]

39. With respect to its work programme, the SCTE focused on the first, third and sixth items, building whenever possible on the work of the EMIT Group. Under item 1, the Sub-Committee examined the use of trade measures for environmental purposes, particularly those applied in the context of multilateral environmental agreements and those applied specifically to non-parties to those agreements. Delegations began

reviewing the potential advantages and disadvantages of *ex ante* and *ex post* approaches to establishing the relationship of these measures to the provisions of the multilateral trading system. With regard to item 3, delegations began reviewing the use of environmental taxes, in particular in the context of GATT disciplines on border tax adjustment, and examined further environmental regulations and standards, notably those related to eco-labelling, on the basis of the work that had already been undertaken on this subject by the EMIT Group. Under item 6 of the work programme delegations highlighted for further examination issues such as the effects of tariff escalation, non-tariff barriers and trade distorting subsidies on the environment, export diversification and its relationship to environmental protection, market opportunities for environmentally friendly products particularly from developing countries, and the importance of technology transfer, technical and financial assistance in pursuit of sustainable development.

40. The SCTE transmitted its working documents and reports to the WTO's Committee on Trade and Environment.

3. Work of the Committee on Trade and Environment

41. As stipulated in the Marrakesh Ministerial Decision on Trade and Environment, the General Council of the WTO established the Committee on Trade and Environment (CTE) at its first meeting, held on 31 January 1995. It was agreed that the CTE would be open to all Members of the WTO and would report to the first biennial WTO meeting of the Ministerial Conference, when its work and terms of reference would be reviewed, in the light of recommendations by the Committee itself. The General Council nominated Ambassador J. C. Sanchez Arnau (Argentina) as Chairman of the CTE.

(a) Work of the CTE until the Singapore Ministerial Meeting

42. The CTE held its first meeting on 16 February 1995. It adopted a programme of work whereby each meeting would focus on some of the ten agenda items. CTE Members also agreed that meetings would be organized such that, once discussion of the items constituting the focus of the meeting had been completed, delegations could address, if they wished, the item(s) that had been discussed at the previous meeting. The work of the CTE was assisted by background and analytical papers prepared by the Secretariat, as well as documents submitted by delegations.

43. The CTE initially extended observer status to those intergovernmental organizations (IGOs) which had had observer status in the SCTE: the United Nations (UN), the United Nations Conference on Trade and Development (UNCTAD), the World Bank, the International Monetary Fund (IMF), the United Nations Environment Programme (UNEP), United Nations Development Programme (UNDP), the Commission for Sustainable Development (CSD), the Food and Agriculture Organization (FAO), the International Trade Centre (ITC), the Organization for Economic Cooperation and Development (OECD), and the European Free Trade Association (EFTA).

44. Until May 1996, CTE Members completed two full rounds of analysis of each individual item of the agenda.[42] At the May 1996 stocktaking exercise, it was noted that

> In preparing for the Singapore Ministerial Conference, the CTE has held a general debate on all items of its agenda. Some agenda items have been disaggregated, some specific issues and problems have been identified. The general debate clarified and promoted understanding of some issues and also permitted the identification of divergences of view. In some cases more analytical work is required. As a result of this process, the CTE is now in a position to centre its attention on specific issues, including issues covered by proposals submitted or to be submitted by Members, keeping in mind the need for a balanced and focused approach to the whole agenda.[43]

45. The CTE then focused its activities on the preparation of its report to the first Ministerial Conference in Singapore. Members agreed that the report had to be comprehensive, balanced among the agenda items and among the different "schools of thought" and perceptions of the issues under debate. The document "would include conclusions and recommendations if any".[44] The CTE Report to the Singapore Ministerial Conference was adopted on 8 November 1996, with the understanding that it "did not modify the rights and obligations of any WTO Member under the WTO Agreements".[45] As noted by the Chairman, this statement made it possible for a number of delegations to join the consensus and approve the report.[46] The Report contains a brief introductory section which sketches the CTE's establishment and outlines its work programme; a second section presents the discussions and describes

the documents submitted by delegations; the third section includes the conclusions and recommendations.[47]

46. At Singapore, Trade Ministers endorsed the Report and directed the CTE to continue its work under its current mandate:

> The Committee on Trade and Environment has made an important contribution towards fulfilling its Work Programme. The Committee has been examining and will continue to examine, *inter alia,* the scope of the complementarities between trade liberalization, economic development and environmental protection. Full implementation of the WTO Agreements will make an important contribution to achieving the objectives of sustainable development. The work of the Committee has underlined the importance of policy coordination at the national level in the area of trade and environment. In this connection, the work of the Committee has been enriched by the participation of environmental as well as trade experts from Member governments and the further participation of such experts in the Committee's deliberations would be welcomed. The breadth and complexity of the issues covered by the Committee's Work Programme shows that further work needs to be undertaken on all items of its agenda, as contained in its report. We intend to build on the work accomplished thus far, and therefore direct the Committee to carry out its work, reporting to the General Council, under its existing terms of reference.[48]

(b) The Singapore Report

47. The Report recalls that the work of the CTE was guided by the consideration contained in the Ministerial Decision that there should not be nor needed to be any policy contradiction between upholding and safeguarding an open, equitable and non-discriminatory multilateral trading system on the one hand and acting for the protection of the environment on the other. These two areas of policy-making were both important and they should be mutually supportive in order to promote sustainable development. Discussions demonstrated that the multilateral trading system had the capacity to further integrate environmental considerations and enhance its contribution to the promotion of sustainable development without undermining its open, equitable and non-discriminatory character; implementation of the results of

the Uruguay Round negotiations would represent already a significant contribution in that regard.

48. The CTE's discussions were also guided by the consideration that the competence of the multilateral trading system was limited to trade policies and those trade-related aspects of environmental policies which could result in significant trade effects for its Members. It was recognized that achieving the individual as well as the joint objectives of WTO Member governments in the areas of trade, environment and sustainable development required a coordinated approach that drew on interdisciplinary expertise. In that regard, policy coordination between trade and environment officials at the national level had an important role to play. Work in the CTE was helping to better equip trade officials to make their contribution in this area.

49. The Report states that WTO Member governments were committed not to introduce WTO-inconsistent or protectionist trade restrictions or countervailing measures in an attempt to offset any real or perceived adverse domestic economic or competitiveness effects of applying environmental policies; not only would this undermine the open, equitable and non-discriminatory nature of the multilateral trading system, it would also prove counterproductive to meeting environmental objectives and promoting sustainable development. Equally, and bearing in mind the fact that governments had the right to establish their national environmental standards in accordance with their respective environmental and developmental conditions, needs and priorities, WTO Members noted that it would be inappropriate for them to relax their existing national environmental standards or their enforcement in order to promote their trade. As noted by OECD Ministers in 1995, there was no evidence of a systematic relationship between existing environmental policies and competitiveness impacts, nor of countries deliberately resorting to low environmental standards to gain competitive advantages.

50. The CTE worked intensively on the issue of the *relationship between trade measures in multilateral environmental agreements (MEAs) and the multilateral trading system* (items 1 and 5). It examined whether there was a need to clarify the scope that existed under WTO provisions to use such measures. Various proposals were made in that regard. However, the report concluded that there was no agreement for the time being to

modify WTO provisions in order to provide increased accommodation in this area. Many delegations shared the view that WTO provisions already provided broad scope for trade measures to be applied pursuant to MEAs in a WTO-consistent manner.

51. In its conclusions and recommendations on this issue, the Report endorsed and supported multilateral solutions as the best and most effective way for governments to address global and transboundary environmental problems; it pointed to the clear complementarity that existed between this approach and the work of the WTO in seeking multilateral solutions to trade concerns. It acknowledged that trade measures could, in certain cases, play an important role, particularly where trade was a direct cause of the environmental problem; trade measures played an important role in some MEAs in the past, and they could be needed to play a similarly important role in the future. But, it also pointed out that trade restrictions were not the only nor necessarily the most effective policy instrument to use in MEAs: adequate international cooperation provisions, including financial and technology transfers and capacity building, were often decisive elements of a policy package for an MEA.

52. The CTE also examined carefully some characteristics of the trade measures used in MEAs. It concluded in particular that problems were unlikely to arise in the WTO over trade measures agreed and applied among Parties to an MEA. However, concerns were expressed regarding measures applied to MEA non-signatories. The Report stated that, in the negotiations of a future MEA, particular care should be taken over how trade measures might be considered for application to non-parties.

53. Regarding the relationship between WTO dispute settlement procedures and those found in MEAs, the report recognized that WTO Members had the right to bring disputes over the use of a trade measure taken pursuant to MEAs to the WTO dispute settlement system. However, disputes arising over the use of a trade measure applied pursuant to an MEA between two WTO Members which were both signatory to an MEA should be resolved through the dispute settlement mechanism available under that MEA.

54. The CTE report stressed in several instances the importance of ensuring policy coordination between trade and environment experts. First and foremost, policy coordination had to take place at the national

level, in order to prevent governments from entering into conflicting obligations in different treaties they were signatories to: this was best done at the negotiating and drafting stage. At the international level, the report encouraged cooperation between the WTO and relevant institutions.

55. The "unilateral" trade measures taken for environmental purposes were also under scrutiny. Most of the delegations which intervened in the CTE on this issue considered that GATT Article XX did not permit a Member to impose unilateral trade restrictions that were otherwise inconsistent with its WTO obligations, for the purpose of protecting environmental resources that were outside its jurisdiction. Another opinion expressed in the CTE was that nothing in the text of Article XX indicated that it only applied to protection policies within the territory of the country invoking the provision.

56. A number of *trade-related environmental policies* not covered elsewhere in the work programme of the CTE were discussed under item 2. Property rights, tradable emission permits, fiscal instruments, emission taxes, liability system, deposit-refund systems and environmental subsidies have been mentioned. Moreover, there was an exchange of views on the use by governments of environmental reviews of trade agreements, and of the relationship and compatibility of general trade and environmental policy-making principles.

57. The CTE undertook only a preliminary examination of *the relationship between WTO provisions and environmental taxes and charges* (item 3(a)). Various views were presented on the potential trade effects and general economic and environmental effectiveness of levying environmental taxes and charges. The application of WTO rules on border tax adjustment to environmental taxes and charges was also examined.

58. On *eco-labelling* (item 3(b)), discussions focused on voluntary eco-labelling programmes, including those based on life cycle approaches, and their relationship to the Agreement on Technical Barriers to Trade. CTE Members recognized that well-designed eco-labelling programmes could be effective instruments of environmental policy to develop environmental awareness of consumers, and assist them in making informed choices. But, at the same time, concerns were expressed about their possible trade effect: the multiplication of eco-labelling schemes with different criteria and requirements, or the fact that they could reflect the environmental conditions, preferences and priorities prevailing in

the domestic market might have the effect of limiting market access for overseas suppliers.

59. CTE Members noted that increased transparency could help deal with trade concerns regarding eco-labelling schemes. It could also help to meet environmental objectives by providing accurate and comprehensive information to consumers. Transparency should be ensured in the preparation, adoption and application of the programme, and all interested parties from other countries had to be afforded an opportunity to participate in the preparation of the programme. The Report stressed the importance of WTO Members respecting the provisions of the TBT Agreement and its Code of Good Practice. Further discussion was needed, however, on how criteria based on non-product related processes and production methods should be treated under the TBT Agreement.

60. Regarding the *transparency of trade measures used for environmental purposes* (item 4), CTE Members concluded that no modifications to WTO rules were required for the time being. Transparency is not an end in itself and trade-related environmental measures should not be subject to more onerous transparency requirements than other measures that affected trade. In relation with measures notified under the WTO, the CTE suggested that WTO Members should supply information to other Members, especially developing countries, about market opportunities created by environmental measures. Finally, the Report mandated the WTO Secretariat to compile all notifications of trade-related environmental measures and collate them in a single database accessible to WTO Members.

61. The CTE discussed how the WTO could contribute to *making international trade and environmental policies mutually supportive for the promotion of sustainable development* (item 6). There was a concern that environmental measures could adversely affect the competitiveness and market access opportunities of small and medium-sized enterprises, especially in developing and least-developed countries. Among its conclusions, the CTE emphasized the importance of market access opportunities in assisting those countries to obtain the resources to implement adequate developmental and environmental policies, diversify their economies and provide income-generating activities. Improving market access opportunities and preservation of an open and non-discriminatory trading system was essential for supporting countries in their efforts to ensure

sustainable management of their resources. At the same time, however, the CTE underlined the necessity for countries to implement appropriate environmental policies in order to ensure that trade-induced growth was sustainable.

62. The CTE also discussed whether and how the removal of trade restrictions and distortions, such as high tariffs, tariff escalation, export restrictions, subsidies and non-tariff measures, could benefit both the multilateral trading system and the environment. The Committee had focused first on the agriculture sector, but it was agreed to extend this analysis to other sectors, such as tropical timber and natural resource-based products, textiles and clothing, fisheries, forest products, environmental services and non-ferrous metals, taking into account country-specific natural and socio-economic conditions.

63. *Domestically prohibited goods* (item 7) was an issue of serious concern to some developing and least-developed countries which considered that they did not have sufficient timely information about the characteristics of these products, nor the technical capacity to make informed decisions about importing them.

64. The CTE noted that a number of international instruments, dealing *inter alia* with the monitoring and control of trade in certain DPGs, entered into force and others were under negotiation (reference was made to the Basel Convention on the Control of Transboundary Movements of Hazardous Wastes and their Disposal, the preparation under the Amended London Guidelines of an internationally legally-binding instrument for the application of the prior-informed consent procedures for certain hazardous chemicals in international trade). WTO should consider to fully participate in the activities of other organizations which have the relevant expertise for providing technical assistance in this field.

65. The CTE stressed the important role that technical assistance and transfer of technology could play in this field, both in tackling environmental problems at their source and in helping to avoid unnecessary additional trade restrictions on the products involved. The CTE will continue to examine what contribution WTO could make in this area, bearing in mind the need not to duplicate work of other specialized agencies. In the meantime, the WTO Secretariat will survey the information already available in the WTO on trade in DPGs, and WTO

Members are encouraged to submit to the Secretariat any additional information they have which could help drawing up a comprehensive picture of the situation throughout the WTO.

66. The CTE started work on the relationship of the *Agreement on Trade-Related Aspects of Intellectual Property Rights* (TRIPS) to the environment (item 8). It discussed the role of the TRIPS Agreement in the generation, access to and transfer of environmentally sound technology, and its relations with MEAs, in particular the Convention on Biological Diversity.

67. The Report noted that the TRIPS Agreement already played an essential role in facilitating access to and transfer of environmentally-sound technology and products. Positive measures, such as access to and transfer of technology, could be effective instruments to assist developing countries to meet MEAs' objectives. Delegations disagreed as to whether some provisions of the TRIPS Agreement needed to be amended in order to facilitate the international transfer of technology. It identified several areas on which it intended to focus its future work: (i) facilitating the generation of environmentally sound technology and products; (ii) facilitating their access and transfer; (iii) the creation of incentives for the conservation of biological diversity, the sustainable use of its components, and the fair and equitable sharing of the benefits arising out of the use of genetic resources, which included the protection of knowledge, innovations and practices of indigenous and local communities.

68. Preliminary discussion took place on the work programme envisaged in the *Decision on Trade in Services and the Environment* (item 9). So far, it did not lead to the identification of any environmental measures that Members might need to apply to services trade which would not be covered adequately by the provisions of the GATS [General Agreement on Trade in Services] Agreement, in particular Article XIV(b).

69. The CTE recognized that there was a need to respond to public interest in WTO activities in the area of trade and environment. Regarding the *relationship with non-governmental organizations* (item 10), CTE Members considered that the primary responsibility for closer consultation and cooperation lay at the national level. Nevertheless, it recommended that the WTO Secretariat continue its interaction with NGOs, for example through the organization of informal meetings. The CTE took note and endorsed the Decisions of the General Council of 18 July

1996 on "Procedures for the circulation and derestriction of WTO documents" and on "Guidelines for arrangements on relations with non-governmental organizations". In order to improve public access to WTO documentation, it recommended that all CTE working documents which were still restricted be derestricted, and encouraged Members to agree to derestrict the papers and non-papers they submitted.

(c) Work of the CTE since the
Singapore Ministerial Meeting

70. In 1997 and 1998, the CTE continued to work under the chairmanship of, respectively, Ambassador B. Ekblom (Finland) and Ambassador C. M. See (Singapore), with the mandate and terms of reference contained in the Marrakesh Decision. Since Singapore, CTE Members have adopted a thematic approach (the so-called "cluster approach"), which has allowed the items of the work programme to be addressed in a systematic and more focused manner. A full account of the debates can be found in the minutes of the meetings, and a summarized version is available in the *Trade and Environment Bulletins*.[49]

71. A first cluster regroups those items relevant to the theme of market access (i.e. items 2, 3, 4, and 6). Under *item 2*, Members had an initial exchange of views on the environmental review of trade agreements. With respect to *item 3(b)*, Members focused on the effects of eco-labelling programmes on market access and their relation with WTO rules, in particular the TBT Agreement; concrete examples of eco-labelling programmes, presented by delegations, were also discussed. Under the same item, the application of WTO rules to environmental taxes and charges was also raised. In order to fulfil the recommendations contained in the Singapore Report with respect to *item 4*, the CTE established a WTO Environmental Database (EDB) which compiles all environment-related notifications made under various WTO instruments; the EDB is regularly up-dated by the Secretariat.[50] A detailed examination of the potential economic and environmental benefits of removing trade restrictions and distortions took place under *item 6*. CTE Members examined the environmental and trade effects of various types of measures—tariff escalation, subsidies, non-tariff measures—in specific sectors—agriculture, energy, fisheries, forestry, non-ferrous metals, textiles and clothing, leather and environmental services. The

Secretariat contributed to the analysis by preparing a background paper, outlining for each sector the most prevalent trade restrictions and distortions, as well as the environmental benefits associated with their elimination.[51]

72. A second cluster contains the items related to the linkages between the multilateral environment agenda and the multilateral trade agenda (i.e. items 1, 5, 7 and 8). Discussions under *items 1 and 5* focused on the interaction between WTO rules and MEAs containing trade provisions, and various ways of accommodating the two sets of rules. In this respect, the CTE held two informal sessions with a number of Secretariats of multilateral environmental agreements relevant to its work, in order to inform WTO Members on the latest developments in these instruments and help them to better understand the relationship between the environmental agenda and the trade agenda. On *item 7,* discussions continued on the possible modalities of a notification scheme for DPGs. As to *item 8,* CTE Members examined the various aspects of the relationship between the Convention on Biological Diversity and the TRIPS Agreement; they also exchanged views on the effects of the TRIPS Agreement on technology transfer, in particular environmentally-sound technology.

73. With respect to *item 9,* Members exchanged views on the possible benefits for both trade and the environment of liberalizing environmental services. Options for increasing the transparency of the CTE's work and for improving relations with civil society were examined under *item 10.*

74. The CTE has currently granted observer status to twenty inter-governmental organizations, i.e. those which had been granted observer status at the first meeting, as well as: African, Caribbean and Pacific Group of States (ACP Group), Convention on Biological Diversity (CBD), Convention on International Trade in Endangered Species of Wild Fauna and Flora (CITES), International Organization for Standardization (ISO), International Plant Genetic Resources Institute (IPGRI), Latin American Economic System (SELA), United Nations Industrial Development Organization (UNIDO), World Customs Organization (WCO), World Intellectual Property Organization (WIPO).[52]

75. In 1999, the first meeting of the CTE was held on 18 and 19 February and addressed the market access cluster. The next meetings will take place in June and October.

B. Environment-Related Provisions in WTO Agreements

76. The environment was not, as such, a subject of negotiations during the Uruguay Round. At the beginning of the eighties, the protection of the environment was not as high on the political agenda of governments and, except for the issue of domestically prohibited goods, no attempt was made to include the subject in the programme of negotiations. Environmental considerations were, nevertheless, not totally absent from the preoccupations of negotiators and are reflected in several WTO instruments. Environment is also proving to be a cross-cutting issue and questions related to environmental concerns have arisen in various WTO bodies, such as the General Council, the Committee on Technical Barriers to Trade, the Council for TRIPs and the Council for Trade in Services.

1. The Marrakesh Agreement Establishing the World Trade Organization

(a) The Preamble

77. The Agreement Establishing the World Trade Organization (the "WTO Agreement") envisages a single institutional framework for the multilateral trading system which encompasses the GATT 1947, as modified by the Uruguay Round, and other agreements and associated legal instruments resulting from the Uruguay Round. The first paragraph of the Preamble to the WTO Agreement includes, for the first time in the context of the multilateral trading system, reference to the objective of sustainable development and to the need to protect and preserve the environment. It states:

> *Recognizing* that their relations in the field of trade and economic endeavour should be conducted with a view to raising standards of living, ensuring full employment and a large and steadily growing volume of real income and effective demand, and expanding the production of and trade in goods and services, while allowing for the optimal use of the world's resources in accordance with the objective of sustainable development, seeking both to protect and preserve the environment and to enhance the means for doing so in a manner consistent with their respective needs and concerns at different levels of economic development, . . .

78. In the *Shrimp* case, the Appellate Body considered that the first preambular paragraph of the WTO Agreement is relevant for the interpretation of provisions contained in the various WTO agreements, such as GATT Article XX. By explicitly recognizing the "objective of sustainable development", the preamble shows that "the signatories to the Agreements were, in 1994, fully aware of the importance and legitimacy of environmental protection as a goal of national and international policy". The Appellate Body further noted that the language of the WTO preamble

> demonstrates a recognition by WTO negotiators that optimal use of the world's resources should be made in accordance with the objective of sustainable development. As this preambular language reflects the intentions of negotiators of the *WTO Agreement,* we believe that it must add colour, texture and shading to our interpretation of the agreements annexed to the *WTO Agreement,* in this case the GATT 1994.[53]

(b) Arrangements with non-governmental organizations (NGOs)

79. Article V:2 of the Marrakesh Agreement Establishing the World Trade Organization enables the General Council to "make appropriate arrangements for effective cooperation with other intergovernmental organizations that have responsibilities related to those of the WTO". Pursuant to this provision, the General Council adopted, on 18 July 1996, a decision entitled "Guidelines for arrangements on relations with non-governmental organizations", where Members recognize the rôle NGOs can play in increasing the awareness of the public in respect of WTO activities and agree to improve transparency and develop communication with NGOs. Members also agree to ensure that more information about WTO activities is made available, in particular by derestricting documents more promptly than in the past, and direct the Secretariat to play a more active rôle in its direct contacts with NGOs, for instance by organizing symposia on specific WTO-related issues. Pointing to the "special character of the WTO, which is both a legally binding intergovernmental treaty of rights and obligations among its Members and a forum for negotiations", the General Council states that "there is currently a broadly held view that it would not be possible for NGOs to be directly involved in the work of the WTO or its meetings"

and notes that the primary responsibility for interacting with NGOs lies at the national level.[54]

80. At the same time, the General Council adopted new rules to facilitate the derestriction of WTO documents. It agreed that working documents, background notes by the Secretariat and minutes of meetings of all WTO bodies shall be considered for derestriction six months after the date of their circulation. Notwithstanding the six months rule, any Member may, at the time it submits any document for circulation to WTO Members, indicate to the Secretariat that the document be issued as unrestricted. Panel and Appellate Body reports are derestricted at the same time they are circulated to WTO Members.[55]

81. These decisions apply to all WTO bodies but are particularly relevant for the work of the CTE and other environment-related issues in the WTO, which have generally attracted most of the public attention.

2. The General Agreement on Tariffs and Trade

82. Article XX of the GATT allows a government to depart, under certain conditions, from its obligations under the Agreement. The relevant part of Article XX reads as follows:

> Subject to the requirement that such measures are not applied in a manner which would constitute a means of arbitrary or unjustifiable discrimination between countries where the same conditions prevail, or a disguised restriction on international trade, nothing in this Agreement shall be construed to prevent the adoption or enforcement by any contracting party of measures:
>
> (b) necessary to protect human, animal or plant life or health;
> (g) relating to the conservation of exhaustible natural resources if such measures are made effective in conjunction with restrictions on domestic production or consumption.

83. During the Uruguay Round, at the last formal meeting of the Negotiating Group on GATT Articles, Austria proposed that Article XX should be amended by adding the term "environment" in paragraph (b) in order to appropriately reflect the increasingly important relationship between trade and the environment. Austria noted that "[t]he inclusion of the notion [of environment] in Article XX(b) might just be one possibility worth exploring" but recognized it was too late to start

working on it in the Negotiating Group. No effect was given to this proposal.[56]

84. GATT/WTO panels and the Appellate Body have examined Article XX in various disputes which are presented in Section IV of this Note.[57]

3. The Agreement on Technical Barriers to Trade

(a) Main features of the Agreement

85. The WTO Agreement on Technical Barriers to Trade ("TBT Agreement"), which governs the preparation, adoption and application of product technical requirements, and of procedures used for the assessment of compliance with them, was finalized during the Uruguay Round. It builds upon and strengthens the 1979 Standards Code that was negotiated during the Tokyo Round. This Agreement is particularly relevant for the trade aspects of environmental policy-making.

86. The TBT Agreement divides product technical requirements into two categories, technical regulations and standards. The main distinction which the Agreement establishes between the two is that compliance with the former is mandatory, while compliance with the latter is voluntary. The Agreement recognizes that countries should not be prevented from taking measures necessary to pursue various policy purposes, such as the protection of public health or the environment, and that each country has the right to set the level of protection it deems appropriate. Governments are, however, required to apply technical regulations and standards in a non-discriminatory way (which means meeting the requirements of the most-favoured-nation and national treatments). Governments must also ensure that technical regulations and standards do not create unnecessary obstacles to trade. This means that mandatory technical regulations must not be more trade-restrictive than necessary to fulfil a legitimate objective, taking into account the risks non-fulfilment of that legitimate objective would create. In an illustrative list of legitimate objectives, the Agreement mentions national security requirements, the prevention of deceptive practices, the protection of human health or safety, animal or plant life or health, or the environment.

87. The Agreement encourages—but does not require—countries to use international standards whenever possible, in order to limit the proliferation of different domestic technical requirements. When a WTO

Member considers that the relevant international standard would not appropriately fulfil the objective pursued, for instance because of fundamental climatic or geographical factors or fundamental technological problems, this Member can use the technical regulation or standard which suits its needs.

88. One of the key features of the TBT Agreement is that it provides a high degree of transparency, which allows economic operators to adjust to technical requirements in export markets. Notification obligations include, *inter alia,* notifying draft technical regulations, conformity assessment procedures and standards, and providing other Members with sufficient time to comment on them, and notifying more generally the domestic measures taken to implement the provisions of the TBT Agreement. Notification requirements are complemented by the establishment of national "enquiry points" which provide, on request, further information about technical regulations, standards and conformity assessment procedures. Regular meetings of the TBT Committee further contribute to ensuring the transparent implementation of the Agreement.

89. In the WTO, the majority of trade-related environmental measures have been notified under the TBT Agreement. Since the entry into force of the Agreement, on 1 January 1995, about 2300 notifications have been received, of which some 11 per cent are environment-related. In this category, we find measures for pollution abatement, waste management, energy conservation; standards and labelling (including eco-labels); handling requirements; economic instruments and regulations; measures for the preservation of natural resources, and measures taken for the implementation of multilateral environmental agreements.[58]

90. Finally, the TBT Agreement provides that a panel called to examine a dispute between Members may establish, at its own initiative or at the request of a party to the dispute, a technical expert group. Participation in such a group will include persons of professional standing and experience in the field of question.

(b) Eco-labelling in the TBT Committee

91. Eco-labelling is the main environment-related issue which has been raised in the TBT Committee where discussions took place in parallel with those held on the same subject in the CTE. The two Committees held a joint informal meeting on this subject matter.

92. The issues raised in the TBT Committee with respect to eco-labelling are generally similar to those discussed in the CTE.[59] They include the applicability of the TBT Code of Good Practice to voluntary eco-labelling programmes, the extent to which eco-labelling programmes based on non-product related processes and production methods (PPMs) are covered by the TBT Agreement, the effects of eco-labelling programmes on international trade, and questions linked to the implementation and management of those programmes (selection of criteria, transparency, etc). As in the CTE, no conclusion has been reached on these issues, which are, therefore, still open.

93. At the first triennial review of the TBT Agreement, in 1997, the Committee agreed on some measures which should be taken to improve the transparency of, and compliance with, the Code of Good Practice. Among those measures, it was agreed that "without prejudice to the views of Members concerning the coverage and application of the Agreement, the obligation to publish notices of draft standards containing voluntary labelling requirements under paragraph L of the Code is not dependent upon the kind of information provided on the label." [60] This statement is directly relevant to eco-labelling programmes.

4. The Agreement on Sanitary and Phytosanitary Measures

94. The Agreement on Sanitary and Phytosanitary Measures ("SPS Agreement") was negotiated during the Uruguay Round. Before its entry into force, national food safety, animal and plant health measures affecting trade were subject to GATT rules, such as Article I (most-favoured-nation treatment), Article III (national treatment) and Article XX (general exceptions). The 1979 Agreement on Technical Barriers to Trade also covered technical requirements resulting from food safety and animal and plant health measures. However, it was considered that these provisions did not adequately address the potential problems posed by SPS measures.

95. Governments enforce sanitary and phytosanitary measures to ensure that food is free from risks arising from additives, contaminants, toxins or disease-causing organisms, to prevent the spread of plant-, animal- or other disease-causing organisms; and to prevent or control pests. They are applied to domestically produced food or local animal and plant diseases, as well as to products coming from other countries.

The SPS Agreement recognizes the legitimate right of governments to maintain the level of health protection they deem appropriate but ensures at the same time that this right is not abused and does not result in unnecessary barriers to international trade.

96. Governments are encouraged to harmonize their SPS requirements, i.e. to base them on international standards, guidelines or recommendations developed by international organizations, such as the joint FAO/WHO Codex Alimentarius Commission, the International Office of Epizootics and the International Plant Protection Convention. Governments are, nevertheless, entitled to set more stringent national standards in case the relevant international norms do not suit their needs; however, the SPS measures must be based on a scientific justification or on an assessment of the risks to human, animal or plant life or health. The procedures and decisions used by a country in a risk assessment will be made available upon request by other countries. The Agreement explicitly recognizes the right of governments to take precautionary provisional measures when scientific evidence is lacking, while seeking further information.

97. SPS measures must be applied in a non-discriminatory manner, although adapted to the health situations of both the area from which a product comes and the area to which it is destined. When governments have at their disposal various alternative measures, which are economically and technically feasible, they should choose measures which are not more trade restrictive than necessary to achieve the desired level of protection.

98. In order to increase transparency of SPS measures, governments are required to notify other countries of those measures which restrict trade and to set up so-called "enquiry points" to respond to requests for more information. The SPS Committee provides WTO Members with a forum to exchange information on all aspects of the implementation of the SPS Agreement, review compliance with it and maintain cooperation with the appropriate technical organizations. When a trade dispute arising over the use of a SPS measure involves scientific or technical issues, the Agreement stipulates that the panel should seek advice from experts.

5. The Agreement on Agriculture

99. In general, reducing domestic supports and export subsidies should lead to less intensive and more sustainable production with

reduced use of agricultural inputs like pesticides and fertilisers, leading to improvements in the environment.

100. The Agreement on Agriculture provides for the long-term reform of trade in agricultural products and domestic policies. It increases market orientation in agricultural trade by providing for commitments in the areas of market access, domestic support and export competition. A significant aspect of the Agreement is the commitment to reduce domestic support for agricultural production, particularly in the form of production-linked agricultural subsidies.

101. Protection of the environment is an integral part of the Agreement on Agriculture. The sixth paragraph of the preamble states that commitments made under the reform programme should have regard for the environment while Article 20 requires that the negotiations on the continuation of the reform programme take account of non-trade concerns, which includes the environment.

102. More specifically, Annex 2 of the Agreement, which lists the different types of subsidies which are not subject to reduction commitments, covers a number of different types of measures relevant to the environment. These include direct payments to producers and government service programmes for research and infrastructural works under environmental programmes. Eligibility for the direct payments must be based on clearly-defined government environmental or conservation programmes and the amount of payments are limited to the extra costs or loss of income involved in complying with the programme.

103. It should be noted that Members are free to introduce new, or amend existing, Annex 2 measures subject only to the general requirement that they have no, or at most minimal, trade-distorting effect and that they come under publicly funded government programmes.

6. The Agreement on Subsidies and Countervailing Measures

104. The Agreement on Subsidies and Countervailing Measures ("SCM Agreement") identifies three categories of subsidies, depending on their effect on international trade, and provides for different types of remedy for each category: (i) prohibited subsidies are subject to an accelerated dispute settlement procedure and a Member found to grant or maintain such a subsidy must withdraw it without delay; (ii) actionable subsidies, i.e. subsidies other than prohibited and non-actionable subsidies, can in

principle be granted or maintained, but may be challenged in WTO dispute settlement or subject to countervailing action if they cause adverse effects to the interests of other Members; (iii) non-actionable subsidies (i.e. non-specific subsidies and defined specific subsidies) are not subject to countervailing action nor to dispute settlement challenge.

105. Subsidies to promote adaptation of existing facilities to new environmental requirements fall into the third category. Subject to certain conditions, up to 20 per cent of the cost of adaptation would be considered a non-actionable subsidy.

7. The Agreement on Trade-Related Aspects of Intellectual Property Rights

106. The Agreement on Trade-Related Aspects of Intellectual Property Rights ("TRIPS Agreement") provides a common set of rules for the protection and enforcement of intellectual property rights. Article 27 of the TRIPS Agreement defines "patentable subject matter". Specific reference to the environment is made in Article 27.2 which allows Members to exclude from patentability inventions, the prevention of whose commercial exploitation within their territory is necessary to protect, *inter alia,* human, animal or plant life or health or to avoid serious prejudice to the environment. Paragraph 3 of Article 27 further provides that Members may exclude from patentability plants and animals other than micro-organisms, as well as essentially biological processes, other than microbiological processes, for the production of plants or animals. Members must, however, provide for the protection of plant varieties either by patents or by an effective *sui generis* system or by a combination thereof.

107. Article 27.3(b) of the TRIPS Agreement will be reviewed in 1999. In this context, the TRIPS Council agreed, at its December 1998 meeting, that, in order to initiate the review, those Members which are already under an obligation to apply Article 27.3[61] shall provide, by 1 February 1999, information on how the matters addressed in this provision are presently treated in their national law; other Members are invited to provide this information on a best endeavour basis. An illustrative list of questions to be drawn up by the Secretariat will help Members in preparing their contributions. The Secretariat will also contact the FAO, the Secretariat of the Convention on Biological Diver-

sity and UPOV [Union for the Protection of New Varieties of Plants] to request factual information on their activities of relevance.

8. The General Agreement on Trade in Services

(a) Article XIV of the GATS

108. The General Agreement on Trade in Services ("GATS") contains in Article XIV a general exceptions clause which is modelled on Article XX of the GATT. The chapeau of that provision is basically identical to that of GATT Article XX and environmental concerns are addressed in a paragraph (b) which is similar to paragraph (b) of Article XX.

109. Anticipating interpretative questions regarding the scope of Article XIV of the GATS, the Council for Trade in Services adopted at its first meeting a Ministerial Decision on Trade in Services. The Decision acknowledges that measures necessary to protect the environment may conflict with the provisions of the Agreement and notes that it is not clear that there is a need to provide for more than is contained in Article XIV(b). In order to determine whether any modification of Article XIV of the Agreement is required to take account of such measures, the Council for Trade in Services consequently decided to request the Committee on Trade and Environment "to examine and report, with recommendations if any, on the relationship between services trade and the environment including the issue of sustainable development. The Committee shall also examine the relevance of intergovernmental agreements on the environment and their relationship to the Agreement".[62]

110. Discussion to date in the CTE on this item has not led to the identification of any environmental measure applied to services trade that would not be covered adequately by GATS provisions, in particular Article XIV(b). This item remains under examination in the CTE and WTO Members are invited to submit any relevant information in that regard.[63]

(b) Environmental services[64]

111. The Services Sectoral Classification List annexed to the GATS was developed during the Uruguay Round[65] and was largely based on the United Nations Central Product Classification (CPC) system. The environmental services sector contained in the List includes four categories:

—A. Sewage services (CPC 9401)
—B. Refuse disposal services (CPC 9402)
—C. Sanitation and similar services (CPC 9403)
—D. Other

112. The fourth category ("other") can be understood to include the environmental services of the CPC which are not specifically referred to in the List, i.e. cleaning of exhaust gases (CPC 9404); noise abatement services (CPC 9405); nature and landscape protection services (CPC 9406) and other environmental protection services (9409). In discussing environmental services in GATS Council, some WTO Members suggested that it may be necessary to rethink the existing classification contained in the Services Sectoral Classification List.[66]

113. So far, some fifty WTO Members (counting the EC Member States individually) have made commitments under at least one of the four sub-sectors. The number of commitments is nearly equal for each of the individual four sub-sectors. Limitations on market access and national treatment with respect to the four modes of supply must however be kept in mind in order to assess the liberalizing content of those commitments. It must also be kept in mind that other services sectors may be directly relevant for the environment (research, engineering, construction, etc.).

114. In 1998, the Council for Trade in Services initiated an exchange of information exercise on various services sectors, the purpose of which was to facilitate the access of all Members, in particular developing country Members, to information regarding laws, regulations and administrative guidelines and policies affecting trade in services. The sectoral discussions focused in particular on the manner in which the services in question are traded and regulated, in order to enable Members to identify negotiating issues and priorities, in preparation for the further negotiations foreseen in Article XIX (Negotiation of Specific Commitments) of the GATS.

115. In discussing trade liberalization in environmental services, delegations noted that the environmental industry was playing a significant role in their economies and that trade in the area was growing from previously low levels; however, only a limited number of Members had made commitments in this sector. Members also described their own

regimes, stressing liberalizing trends. Nevertheless, public sector production and public procurement remain important in this sector. They
also pointed to different types of market access restrictions, such as
discriminatory taxes, subsidies and non-recognition of foreign qualifica-
tion, restrictions on trade in complementary sectors like construction,
inadequate protection of intellectual property rights, restrictions on
investment and movement of natural persons. The characteristics of
regulatory mechanisms, including environmental regulations, and their
effects on trade in environmental services were also addressed.[67]

9. The Understanding on Rules and Procedures Governing the Settlement of Disputes

(a) Expert advice and public disclosure of submissions

116. The Understanding on Rules and Procedures Governing the
Settlement of Disputes ("DSU") lays down detailed procedures WTO
Members have to follow to settle trade disputes arising out of the
implementation of any WTO agreement.

117. The DSU provides that, in its examination of the case, a panel may
seek information and technical advice from any individual or body which it
deems appropriate. Panels may seek information from any relevant source
and may consult individual experts, or a group of experts, on certain aspects
of the matter under dispute. This possibility was used, for instance, by the
panel in the *Shrimp* case to consult biologists and fishery experts on certain
questions related to sea turtle biology and conservation.[68]

118. Documents submitted to a panel in the course of dispute settlement proceedings are in principle confidential. Nothing in the DSU,
however, precludes a party to a dispute from disclosing statements of its
own position to the public. Moreover, in order to increase transparency,
a party to a dispute which submits a confidential submission to the panel
must, upon request of another Member to the dispute, provide a non-
confidential summary of this text that could be disclosed to the public.

(b) Panel proceedings and non-requested information

119. In the *Shrimp* case, the Appellate Body had to decide whether
the right to seek information under Article 13 of the DSU included
the right for a panel to accept non-requested information from non-
governmental sources. In the first instance, the Panel, which had received

two *amicus briefs* from two non-governmental organizations, had considered that accepting non-requested information from non-governmental sources would be incompatible with the provisions of the DSU as currently applied.[69] The Panel, however, gave the parties to the dispute the opportunity to endorse the *amicus briefs*, or part of them, as part of their own submissions.

120. The Appellate Body disagreed with the interpretation given by the Panel to Article 13. It considered that the DSU accords a panel "ample and extensive authority to undertake and to control the process by which it informs itself both of the relevant facts of the dispute and of the legal norms and principles applicable to such facts." The Appellate Body reproached the Panel for reading the word "seek" in too literal a manner, and specified

> [i]n the present context, authority to *seek* information is not prop-erly equated with a *prohibition* on accepting information which has been submitted without having been requested by a panel. A panel has the discretionary authority either to accept and consider or to reject information and advice submitted to it, *whether requested by a panel or not.* The fact that a panel may *motu proprio* have initiated the request for information does not, by itself, bind the panel to accept and consider the information which is actually submitted. The amplitude of the authority vested in panels to shape the processes of fact-finding and legal interpretation make [*sic*] clear that a panel will *not* be deluged, as it were, with non-requested material, *unless that panel allows itself to be so deluged.*[70]

121. The Appellate Body nevertheless considered that the actual disposition of the briefs by the panel in this case (i.e. giving the parties to the dispute the possibility to endorse them as part of their own submissions) did not constitute either legal error or abuse of the Panel's discretionary authority.[71]

IV. SECRETARIAT'S ACTIVITIES

A. Trade and Environment Bulletins

122. Since April 1993, the Secretariat regularly issues the *Trade and Environment Bulletin.* So far, more than thirty bulletins have kept readers regularly informed about the work of the EMIT Group, the SCTE and

the CTE. The Bulletins have also provided information on GATT/WTO's follow-up to the UN Conference on Environment and Development, environmental issues emerging from the Uruguay Round, environment-related trade disputes and any other relevant news. These publications aim at facilitating public understanding and awareness of the trade and environment policy agenda.

123. The *Trade and Environment Bulletin* is available on request at the Information and Media Relations Division of the WTO, or can be consulted on the WTO homepage at http://www.wto.org.

B. Symposia with Non-Governmental Organizations

124. Since 1994, the WTO Secretariat has organized yearly (with the exception of 1995) a Symposium on Trade, Environment and Sustainable Development. These symposia, which are held under the Secretariat's own responsibility, are generally attended by participants representing environment, development, consumer NGOs, industry interests, academics, as well as WTO Member governments. Voluntary financial assistance provided by some WTO Member countries or by private institutions has facilitated the participation of developing country NGOs.

125. The main objectives of the symposia are to keep civil society informed of the work underway in GATT/WTO on trade and environment, and to allow experts in the field to examine and debate the inter-linkages between trade, environment and sustainable development. The symposia were all organized on the same pattern: presentations from invited panellists on specific topics were followed by an informal debate among all participants. Various themes, covering the different facets of the trade and environment relationship, were on the agenda of each symposium, for instance, the synergies between trade liberalization and the environment, the relationship between multilateral environmental instruments and the WTO, the work of the CTE, WTO relations with civil society, etc. No attempt was made to summarize views or to identify consensus positions.

C. New Initiatives Taken by the Director-General

126. The WTO Secretariat receives every day a large number of requests for information from NGOs, including environmental organizations,

which are promptly responded to. Moreover, the Secretariat staff meets with NGOs on a regular basis—both individually or as part of organized events.

127. During the General Council on 15 July 1998, the Director-General informed Members of certain new steps he was taking to enhance the transparency of the WTO and improve the dialogue with civil society. These initiatives were implemented by October 1998. They include (i) regular briefings by the Secretariat on WTO activities, along the lines of the briefings already offered to the media, but tailored to the particular interests and perspectives of the NGO community; (ii) the creation of a NGO section on the WTO web site, containing information of particular interest to civil society;[72] (iii) a monthly list of NGO position papers received by the Secretariat is circulated for the information of Members who can receive them upon request; (iv) the Director-General has initiated a process of regular informal meetings with different NGO representatives, with the goal of improving and enhancing mutual understanding.

D. Trade and Environment Regional Seminars

128. In 1998 and early 1999, the Secretariat held six regional seminars on trade and environment for government officials from developing and least-developed countries, and economies in transition. These seminars were organized in the Asia/Pacific region, the Caribbean, South America, Central Europe and Central Asia, and Africa (French-speaking and English-speaking). A seventh seminar will be held for the Middle East in the spring.

129. The objective of those seminars is to raise awareness on the links between trade, environment and sustainable development, and to enhance the dialogue between trade and environment policymakers. Participating countries were represented by officials from Ministries of either Trade or Foreign Affairs (whichever is responsible for WTO matters) and from Ministries of Environment.

130. Presentations made by WTO Secretariat officials during three days addressed the various aspects of the trade and environment interrelationship, the relevant rules of the WTO, as well as specific concerns arising in each region.

131. These seminars were funded by the governments of Hong Kong, China; the Netherlands; and Norway.

Notes

1. This document was prepared by the World Trade Organization Secretariat to provide participants to the High Level Symposium on Trade and Environment held in March 1999 with an overview of the various environment-related activities in GATT 1947 and in the WTO. Prepared under the Secretariat's own responsibility, this Note is not meant to reflect WTO members' views or to interpret WTO agreements.

2. Doc. L/3538.

3. Doc. C/M/73.

4. Ibid.

5. Doc. C/M/74.

6. Ibid.

7. Doc. C/M/75.

8. Austria, Finland, Iceland, Norway, Sweden, Switzerland.

9. Doc. MTN.TNC/W/47, 3 December 1990.

10. Doc. SR.46/2.

11. GATT Council meeting of 6 February 1991, Doc. C/M/247. The issue was also on the agenda of the 12 March 1991 Council meeting, Doc. C/M/248.

12. GATT Council meeting of 6 February 1991, Doc. C/M/247.

13. Council meeting of 24 April 1991, Doc. C/M/249, 22 May 1991.

14. *Outline of Points for Structured Debate on Environmental Measures and Trade,* Doc. Spec (91) 21, 29 April 1991.

15. The structured debate took place during the Council meeting of 29–30 May 1991. A summary of the interventions made during the meeting is contained in C/M/250. The statements have been issued *in extenso* in the series Spec (91) 27 to Spec (91) 56.

16. Communication by Malaysia on behalf of the ASEAN contracting parties (Indonesia, Singapore, Thailand, and the Philippines), Doc. L/6859, 29 May 1991.

17. Council meeting of 11 July 1991, Doc. C/M/251.

18. Council meeting of 8 October 1991, Doc. C/M/252, 4 November 1991.

19. Council meeting of 12 November 1991, Doc. C/M/253.

20. For an account of the debates held under each agenda item, see the reports of the meetings, contained in the series TRE/1 to TRE/14. See also the Report of the Chairman to the 48th and 49th Sessions of the CONTRACTING PARTIES, respectively contained in Docs. SR.48/2, point 6(b), 5 January 1993, and L/7402, 2 February 1994.

21. *Report by Ambassador H. Ukawa (Japan), Chairman of the Group on Environmental Measures and International Trade, to the 49th Session of the CONTRACTING PARTIES,* L/7402, 2 February 1994. This document provides a detailed summary of the debate under each of the three agenda items.

22. *Trade and Environment*, Factual Note by the Secretariat, L/6896, 18 September 1991.

23. GATT, *International Trade 90-91*, vol. I, pp. 19–47.

24. Council meeting of 14 July 1992, Doc. C/M/258.

25. Forty-Eighth Session of the CONTRACTING PARTIES, 2 December 1992, SR.48/1. See also Docs. C/M/259 and C/M/260.

26. Reports of the EMIT Group discussions on the UNCED follow-up can be found in TRE/12, 30 July 1993, TRE/13, 21 October 1993, TRE/14, 17 February 1994, + TRE/14/Corr. 1 and in the *Report by Ambassador H. Ukawa (Japan), Chairman of the Group on Environmental Measures and International Trade, to the 49ᵗʰ Session of the CONTRACTING PARTIES,* L/7402, 2 February 1994.

27. Council meeting of 22 February 1994, Doc. C/M/269.

28. This section is based on two background notes by the Secretariat: *Trade and Environment*, L/6896, 18 September 1991, and *Exports of Domestically Prohibited Goods,* PC/SCTE/W/7, 22 December 1994.

29. Ministerial Declaration, adopted 28 November 1982, BISD 29S/9.

30. L/5907, 22 November 1985.

31. Ministerial Declaration on the Uruguay Round, Declaration of 20 September 1986, BISD 33S/30.

32. MTN.TNC/8(MIN), 17 January 1988, pp. 11–12.

33. L/6553, 21 July 1989.

34. Ibid.

35. The minutes of the meetings of the Working Group are contained in Docs. Spec (89) 48 and 52; Spec (90) 3, 12, 20, 27, 36, and 39; and Spec (91) 3, 4, 23, 60, and 62.

36. *Technical Note on Domestically Prohibited Goods,* Communication by Cameroon, Côte d'Ivoire, Nigeria, Sri Lanka, and Zaire, MTN.GNG/W/18, 17 November 1998; *Outline of a Possible GATT Framework of Rules in the Area of Domestically Prohibited Goods and Other Hazardous Substances,* Communication by Nigeria and Cameroon, DPG/W/8, 30 March 1990; *Understanding on Trade in Domestically Prohibited Goods and Other Hazardous Substances,* Communication by the European Community, DPG/W/9, 12 April 1990.

37. L/8672, 2 July 1991.

38. MTN.TNC/W/123, 13 December 1993.

39. MTN.TNC/45(MIN), 6 May 1994.

40. See the Ministerial Decision on Trade and Environment (14 April 1994) taken on the occasion of signing the Final Act embodying the results of the Uruguay Round of Multilateral Trade Negotiations at Marrakesh on 15 April 1994.

41. See Docs. PC/SCTE/M/1 to PC/SCTE/M/5. See also Doc. PC/R, 31 December 1994.

42. See document series WT/CTE/M/1 to 13.

43. *Results of the Stocktaking Exercise,* adopted at the 28–29 May 1996 Meeting, WT/CTE/W/33, 4 June 1996.

44. Ibid.

45. *Report of the Meetings Held on 30 October and 6–8 November 1996,* Doc. WT/CTE/M/13, 22 November 1996.

46. Meeting of the General Council held on 7, 8 and 13 November 1996, WT/GC/M/16, 6 December 1996.

47. *Report (1996) of the Committee on Trade and Environment,* WT/CTE/1, 12 November 1996, Section III of the Report (Conclusions and Recommendations).

48. *Singapore Ministerial Declaration,* adopted on 13 December 1996, WT/MIN(96)/DEC, 18 December 1996, para. 16.

49. WT/CTE/M/14 to WT/CTE/M/18 and PRESS/TE 018 to 027.

50. WT/CTE/W/77, 9 March 1998, and WT/CTE/W/78, 9 March 1998.

51. *Environmental Benefits of Removing Trade Restrictions and Distortions,* Note by the Secretariat, WT/CTE/W/67, 7 November 1997.

52. Document WT/CTE/W/41/Rev.3, 2 December 1998.

53. *United States–Import Prohibition of Certain Shrimp and Shrimp Products,* Appellate Body Report, WT/DS58/AB/R, circulated on 12 October 1998, in particular paras. 129 and 152.

54. *Guidelines for Arrangements on Relations with Non-Governmental Organizations,* WT/L/162, 23 July 1996.

55. *Procedure for the Circulation and Derestriction of WTO Documents,* WT/L/160/Rev.1, 26 July 1996.

56. Paragraph (b) of Article XX, as amended by the Austrian proposal, would read: "necessary to protect the environment, human, animal or plant life or health". MTN.GNG/NG7/W/75, 1 November 1990.

57. For a more detailed account of the dispute settlement practice which has built on this provision, see also Doc. WT/CTE/W/53/Rev.1, 26 October 1998 + Corr.1, 27 November 1998.

58. For more details on this subject, see *Item 4: Provisions of the Multilateral Trading System with Respect to the Transparency of Trade Measures Used for Environmental Purposes and Environmental Measures and Requirements Which Have Significant Trade Effects,* Note by the Secretariat, WT/CTE/W/77, 9 March 1998.

59. *Communication from Canada,* G/TBT/W/9, 5 July 1995; *Negotiating History of the Coverage of the Agreement on Technical Barriers to Trade with Regard to Labelling Requirements, Voluntary Standards, and Processes and Production Methods Unrelated to Product Characteristics,* G/TBT/W/11—WT/CTE/W/10, 29 August 1995; *US Proposal Regarding Further Work on Transparency of Eco-Labelling,* G/TBT/W/29, 18 June 1996; *Draft Decision on Eco-Labelling,* G/TBT/W/30—WT/CTE/W/38, 24 July 1996; *Environmental Labels and Market Access: Case Study on the Colombian Flower-Growing Industry—Document from Colombia,* G/TBT/W/60, 9 March 1998; *Forests: A National Experience—Contribution by Canada,* G/TBT/W/61—WT/CTE/W/81, 11 March 1998. See also G/TBT/M/2, 4 October 1995, G/TBT/M/3, 5 January 1996, G/TBT/M/4, 10 June 1996, G/TBT/M/5, 19 September 1996, G/TBT/M/11, 27 May 1998.

60. *First Triennial Review of the Operation and Implementation of the Agreement on Technical Barriers to Trade,* G/TBT/5, 19 November 1998.

61. These are developed countries other than some with economies in transition, as well as developing and transition economy countries which joined the WTO after 1 January 1995.

62. S/L/4, 4 April 1995.

63. See *Report (1996) of the Committee on Trade and Environment,* WT/CTE/1, 12 November 1996, paras. 210–211.

64. For more details, see *Environmental Benefits of Removing Trade Restrictions and Distortions,* Note by the Secretariat, WT/CTE/W/67/Add.1, 13 March 1998, and *Environmental Services,* Background Note by the Secretariat, S/C/W/46, 6 July 1998.

65. MTN.GNS/W/120.

66. Council for Trade in Services, *Report of the Meeting Held on 22 and 23 July 1998,* Note by the Secretariat, S/C/M/29, 24 August 1998.

67. Council for Trade in Services, *Report of the Meeting Held on 22 and 23 July 1998,* Note by the Secretariat, S/C/M/29, 24 August 1998.

68. Panel Report on *United States–Import Prohibition of Certain Shrimp and Shrimp Products,* WT/DS58/R, circulated on 15 May 1998.

69. Ibid., para. 7.8.

70. Appellate Body Report on *United States–Import Prohibition of Certain Shrimp and Shrimp Products,* WT/DS58/AB/R, circulated on 12 October 1998, paras. 106–107 (emphasis in the text).

71. Ibid., para. 109.

72. This section is at <http://www.wto.org/wto/ngo/contact.htm>

Appendix II

Key Trade and Environment Issues, Problems, and Possible Solutions

Veena Jha and René Vossenaar

Table II.1.   The trade and environment agenda

| | Solution | |
Problem	WTO	Outside WTO
The trade and environment debate lacks **balance** and does not pay adequate attention to concerns of developing countries	The CTE should continue to discuss all relevant issues and further strengthen the development dimension in its deliberation. CTE should pay particular attention to issues of interest to developing countries. Seattle Ministerial Declaration should go beyond UNCED commitments and formulate the rights and obligations of WTO members in view of these commitments.	Strengthen the role of UNCTAD, UNEP, and other international and regional organizations in trade and environment issues. Developing countries should seek to strengthen the development dimension, in particular at UNCTAD X and the 8th session of the Commission on Sustainable Development (which will consider the cross-sectoral theme Financial Resources/ Trade and Investment and / Economic Growth). Develop a broad programme of capacity-building on trade and sustainable development.
There is continued pressure to accommodate **the extra-territorial use of unilateral trade measures** on environmental grounds.	Ministerial Declaration should firmly reject extra-territorial use of unilateral trade.	Reiterate the Rio Declaration (in particular Principle 12) and Agenda 21. Promote bilateral and multilateral cooperation.
Pressures for a modification or interpretation of GATT **Article XX** to provide further accommodation of discriminatory trade measures pursuant to multilateral environmental agreements (MEAs) pose a risk to developing countries.	The CTE should continue to discuss the relationship between the trade provisions in MEAs and the provisions of the multilateral trading system (see table II.5 below). Issues such as the definition of MEAs, the necessity and effectiveness of trade measures, and the role of supportive measures should receive further attention at the CTE.	Strengthened policy coordination at the national level. Cooperation between the secretariats of WTO, UNEP, MEAs, and UNCTAD.

Table II.1.   The trade and environment agenda (*continued*)

Problem	Solution	
	WTO	*Outside WTO*
There is pressure to accommodate certain trade measures based on non-product-related **processes and production methods (PPMs)** in the multilateral trading system. This would have potentially adverse implications for developing countries.	WTO should assess what would be the "risk of non-fulfilment" of environmental objectives in these cases.	International cooperation, supportive measures, and multi-stakeholder approaches are the preferred ways to support the use of environmentally friendly PPMs in developing countries. Developing countries may wish to engage in the development of a set of criteria on eco-labelling in terms of transparency and the avoidance of trade barrier effects.
There are differing views on whether and in which cases the WTO should provide greater scope for the use of the **precautionary principle**. There is a need to prevent the abuse of the precautionary principle for protectionist purposes.	There is a need to consider the extent to which a combination of the precautionary principle and the concept of proportionality could address environment and trade concerns. There should be greater attention to the appropriate use of the precautionary principle to address possible risks of trade in genetically modified organisms (GMOs).	Develop criteria for the appropriate use of the precautionary principle.
Clarifying issues on the basis of the development of **case-law** (through the dispute settlement mechanism) may fail to meet a broad-based consensus.	The CTE should continue to seek to build consensus of views, including through cooperation with MEA secretariats. Through the review process of the Dispute Settlement Understanding, developing countries should seek clarification of the scope and terms of reference of the Appellate Body and its rulings.	Build consensus on principles and approaches aimed at preventing environment-related conflicts. Include the concept of proportionality of trade measures while deciding on the package of measures to be used by MEAs.

Table II.2.   Mainstreaming environment in WTO Agreements

Problem	Solution	
	WTO	*Outside WTO*
The **risks and opportunities** for developing countries of "mainstreaming" environment in several WTO Agreements **are not well understood.**	Developing countries should seek to strengthen the role of the CTE in enhancing understanding of trade and environment linkages and participate effectively in its deliberations. Developing countries should also engage in more intensive discussions on issues of their interest.	Technical cooperation for capacity-building.
Mainstreaming environment into several WTO committees could make it **more complicated for developing countries to participate effectively** in WTO deliberations on trade and environment issues.	Maintain a key role for the CTE.	Technical cooperation for capacity-building.
Diffusing the environmental agenda to several WTO committees could **erode the balance** in the WTO work programme on trade and environment, as established in the CTE.	Maintain a key role for the CTE.	Improve implementation of supportive measures such as capacity-building, finance, and access to and transfer of technology.

Table II.3.   Market access issues

	Solution	
Problem	*WTO*	*Outside WTO*
Compliance with **environmental requirements and sanitary and phytosanitary (SPS) measures** may pose certain problems to developing country producers, particularly small and medium enterprises (SMEs).	Developing countries, particularly the LDCs, should take full advantage of possibilities to request technical assistance to comply with SPS measures, standards, and regulations. Improve provisions on special and differential treatment (S&D). Examine the role of sound science and risk of "non-fulfilment" of these objectives. Examine the necessity and effectiveness of such measures, especially when they relate to PPMs.	Improve awareness and channels of information. Strengthen infrastructure, especially testing facilities in developing countries to comply with SPS measures and environmental requirements. Regional cooperation on standards. Enhanced participation of developing countries in the work of the ISO and other organizations for standardization, including through regional cooperation and representation.
SMEs may have special difficulties in responding to environmental challenges.	The implications for SMEs in the context of the Agreement on Trade-related Investment Measures (TRIMS) and in the Subsidies Agreement should be examined.	The above-mentioned measures should pay special attention to the needs of SMEs. SMEs should seek alliances with other SMEs and with large firms to strengthen their capacity to respond to environmental challenges and to maintain or increase competitiveness.
There is **insufficient WTO discipline** for certain environmental measures, with a potential impact on exports from developing countries.	Devise a mechanism under existing Code of Good Practices to avoid the use of trade discriminatory measures based on PPM-related requirements. Consider the scope for applying greater WTO discipline to those policies of local governments that may have a potentially significant adverse	Promote cooperation and develop supportive measures to address environmental problems and to promote sustainable development.

(Table continues on next page)

Table II.3.   Market access issues (*continued*)

	Solution	
Problem	*WTO*	*Outside WTO*
	impact on developing country exports (such as bans on the use of tropical timber imposed by several munici-palities), for example in the context of the Plurilateral Agreement on Public Procurement.	
There is a need to streamline **trading opportunities for environmentally preferable products (EPPs).**	Examine systemic factors that may create certain obstacles to developing country efforts to take full advantage of trading opportunities for EPPs (for example with regard to providing protection for intellectual property rights (IPRs)). Examine how the multilateral trading system can provide incentives for trade in "environmentally friendly" products from developing countries without creating new forms of conditionality.	Strengthen infrastructure. Regional cooperation. Umbrella certification. Development of trademarks. Business partnerships.

Table II.4.   "Win–win" scenarios

	Solution	
Problem	*WTO*	*Outside WTO*
"**Win–win**": trade liberalization, including the elimination of export subsidies provided by developed countries, may result in new trading opportunities for developing countries. In some sectors, however, the extent to which the elimination of trade restrictions and distortions in developed countries will result in economic benefits for the developing countries is uncertain.	The WTO should promote the reduction or elimination of subsidies that are clearly environmentally harmful, particularly those that may result in trade benefits for developing countries. Due attention should be paid to possible adverse short-term economic effects on certain developing countries.	Research on the implications of the elimination of trade restrictions and distortions for developing countries. Anticipate possible short-term negative economic effects on certain developing countries that may arise from the elimination of certain subsidies, and, where appropriate, explore ways to provide compensation or other forms of assistance.

Table II.5.   Multilateral environmental agreements

Problem	*Solution*	
	WTO	*Outside WTO*
Efforts to clarify the relationship between certain provisions in multilateral environmental agreements (MEAs) and the provisions of the multilateral trading system focus on **only part of the relationship.**	Trade measures and supportive measures should be considered in conjunction. Full consideration should be given to the concerns of many developing countries and NGOs about differences in the concepts and regimes in the Convention on Biodiversity (CBD) on the one hand and the WTO TRIPS Agreement on the other.	The CBD should develop clear guidelines and mechanisms on protection of traditional knowledge.
The **economic and social implications of certain trade measures** for countries at different levels of development are not well understood.	The CTE should continue to examine this issue.	Improve the imple-mentation of supportive measures under MEAs. Promote multi-stakeholder panels at the national level as well as study groups at the inter-national level to identify efficient and development-friendly solutions.

Table II.6.   Environmentally sound technologies

	Solution	
Problem	*WTO*	*Outside WTO*
Insufficient progress has been made in improving access to and transfer of environmentally sound technologies (ESTs) to developing countries.	Review implementation of Articles 66.2 (in favour of LDCs) and 67 (in favour of developing countries) of the TRIPS Agreement. Also examine how lack of progress could be taken into account in the context of the dispute settlement mechanism.	Enhance implementation of Agenda 21 provisions and recommendations on transfer of technology.
Although it has already been recognized that the international community should promote transfer of ESTs and provide funds for the "incremental costs" of technology-switching to address **global environmental problems,** there have been problems in implementation.	There is a need to examine the contribution that the multilateral trading system can make to effective implementation of provisions on transfer of ESTs.	Improve the implementation of transfer of technology provisions in MEAs.
	The relationship between IPR protection and the transfer of specific ESTs required to comply with obligations under MEAs should continue to be examined.	Design and implement innovative ways to promote the transfer of ESTs.
Currently, there are no comparable international mechanisms for the facilitation of ESTs that are appropriate for addressing **local environmental problems.**	The multilateral trading system should encourage transfer of ESTs to developing countries by utilizing existing mechanisms and provisions of the TRIPS Agreement.	Promote the diffusion of ESTs to developing countries, e.g. through "green" credit lines, multilateral and bilateral cooperation, business partnerships, etc.

Table II.7.   TRIPS and biodiversity

	Solution	
Problem	*WTO*	*Outside WTO*
There may be **inconsistencies** between certain provisions of the CBD and those of the WTO TRIPS Agreement. Provisions in the CBD may better represent the interests of developing countries.	Priority should be given to further examination of this relationship in the WTO. The CBD should take primacy over the TRIPS Agreement in the areas of biological resources and traditional knowledge systems.	Discussions on benefit-sharing as outlined in the Biodiversity Agreement should take place at the national and, where appropriate, regional levels.
The WTO TRIPS Agreement may provide **insufficient room for appropriate protection of the traditional, communal systems of innovation** in the developing countries. Consequently, the intellectual property of producers and communities may be denied recognition, and hence protection.	There is a need to consider systems such as FAO 1983 that protects land races and traditional medicinal plants as intellectual property. There is a need for further studies on the options for providing protection to indigenous knowledge.	There is a need to devise suitable *sui generis* methods for the protection of traditional knowledge at the national and regional levels. There is also a need to develop a database in terms of the geographical appellation of a number of products that are known to originate in a specific country or region.
Patenting of life forms may have adverse economic and social effects in the developing countries.	The review of the TRIPS Agreement should ensure that the rights of sovereign states to exclude all life forms and related knowledge from IPR systems are not eroded. There is a need to study the application of Article 27.2, which can exclude from patentability technologies that can harm the environment.	

Table II.7.   TRIPS and biodiversity (*continued*)

| | Solution | |
Problem	WTO	Outside WTO
The 1999 review of Article 27.3(b) of the TRIPS Agreement may have serious implications for developing countries by narrowing the window on *sui generis* and other forms of intellectual property protection that are not based on patents.	Developing countries may seek additional time for examining the full implications of Article 27.3(b) as well as for a consideration of different options for implementing *sui generis* systems. WTO should recognize that patenting of traditional knowledge may be inappropriate for their protection and the protection of associated biodiversity.	It is important to examine issues such as *sui generis* systems, the patenting of life forms, and the patenting of micro-organisms on a national and regional basis.

Table II.8.   The issue of exports of domestically prohibited goods

	Solution	
Problem	*WTO*	*Outside WTO*
Products that are prohibited for sale or severely restricted in the domestic market of other countries (**DPGs**) may nevertheless be exported to developing countries, without information being provided of health and environmental risks. Developing countries may lack infrastructure to control imports of DPGs. A number of multilateral agreements and instruments regulate trade in DPGs. These include the Rotterdam Convention on Prior Informed Consent, the proposed Convention on Persistent Organic Pollutants (POPS), and the Basel Convention. However, there may still be gaps, for example in terms of product coverage and membership.	Although duplication of the work of multilateral agreements and instruments is to be avoided, the CTE should further examine whether existing intruments, such as the prior informed consent (PIC) procedures, are sufficient from the perspective of developing countries, in particular with regard to product coverage and procedures. The CTE recommendations on technical assistance should be fully implemented. The DPG notification system that had been in existence between 1982 and 1990 should be revived.	Multilateral agreements and instruments to deal with exports of DPGs should be further improved. Developed countries should strengthen legislation and take further initiatives to mitigate adverse environmental effects of trade in DPGs. Mechanisms should be developed on a regional basis for exchanging information on DPGs. Mechanisms should be developed on a regional basis between customs officers for controlling trade in DPGs.

Table II.9.   Environmental impacts of trade policies and agreements

	Solution	
Problem	*WTO*	*Outside WTO*
Changes in patterns of production associated with trade liberalization, in the absence of adequate environmental and macro-economic policies, may have **adverse environmental and social effects.**	This issue needs to be further discussed in the CTE. WTO members may be encouraged to integrate environmental and developmental considerations in economic and trade policies. Promote the diffusion of ESTs to developing countries.	National governments should anticipate these effects and ensure that trade liberalization is accompanied by appropriate environmental and macro-economic policies. Developing countries should promote increased awareness of trade and environment issues across all sectors at the national and regional levels. Developing countries should be assisted in strengthening their capacities to integrate environmental considerations into economic policies. UNEP, in cooperation with UNCTAD, should examine methodologies and develop parameters that could be used at the national level, as well as provide technical assistance for capacity-building. UNEP and UNCTAD should continue to cooperate in the development of pilot projects.
In certain cases calls for environmental impact assessments (EIAs) could be motivated by **protectionist purposes.**	This issue needs to be further discussed in the CTE.	International cooperation, for example in the areas of capacity-building and transfer of technology, are effective in reducing possible adverse environmental effects associated with increased export production in developing countries as a result of trade liberalization.

(Table continues on next page)

Table II.9.   Environmental impacts of trade policies and agreements (*continued*)

Problem	Solution	
	WTO	*Outside WTO*
Pressures to attach a commitment to carry out EIAs to the launching and conduct of a possible **new round of multilateral trade negotiations** may add new dynamics to the process.	The WTO may encourage national governments to carry out EIAs, but these should not be "multilateralized" in the WTO.	EIAs should be carried out under the responsibility of the government in the country where major changes in production are likely to occur; technical cooperation may be useful; possible trade-offs between trade and environmental objectives should be resolved at the national level, including through multi-stakeholder approaches.

Contributors

Arthur E. Appleton, J.D., Ph.D., attorney, Lalive & Partners (Geneva). Dr. Appleton is the author of *Environmental Labeling Programmes: International Trade Law Implications,* Kluwer Law International (1997). He is admitted to practice in Washington, DC, and Maryland (USA), and served as lead counsel for three of the developing countries in the appellate phase of the *Shrimp-Turtle* dispute.

Duncan Brack has worked on trade and environment issues at the Royal Institute of International Affairs (Chatham House) since 1995, and has been Head of the Energy and Environment Programme there since September 1998. He has written mainly on multilateral environmental agreements and on international environmental crime.

James Cameron, barrister, Director, Foundation for International Environmental Law and Development, Professor of Law at the College of Europe, Lecturer in Law at SOAS, University of London, adviser to the UK Foreign Secretary Robin Cook MP on global environmental policy, and Of Counsel to Baker & McKenzie, the international law firm. Mr. Cameron is the author and editor of numerous articles and books.

W. Bradnee Chambers, M.A., L.L.M., is an Associate Fellow and Coordinator of the Environmental Governance and Multilateralism Programme of the Institute of Advanced Studies, United Nations University, Tokyo. Mr. Chambers specializes in public international law and works on environmental treaty and international economic legal issues.

Steve Charnovitz practises law at Wilmer, Cutler & Pickering in Washington, DC. He was previously Director of the Global Environment & Trade Study at Yale University (1995–1999), Policy Director of the US Competitiveness Policy Council (1991–1995), and Legislative Assistant to the Speaker of the US House of Representatives (1987–1991). He received a B.A. and J.D. from Yale University and an M.P.P. from the Kennedy School of Government.

William J. Davey is Edwin M. Adams Professor of Law at the University of Illinois College of Law. From 1995 to 1999 he was the Director of the Legal Affairs Division of the World Trade Organization. Professor Davey is the author of *Pine & Swine: Canada–United States Trade Dispute Settlement* (1996), *Legal Problems of International Economic Relations* (1995, with Jackson and Sykes; 1986, with Jackson), *European Community Law* (1993, with Bermann, Goebel, and Fox), and *Handbook of WTO/GATT Dispute Settlement* (1991–1998, with Pescatore and Lowenfeld), as well as of various articles on international trade law issues.

Daniel C. Esty is a Professor of Environmental Law and Policy at the Yale Law School and the Yale School of Forestry and Environmental Studies. He is also Director of the Yale Center for Environmental Law and Policy and Associate Dean of the Yale School of Forestry and Environmental Studies. Professor Esty is the author or editor of several books and numerous articles, including *Thinking Ecologically: The Next Generation of Environmental Policy* (1997, ed. with M. Chertow), *Sustaining the Asia Pacific Miracle: Environmental Protection and Economic Integration* (1997, with A. Dua), and *Greening the GATT: Trade, Environment, and the Future* (1994).

Veena Jha, Ph.D., economics, is the project coordinator of UNCTAD in New Delhi, which is affiliated to the UNCTAD International Trade Division, Geneva. Dr. Jha has been a lecturer and researcher at Queen's College, Oxford, the University of London, the Lady Spencer Churchill School of Management at Wheatley, and the University of Delhi. She has published several articles on trade and environment issues in journals and other publications and edited books including *Trade, Environment and Sustainable Development: A South Asian Perspective* and *Eco-labelling and International Trade*.

Doaa Abdel Motaal is Economic Affairs Officer in the Trade and Environment Division in the World Trade Organization. She has an M.Phil. degree from the University of Cambridge in Environmental Planning and a B.A. degree from Swarthmore College, Pennsylvania, in Economics. Her responsibilities in the WTO include researching different facets of the trade and environment linkage and facilitating negotiations among WTO member countries.

Rubens Ricupero was appointed as UNCTAD's fifth Secretary-General in September 1995. In the course of a long Brazilian government career, he was Minister of Environment and Amazonian Affairs in 1993, and then Minister of Finance in 1994. Mr. Ricupero has held several diplomatic and academic posts, including Ambassador, Permanent Representative to the United Nations in Geneva (1987–1991), Ambassador to the United States of America (1991–1993), and professorships at the University of Brasilia and at the Rio Branco Institute. He is also the author of several books and essays on international relations, problems of economic development, and international trade and diplomatic history.

Gary P. Sampson has a Ph.D. in economics. He is Visiting Academic at the London School of Economics and Visiting Senior Professor at the Institute of Advanced Studies, United Nations University, Tokyo. He also teaches at INSEAD and the Melbourne Business School. Until early 1999, Professor Sampson was director of a number of divisions of the GATT and WTO, most recently the Trade and Environment Division.

David K. Schorr has been with the Worldwide Fund for Nature (WWF) since 1993, where he currently directs the Sustainable Commerce Program. Mr. Schorr has played a direct role in a variety of trade and environment issues, including serving as chair of the NAFTA-related US National Advisory Committee and as a staff member of the President's Advisory Committee on Trade Policy and Negotiations. Prior to joining WWF, Mr. Schorr practised and taught law in Washington, DC. He is a graduate of Yale Law School and Oberlin College.

Magda Shahin, Ph.D. in economics from Cairo University, is Deputy Assistant Minister of Foreign Affairs for International Economic Relations, Egypt. Parallel to her diplomatic function, Mrs. Shahin is Assistant Professor of International Economics at the American University in Cairo (AUC). Mrs. Shahin has served on the delegation of the Egyptian government to numerous United Nations conferences and as a Councillor at the Egyptian Mission to the United Nations in New York. She has also held the post of Deputy Chief of Mission at the Egyptian Mission to the United Nations in Geneva.

René Vossenaar is Chief of the Trade, Environment and Development Section of the Division on International Trade in Goods and Services, and Commodities (DITC) of UNCTAD. Previously he was a researcher at the University of Tilburg in the Netherlands and worked for several years with the Economic Commission for Latin America and the Caribbean (ECLAC) in Santiago, Buenos Aires, and Brasilia. He has published several articles on trade and environment in the OECD and other publications.

Index

Page numbers for entries occurring in endnotes and tables are followed by n and t, respectively.